CENSUS OF INDIA 1911

Census of India 1871-1951, 9 Sets In 384 Bindings (9788121258876) Rs. 700000

Census of India 1911, 23 Vols. In 41 Bindings (9788121271271) Rs. 69000

1. India - Report (9788121275071) Rs. 2475 (Vol. I, Pt. 1)
2. India - Tables (9788121275057) Rs. 2225 (Vol. I, Pt. 2)
3. Andaman and Nicobar Islands - Report & Tables (9788121275033) Rs. 900 (Vol. II, Pt. 1 & 2)
4. Assam - Report (9788121275019) Rs. 1000 (Vol. III, Pt. 1)
5. Assam - Tables (9788121274999) Rs. 1300 (Vol. III, Pt. 2)
6. Baluchistan - Report & Tables (9788121274975) Rs. 950 (Vol. IV, Pt. 1 & 2)
7. Bengal, Bihar And Orissa And Sikkim - Report (9788121274951) Rs. 3100 (Vol. V, Pt. 1)
8. Bengal - Tables (9788121274937) Rs. 2250 (Vol. V, Pt. 2)
9. Bihar And Orissa - Tables and Bengal And Sikkim - Chapter I of Administrative Volume (9788121274913) Rs. 1800 (Vol. V, Pt. 3 & 4)
10. City of Calcutta - Report and Tables and Administrative (9788121274876) Rs. 1300 (Vol. VI, Pt. 1 & 2 & 3)
11. Bombay - Report (9788121274814) Rs. 1950 (Vol. VII, Pt. 1)
12. Bombay - Imperial Tables and Administrative Report (9788121274791) Rs. 3300 (Vol. VII, Pt. 2 & 3)
13. Bombay (Town And Island) - Report And Tables (9788121274753) Rs. 1250 (Vol. VIII, Pt. 1 & 2)
14. Burma - Report (9788121274739) Rs. 2250 (Vol. IX, Pt. 1)
15. Burma - Tables (9788121274715) Rs. 1480 (Vol. IX, Pt. 2)
16. Central Provinces And Berar - Report (9788121274692) Rs. 1475 (Vol. X, Pt. 1)
17. Central Provinces And Berar - Tables (9788121274678) Rs. 1900 (Vol. X, Pt. 2)
18. Coorg - Report And Tables Madras - Report (9788121274630) Rs. 1740 (Vol. XI & Vol. XII, Pt. 1)
19. Madras - Imperial And Provincial Tables (9788121274616) Rs. 1500 (Vol. XII, Pt. 2)
20. Madras - Administrative Report and city of Madras (9788121274593) Rs. 630 (Vol. XII, Pt. 3 & 4)
21. North - West Frontier Province - Report & Tables (9788121274579) Rs. 2150 (Vol. XIII, Pt. 1 & 2)
22. Punjab - Report (9788121274555) Rs. 3000 (Vol. XIV, Pt. 1)
23. Punjab - Tables (9788121274531) Rs. 2200 (Vol. XIV, Pt. 2)
24. Punjab - Appendices To The - Imperial Tables (9788121274517) Rs. 950 (Vol. XIV, Pt. 3)
25. United Provinces of Agra And Oudh - Report (9788121274494) Rs. 2225 (Vol. XV, Pt. 1)
26. United Provinces of Agra And Oudh - Tables (9788121274470) Rs. 4000 (Vol. XV, Pt. 2)
27. United Provinces of Agra And Oudh - Provincial Tables And Appendices (9788121274456) Rs. 570 (Vol. XV, Pt. 3)
28. Baroda - Report (9788121274432) Rs. 2000 (Vol. XVI, Pt. 1)
29. Baroda State - The Imperial Tables (9788121274418) Rs. 850 (Vol. XVI, Pt. 2)
30. Central India Agency - Report And Tables (9788121274395) Rs. 1470 (Vol. XVII)
31. Cochin - Report And Imperial Tables (9788121274371) Rs. 1150 (Vol. XVIII, Pt. 1 & 2)
32. Hyderabad State - Report (9788121274357) Rs. 890 (Vol. XIX, Pt. 1)
33. Hyderabad State - Imperial And Provincial Tables (9788121274333) Rs. 1750 (Vol. XIX, Pt. 2)
34. Kashmir - Report (9788121274319) Rs. 950 (Vol. XX, Pt. 1)
35. Kashmir - Tables (9788121274296) Rs. 1170 (Vol. XX, Pt. 2)
36. Mysore - Report (9788121274272) Rs. 1200 (Vol. XXI, Pt. 1)
37. Mysore - Tables (9788121274258) Rs. 1500 (Vol. XXI, Pt. 2)
38. Rajputana And Ajmer-Merwara - Report (9788121274234) Rs. 1470 (Vol. XXII, Pt. 1)
39. Rajputana And Ajmer-Merwara - Tables (9788121274210) Rs. 1700 (Vol. XXII, Pt. 2)
40. Travancore - Report (9788121274197) Rs. 1870 (Vol. XXIII, Pt. 1)
41. Travancore - Imperial Tables (9788121274173) Rs. 870 (Vol. XXIII, Pt. 2)

Owing to the antiquity and rarity of this book, certain pages are regrettably absent, and readability is compromised due to the blurring of the original text. If you possess any insights regarding the availability of these missing sections, kindly inform us. Your assistance is crucial in ensuring the completion of this significant work for the benefit of future generations.

CENSUS OF INDIA, 1911

VOLUME - XVIII

COCHIN

PART I - REPORT
PART II - IMPERIAL TABLES

C. ACHYUTA MENON

GYAN

Published by

Gyan Publishing House
5, Ansari Road
Daryaganj, New Delhi-110002
Phone: 011-47034999, 9811692060
E-mail: books@gyanbooks.com

Distribution Network
gyanbooks.com
India, USA, Canada, UK, Australia

ISBN: 978-81-212-7127-1 (Set) 23 Vols. In 41 Bindings

ISBN: 978-81-212-7437-1 (PB) Vol. XVIII, Pt. I & II

First Published, 1912

2nd Impression 2024

Printed at: Gyan Press, Delhi.

CENSUS OF INDIA 1911

CENSUS OF INDIA, 1911.

VOLUME XVIII.

COCHIN.

PART I.—REPORT.

PART II.—IMPERIAL TABLES.

BY

C. ACHYUTA MENON, B. A.

SUPERINTENDENT OF CENSUS OPERATIONS, COCHIN STATE.

ERNAKULAM.

PRINTED AT THE COCHIN GOVERNMENT PRESS.

1912.

DETAILED TABLE OF CONTENTS.

PART I.—REPORT.

INTRODUCTION.

CHAPTER I.—Distribution of the population.

SUBSIDIARY TABLES.

CHAPTER II.—Movement of population.

SUBSIDIARY TABLES.

CHAPTER III.—Birth place.

SUBSIDIARY TABLES.

CHAPTER IV.—Religion.

SUBSIDIARY TABLES.

CHAPTER V.—Age

SUBSIDIARY TABLES.

CHAPTER VI.—Proportion of sexes

SUBSIDIARY TABLES.

CHAPTER VII.—Civil condition

CHAPTER VIII.—Education.

CHAPTER IX.—Language.

CHAPTER X.—Infirmities.

CHAPTER XI.—Caste, Tribe and Race.

CHAPTER XII.—Occupation.

PART II.—Imperial Tables.

MAPS.

DIAGRAMS.

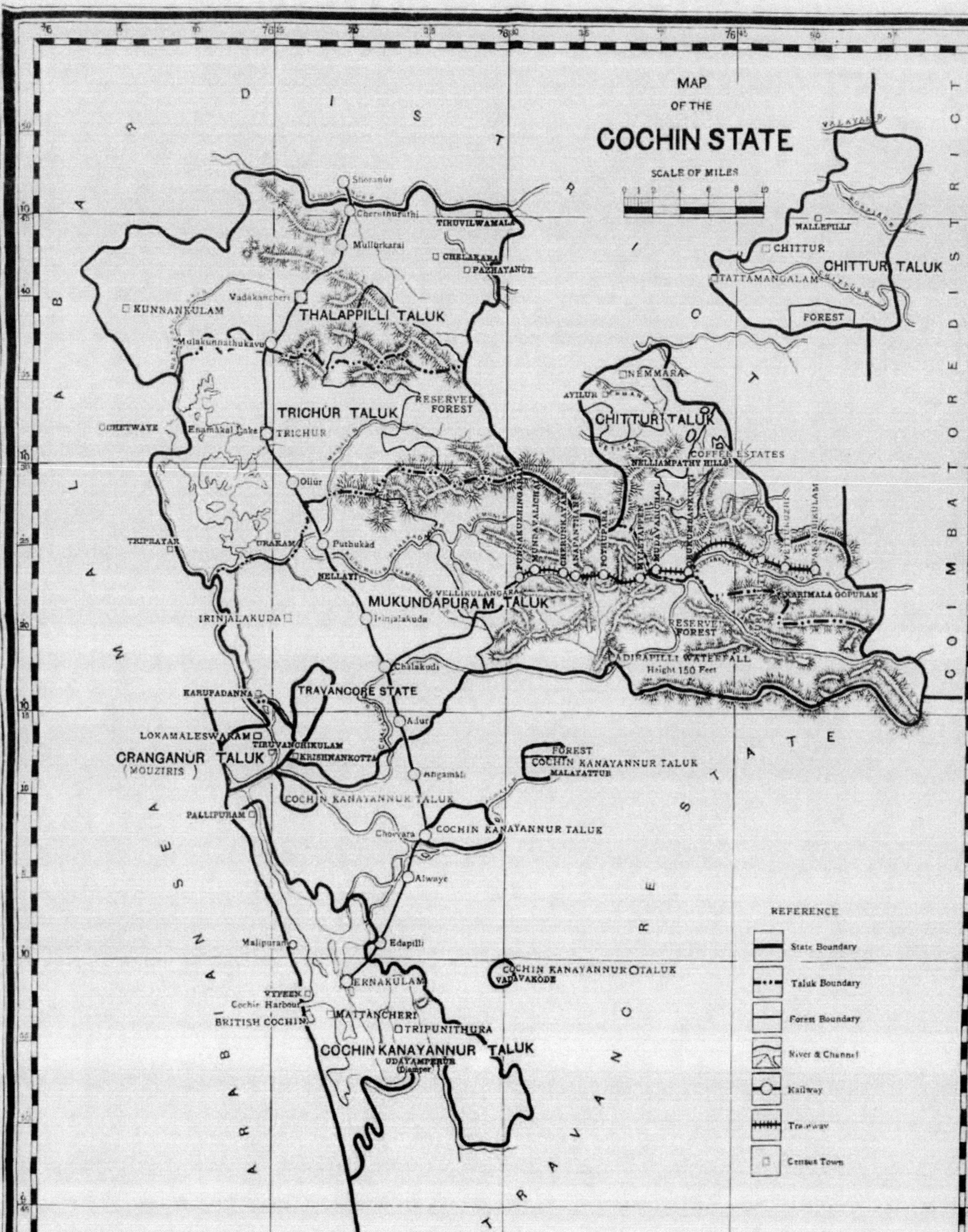
MAP
OF THE
COCHIN STATE
SCALE OF MILES
THALAPPILLI TALUK
TRICHUR TALUK
CHITTUR TALUK
MUKUNDAPURAM TALUK
CRANGANUR TALUK
(MOUZIRIS)
COCHIN KANAYANNUR TALUK
TRAVANCORE STATE
BRITISH COCHIN
RESERVED FOREST
COFFEE ESTATES
NELLIAMPATHY HILLS
ADIRAPILLI WATERFALL
Height 150 Feet
KARIMALA GOPURAM
Shoranur
Cheruthuruthi
TIRUVILWAMALA
Mullurkarai
CHELAKARA
PAZHAYANUR
Vadakancheri
KUNNANKULAM
Mulakunnathukavu
Enamakal Lake
TRICHUR
CHETWAYE
Ollur
TRIPRAYAR
URAKAM
Puthukad
NELLAYI
VELLIKULANGARA
IRINJALAKUDA
Irinjalakuda
Chalakudi
KARUPADANNA
LOKAMALESWARAM
TIRUVANCHIKULAM
KRISHNANKOTTA
Adur
Angamali
FOREST
MALAYATTUR
PALLIPURAM
Chovvara
Alwaye
Malipuram
Edapilli
ERNAKULAM
VADAVAKODE
VYPEEN
Cochin Harbour
MATTANCHERI
TRIPUNITHURA
UDAYAMPERUR
NEMMARA
AYILUR
NALLEPILLI
CHITTUR
TATTAMANGALAM
ARABIAN SEA
MALABAR DISTRICT
COIMBATORE DISTRICT
TRAVANCORE STATE
REFERENCE
State Boundary
Taluk Boundary
Forest Boundary
River & Channel
Railway
Tramway
Census Town
Register No. 515
Copies. 400
Photo Print Land Records Office Trichur
1087

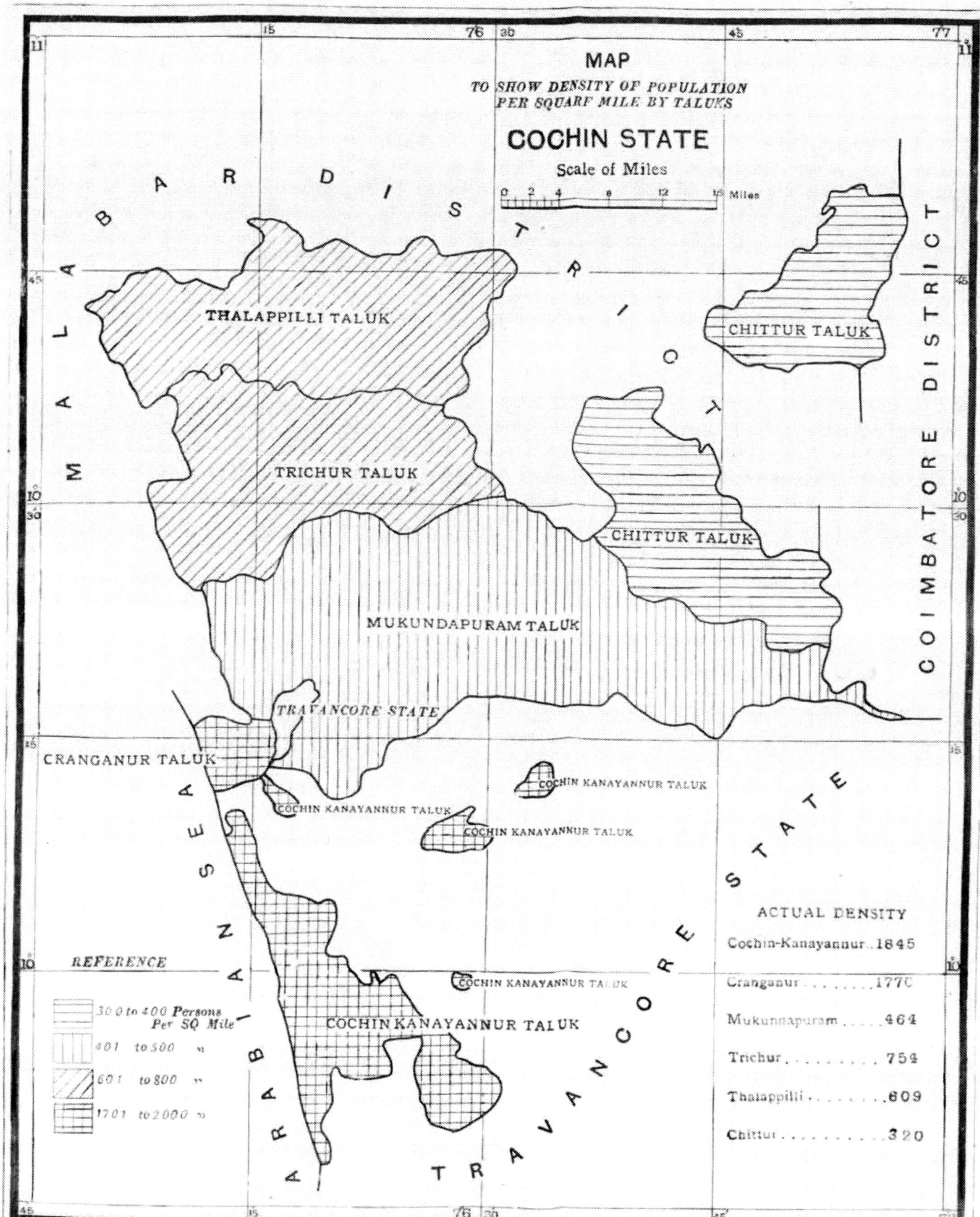

Register No. 811
Copies 400

Photo Print Land Records Office, Trichur.

1087

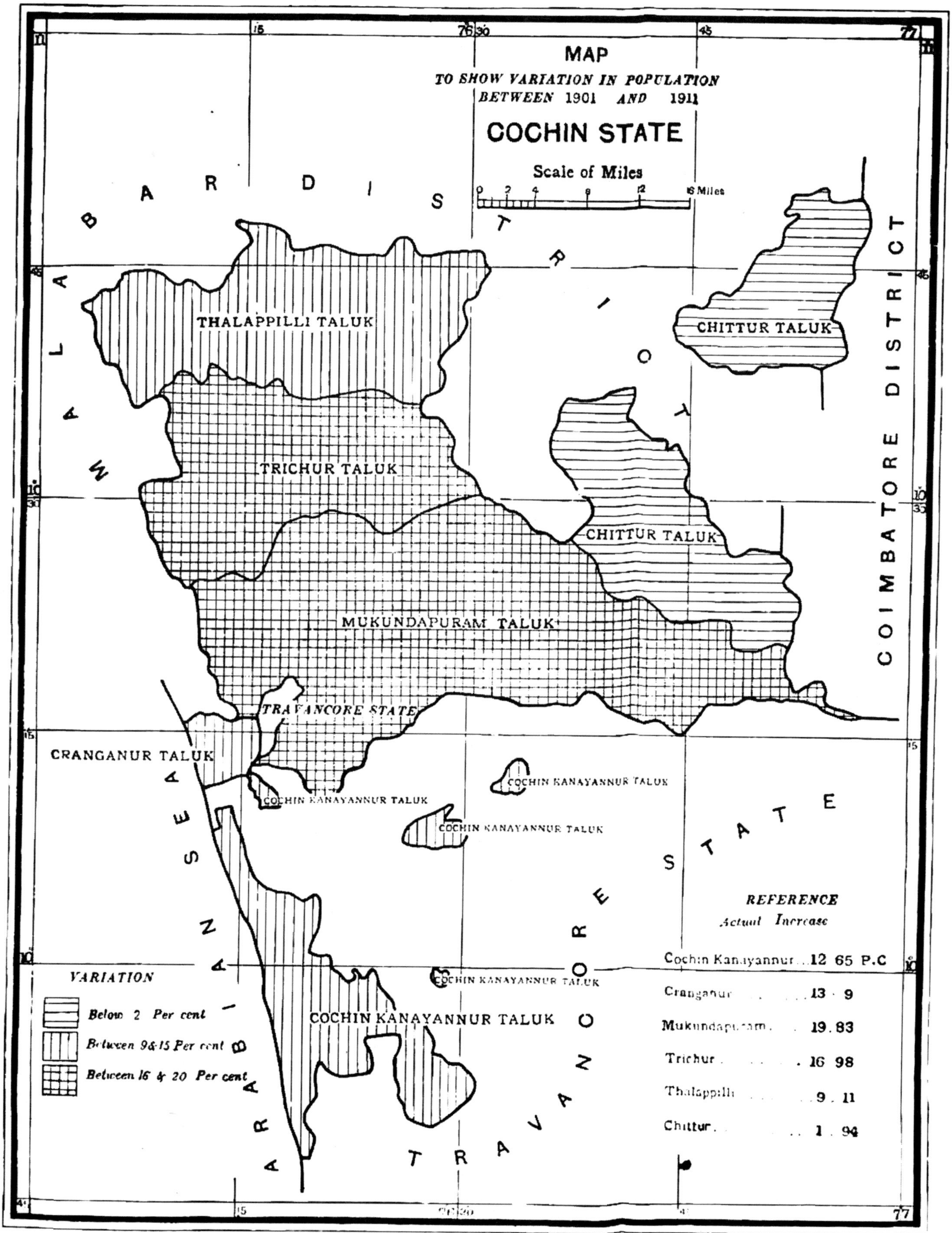

Register No.612
Copies 400

1087

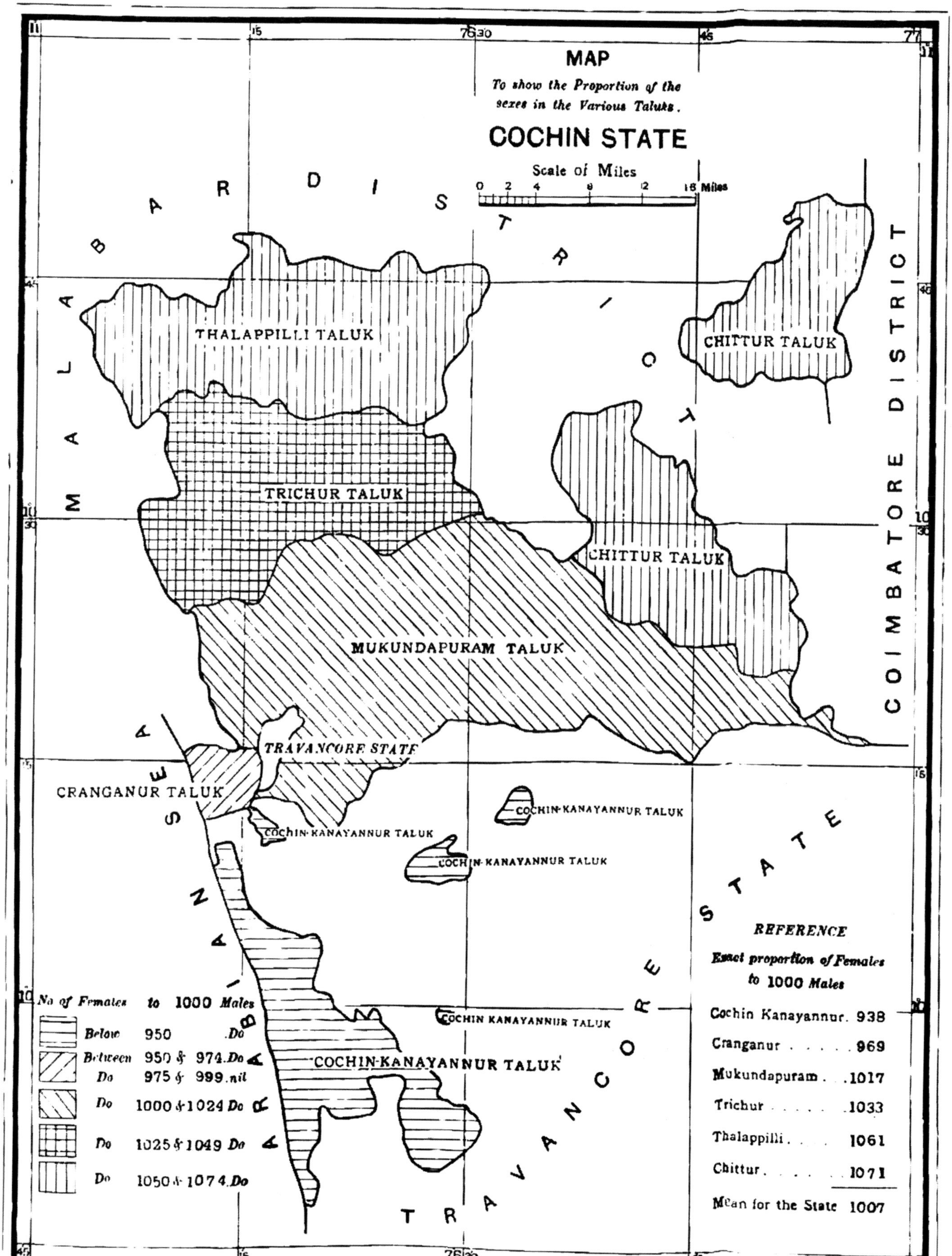

Register. No. 613
Copies 400

Photo Print Land Records Office, Trichur.
1087

DIAGRAM No. 1.

SHOWING THE URBAN AND RURAL POPULATION IN EACH TALUK.

Urban population ◆◆◆ : rural population ◇◇◇. Each diamond represents 5,000 persons.

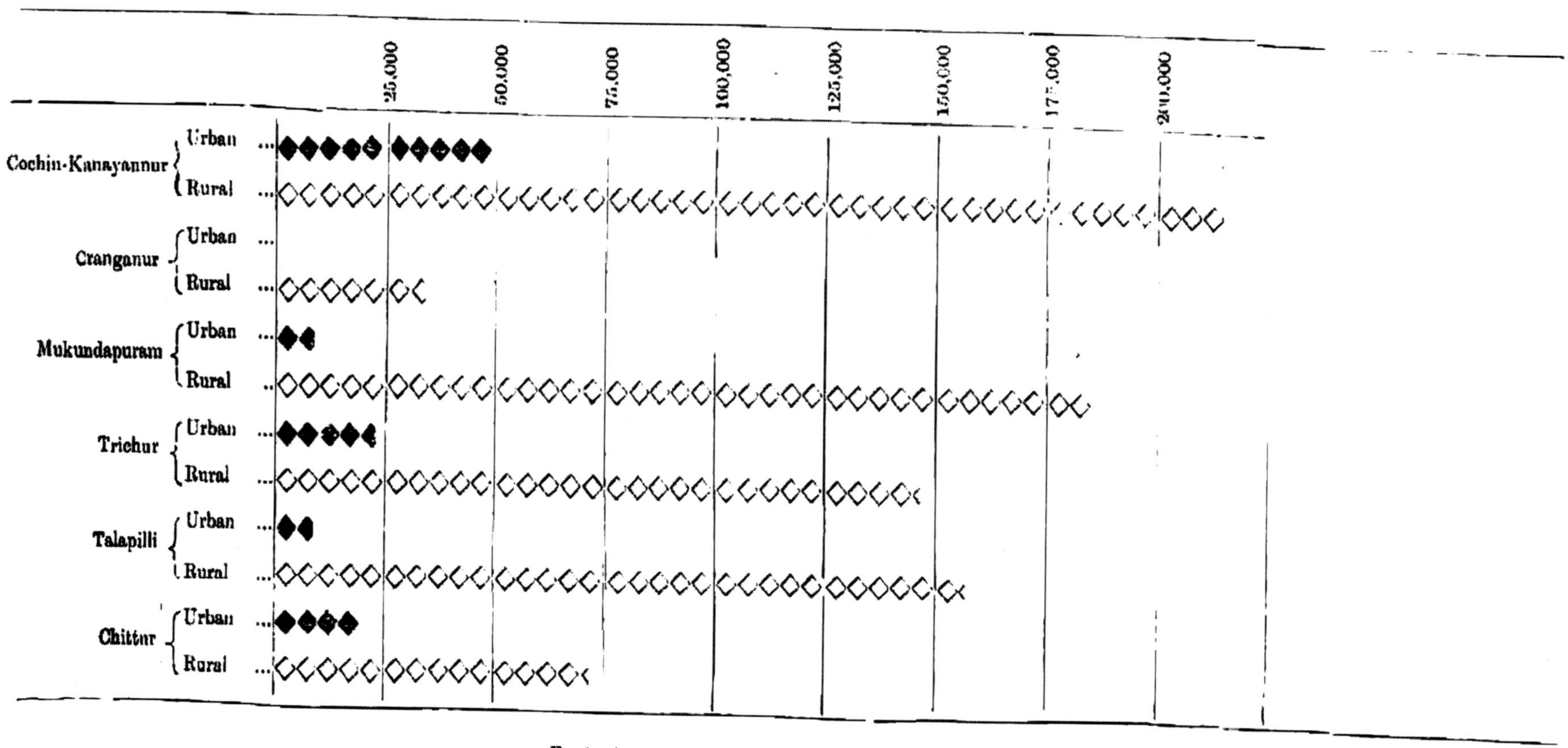

For further particulars see Chapter I and Table III.

DIAGRAM No. 2.

SHOWING THE POPULATION OF EACH TALUK AT EACH OF THE FIVE CENSUSES OF 1875, 1881, 1891, 1901 and 1911.

Each diamond represents 10,000 persons.

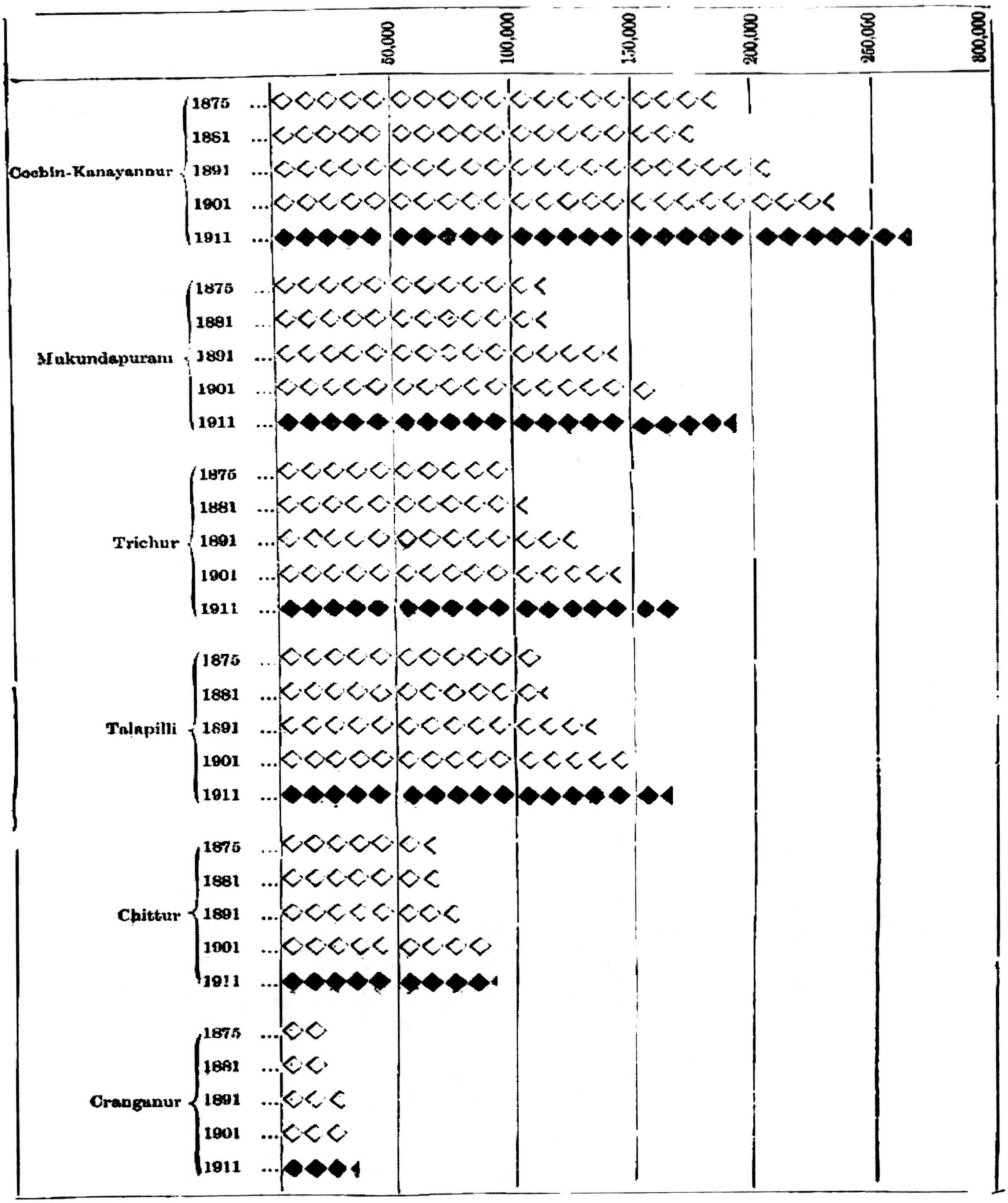

For further particulars see Table II and Chapter II.

DIAGRAM NO. 3.

SHOWING THE NUMBER OF PERSONS IN EVERY 1,000 IN EACH TALUK WHO ARE HINDUS, CHRISTIANS AND MUSALMANS.

Hindus ◆◆◆ **: Christians** ◇◇◇ **: Musalmans** ◆◆◆. **Each diamond, etc., represents 20 persons.**

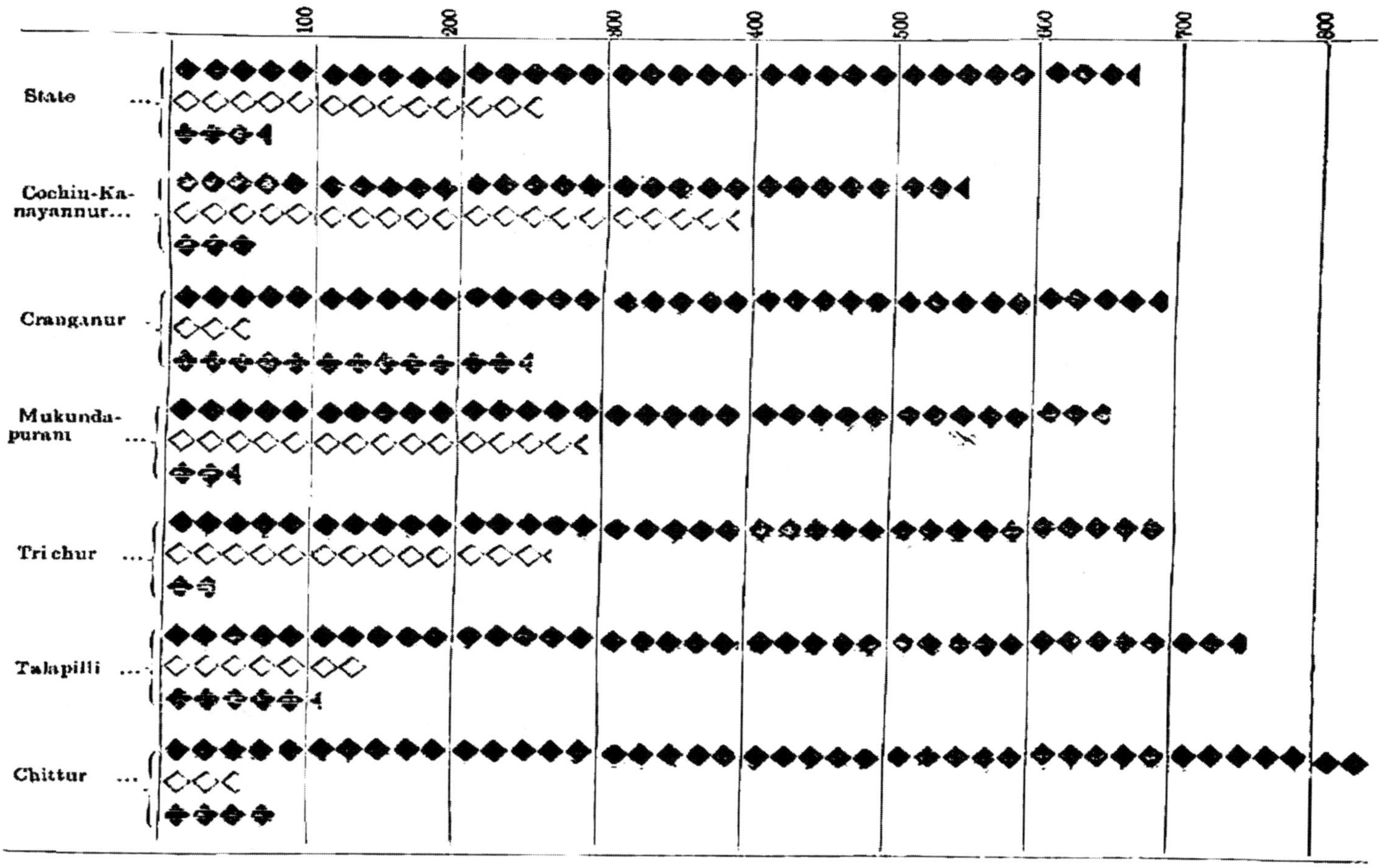

For further particulars see Table VI and Chapter IV.

DIAGRAM. No. 4.

SHOWING FOR CERTAIN AGE PERIODS THE NUMBER IN 1,000 HINDUS, CHRISTIANS AND MUSALMANS, WHO ARE UNMARRIED ◇◇◇, MARRIED ◆◆◆, AND WIDOWED ◆◆◆.

Each diamond, etc., represents 20 persons.

MALES.

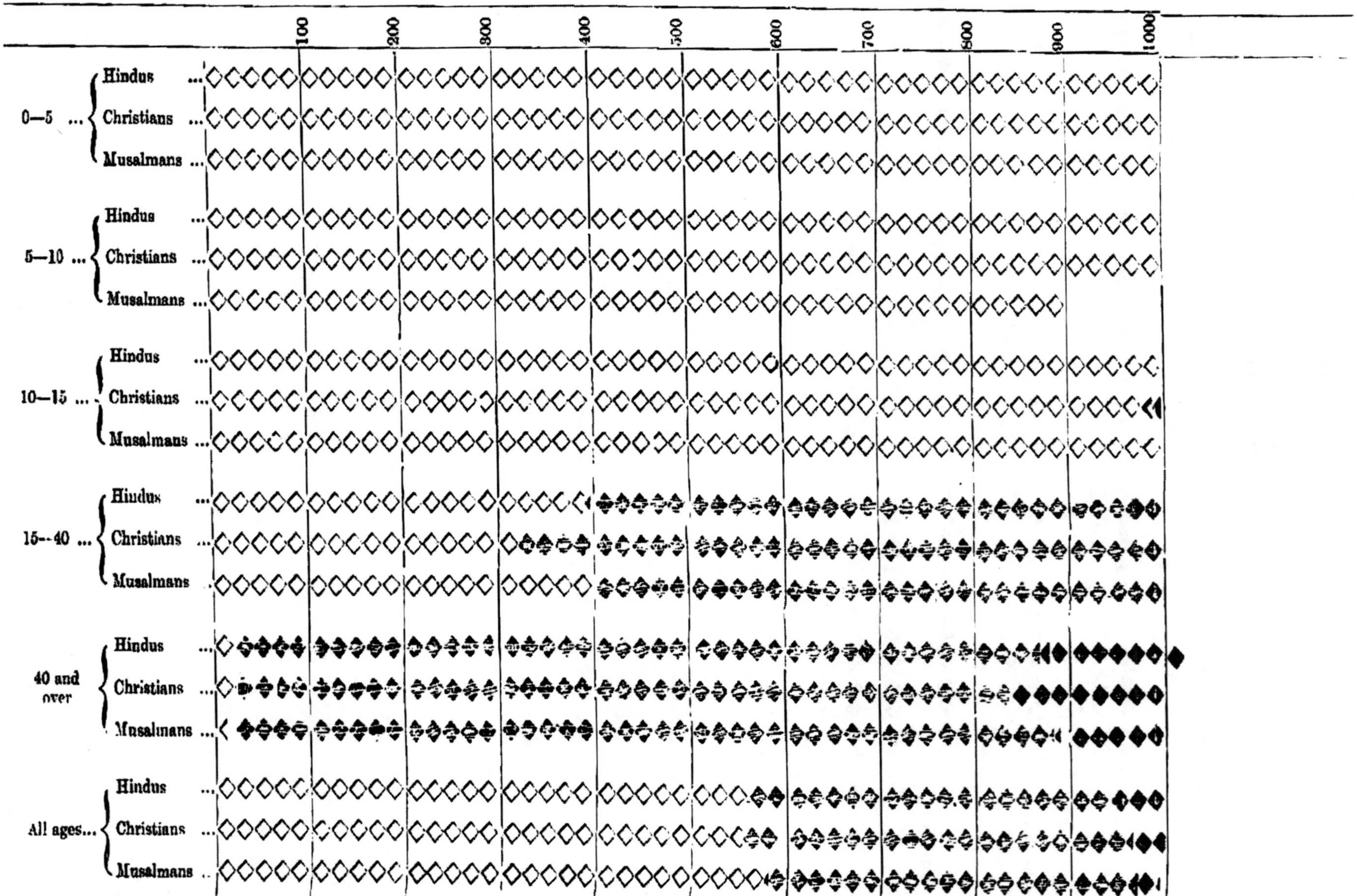

For further particulars see Table VII and Chapter VII.

DIAGRAM No. 4,—*Cont.*

FEMALES.

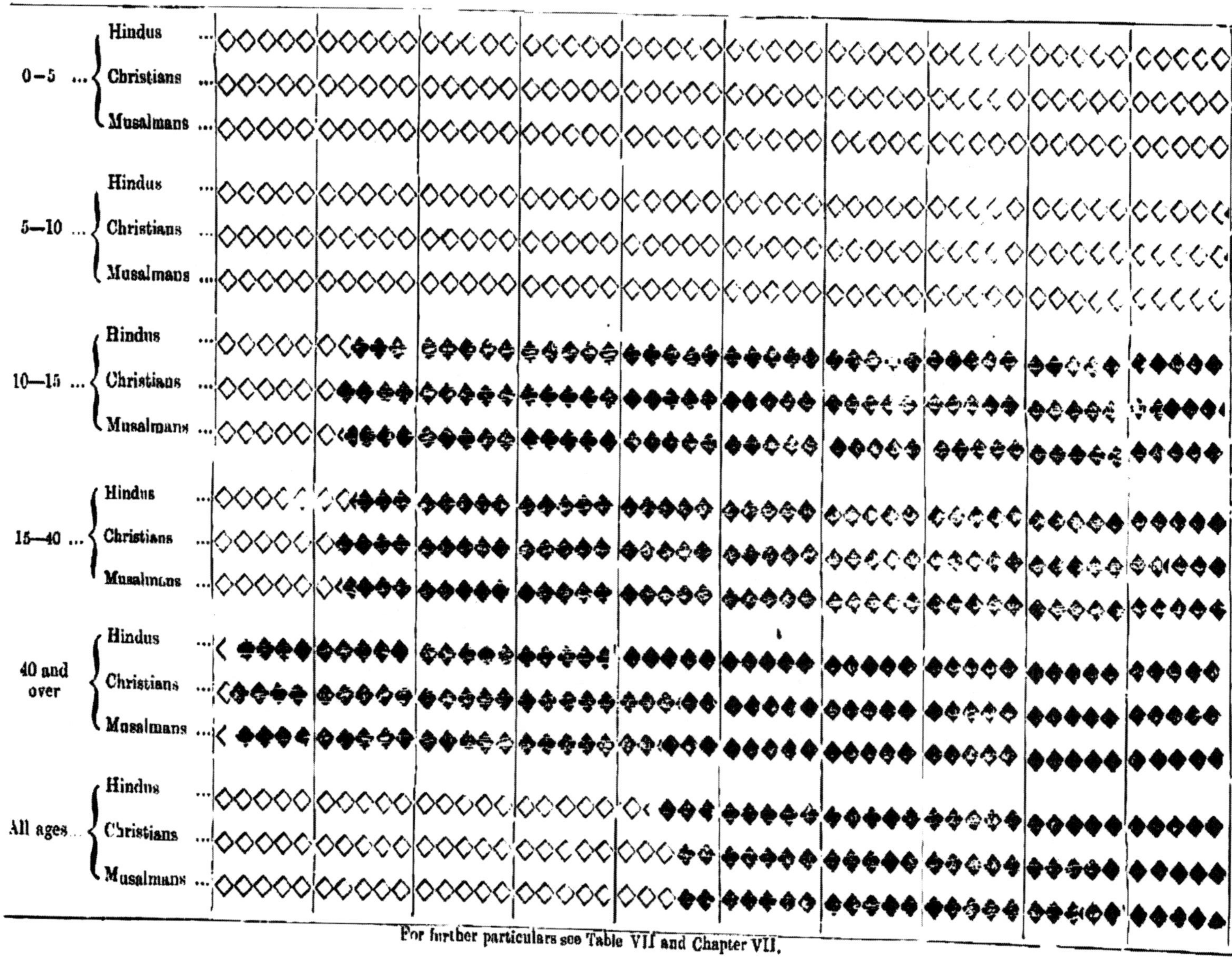

For further particulars see Table VII and Chapter VII.

DIAGRAM No. 5.

SHOWING THE NUMBER IN EVERY 1,000 HINDUS, CHRISTIANS AND MUSALMANS IN EACH OF CERTAIN AGE PERIODS WHO ARE LITERATE

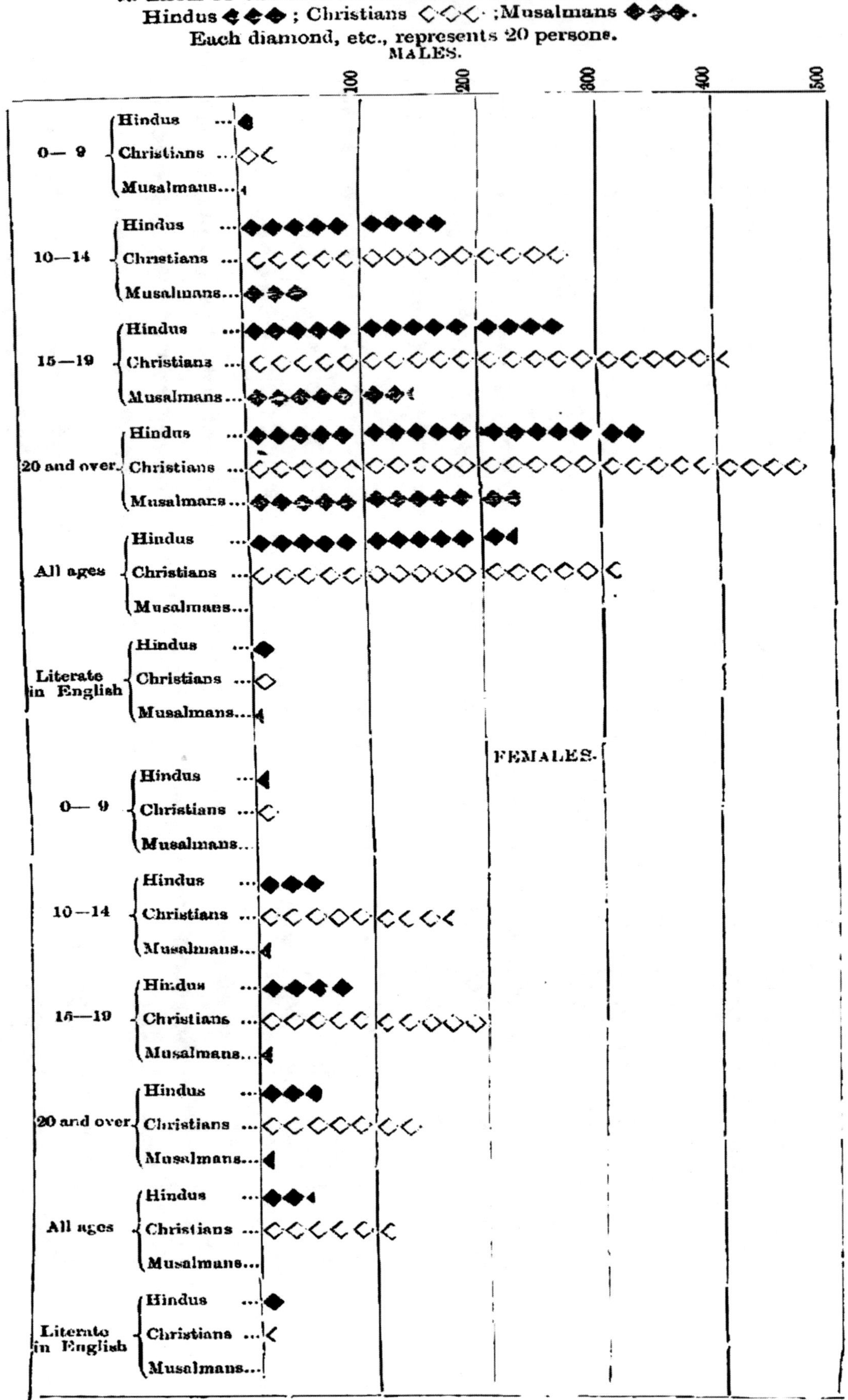

For further particulars see Table VIII and Chapter VIII.

DIAGRAM No. 6.

SHOWING THE NUMBERS IN EVERY 1,000 OF THE CASTES IN TABLE IX WHO ARE

The total number of diamond represents the aggregate number in 1,000 persons of each caste who are literate

MALES

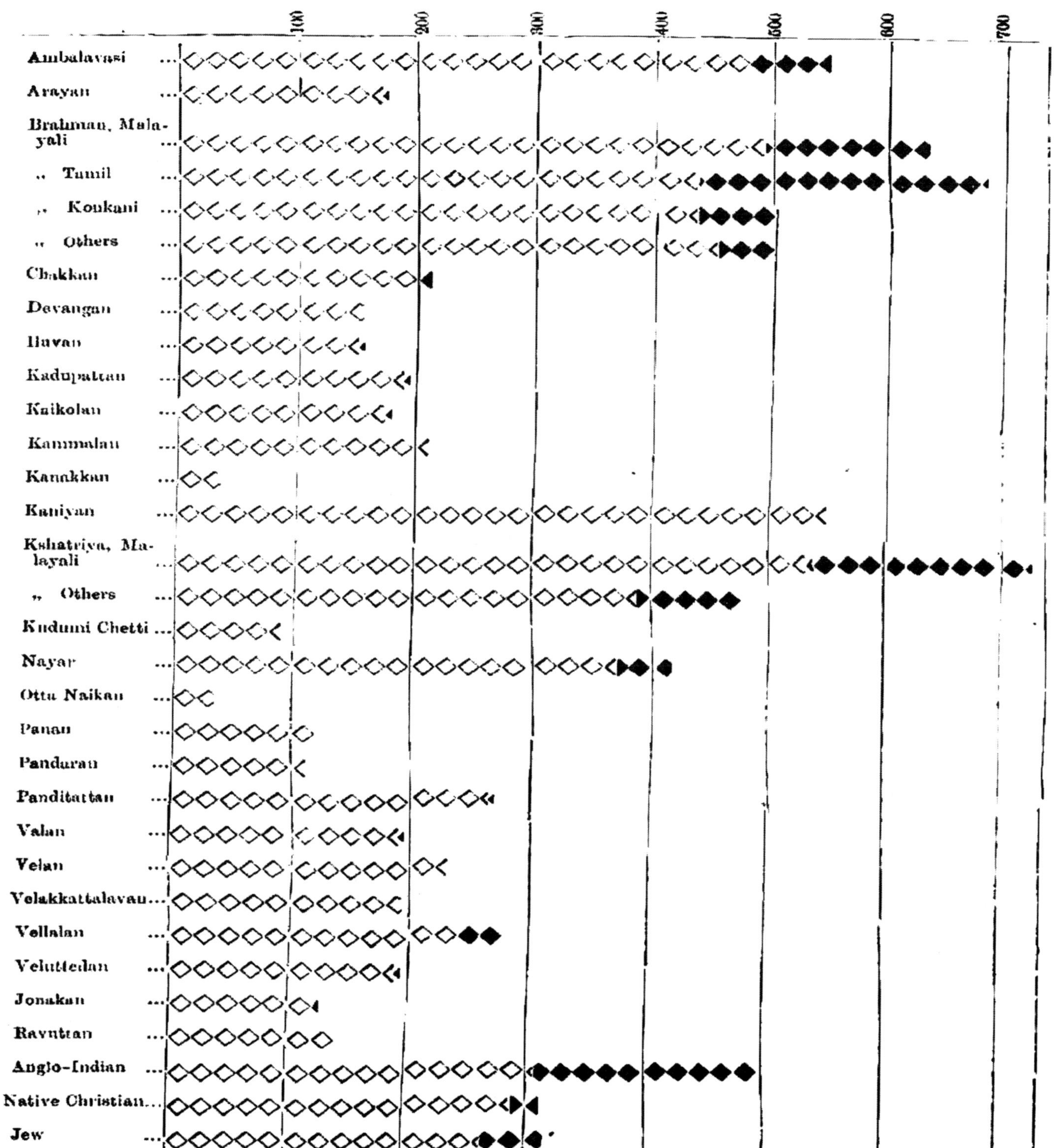

For further particulars see Table IX and Chapter VIII. Of the castes mentioned in the former those that

DIAGRAM No. 6.—*continued.*

LITERATE AND THE NUMBERS OF THOSE WHO ARE ALSO LITERATE IN ENGLISH.

FEMALES.

while the black diamonds represent the number who are literate in English. Each diamond represents 20 persons.

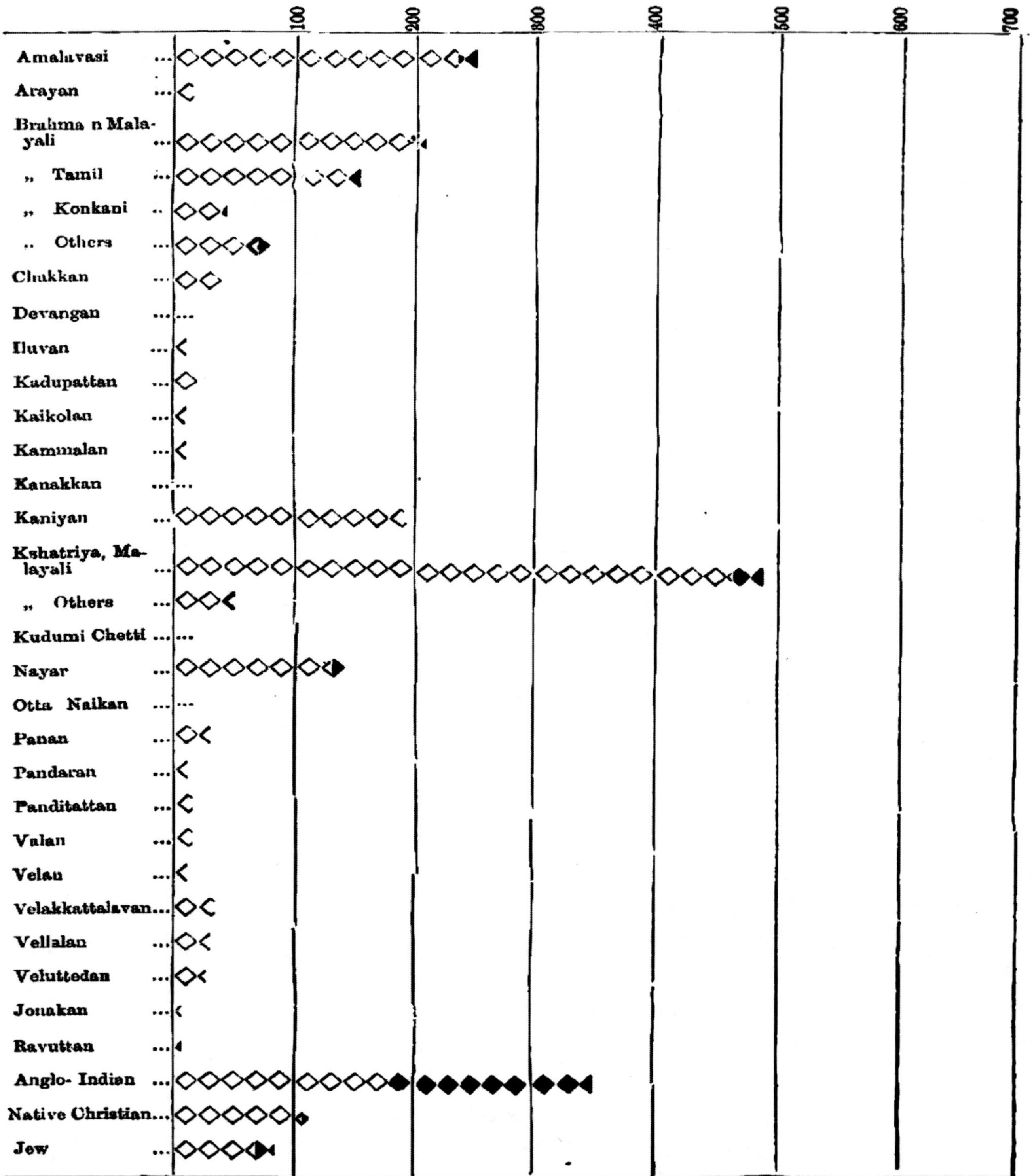

have only less than 20 literates in 1,000 have been omitted from the above diagram.

DIAGRAM No. 7

SHOWING THE MALES ◆◆◆ AND FEMALES ◇◇◇ IN EVERY 100,000 OF THE POPULATION OF EACH TALUK WHO ARE INSANE, DEAF-MUTES, BLIND AND LEPERS RESPECTING.

Each diamond represents 5 persons.

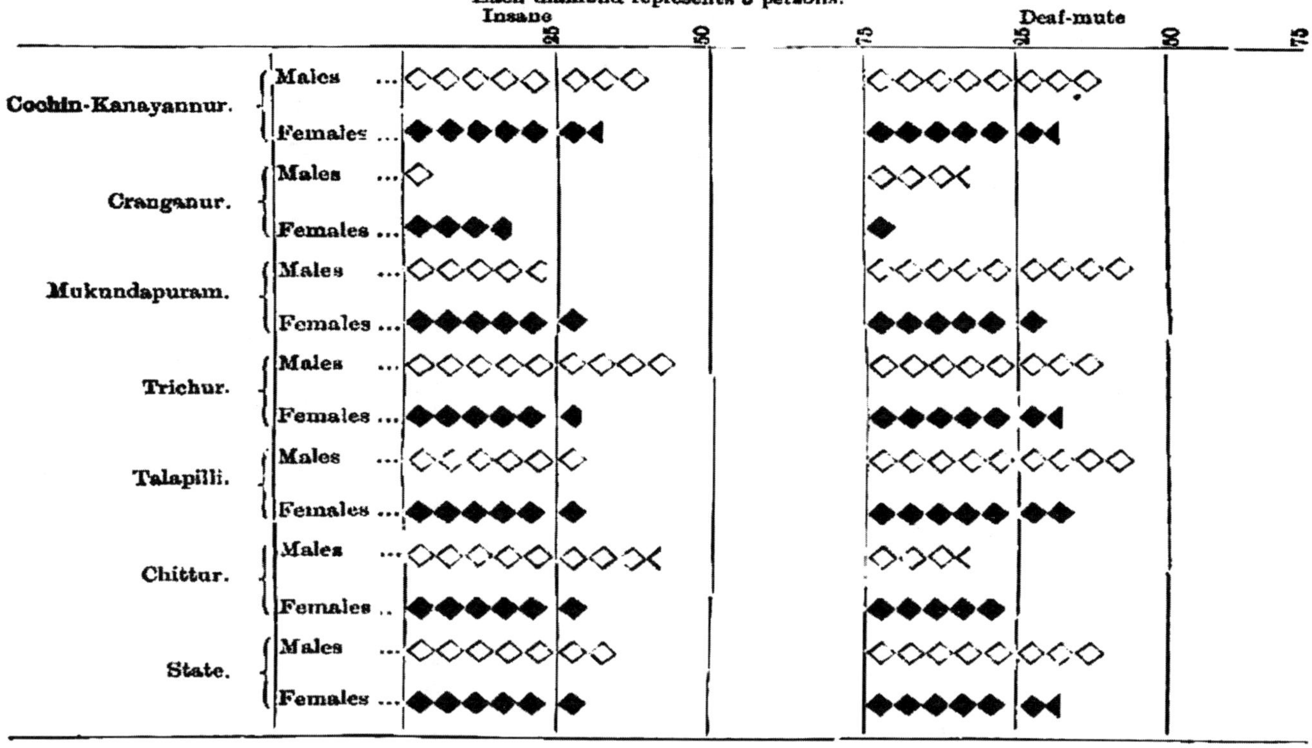

Each diamond represents 10 persons.

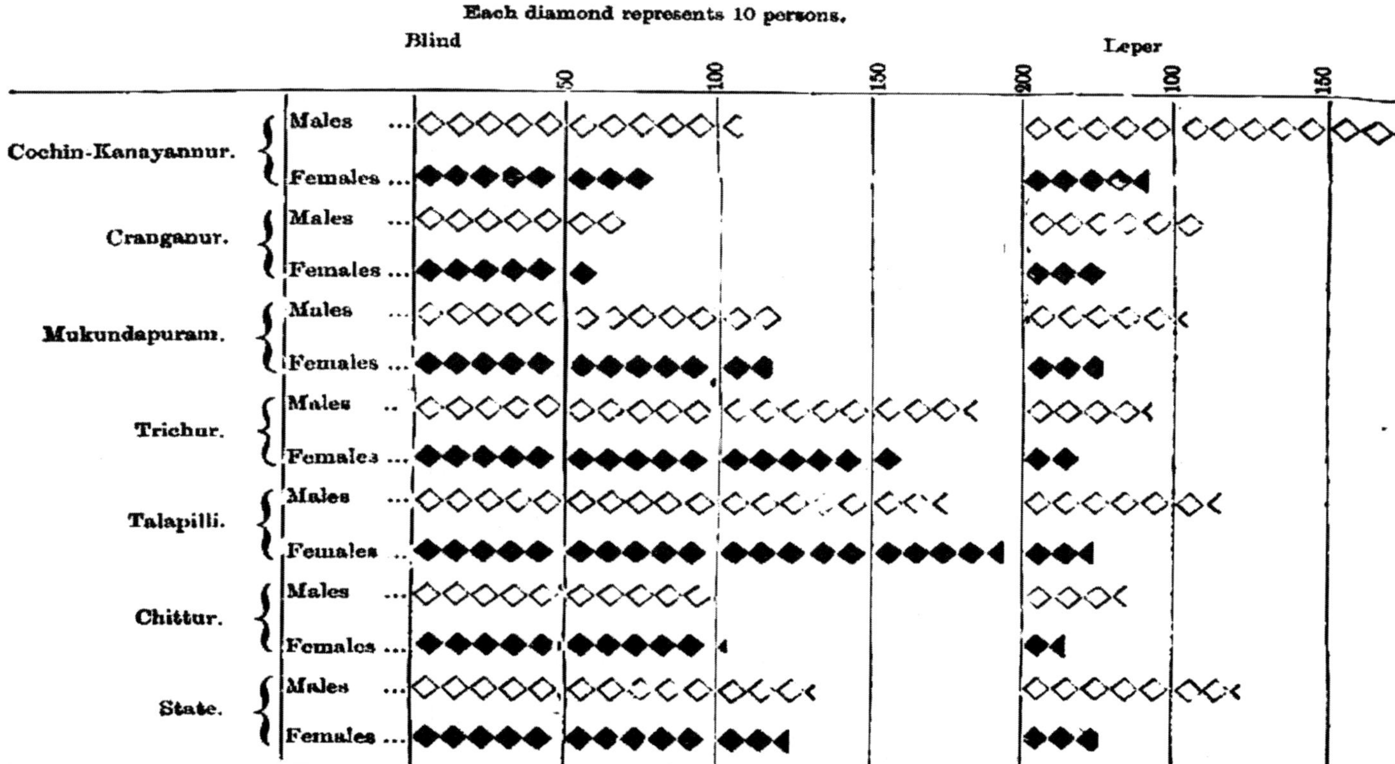

For further particulars see Table XII and Chapter X.

DIAGRAM No. 8

SHOWING THE STRENGTH OF THE LARGER CASTES, TRIBES AND RACES.

Each diamond represents 5,000 persons.

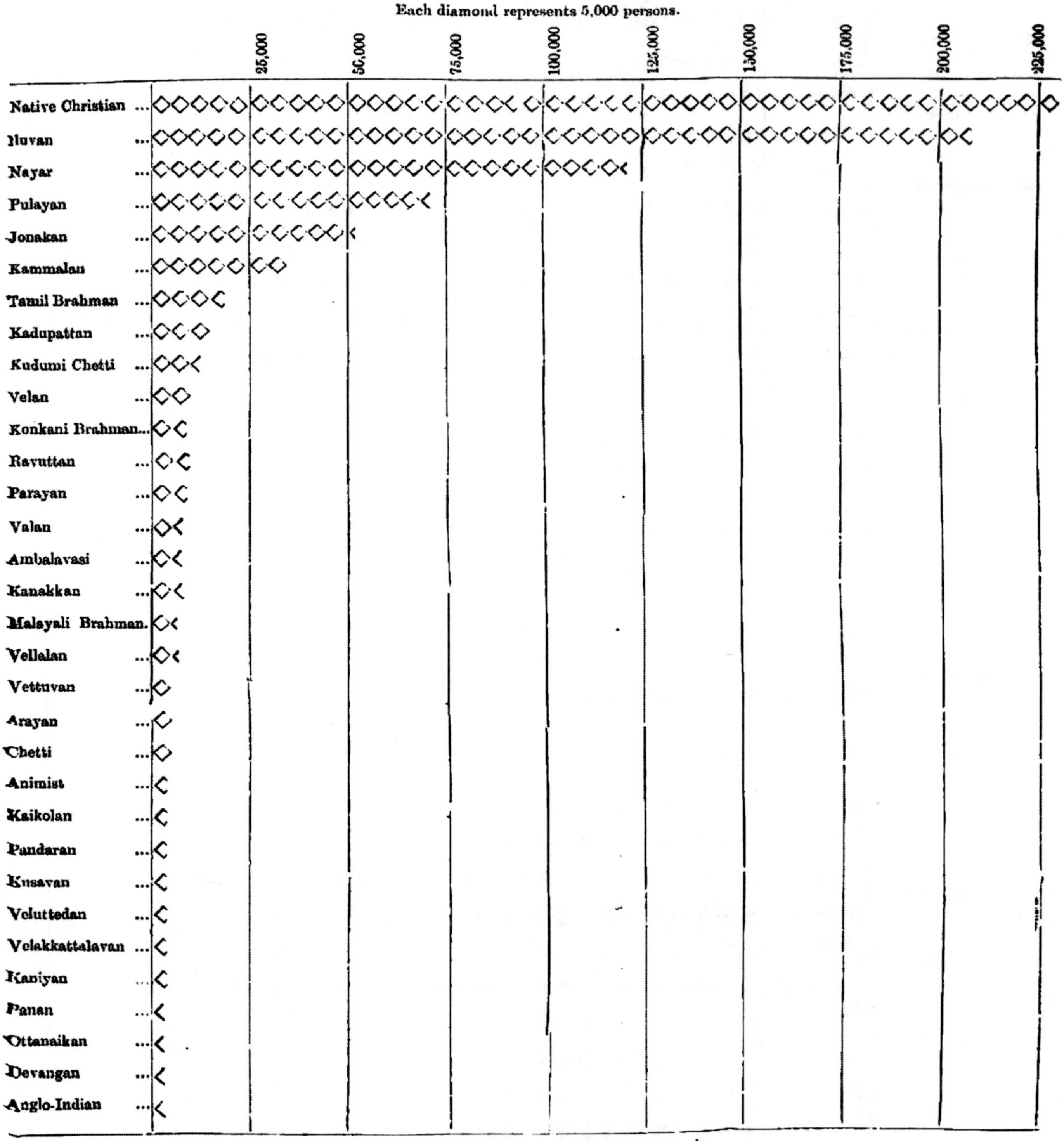

For further particulars see Table XIII and Chapter XI.

DIAGRAM No. 9

SHOWING FOR EACH OF THE SELECTED CASTES (*a*) THE NUMBER IN EVERY 1,000 FEMALE UNDER THE AGE OF 12 WHO ARE EITHER MARRIED OR WIDOWS ◆◆◆ : AND (*b*) THE NUMBER IN EVERY 1,000 FEMALES OF ALL AGES WHO ARE WIDOWS ◇◇◇.

Each diamond represents 10 persons.

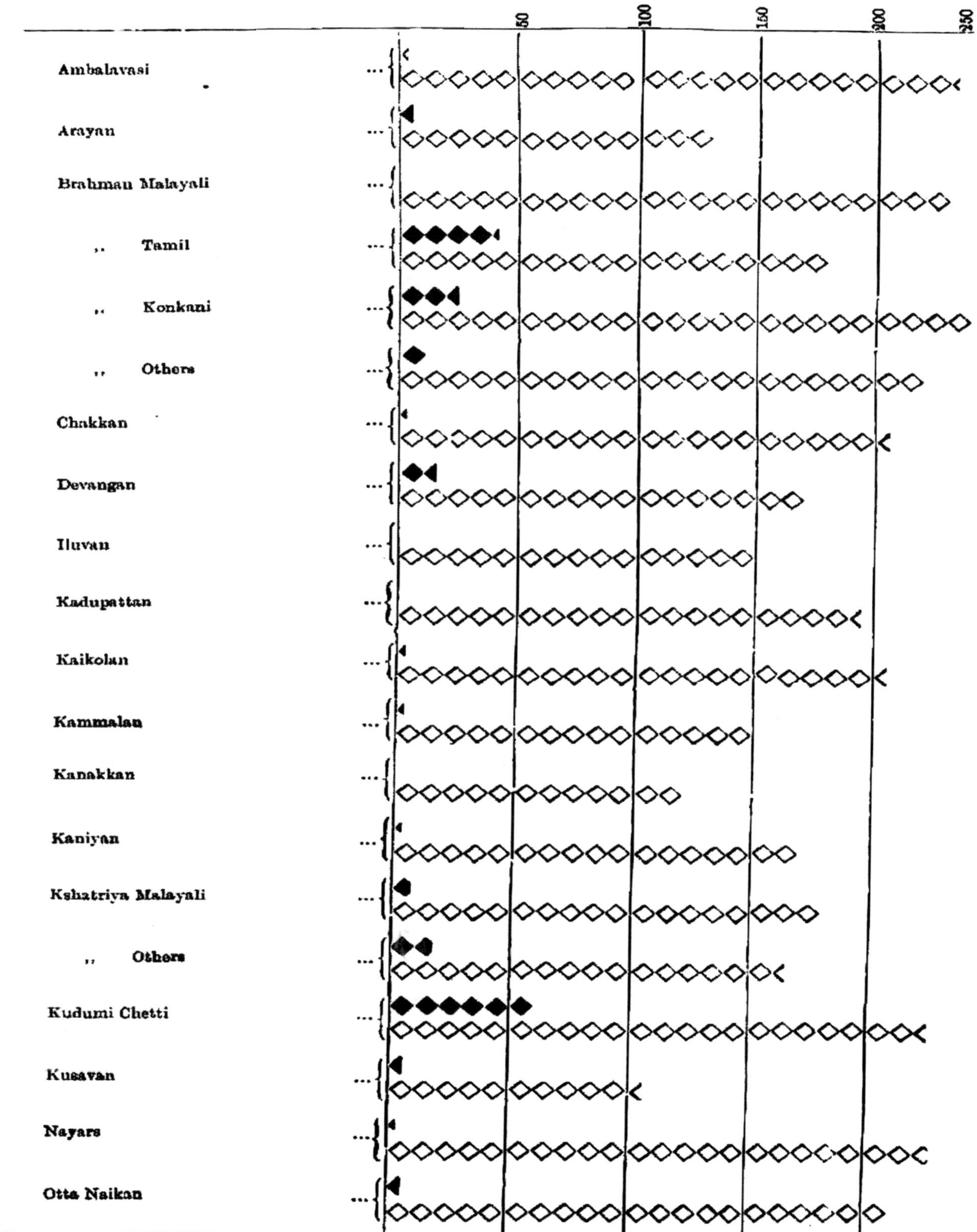

DIAGRAM No. 9.—*continued.*

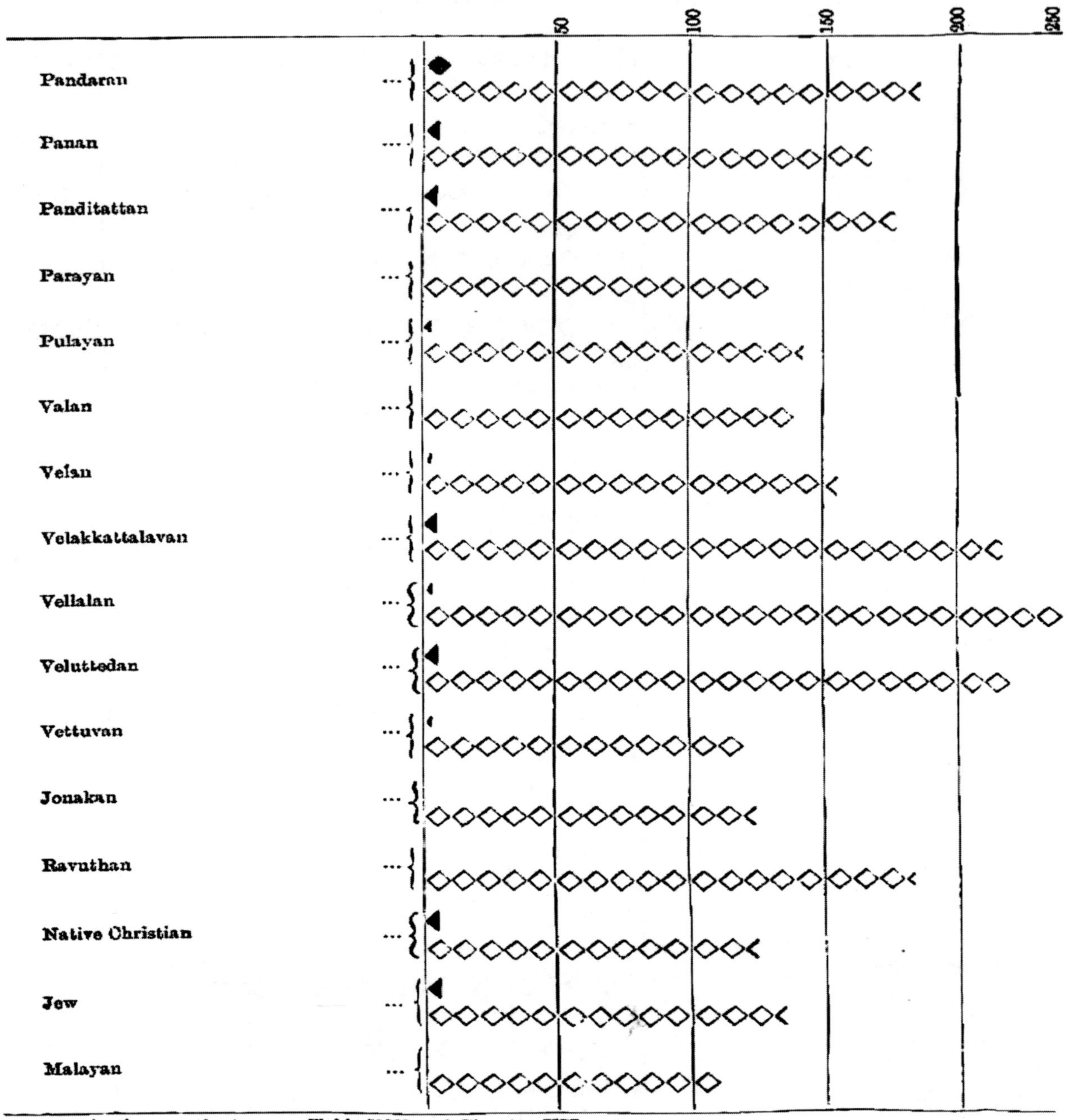

For further particulars see Table XIV and Chapter VII.

DIAGRAM No. 10.

SHOWING THE NUMBER OF PERSONS SUPPORTED BY EACH "ORDER" OF OCCUPATION IN EVERY 1,000 OF THE POPULATION.

Each diamond represents 10 persons.

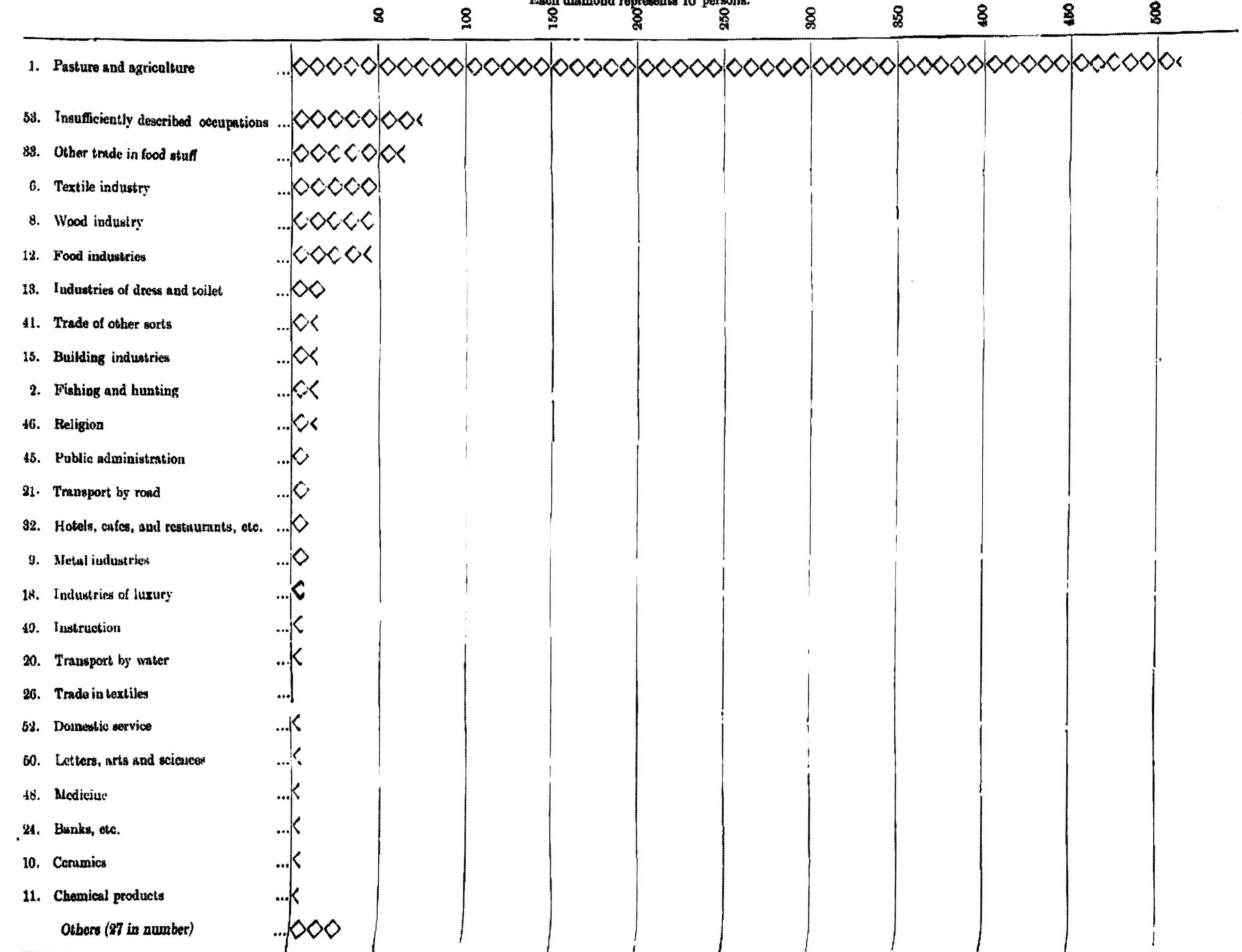

For further particulars see Table XV—A and Chapter XII.

DIAGRAM NO. 11

SHOWING THE PERCENTAGE OF ACTUAL WORKERS IN EACH "ORDER" OF OCCUPATIONS TO THE TOTAL NUMBER OF PERSONS SUPPORTED BY THAT ORDER.

Each diamond represents 2 per cent.

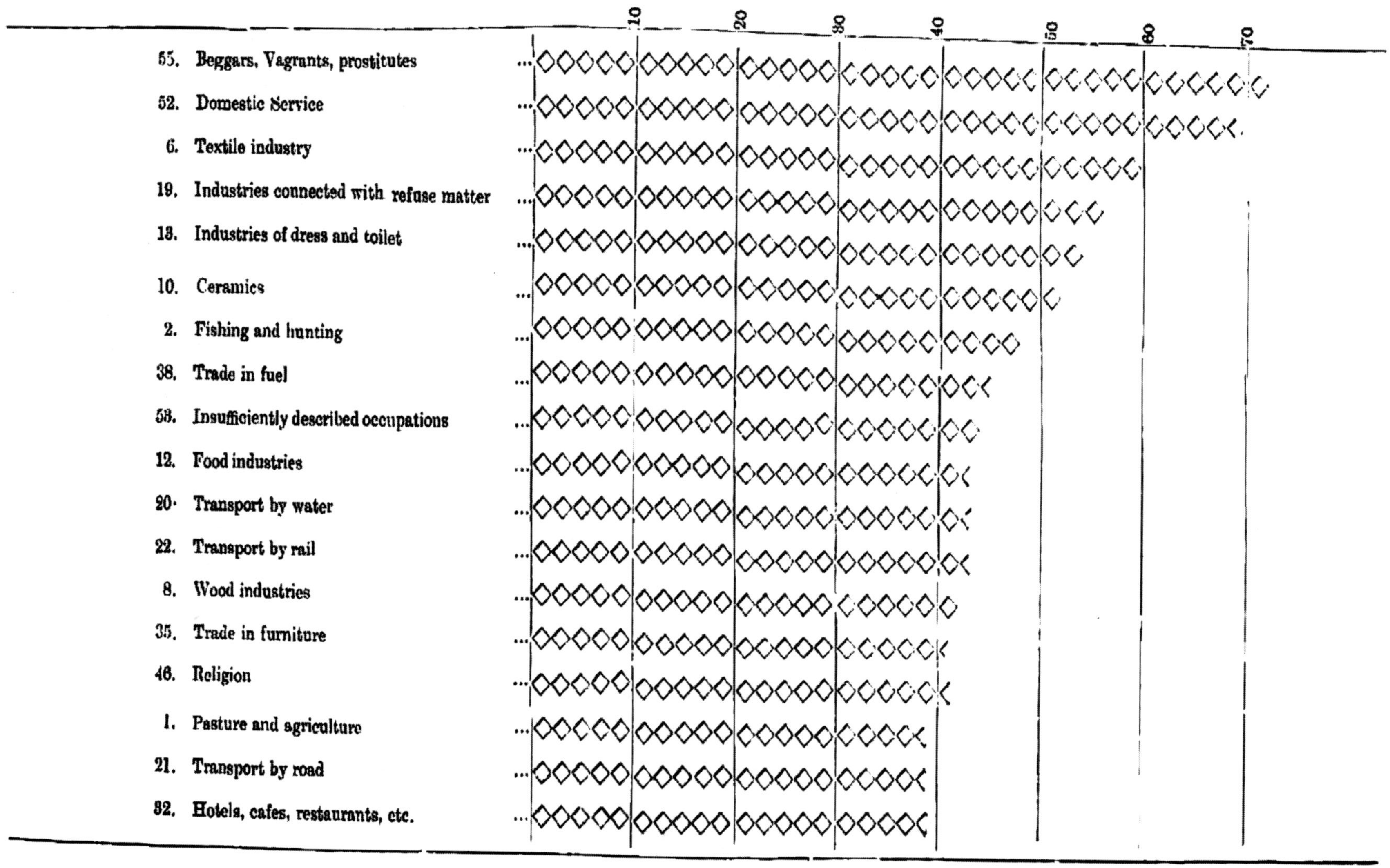

DIAGRAM No. 11—*continued.*

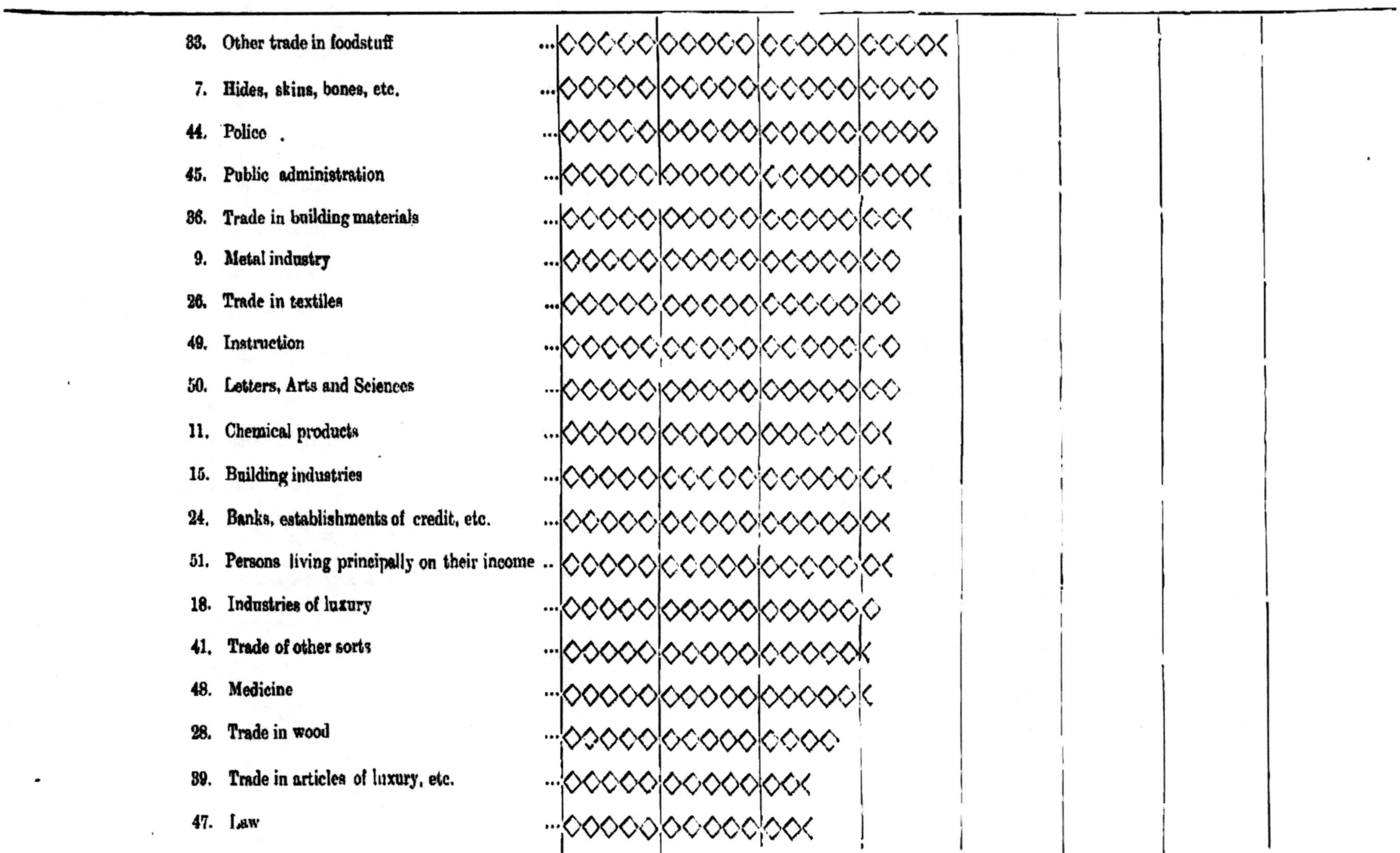

For further particulars see Table XV and Chapter XII. The orders in which the number of actual workers is small are omitted from the above diagram.

DIAGRAM No. 12.

SHOWING THE PERCENTAGE OF FEMALE ACTUAL WORKERS IN EACH "ORDER" OF OCCUPATION TO THE TOTAL ACTUAL WORKERS IN THAT ORDER.

Each Diamond represents 2 per cent.

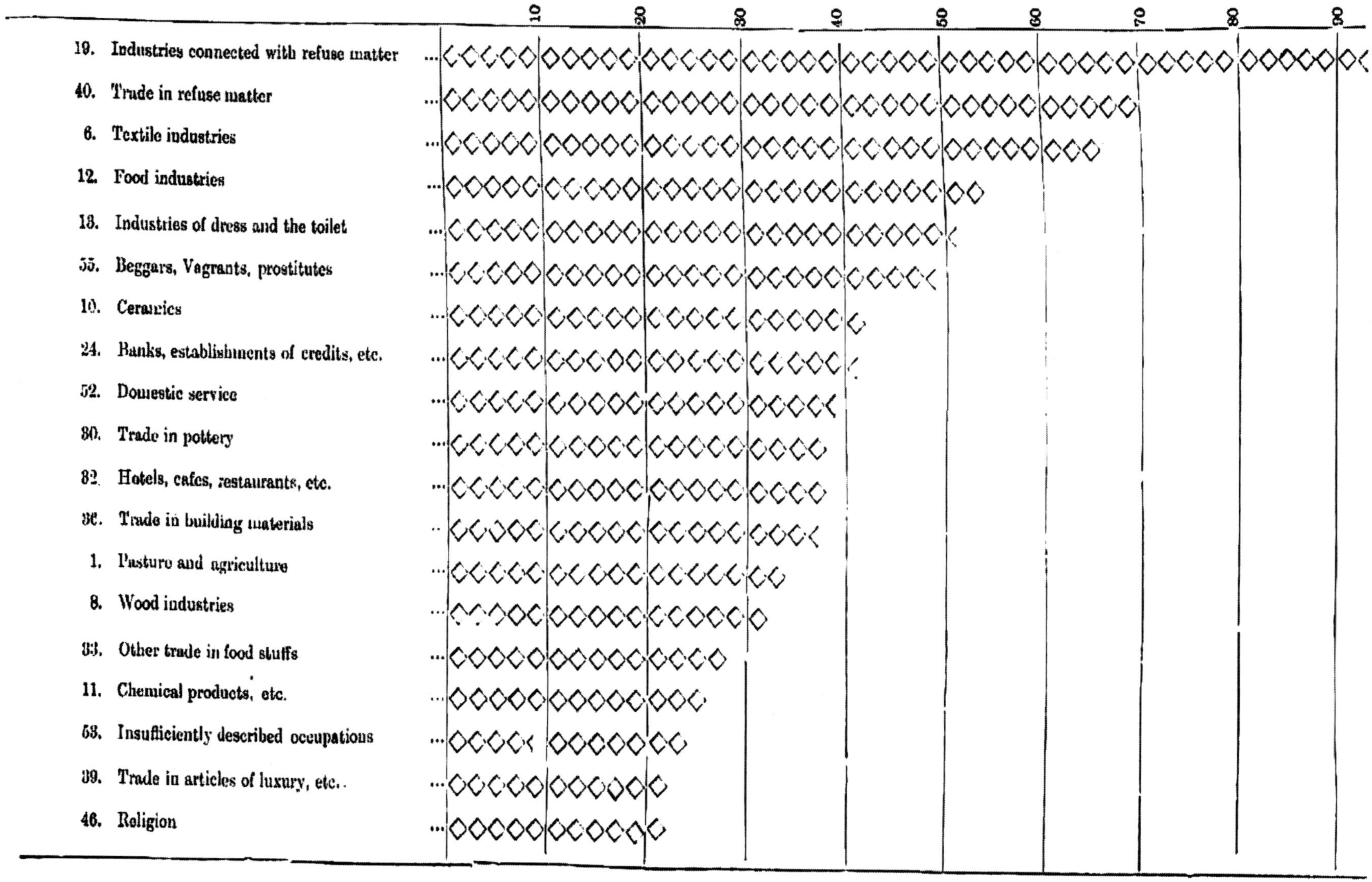

DIAGRAM No. 12—*continued.*

35. Trade in furniture
2. Fishing and hunting
48. Medicine
49. Instruction
9. Metal industry
7. Hides, skins, bones, etc.
38. Trade in fuel
21. Transport by road
41. Trade of other sorts
50. Letters, and arts and sciences
15. Building industries
45. Public administration
54. Inmates of jails, asylums, and hospitals
51. Persons living principally on their income
26. Trade in textiles
37. Trade in means of transport
18. Industries of luxury, etc.

For further particulars see Table XV and Chapter XII. The orders in which the females employed form less than 2 per cent. of the total actual workers are omitted from the above Diagram.

PART I.

REPORT.

REPORT

ON THE

CENSUS OF COCHIN, 1911.

INTRODUCTION.

The Census. The Census with which this Report deals was the fifth systematic enumeration of the population of the State and the fourth taken simultaneously with that of British India, the first being in 1875, while the first Census of British India was taken in 1871. Prior to 1875, estimates of the population were made in 1820, 1836, 1849 and 1858 through the agency of the ordinary village staff, but these were but rough estimates rather than actual computations, and the returns were therefore of but little value from an administrative or scientific point of view. The Census under report was taken on the morning of the 11th March 1911, except in the case of travellers and the houseless poor, who were enumerated during the previous night, and also in that of the hill tribes, who were enumerated leisurely between the 5th and the 10th March. A full account of the procedure adopted in connection with the taking of the Census and the compilation of the results is given in a separate Report: a summary of a few of the more important facts connected with the operations is however given below.

Census divisions and agency. 2. At the previous Censuses the Desam was taken as the unit, that is, the smallest area for which separate statistics were compiled. But the Desams, of which there were 652, were not satisfactory units for Census purposes owing to the great disparity in area and population presented by several of them. Advantage was therefore taken of the recent Survey and Settlement to split up the State into 273 villages, more or less uniform in extent, and these villages were accordingly taken as the units for the purposes of the present Census. The average extent of a village excluding the forest area is nearly 2,000 acres. The State was for Census purposes divided into nine *Charges*, each of the six taluks and the three Municipal towns being treated as a Charge. The Tahsildars of the taluks and the Presidents of the Town Councils were appointed Superintendents of the several Charges. The Charges in their turn were subdivided into 319 *Circles*, each of which was placed under a Supervisor. The Supervisors were mostly recruited from among Government servants and teachers of aided schools, all of whom, with the exception of two or three, were English-knowing men. The Circles were again split up into 5,000 *Blocks*, an Enumerator being appointed to take the Census of each block. The majority of the Enumerators were Government servants and teachers of recognised schools, while the rest were private gentlemen or clerks and accountants of merchants, Devasvams and Janmis. The work throughout was carried out by unpaid agency. In 1901, the non-official Enumerators were given a small remuneration, which amounted in the aggregate to Rs. 1,310, while in 1891 the amount went up to Rs. 6,286. The average number of occupied houses in a block was 33, and the average number of blocks in a circle 16.

3. The first step towards the taking of the Census was the numbering of houses and the preparation of house lists. A house was defined as the dwelling place of one or more families with their resident servants, having a separate principal entrance from the common way. When all the houses have been numbered, a statement showing the number of houses in each village and the number of each grade of Census officers required in each Charge was prepared by the Charge Superintendent and submitted to the Census Superintendent for approval. The work of numbering the houses and the preparation of house lists was carried out by Sanitary Inspectors and Maistries in Municipal towns and by village officers elsewhere between the 15th of August and the end of September. Advantage was taken of this opportunity to take a correct Census of agricultural stock in the State. The officers engaged in numbering houses were required to obtain then and there a return from each house-holder of the agricultural stock owned by him.

House numbering.

4. The next step was the preparation of the preliminary record, that is, the entry in the enumeration schedule of the prescribed particulars regarding all persons ordinarily resident in each house. The period intervening between the commencement of this work and the completion of house numbering was taken up in drilling the Census officers. Classes were held by me in different centres for the instruction of Supervisors in October and November, and the Supervisors in their turn held classes for the instruction of Enumerators in December. Everything possible was done to give the Supervisors and Enumerators a thorough knowledge of their duties, and consequently mistakes and inaccuracies in the entries were reduced into a minimum. The preliminary enumeration was commenced on the 25th January in rural tracts and on the 5th February in towns, and was completed in about fifteen days. The original entries were made on plain paper, and the rough drafts so prepared were shown to and corrected by the Supervisors before they were entered in the schedule books. The correctness of the entries made by the Enumerators were thoroughly tested by the Supervisors during the period intervening between the preparation of the rough drafts and the final Census I went through about 20 per cent of the schedule books myself.

The preliminary record.

5. The final enumeration, or the actual Census, was taken on the morning of the 11th March between daybreak and noon, when each Enumerator went round his block and brought the record up to date by striking out the entries relating to persons no longer present and entering the necessary particulars for new arrivals. Special arrangements were made for the enumeration of travellers by road and canal, the sea-going population and the houseless poor, while travellers by rail were enumerated by the Railway authorities, who, after preparing the provisional totals, despatched the enumeration books to my office. An industrial Census was also taken on the same day in special schedules which were previously filled up by the owners, managers or agents of factories, mills, etc., in which at least 20 persons were employed. Special Enumerators were told off to collect these schedules after correcting them with reference to the actual state of things on the 11th March.

The actual Census.

6. On the afternoon after the Census the Enumerators met their Supervisors at a place previously agreed upon, and prepared an abstract showing the number of houses and of persons, male and female, in their blocks. The Supervisor, after getting the abstracts checked by a second enumerator and having checked them himself, compiled a summary for his circle and despatched it by the quickest route to the charge superintendent, who checked the circle abstracts and posted them in a charge summary, and despatched the latter to the Central office, where provisional totals for the State were compiled from the charge summaries. The first charge summary to arrive was that of the Trichur town and the last that of the Cochin-Kanayannur taluk, which

Provisional Totals.

were received on the 11th and 14th March respectively. The provisional totals for the State were ready on the 14th, and were telegraphed to the Census Commissioner for India at Simla and the Provincial Superintendent at Madras on the same day. The total population as shown by those provisional figures was 918,639, or 529 more than the figure eventually arrived at after detailed tabulation in the Central office. The difference between the two totals was thus only ·057 per cent., or 57 persons in 100,000, as against 393 in the same number in 1901.

Abstraction and Tabulation.

7. The Central office for the abstraction and tabulation of the information contained in the schedules was opened on the 16th March, and work was commenced on the next day. The office consisted at first of five Supervisors, five Assistant Supervisors, 49 abstraction clerks and three office clerks, but their number was gradually reduced till there remained only one Supervisor and one office clerk in January 1912. For abstracting and tabulating the entries in the schedules, what is known as the slip or card system, the invention of the Hungarian statistician Herr Von Mayr was adopted as on the last occasion, a description of which is given in the Administrative Volume. The work ot copying the slips and checking them was completed exactly in two months by 49 clerks, while that of sorting the slips for the different Tables, in which 33 clerks were engaged, was carried out in a little over three months. The compilation and fair-copying of the figures from the Sorters' tickets took a smaller office, consisting only of Supervisors and Assistant Supervisors, some two months more to complete it.

Cost of the Census.

8. The total cost of the Census from the date of my appointment on the 15th December 1909 up to the middle of February 1912 amounted to Rs. 20,590, and an expenditure of about Rs. 2,500 will have to be incurred before the work is finally completed. The total expenditure will thus amount to Rs. 23,094, or Rs. 25—2—5 per thousand of the population, as against Rs. 15,303, or Rs. 18—13—6 per thousand in 1901. Of the total expenditure, the sum of Rs. 10,420 represents the cost of taking the Census, while the balance Rs. 12,674 was expended on the work of abstraction, tabulation, report writing, etc. The increase in the expenditure, as compared with that of the previous Census, was due to the higher pay of the Superintendent. If only his deputation allowance is taken into account in calculating the cost of the Census, as is done in the British Provinces, the expenditure will amount to only Rs. 11,494, or Rs. 12—8—4 per thousand. It has also to be remembered that during a considerable period of his deputation the Superintendent was not engaged exclusivly in Census work but had other duties to attend to. The house lists and a few minor forms were printed at the Cochin Government Press, while all the other forms, including the schedules, slips, sorters' tickets, tabulation and compilation registers, were furnished by the Madras Government at a cost, including transport charges, of Rs. 486.

Acknowledgments.

9. Before concluding this introduction I have to express my grateful thanks to the various officers, especially the Tahsildars and the Presidents of Town Councils, for their cordial co-operation at all the stages of the operations. Fully occupied as the latter already were with their ordinary duties, their work as Charge Superintendents was obviously a heavy additional burden to them, notwithstanding which, with hardly an exception, they ungrudgingly devoted a considerable portion of their time to Census work for over six months, and the accuracy of the enumeration and the promptitude with which it was carried out were in no small measure due to their whole-hearted devotion to the work. In the Central office where abstraction and tabulation were carried out, the strain was particularly heavy, especially for the Supervisors and their assistants, but they one and all did their work cheerfully and satisfactorily. Where all did well, it would be invidious to particularise, but the work of P. Krishna

Variyar, B. A., who was with me from the 16th March up to the 16th January 1912 and who, besides doing his ordinary work as Supervisor, compiled almost all the Subsidiary Tables, deserves special mention.

The Report.

10. The following Report does not profess to do anything more than to deal with the figures contained in the final and Subsidiary Tables and to gather up the more obvious inferences deducible from them. Information already available in a permanent form in the previous Census Reports, recent Administration Reports, the Cochin State Manual, the Cochin Castes and Tribes, etc., will not be found repeated in this Report. Bearing in mind the instructions of the Census Commissioner for India, I have made every attempt to reduce the bulk of the Report to reasonable dimensions.

CHAPTER I.

DISTRIBUTION OF THE POPULATION.

Divisions of the State.

11. In the scheme of natural divisions in which the different parts of India are grouped, Cochin, together with Travancore and the British Districts of Malabar and South Canara, comes under what is known as the West Coast Division. The State lies between 9° 48′ and 10° 50′ N. Latitude and 76° 5′ and 76° 58′ E. Longitude, and consists of two disconnected parts, the larger lying along the coast and the smaller comprising the chief portion of the Chittur taluk and entirely encircled by British territory. The eastern half of the former part is covered with forests and is practically uninhabited, while the rest of the State is thickly populated, the sea-board being more so than the interior. The State is divided into six taluks, Cochin-Kanayannur, Cranganur, Mukundapuram, Trichur, Talapilli and Chittur. Cochin and Kanayannur were separate taluks at the previous Censuses, but they were amalgamated in 1907. As however this amalgamation did not involve any territorial re-distribution, no adjustment of the figures of the previous Censuses is required for purposes of comparison.

Area and population.

12. The general statistics of the area and population of each taluk will be found in Imperial Table I. The total area of the State, according to the Great Trigonometrical Survey, is 1,361½ square miles, and the population, according to the recent Census, is 918,110. The largest taluk is Mukundapuram, which has an area of 418 square miles, while the most populous taluk is Cochin-Kanayannur, which, though only 156½ square miles in extent, has 264,828 inhabitants. The smallest and the least populous taluk is Cranganur, whose area and population are 19 square miles and 33,193 respectively.

Density of the population.

13. Subsidiary Table I at the end of this Chapter shows the mean density of the population per square mile, together with statistics relating to cultivation. The density has now risen to 675 per square mile, which is equalled or exceeded but by few States or Districts in India. As Travancore, Malabar and South Canara have only a density of 438, 520 and 297 respectively, Cochin stands highest in point of density among the tracts comprised in the natural division "West Coast." No district in the Madras Presidency has a greater density than Cochin, while no State in India even approaches it in density. The density of the Madras Presidency as a whole is only 292. No country in Europe has such a density as Cochin, England and Wales, the most densely peopled country in Europe, having a density of only 619 per square mile.

Density by taluks.

14. The density varies in the different taluks of the State and much more so in the different villages, those bordering the sea and the backwater being much more densely peopled than those in the interior with their reserved forests and other uninhabitable tracts. Cochin-Kanayannur and Cranganur belong to the former category, having a density of 1852 and 1747 respectively, and are thus the most densely peopled taluks in Southern India, while Mukundapuram and Chittur, the major portion of which is covered with forests, have only a density of 464 and 320 respectively. In the sea board tract, except for a few paddy flats, there is hardly any uninhabitable or uninhabited area, the whole extent consisting almost entirely of extensive cocoanut plantations, thickly dotted with houses throughout. One of the continental

writers on the Indian Census, Vidal de La Blache, attributes the great density of this tract to the copious rainfall it receives. "The close connection between rainfall and density", he says, "is even more apparent in the south, where a narrow strip of coast-line exposed to the full force of the monsoon has an enormous density, amounting in some parts of Cochin to the phenominal figure of 75 per kmq". While admitting that this density is to some extent due to rainfall, I would attribute the "enormous density" of the sea-board mainly to the adaptibility of its soil to the generous growth of the cocoanut palm. The rest of the State (excepting Chittur) receives as much rain as the sea-board, but is not so densely peopled. In the former there are extensive rice fields which are not and cannot be inhabited, while the cultivation of cocoanut trees does not interfere with the rearing of homesteads in their midst. The cultivation of the tree and the manufacture of articles out of its produce, such as *copra*, oil, coir, toddy, arrack, etc., afford ample occupation to the large numbers of people living in this tract.

Towns and villages.

15. It is first necessary to explain what is meant by the expressions towns and villages. The definition of a town was practically the same as in the previous years, and comprised all Municipalities of whatever population, and every other continuous collection of houses permanently inhabited by not less than 5,000 persons, which the Census Superintendent, having regard to the character and relative density of its population, the importance of the place as a centre of trade and its historic associations, might decide to treat as town. Nine places were accordingly treated as towns, or two more than in 1901, Tripunittura and Nemmara being treated as towns for the first time. The rest of the State, excluding the reserved forests, is divided into 273 villages, more or less uniform in size, but with population varying considerably according to their character and situation. The villages bordering the sea and the back-water are very densely populated, and those in the interior are less so, while the villages situated on the confines of the forests are very sparsely inhabited. Our villages are but administrative units and not compact residential villages of the type common on the eastern side of the Ghats. Some of them contain one or more residential villages, while others contain only a few detached houses scattered over a large area. In the great majority of residential villages the houses have their own compounds with trees and garden lands attached, but in a few of them, where native Christians or non-indigenous Hindus preponderate, the houses are closely packed together on a small site, but not so closely as on the East Coast. The depressed classes generally live in detached huts on the confines of rice fields.

Distribution of the population between towns and villages.

16. The distribution of the population between towns and villages is shown by taluks in Imperial Table I and Subsidiary Table III, from which it will be seen that 12 per cent of the people of the State live in towns, as against 10·7 per cent in 1901, the percentages for Travancore, Malabar and the Madras Presidency as a whole being 6·2, 8 and 11 respectively. Only three of the towns—Ernakulam, Mattancheri and Trichur-are completely urban in their character, and contain over 20,000 inhabitants each, while the remaining six are partly urban and partly rural in their appearance, and contain between them only 38 per cent of the urban population. All these towns are of comparatively recent growth, as the Malayalis have from time immemorial been averse to living in closely built villages. The extension of industrial and other business concerns however has in recent years drawn the people to certain convenient centres and made them congregate there. This tendency is becoming more and more marked now-a-days, the urban population having increased by nearly 26 per cent *, although the population of the State as a whole has increased only by 13 per cent.

* The increase is only 14·2 per cent if Tripunittura and Nemmara, which were treated as towns for the first time in 1911, are excluded.

Urban population by religion.

17. The growth of towns in Cochin, as on the West Coast generally, is mainly due to the habits of living and enterprise of native Christians, Musalmans and non-indigenous Hindus, chiefly Tamil Brahmans, so that they preponderate over the indigenous Hindus in towns, specially in the more important ones. Though the Hindus form 67 per cent of the total population of Cochin, they form but 50 per cent of the population of the more important towns, *viz.*, Ernakulam, Mattancheri and Trichur, and even among these about one-half belong to non-indigenous castes, chiefly Tamil and Konkani Brahmans. Again, only 10 per cent of the Hindus live in towns, while the percentages of Musalmans and Christians living in towns are 16 and 15 respectively. The great majority of the Jews also live in towns. There is not a single animist in any of the towns.

Houses.

18. For Census purposes a house was defined to be the dwelling place of one or more families, with their resident servants, having a separate principal entrance from the common way. As the great majority of houses in Cochin, whether they be the well built mansions of the richer classes or the flimsy huts of the poor, stand in their own premises, no great difficulty was experienced in applying this definition correctly. A few mistakes were committed here and there in numbering the houses, especially in crowded places, where houses are built close to each other on the street system, but they are far too few to affect the statistics materially. The typical Malayali house is the *Nalukettu*, a quadrangular building consisting of four blocks, with a square or oblong court-yard in the centre, known as the *Nadumittam*. The house is surrounded on all sides by a well swept court-yard, which is again surrounded by a compound in which fruit trees and plantains and other vegetables are grown, and which is bounded by masonry walls or by mud walls with fences. The entrance to the compound is through a *Padipura*, or gate house. Though this is the type of the Malayali building, the details of course vary according to the circumstances of the inmates. The dwelling of a wealthy family may consist of two or more *Nalukettus*, and one or more blocks of the building may be two-storeyed. The poorer houses consist of only one of the four blocks with or without varandas or portico. The better classes of houses are built of laterite plastered with chunnam, and the roofs are generally tiled, but are in some cases thatched with plaited cocoanut leaves or the leaves of the palmyra. The poorer houses are built of mud, whitewashed or coloured red, and the roofs thatched with plaited leaves or straw; but in the sandy tracts wooden planks or bamboo mats take the place of mud walls. Terraced buildings are almost unknown, the heavy rainfall of this coast rendering terraced roofs unsafe.

House room.

19. Talukwar statistics showing the average number of persons living in each house and the average number of houses per square mile are given in Subsidiary Table VI. Occupied houses, which numbered 163,286, or 17,401 more than in 1901, increased by 12 per cent during the decade, as against an increase of 13 per cent in the population, so that there had been no material change in the average number of persons per house, the number being 5·6, against 5·5 ten years ago. In Travancore, in Malabar and in the Presidency generally, occupied houses increased by 14, 8·2 and 9·8 per cent respectively, and the population by 16, 7·8 and 8·3 per cent, the average number of persons per house being 5·2, 5·6 and 5·3 respectively. Houses are naturally more crowded in towns than in villages, the average for the former being 6·2 and for the latter 5·5. The average number of houses to a square mile was 120, as against 107 in 1901, and varies according to the density of population. The average for Cochin-Kanayannur and Cranganur considerably exceeds, and that for Talapilli, Mukundapuram and Chittur falls short of, the State average. The figures for Travancore, Malabar and the Presidency are 87, 92 and 55 respectively. The average number of persons per house cannot be taken as indicating the size of the families. In a great majority

of the population of the State, especially among those who follow the *Marumakkattayam* law of inheritance, the joint family system prevails in almost its prestine vigour. Among the Nambudiris, for instance, partition is almost unknown, while among the Ambalavasis, Nayars and others it is but of rare occurrence, though of late the people have begun to show a tendency towards partition, especially in the case of overgrown families. There are several families in Cochin containing over a hundred members, but the average strength of a joint family is of course considerably less than this, and may be taken to be between 12 and 20. In the case of most such families the members generally dine together but live in two or more detached buildings, which were treated as separate houses for Census purposes.

Unoccupied buildings.

20. The number of unoccupied houses was 13,175, or 7,134 less than in 1901. The decrease was probably due to the conversion of unoccupied buildings into residences owing to the increase of population. Of the unoccupied buildings, 2,667 are places of worship, the rest being public buildings, shops, etc.

SUBSIDIARY TABLE I

I. Density, Water supply and Crops.

District and Natural Division "West Coast, Madras State"	Mean density per square mile in 1911	Percentage of total area		Percentage of cultivated area which is irrigated	Normal rainfall	Percentage of cultivated area under			
		Cultivable	Cultivated			Rice	Wheat	Pulses	Other Crops
1	2	3	4	5	6	7	8	9	10
Cochin State	**675**	**00·80**	**56·24**	**4·08**	*** 103·44**	**42·08**	..	..	**57·92**
Cochin Kanayannur ..	1,852	00·79	80·24	..	99·20	43·00	..	..	57·00
Cranganur ..	1,747	..	78·87	..	98·69	30·82	..	..	69·18
Mukandapuram ..	464	1·41	47·47	..	110·51	42·88	..	..	57·12
Trichur ..	754	..	66·22	..	120·16	50·88	..	..	49·12
Talapilli ..	609	1·42	63·77	..	112·59	36·65	..	...	63·35
Chittur ..	320	00·03	40·50	27·06	79·50	38·02	..	..	61·98

* Average rainfall for the State.

SUBSIDIARY TABLE II.

Distribution of the population classified according to density.

[District and] Natural Division West Coast Madras State	Talukas with a population per square mile of															
	under 150		150–300		300–450		450–600		600–750		750–900		900–1050		1050 and over	
	Area	Population 000's omitted	Area	Population 000's omitted	Area	Population 000's omitted	Area	Population 000's omitted	Area	Population 000's omitted	Area	Population 000's omitted	Area	Population 000's omitted	Area	Population 000's omitted
1	2	3	4	5	6	7	8	9	10	11	12	13	14	15	16	17
Cochin State	..	..	..	..	**285** *20·94*	**91** *9·94*	**418** *30·72*	**194** *21·12*	**271** *19·91*	**165** *17·99*	**225** *16·53*	**170** *18·49*	..	..	**162** *11·90*	**298** *34·46*
Cochin-Kanayannur ..	..	...	..	..		..	..	..	..	..	..	..	..	..	143 *10·50*	265 *28·84*
Cranganur ..	..	..	..	..	..	..	..	..	..	..	..	..	..	..	19 *1·40*	33 *3·62*
Mukundapuram	..	..	..	..	..	..	418 *30·72*	194 *21·12*	..	..	..	..	..	..	..	..
Trichur ..	..	..	..	..	..	..	..	..	..	..	225 *16·53*	170 *18·49*	..	..	..	..
Talapilli ..	..	..	..	..	..	..	..	..	271 *19·91*	165 *17·99*	..	..	..	..	..	..
Chittur ..	..	..	..	..	285 *20·94*	91 *9·94*	..	..	..	..	..	..	..	..	..	..

SUBSIDIARY TABLE III.

III. Distribution of the Population between Towns and Villages.

(District and) Natural Division "West Coast" Madras State.	Average population per		Number per mille residing in		Number per mille of urban population residing in towns with a population of				Number per mille of rural population residing in villages with a population of.			
	Town.	Village.	Towns.	Villages.	20,000 and over	10,000 to 20,000	5,000 to 10,000	Under 5,000	5,000 and over	2,000 to 5,000	500 to 2,000	Under 500
1	2	3	4	5	6	7	8	9	10	11	12	13
Cochin State ..	**12,217**	**2,951**	120	877	621	..	289	90	327	499	168	3
Cochin-Kanayannur ..	**16,560**	**5,815**	188	812	900	..	..	100	775	182	41	2
Cranganur ..	..	**6,638**	..	1,000	..	..	..	..	917	83	..	..
Mukundapuram ..	**8,699**	**3,066**	45	948	..	..	1,000	..	190	689	114	..
Trichur ..	**23,574**	**2,030**	139	861	1,000	..	..	..	40	600	349	11
Talapilli ..	**8,336**	**2,118**	50	950	..	..	1,000	..	33	674	293	..
Chittur ..	**6,555**	**2,812**	215	770	..	..	748	252	294	554	125	8

Note:— From the Rural population of Mukundapuram Taluk 1,284 persons and from that of Chittur Taluk 1,329 persons are excluded, since they live neither in towns nor in villages.

SUBSIDIARY TABLE IV.

IV. Number per mille of the total population and of each main religion who live in Towns.

(District and) Natural Division "West Coast" Madras State	Number per mille who live in Towns.						
	Total population	Hindu	Musalman	Christian	Jain	Parsi	Jew
1	2	3	4	5	6	7	8
Cochin State	120	103	162	150	992	1,000	781
Cochin-Kanayannur ..	188	179	441	153	1,000	...	862
Cranganur ..	..	..	..	..	..	..	..
Mukundapuram ..	45	39	53	57	..	..	..
Trichur ..	139	102	190	231	..	1,000	1,000
Talapilli ...	50	22	2	242	..	..	..
Chittur ..	215	230	242	39	..	..	..

SUBSIDIARY TABLE V.

Towns classified by population.

Class of Town	Number of towns of each class in 1911	Proportion (per mille) to total urban population	Number of females per 1,000 males	Increase per cent in the population of towns as classed at previous censuses				Increase per cent in urban population of each class from 1875 to 1911	
				1901 to 1911	1891 to 1901	1881 to 1891	1875 to 1881	(a) in towns as classed in 1875	(b) in the total of each class in 1911 as compared with the corresponding total in 1875
1	2	3	4	5	6	7	8	9	10
Total ...									
I. 100,000 and over..	...	...	...	...	...	...	...	...	...
II. 50,000-100,000...	...	...	...	...	...	...	...	...	...
III. 20,000- 50,000...	3	622	863	6·53	...	...	...	...	...
IV. 10,000- 20,000...	...	...	...	51·26	19·71	17·46	5·14	75·42	...
V. 5,000- 10,000...	4	288	1,051	6·04	16·87	11·47	13·58	47·07	170·98
VI. Under 5,000 ...	2	*90	947	...	...	13·86	1·78	56·24	6·94

* Treated as towns for the first time in 1911.

SUBSIDIARY TABLE VI.

Persons per house and houses per square mile.

(District and) natural Division "West Coast," Madras State.	Average number of persons per house				Average number of houses per square mile.			
	1911	1901	1891	1881	1911	1901	1891	1881
1	2	3	4	5	6	7	8	9
Cochin State ...	5·62	5·57	5·43	4·79	120	107·15	97·82	92·08
Cochin-Kanayannur ...	5·50	5·50	5·19	4·53	336	297·47	278·71	274·50
Cranganur ...	5·48	5·24	5·58	4·64	322	296·32	269·65	240·91
Mukundapuram ...	5·68	5·56	5·52	4·75	82	69·61	63·07	57·97
Trichur ...	5·95	5·84	6·02	5·28	127	110·47	95·11	88·11
Talapilli ...	5·81	5·75	5·76	5·15	105	97·02	85·46	81·09
Chittur ...	5·05	5·15	4·58	4·41	63	60·96	60·34	58·82

CHAPTER II.

MOVEMENT OF POPULATION.

21. The statistics of the population as it stood on the 11th March 1911 have been considered in the previous Chapter. The present Chapter deals with the variations that had taken place since 1875. The phrase "movement of the population" is sanctioned by statistical usage to denote the net result of the two factors which determine the strength of the population at any given time, namely, the proportion of births to deaths and the proportion of emigration to immigration. It is the effect of these factors and the state of affairs which results from these opposing forces that will be considered in this Chapter.

Introductory.

22. No reliable information is available regarding the early population of the State, as no early writers, so far as I know, have dealt with the subject. The first estimate of the population, which was but a rough one made through the agency of the ordinary village staff, was made in 1820, when the population numbered 223,003. The population has thus increased by over 300 per cent. during the last 91 years. Though this estimate was probably below the mark, there can be no doubt that the population has been steadily increasing at a somewhat rapid rate ever since the State came under British supremacy, which put an end to the constant internecine wars and factions fights, which were the characteristic features of the history of Cochin during the pre-British period. Large tracts of territory, which were, within the memory of men still living, covered with dense forests abounding in big game, are now either extensive rice fields or well stocked garden lands dotted with homesteads. A statement showing the results of all attempts to determine the population since 1820 is subjoined. The increase of 50 per cent. in the population in the seventeen years ending with 1875, the year of the first systematic Census, shows that the population was under-estimated on all the previous occasions. The decrease of population in 1881 and the large increase during the subsequent decade appear to have been due to short counting in that year, as is shown in the Report on the Census of 1891.

Growth of population.

Year of the Census.	Interval between successive Censuses.	Population.	Per cent. of increase (+) or decrease (—)
1820		228,003	
1836	16 years	288,176	+ 29
1849	13 ,,	356,802	+ 24
1858	9 ,,	399,056	+ 12
1875	17 ,,	601,114	+ 50
1881	6 ,,	600,278	— ·14
1891	10 ,,	722,906	+ 20·4
1901	10 ,,	812,025	+ 12·3
1911	10 ,,	918,110	+ 13·6

23. The decade preceding the present Census has comparatively been a very prosperous one, and consequently very favourable for the growth of population There had been no wide-spread outbreaks of epidemics, such as cholera or small-pox, in any part of the State, nor did the plague make its appearance anywhere. During the decade taken as a whole the monsoon rains proved fairly copious and regular: at no time was scarcity felt in an acute form. On the other hand, the State made notable industrial development during the decade, which has appreciably increased the prosperity of the people. The Railway was introduced at the beginning of the decade, and the

Condition of decade 1901 to 1911.

line runs right across the middle of the State from one end of it to the other. The thorough and systematic exploitation of the forests synchronized with the introduction of the railway, and the Forest Steam Tramway, 50 miles long, was constructed through virgin forests hitherto inaccessible to serve as an outlet for their produce. Two timber saw mills, three or four cocoanut oil mills, a weaving mill and a number of brick and tile factories were opened during this period, and the forests were opened up for rubber plantation on a large scale. The result of these circumstances has been a steady growth of population at what may be considered a normal rate.

Statistics of births and deaths.

24. As pointed out by the Census Commissioner for India, if the registration of births and deaths were accurate, it would be easy to ascertain the population of a tract at any given time (except in so far as it is affected by migration) by adding to the statistics of the last Census the excess of births over deaths since reported. But unfortunately the registration of vital statistics has been far from being satisfactory, though some improvement was effected in it recently. The registration was initiated in the State in 1895-6, and was carried out by Pravritti (village) officers. The Pravritti was the administrative unit for purposes of registration as well as revenue collection, but the average Pravritti comprised an area of about thirty square miles and a population of over 17,000. It was thus manifestly impossible for the village officers to carry out the work with any degree of exactitude, especially in the absence of any legislation to compel house-holders to report births and deaths in their families. Since the completion of the revenue survey and settlement, the State was divided into a much larger number of revenue villages, each village having an average extent of three to four square miles and a population of about 5,000, and a Births and Deaths Regulation was passed five years ago. The registration has consequently become more satisfactory in recent years, but it is still far from being perfect. The statistics of the decade on the whole are worthless from an actuarial point of view. It will be seen from Subsidiary Table III that deaths exceeded births by 971 during the decade, while the Census returns show that the population actually increased during this period by over 106,000. The increase was entirely due to the natural fecundity of the population, as the effect of migration during the decade has been a loss to the State as compared with that of the previous one.

Migration.

25. Migration is the second factor that affects the movement of the population. In the absence of any officially recorded statistics of emigrants and immigrants, the only means of ascertaining the result of migration is to note the number of persons born outside the State but enumerated in Cochin and *vice versa*, and deduct the smaller figure from the greater. These figures do not however represent actual immigration and emigration, as many of those so enumerated may have been only mere travellers or temporary sojourners for short periods. Such as they are, the statistics for the past decade are given in Subsidiary Table II, and in part in Imperial Table XI. It will be seen from the former that 47,266 persons, or 5·1 per cent. of the total population, were outside-born, against 50,054, or 6·1 per cent. in 1901. The number of Cochin-born persons enumerated outside the State, so far as can be gathered from the statements furnished by the Provincial Superintendents, was 25,047, as against 14,790 at the previous Census. The result of migration has thus a gain to Cochin of 22,219, against a gain of 35,264 in 1901. At the time of the previous Census the construction of the Cochin State Railway was in progress, which attracted a large number of workmen and others temporarily to the State, and this probably accounts for the larger number of outside-born persons enumerated here than on the present occasion. The increase in the number of emigrants, as

compared with that of 1901, is probably due to the fact that, owing to the increasing pressure of the population on the soil, the people have begun, though very slowly, to move beyond the State in search of fresh fields and pastures new.

Growth of population during the past decade.

26. At the beginning of the decade preceding the present Census the population of the State numbered 812,025, while at the end of it it numbered 918,110. The population thus increased during the decade by 106,085, or 13·06 per cent., which is slightly higher than the rate of increase in the preceding decade, namely 12·33 per cent. The increase during the same period was 16·2 per cent. in Travancore, 7·8 per cent. in Malabar, 8·3 per cent. in the Madras Presidency and 7·1 per cent. in the Indian Empire. As the last three Censuses were the most accurate of all those taken in Cochin, the increase shown during each of the last two decades, namely, about 13 per cent., or a little over one per cent. per annum, may be taken as the normal rate of increase in Cochin. According to some prominent statisticians and economists, this is the rate of increase that is the best from a national point of view, at once stimulating activity and not overrunning or even pressing upon the means of subsistence. Considering the fertility and general prosperity of the State and the immunity that it has always enjoyed from famine, plague and other causes that arrest the growth of population, it is but natural that its population should grow at the rate at which it grows in all prosperous countries. The rate of progress however has not been uniform in all the taluks. In Cochin-Kanayannur and Cranganur the increase approximates very nearly to the mean increase of the State, while that in Mukundapuram (20 per cent.) and Trichur (17 per cent.) considerably exceeds it. This is due to the fact that the circumstances mentioned in paragraph 23, such as the introduction of the Railway, the construction of the Forest Tramway and the opening up of the forests for rubber cultivation, have benefited these two taluks more than the others, and have attracted people from other taluks thereto. The Talapilli taluk lags behind the other taluks in industrial development, which probably accounts for the increase of its population being only 9 per cent. The increase in Chittur is a little less than 2 per cent., which is mainly due to two causes, one natural and the other accidental. A considerable portion of the taluk is feverish, which naturally arrests the growth of population. While the population has increased by nearly 53 per cent. in the State since 1875, it has increased only by 38 per cent. in Chittur. The fact that the Census was taken ten days later than the Census of 1901 has to some extent contributed to the apparent low rate of increase. The coffee planting industry is almost confined to this taluk, and most of the workmen and others leave the estates at the end of February and the beginning of March. On examining the schedules I found that hundreds of names recorded at the preliminary enumeration on the Nelliampatis were scored out at the final, as many of the workmen left the station between these two stages of the Census. While the population of the Nelliampatis, the planting district, was 3,018 in 1901, it was only 794 in 1911.

Variation in population since 1875.

27. As already pointed out, the first systematic Census was taken in 1875, when the population stood at 601,114. The population has thus risen by 316,996 during the past thirty-six years, the rate of increase being 52·7 per cent., against 48 per cent. in Travancore, 33·3 per cent. in Malabar and 32·6 per cent. in the Presidency. The rate of increase varies in the different taluks, the mean rate being considerably exceeded by Cranganur, Mukundapuram and Trichur, while in the other taluks the increase falls short of it. Columns 2 to 5 of Subsidiary Table 1 show the variations of the successive Censuses, from which it will be seen that, while the increase had been steady and uniform in the last two decades, the period 1875 to 1881 showed a decrease of ·14 per cent. and the succeeding decade showed an increase of 20·43 per cent. in

the population. As there were no exceptional circumstances to account for these anamolous variations, they must be set down to incorrect enumeration in 1881, as pointed out in the Report for 1891.

Probable future rates of increase.

28. It seems hazardous to endeavour to prognosticate the rate at which the population will increase in the future in the State as a whole and in the different taluks in particular. It seems safe however to assume that in the absence of any exceptional circumstances the rate disclosed by the last two Censuses, namely, about one per cent per annum, will hold good for several years to come. It is true that the southern taluks are already very densely peopled, but mere figures of density of the population is no guide to the degree to which it is pressing closely on the means of subsistence. The abundance of the cocoanut crop, the manifold industries to which its produce gives rise and the facilities available in the way of communications and markets enable these taluks to support in comfort a population which would starve in a tract where the staple crops are less valuable and less useful for industrial purposes. There are as yet no signs of acute pressure of the population on the soil, and it may therefore be predicted with more or less safety that the population will go on increasing at the normal rate above mentioned and that the population of the State at the end of the current decade will considerably exceed a million.

SUBSIDIARY TABLE I.

I. Variation in relation to density since 1875.

District and natural Division "West Coast" Madras State.	Percentage of variation increase (+) decrease (—)				Net variation 1875 to 1911	Mean density per square mile.				
	1901 to 1911	1891 to 1901	1881 to 1891	1875 to 1881		1911	1901	1891	1881	1875
1	2	3	4	5	6	7	8	9	10	11
Cochin State ...	+18·06	+12·83	+20·48	—0·14	+52·73	676	597	531	441	442
Cochin-Kanayannur ...	+12·66	+13·23	+16·24	—4·78	+41·17	1,852	1,644	1,452	1,249	1,312
Cranganur ...	+13·90	+4·20	+33·48	+2·71	+62·73	1,747	1,534	1,472	1.103	1,074
Mukundapuram ...	+19·63	+11·08	+26·46	+0·21	+68·67	464	387	349	276	275
Trichur ...	+16·98	+12·52	+23·17	+2·90	+66·84	754	645	573	465	452
Talapilli ...	+9·11	+13·01	+18·47	+2·40	+49·47	609	558	494	417	408
Chittur ...	+1·94	+13·66	+16·87	+2·65	+33·41	320	314	276	238	231

SUBSIDIARY TABLE II.

II. Variation in natural population.

District and Natural Division "West Coast" Madras State.	Population in 1911				Population in 1901				Variation per cent. (1901—1911) in natural population Increase (+) Decrease (—)
	Actual Population.	Immigrants	Emigrants	Natural population	Actual population	Immigrants	Emigrants	Natural population	
1	2	3	4	5	6	7	8	9	10
Cochin State ...	918,110	47,266	25,047	895,891	812,025	50,054	14,790	776,761	+15·34

SUBSIDIARY TABLE III.

III. Comparison with vital statistics.

District and natural division "West Coast," Madras State	In 1901—1910 Total number of		Number per cent of population of 1901 of		Excess (+) or Deficiency (—) of births over deaths	Increase (+) or Decrease (—) of population of 1911 compared with 1901	
	Births	Deaths	Births	Deaths		Natural population	Actual population
1	2	3	4	5	6	7	8
Cochin State	88,985	89,906	10·95	11·07	—971	+119,130	+106,085

SUBSIDIARY TABLE IV.

IV. Variation by Taluks classified according to density.

(A) Actual Variation.

Natural Division (West Coast)	Decade	Variation in Taluks with a population per square mile at commencement of decade of							
		Under 150	150 to 300	300 to 450	450 to 600	600 to 750	750 to 900	900 to 1050	Over 1050
1	2	3	4	5	6	7	8	9	10
Cochin State ...	**106,085**	...	...	...	**78**	...	...	...	...
Cochin-Kanayannur ...	29,744	...	...	...	...	...	...	...	208
Cranganur ...	4,058	...	...	...	...	...	...	...	213
Mukundapuram...	32,097	...	...	77	...	...	...	...	...
Trichur ...	24,652	...	...	...	...	109	...	...	...
Talapilli ...	13,799	...	...	...	51	...	...	...	...
Chittur ...	1,740	...	...	6	...	...	...	...	...

(B) Proportional Variation.

Natural Division (West Coast)	Decade	Variation in Taluks with a population per square mile at commencement of decade of							
		Under 150	150 to 300	300 to 450	450 to 600	600 to 750	750 to 900	900 to 1050	1050 and over
1	2	3	4	5	6	7	8	9	10
Cochin State ...	**13·06**	...	...	...	**13·06**	...	...	...	...
Cochin-Kanayannur ...	12·65	...	...	...	...	...	...	...	12·6
Cranganur ...	13·90	...	...	...	...	...	...	...	13·9
Mukundapuram...	19·83	...	...	19·8	...	...	...	...	...
Trichur ...	16·98	...	...	...	...	16·9	...	...	...
Talapilli ...	9·11	...	...	...	9·1	...	...	...	...
Chittur ...	1·94	...	...	1·9	...	...	...	...	...

CHAPTER III

BIRTH PLACE.

Statistics of Birth place.

29. Imperial Table XI gives the statistics of birth place of the population enumerated in Cochin, while the subsidiary tables at the end of this Chapter compare the number of outside-born people enumerated in Cochin and that of Cochin-born people enumerated elsewhere. The most striking feature disclosed by the figures contained in these Tables is the remarkably stay-at-home character of the people of Cochin, as indeed of those of other parts of India. As many as 870,844 persons, or nearly 95 per cent of the population enumerated in this State, were born in it, while only 5 per cent were outsiders residing in the State permanently or temporarily at the time of the Census. The percentages in 1901 were 93·8 and 6·2 respectively. The number of Cochin-born persons enumerated outside the State, so far as can be gathered from the statements furnished by the Provincial Superintendents, was 25,047, against 14,790 in 1901. This increase was chiefly due to emigration of coolies from Cochin to Ceylon, which has been going on to a considerable extent in recent years.

Immigrants into Cochin.

30. Of the 47,266 so called immigrants, 92 per cent are from the contiguous State of Travancore (15,207) and the contiguous British Districts of Malabar (25,342) and Coimbatore (3,026). The great majority even among these have merely stepped over the boundary line, as they are chiefly found in the contiguous taluks of Cochin. Thus, most of the immigrants from Travancore are found in the Cochin-Kanayannur taluk, those from Malabar in Talapilli and Chittur and those from Coimbatore in Chittur. The decrease in the number of immigrants from Coimbatore, as compared with those in 1901, seems to have been due to the exodus of coolies from the Nelliampati coffee plantations just before the final enumeration (vide paragraph 26). The only other Districts which have contributed any noticeable number of immigrants are Tinnevelly and South Canara. The Tinnevelly Brahman merchants used to be and to some extent still are ubiquitous in all parts of the West Coast, with the cotton fabrics manufactured in their District, for which there is a great demand among the Malayali community. But with the increasing demand for, and the increasing production of, similar articles manufactured in the State, they are gradually disappearing from Cochin, their number having decreased from 936 in 1901 to 653 in 1911. The contribution from South Canara is represented mainly by Embrans or Tulu Brahmans, who officiate as priests in many of the temples in the State and whose services are generally indispensable therein. For the decrease in the number of South Canara men, as compared with that of 1901, no obvious reason can be furnished. The Bombay Presidency and the Feudatory States attached to it contribute over a thousand immigrants. They are mostly Baniya and Muhammadan merchants, who are chiefly found in the town of Mattancheri and its neighbourhood and to whose energy and enterprise Cochin owes no small share of its industrial and commercial prosperity. * The immigrants from all parts of India put together number only 47,190.

Emigrants from Cochin.

Full statistics of Cochin-born persons enumerated outside the State are not available. It is well known, for instance, that many such are to be found in the Straits Settlements and other places, but I have not been able to obtain the necessary figures from the Census Superintendents

* The immigrants from the Bombay Presidency are locally spoken of as *Kacchikars* or natives of Cutch, and the enumerators seem to have returned their birth-place indifferently as Bombay or Cutch. This probably accounts for the difference in the figures for 1901 (Bombay, 856 and Cutch, 7) and 1911 (Bombay, 457 and Cutch, 312).

concerned. The available figures show that emigration has been slightly on the increase during the decade, but, like the immigrants, the majority of emigrants also have but stepped over the boundary line, 87 per cent of them being found in Travancore (9,946), Malabar (7,629) and Coimbatore (694). Of the 471 Cochin-born persons enumerated in Madras a good many are students reading for their degrees, and of the 1,032 found in the Bombay Presidency, probably the majority are persons born in Cochin during the temporary sojourn of their parents here. The number of emigrants to other parts of India is inconsiderable. As many as 4,056 Cochin-born people are found in Ceylon. They are mostly coolies, and the majority of them are from the Mukundapuram and Talapilli taluks.

Types of migration.

Of the five types of migration mentioned by the Census Commissioner for India, namely, casual, temporary, periodic, semi-permanent and permanent, the first is the prevailing type of migration from and into Cochin. It consists mainly of minor movements between adjacent villages, and arises largely from the very common practice among the people of taking a wife from another village and from the fact that young married women generally go to their parents' home for their first confinement. In this type of migration females generally preponderate over males, as shown in the margin.* Temporary and periodic migrations vary at different seasons of the year, but they are at no time very considerable in the State, except during the working season in the coffee estates, when large numbers of coolies from Coimbatore resort to the Nelliampatis. Semi-permanent migrants are natives of one place residing and earning their living in another, but retaining their connection with their own homes, where they leave their families and to which they return in their old age and at more or less intervals in the meantime. Such are the immigrants from the Bombay side, Tinnevelly and South Canara, and the emigrants to Madras, Mysore, Bombay and Ceylon. The bulk of such migrants are men as shown in the margin. Permanent migrants are people driven away by overcrowding or induced by the superior attractions of some other place. There are hundreds of immigrants of this nature, but hardly any emigrants.

Immigrants from	No. of females to 100 males.
Travancore	120
Malabar	109
Coimbatore	118
Emigrants to	
Travancore	120
Malabar	114

Immigrants from	No. of females to 100 males.
Bombay	48
Tinnevelly	42
South Canara	19
Emigrants to	
Madras	56
Mysore	60
Bombay	12
Ceylon	7

Loss or gain by migration.

As already pointed out, the total number of immigrants into Cochin of one type or another was 47,266, and that of emigrants 25,047. The net result of migration was thus a gain of 22,219 people to Cochin. In 1901 the gain was 35,264, but in that year no account was taken of the large number of Cochin people found in Ceylon. It seems to be clear however that the outward movement in search of employment elsewhere is on the increase, however slow it may be.

SUBSIDIARY TABLE I.

Immigration.

Natural Division where enumerated "West Coast" Madras State	Born in: Cochin State			Contiguous Districts and States in the Madras Presidency (Malabar, Coimbatore and Travancore)			Other parts of the Madras Presidency including Native States of Mysore and Pudukotta and the French Settlements.			Provinces and States outside the Madras Presidency including the Portuguese Settlement			Outside India		
	Total	Males	Females	Total	Males	Females	Total	Males	Females	Total	Males	Females	Total	Males	Females
1	2	3	4	5	6	7	8	9	10	11	12	13	14	15	16
Cochin State ...	870,844	434,379	436,465	43,575	20,444	23,131	2 240	1,499	741	1,375	959	416	76	61	15

SUBSIDIARY TABLE II.

Emigration

District and Natural Division of birth "West Coast" Madras State.	Enumerated in: Cochin State			Contiguous Districts & States in the Madras Presidency—Malabar. Coimbatore, Travancore and Anjengo.			Other parts of the Madras Presidency including the Native States of Mysore, Pudukotta and the French Settlements.			Provinces and States outside the Madras Presidency including the Portuguese Settlements			Outside India		
	Total	Males	Females	Total	Males	Females	Total	Males	Females	Total	Males	Females	Total	Males	Females
1	2	3	4	5	6	7	8	9	10	11	12	13	14	15	16
Cochin State ...	870,844	434,379	436,465	18,293	8,544	9,749	1,537	944	593	1,161	1,020	141	4,056	3,797	259

SUBSIDIARY TABLE III.

Proportional migration to and from each district.

District and Natural Division "West Coast" Madras State	Number per mille of actual population of: Immigrants: Total	Immigrants: From contiguous districts and States in the Madras Presidency	Immigrants: From other places	Emigrants: Total	Emigrants: To contiguous districts and States in the Madras Presidency	Emigrants: To other places	Number of females to 100 males amongst: Immigrants: From contiguous districts and States in the Madras Presidency	Immigrants: From other places	Emigrants: To contiguous districts and States in the Madras Presidency	Emigrants: To other places
1	2	3	4	5	6	7	8	9	10	11
Cochin State ...	51·5	47·5	4·0	27·3	19·9	7·4	113	47	114	17

SUBSIDIARY TABLE IV.

Migration between the Cochin State and other parts of India and other countries.

PROVINCE OR STATE	IMMIGRANTS TO COCHIN			EMIGRANTS FROM COCHIN			EXCESS (+) OR DEFICIENCY (—) OF IMMIGRATION OVER EMIGRATION	
	1911	1901	Variation	1911	1901	Variation	1911	1901
1	2	3	4	5	6	7	8	9
Grand total	47,266	50,054	—2,788	25,047	14,790	+10,257	+ 22,219	+ 35,264
A—India	47,190	49,997	—2,807	20,991	14,790	+ 6,201	+25199	+ 35,207
i. Madras Presidency	45,696	48,643	—2,947	19,624	...	...	+ 26,072	...
(a) British Territory ...	30,486	33,184	—2,698	9,676	...	...	+20,810	...
Anantapur	...	4	— 4	1	...	...	— 1	...
Anjengo	...	...	...	24	...	...	— 24	...
Bellary	4	6	— 2	8	...	...	— 4	...
Chingelput...	14	28	— 14	32	...	...	— 18	...
Chittoor	...	...	...	9	...	...	— 9	...
Coimbatore	3,026	4,543	—1,517	694	669	+ 25	+ 2,332	+ 3,874
Coorg	1	...	+ 1	35	...	...	— 34	...
Cuddappa	12	2	+ 10	1	...	...	+ 11	...
Ganjam	...	6	— 6	7	...	...	— 7	...
Godavari	6	3	+ 3	10	...	...	— 4	...
Guntur	6	...	+ 6	10	...	...	— 4	...
Kistna	...	7	— 7	29	...	...	— 29	...
Kurnool	16	...	+ 16	18	...	...	— 2	...
Madras	193	261	— 68	471	...	...	— 278	...
Madura	183	169	+ 14	83	...	...	+ 100	...
Malabar	25,342	25,662	— 320	7.629	5,824	+1,805	+ 17,713	+ 19,838
Nellore	2	35	— 33	38	...	...	— 36	...
Nilgiris	31	15	+ 16	140	...	...	— 109	...
North Arcot	22	71	— 49	30	...	...	— 8	...
Ramnad	1	...	+ 1	33	...	...	— 32	...
South Canara	500	716	— 216	124	...	...	+ 376	...
Salem	67	303	— 236	18	...	...	+ 49	...
South Arcot	39	33	+ 6	22	...	...	+ 17	...
Tanjore	199	209	— 10	71	...	...	+ 128	...
Tinnevelly	653	936	— 283	70	...	...	+ 583	...
Trichinopoly	166	168	— 2	54	...	...	+ 112	...
Vizagapatam	3	7	— 4	15	...	...	— 12	...
(b) Feudatory States ...	15,210	15,459	— 249	9,948	...	...	+ 5,262	...
Pudukotta	3	17	— 14	2	...	...	+ 1	...
Travancore...	15,207	15,442	— 235	9,946	7,942	+2,004	+ 5,261	+ 7,500
ii. Other Provinces and States in India	1,377	1,317	+ 60	1,367	...	...	+ 10	--
(a) British Territory	578	1,116	— 538	1,157	...	...	— 579	...
Bengal	47	54	— 7	58	...	...	— 11	...
Bombay	464	857	— 393	1,032	...	...	— 568	...
Burma	...	1	— 1	53	...	...	— 53	...
Central Provinces and Berar ...	12	31	— 19	12	...	...	...	...
North-west Frontier Province..	1	...	+ 1	...	...	...	+ 1	...
Punjab	3	34	— 31	2	...	...	+ 1	...
United Provinces of Agra and Oudh ...	51	139	— 88	...	...	...	+ 51	...
(b) Feudatory States	799	201	+ 598	210	...	...	+ 589	...
Bombay States	611	7	+ 604	...	...	...	+ 7	...
Cutch	342	7	+ 335	...	...	...	+ 7	...
Kathiawar	267	...	+ 267	...	...	...	...	...
Rewa Kantha Agency ...	2	...	+ 2	...	...	...	...	...
Central India Agency ...	38	5	+ 33	...	...	...	+ 5	...
Hyderabad	27	42	— 15	...	...	...	+ 27	...
Mysore	108	127	— 19	206	52	+ 154	— 98	+ 75
Nepal	...	10	— 10	...	...	...	...	...
Rajputana	15	10	+ 5	1	...	...	+ 14	...
Adjmir and Morwara ...	...	...	...	3	...	...	— 3	...
iii. French Settlements ...	11	3	+ 8	...	...	...	+ 11	...
iv. Portuguese Settlement ...	76	34	+ 42	...	...	...	+ 76	...
v. India unspecified ...	30	...	+ 30	...	...	...	+ 30	...
B—Other Asiatic Countries	22	19	+ 3	4,056	...	...	— 4,034	...
Afghanistan	...	2	— 2	...	...	...	...	...
Arabia	...	7	— 7	...	...	...	...	...
Ceylon	13	6	+ 7	4,056	...	...	— 4,043	...
Persia	2	...	+ 2	...	...	...	+ 2	...
Siam	...	1	— 1	...	...	...	...	...
Strait Settlements and Malaya.	4	...	+ 4	...	...	...	+ 4	...
Turkey in Asia	3	2	+ 1	...	...	...	+ 3	...
Turkistan	...	1	— 1	...	...	..	...	...
C—Europe	50	33	+ 17	...	...	...	+ 50	...
D—Africa unspecified	...	2	— 2	...	...	...	...	...
E—America	3	2	+ 1	...	...	...	+ 3	...
F—Australia...	1	...	+ 1	...	...	...	+ 1	...
G—Sea (South Pacific) ...	..	1	— 1	...	...	...	...	...

CHAPTER IV.

RELIGION.

Introductory.

34. Imperial Table VI and Provincial Table II give the strength of all religions returned for each taluk, and Imperial Table XVII shows the various denominations to which the Christians of the State belong. The Subsidiary Tables at the end of this Chapter give the chief facts contained in them in the usual proportional forms. Information of a general nature regarding the religious beliefs of the people and historical accounts of the various religions followed in the State are given more or less fully in the Cochin State Manual and in the Reports on the previous Censuses, especially in that of 1901. It is superfluous to go over these well-beaten paths again : this Chapter will therefore confine itself to a discussion of the statistics in the several tables.

Distribution and variation since 1901.

35. The general distribution of the people by religion, as compared with that of 1901, is shown in the margin. It will be seen from it that two-thirds of the population are Hindus, one-fourth Christians and about 7 per cent are Muhammadans. Only six in a thousand belong to all other religions put together. The most noticeable feature in the figures is the preponderance of Christians over Muhammadans, which is without a parallel anywhere else in India except in Travancore. In the contiguous District of Malabar there is only one Christian to every eighteen Muhammadans, while in Cochin there are nearly four Christians to every Muhammadan. The other noticeable features are the relatively more rapid growth of Christians and Muhammodans, as compared with Hindus, and the stationary condition on the Jewish population. The distribution of the above religions varies greatly in different parts of the State, but these variations will be noticed more fully in the paragraphs dealing with each religion.

Religions	*1911*	*1911.*
Hindus	615,708	554,255
Musalmans	63,832	54,492
Christians	233,092	198,239
Jews	1,175	1,137
Animists	4,177	3,897
Others	136	5

Animists.

36. It will be convenient for various reasons to begin with the Animists. The essentials of their creed it is not easy to define accurately. It is a combination of spiritism and fetichism, and may roughly be described as the belief in the existence of souls or spirits which have acquired the rank of divine beings and become objects of worship. These spirits are conceived as moving freely through earth and air, and, either of their own accord or conjured by some spell, appear to men (*spiritism*). They may also take up their abode temporarily or permanently in some object, whether living or lifeless, which object, as endowed with higher power, is then worshipped or employed to protect individuals and communities (*fetichism*). Though none of these spirits have the attributes, names or local habitations of the Hindu Gods and though high class Hindus will not admit them to be fit subjects for reverence, the dividing line between Hinduism and Animism is very uncertain. For this reason and for the reason that the Animists themselves have no name for their religion, a correct return of their number was found to be exceedingly difficult. The enumerators were therefore instructed to return as Animists all hill tribes (it is among such that pure Animism is found), except those among them who wished to be returned as Hindus. This was a somewhat arbitrary distinction, as there is hardly any difference beween the beliefs and practices obtaining among the Pulayans and Parayans on the one hand and those

obtaining among the Kadans and Malayans on the other, and yet the former were returned as Hindus and the latter as Animists.

Distribution of Animists.

37. The Animists numbered 4,177 at the present Census, as against 3,897 in 1901. They are almost confined to the forest tracts, mainly those of Chittur (2,418) and Mukundapuram (1,061). There are no Animists in Cranganur, the only taluk which has no forest area. The Animists have increased only by 7 per cent during the last decade. This increase may be due to natural causes, or more probably to immigration from Coimbatore and Malabar forests, as, owing to the construction of the forest tramway and the opening up of rubber plantations during the last decade, they are able to obtain a better means of livelihood here than elsewhere. If the Pulayans and others mentioned in the next paragraph are treated as Animists, as properly speaking they should have been, their number will come up to 98,720, or nearly 11 per cent of the total population.

Hindus.

38. What the term Hinduism means is more easily understood than explained, for it is of the vaguest possible description. As a definition of religion or even of race it is more liberal than accurate. As a religious classification, it lumps together the most discordant elements—the pantheism of the Brahmans, the polytheism of the Sudras, the demonolatory of the polluting castes and the fetichism of the slave castes. Viewed in the light of race, it groups the Aryan immigrants from the north with the Dravidian settlers of Southern India and the aboriginal tribes of the hill side. Thinking it desirable to lay down some definite standard to differentiate Hindus from non-Hindus, the Census Commissioner for India has suggested the application of the following tests for the purpose:—(1) the worshipping of the great Hindu gods; (2) the privilege of entering Hindu temples or making offerings at the shrine; (3) good Brahmans acting as priests; (4) degraded Brahmans acting as priests without losing recognition as Brahmans by persons outside the caste; (5) clean castes taking water from them: and (6) the causing of pollution by touch or proximity. These tests do not appear to be decisive in so far, at least, as Malayali Hindus are concerned. An Iluvan or Kammalan, for instance, is undoubtedly looked upon as a Hindu on this coast, but he has none of the privileges above mentioned, except worshipping the great Hindu gods in his own way, and he also causes pollution not only by touch but also by proximity. The position of the Pulayan or Parayan on the other hand is different from that of an Iluvan or Kammalan: there is nothing common between the beliefs, ritual and practice of the former and those of the latter, much less those of the Brahman or the Nayar. It will be more in keeping with the fitness of things from a religious standpoint to separate the classes noted in the margin from the Hindu community and treat them as Animists, as the difference between them and those who were returned as Animists is but shadowy from a religious point of view. Even when they are so separated, the rest of the community is far from being a homogenious one from a religious standpoint, but it will stand one test, the only one that appears to me to be applicable in the case of Malayali Hindus, namely, the recognition of caste as a socio-religious institution.

Kanakkan	7,527
Parayan	8,356
Pulayan	72,787
Pulluvan	110
Valluvan	502
Vettuvan	5,261
Total	**94,543**

Distribution of Hindus.

39. As already pointed out, 67 per cent of the population are Hindus, but if the castes mentioned in the preceding paragraph are transferred to the category of Animists, they form only 57 per cent of the population. The Hindus form the predominant portion of the population not only in the State as a whole but also in every one of the taluks. Their relative strength however varies in the different taluks, Chittur having the

highest proportion (84 per cent) and Cochin-Kanayannur the lowest (55 per cent). Cranganur and Mukundapuram have about the mean State proportion, but Talapilli has 75 and Trichur 70 per cent. The Hindus form the majority in all but twenty-one of the 273 villages of the State and 7 out of the nine towns, the two towns in which they are in a minority are Mattancheri and Kunnamkulam. In the former Christians and Mussalmans together and in the latter Christians alone out-number the Hindus. The Hindus have increased only by 11 per cent during the decade, while the population as a whole has increased by 13 per cent. The lower rate of increase, as compared with that of Christians and Muhammadans, seems to be due to loss by conversion to the latter religions.

Hindu Sects.

40. Statistics of Hindu sects were not collected in the State at the present Census. Among the indigenous Hindus who form about 86 per cent of the Hindu population of the State, sectarian differences are unknown, so much so that most of them are not even aware of their existence elsewhere. They worship Vishnu, Siva and other Puranic gods with equal reverence, as also do the majority of the non-indigenous Hindus found in Cochin. The only considerable section of the Hindus who are not Smartas are the Konkani Brahmans and their Sudras (Kudumi Chettis), who are Vaishnavites, being followers of Madhvacharya.

Christians.

41. The Christians form almost exactly a fourth of the population of the State. They are relatively strongest in Cochin-Kanayannur (38 per cent) and weakest in Cranganur and Chittur (5 per cent). The proportion for Mukundapuram, Trichur and Talapilli are 29, 26 and 14 per cents respectively. They are found everywhere in the State, except in 20 of the villages in the Talapilli Taluk and 6 in the Chittur Taluk, and they preponderate over the Hindus in 13 villages in Cochin-Kanayannur, 3 in Mukundapuram, 1 in Trichur, and 3 in Chittur, and also in the town of Kunnamkulam. The Christians have increased by 17 per cent since the previous Census, the largest relative increase being in Mukundapuram and Trichur. A portion at least of this increase seems to have been due to conversion from Hinduism, the converts being mainly recruited from the classes of Hindus which are lowest in the social scale, who have little to loose and much to gain by forsaking the creed of their forefathers and embracing Christianity or Muhammadanism.

Christian Sects.

42. Christianity is the only religion in the case of which statistics of sects were collected at the present Census. The strength of the various sects, as compared with that of 1901, is given in the margin.

	1911.	*1901.*
Roman Catholic	97,787	79,221
Syrian (Chaldean)	12,157	8,881
Do. (Jacobite)	20,025	17,408
Do. (Reformed)	596	514
Do. (Roman)	100,166	90,142
Protestant	2,361	2,070

The Malabar church, whose existence dates at least from the fourth century, appears to have followed the Nestorian doctrines till the advent of the Portuguese at the beginning of the sixteenth century. Through their exertions, especially those of Archbishop Menezes, the church was brought under the domination of Rome after a prolonged struggle, and adopted the Latin rite in 1599. On the decline of the Portuguese power, the party hostile to Rome again got the upper hand, and elected Thomas, a native Archdeacon, to be their Bishop. This Bishop was consecrated in 1665 by the Patriarch of Antioch, who introduced the Jacobite liturgy and ritual in place of the Nestorian. The adherents of this Bishop are therefore known as Jacobite Syrians. A section of the Syrians however refused to follow Mar Thomas, and still remained subject to Rome. They were however allowed to use the Syriac rite, and are consequently known as Romo-Syrians or Syrian Catholics. The teaching of the missionaries belonging to the Church of England caused a split in the Jacobite Syrian camp in the first half of the nineteenth century, the party favouring the methods of the missionaries having seceded from the authority of the Patriarch of Antioch, and set up a church of their own, owing no allegiance to any foreign eccleciastical authority. They call themselves St. Thomas Syrians after the reputed founder of the Malabar church, but are better known as Reformed Syrians. A split also arose amongst the Romo-Syrians of Trichur by the arrival of a Bishop sent by the Chaldean Patriarch of Babylon in 1874. The action of the Patriarch was condemned, and the Bishop's title to the headship of the Trichur church was repudiated, by the Pope, whereupon several of the parishioners refused to accept him as their Bishop. Those who continued to acknowledge his authority gave up their allegiance to Rome, and placed themselves under the jurisdiction of the Patriarch of Babylon. They call themselves Chaldean Syrians, and are confined to Trichur and its neighbourhood. Roman Catholics or Catholics of the Latin rite are believed to be descendants of converts made during and after the Portuguese period, while those found in the Chittur taluk are recent converts made by Jesuit priests who have their head quarters in Coimbatore. The local heads of the Latin church are the Archbishop of Verapoly and the Bishops of Cochin and Coimbatore, while those of the Romo-Syrian church are the Vicars Apostolic of Trichur and Ernakulam. The Protestants form but a small community, of whom the great majority belong to the Anglican communion. The Church Missionary Society began work in Trichur in 1842 and in Kunnamkulam in 1854, the Church of England Zenana Mission in Trichur in 1881 and the Leipzich Lutheran Mission in Chittur in 1882. These missions have made but little progress, as will be seen from the figures in the margin, and even of this small number, several are sojourners from outside, especially from Travancore.

Muhammadans.

43. The Muhammadans form but 7 percent of the population of the State, as against 31½ per cent in Malabar. This difference is due to the fact that, while the Zamorin favoured the Muhammadans from very early times, his hereditary enemy, the Raja of Cochin, always extended his favour to the Christians. A little over 80 per cent of the Muhammadans are Mappilas, who are the descendants of the offspring of mixed unions or converts from the lower classes. The Ravuttans or Labbais, who are of similar origin but belong to the Tamil countries, form over 13 per cent of the community, and are found chiefly in the Chittur Taluk. The remaining seven per cent are pure Muhammadan immigrants from the north, and consist mainly of Pathans, with a slight sprinkling of Shaiks, Kacchi Memons, Saiyads, Arabs, etc. The Muhammadans are found in all the taluks and in over 200 villages. They are relatively strongest in Cranganur (25 per cent) and weakest in Trichur (3·3 per cent). They have increased by 17 per cent during the past decade. The increase seems to have been due partly to conversion from the lower classes and partly to more accurate enumeration, as the Muhammadans, especially their females, appear to have suffered most by short counting at the previous Censuses.

Jews.

44. The Jews, though small in number, form a very interesting community in Cochin, as they have been settled here for about twenty centuries. They are said to have numbered several thousands a century ago; if so, their number has subsequently dwindled down considerably, and during the last thirty-six years it has remained almost stationary. The great majority of them are found in the towns of Mattancheri and Ernakulam, the rest having their domicile in Chennamangalam in Cochin-Kanayannur and Mala in Mukundapuram. They are not found in any other part of the State. There are two classes of Jews in the State, the White and the Black. The former have preserved their racial purity and light complexion to a remarkable extent, while the latter are hardly distinguishable from the native Muhammadans. Whether the Black Jews were the first settlers on this coast, as claimed by them,

or whether, as contended by the White Jews, they are the descendants of native converts, are disputed questions which will probably remain unsettled for all time.

Urban and Rural Proportions.

45. The distribution of urban and rural population by religion is shown in Subsidiary Table VI. It will be seen from it that the proportion of Hindus is considerably lower in towns than in the country, while that of Muhammadans and Christians is much higher in the former than in the latter, though, in spite of their relatively low proportion in towns, the Hindus still out-number the adherants of all other religions in urban tracts also. The Hindus are more agricultural and also more averse to close neighbourhood than the other classes, which accounts for their preference of a rural to an urban life, while the Muhammadans, Christians and Jews, whose persuits are to a great extent industrial and commercial, are naturally driven to congregate in towns.

Places of Worship.

46. There are 2,667 places of worship in the State, of which 2,286 are Hindu temples and minor shrines, 249 Christian churches and chapels, 125 Muhammadan mosques and 7 Jewish synagogues. The number of temples has increased by nearly 24 per cent during the last decade, churches by 27 per cent and mosques by 34 per cent, while the number of synagogues, like that of Jews, has remained stationary. There is thus one place of worship for every 344 of the population—one temple for every 270 Hindus, one church for every 936 Christians, one mosque for every 510 Muhammadans and one Synagogue for every 168 Jews, the proportion in 1901 being 378, 300, 1,011, 586 and 163 respectively.

SUBSIDIARY TABLE I.

General distribution of the population by religion.

RELIGION AND LOCALITY	Actual number in 1911	Proportion per 10,000 of population in				Variation per cent. (Increase+ Decrease—)			Net variation 1881—1911	
		1911	1901	1891	1881	1901—1911	1891—1901	1881—1891	Actual number	Per cent.
1	2	3	4	5	6	7	8	9	10	11
HINDU.										
Cochin State.	618,708	6,706	6,825·59	6,882·18	7,152·08	+11·08	+11·40	+16·82	+186,884	+43·41
Cochin-Kanayannur...	144,927	5,478	5570·35	5,585·34	5,787·35	+10·67	+12·92	+12·18	+41,562	+40·20
Cranganur ...	28,104	6,961	7,006·86	7,171·82	7,465·39	+13·15	+1·80	+28·23	+7,464	+47·72
Mukundapuram ...	126,978	6,647	6,649·82	6,794·91	7,177·72	+17·99	+8·70	+19·70	+44,282	+53·54
Trichur ...	119,088	7,012	7,116·41	7,223·26	7,373·32	+15·27	+10·85	+20·66	+41,888	+54·19
Talapilli ...	124,918	7,566	7 670·75	7,803·49	8,012·80	7·62	+11·08	+15·27	+34,282	+37·82
Chittur ...	76,748	8,407	8,480·16	8,745·19	8,831·64	1·06	+10·21	+15·23	+16,956	+23·85
CHRISTIAN.										
Cochin State.	233,092	2,589	2,441·29	2,404·61	22,71·68	+17·58	+14·04	+27.47	96,731	+70·98
Cochin-Kanayannur...	102,884	3,888	3,836·08	3,849·53	3,672·62	+14·08	+12·83	+21·84	+37,239	+56·77
Cranganur ...	1,713	561	522·31	509·92	511·70	+12·54	+6·73	+33·02	+ 641	+59·79
Mukundapuram ...	55,990	2,887	2,802·46	2,715·63	2,392·81	+23·45	+14·68	+43·51	+28,422	+103·09
Trichur ...	44,775	2,638	2,513·30	2,437·56	2,365·06	+22 77	+16·01	+26·94	+20 014	+80·82
Talapilli ...	22,927	1,388	1,346·79	1,318·80	1,245·91	+12 50	+15·40	+25·29	+8,884	+62·68
Chittur ...	4,553	582	484·32	485·75	483·30	+11 89	+18·32	+16·96	+1,881	+48·31
MUSALMAN.										
Cochin State.	63,828	695	671·06	641·70	555·47	+17·12	+17·46	+39·12	+30,478	+91·40
Cochin-Kanayannur...	15,715	593	540·28	514·42	475 86	+23·73	+18·92	+25·66	+7,216	+84·90
Cranganur ...	8,376	2 523	2,470·83	2,318·26	2,022·91	+16·33	+11·05	+52·97	+4,138	+97·64
Mukundapuram ...	9,791	505	489·39	483·28	420·53	+23·62	+12·48	+45·32	+4 946	+102·08
Trichur ...	5,618	331	389·41	339·18	261·62	+14·07	+12·59	+59·69	+2 879	+105·11
Talapilli ...	17,052	1,033	961·24	877·71	741·29	+17 23	+23·76	+40·15	+8 667	+103 36
Chittur ...	7,270	796	804·14	769·06	685·06	+0·95	+18·84	+30·63	+2,632	+56·74
ANIMIST.										
Cochin State.	4,177	46	47·99	55·71*	...	+7·18	—3 22	...	...	...
Cochin-Kanayannur...	159	6	9·02	...	...	-23·00	...	...	...	...
Cranganur ...	...	...	...	...	...	...	...	...	...	...
Mukundapuram ...	1,061	55	52·15	...	...	+25·71	...	...	...	...
Trichur ...	323	19	30·87,	...	...	—27 90	...	...	...	...
Talapilli ...	216	13	21·22	...	...	—32·71	...	...	...	...
Chittur ...	2,418	265	231·38	...	...	+16 69	...	...	...	...
JEW.										
Cochin State.	1,175	13	14·00	15·79	20·81	+3 34	—0·44	—8·57	—74	—5·92
Cochin-Kanayannur...	1,063	40	44·11	50·68	64·17	+2·50	—1·42	—8·20	—83	—7·24
Mukundapuram ...	110	6	6·51	6·17	...	+10·00	+11·11	—12·62	+7	+6·79
Trichur ...	2	0·11	...	...	...	...	...	...	...	...
JAIN.										
Cochin State.	129	1	0·06	...	...	+24·80	...	...	...	...
Cochin-Kanayannur...	128	5	0·21	...	...	+24·60	...	...	...	...
Talapilli ...	1	0·06	...	...	...	...	...	...	...	...
PARSI.										
Cochin State.	5	·05	...	...	...	...	...	...	...	...
Trichur ...	5	·29	...	...	...	...	...	...	...	...
BRAHMO.										
Cochin State	2	·02	...	...	...	...	...	...	...	...
Cochin-Kanayannur...	2	·07	...	...	...	...	...	...	...	...

* Figures for the taluks are not available.

SUBSIDIARY TABLE II.

Distribution by Districts of the main religions.

DISTRICT AND NATURAL DIVISION "WEST COAST" MADRAS STATE.	NUMBER PER 10,000 OF THE									
	Hindus.				Muhammadans.				Christians.	
	1911	1901	1891	1881	1911	1901	1891	1881	1911	1901
1	2	3	4	5	6	7	8	9	10	11
Cochin State ..	6,706	6,826·59	6,882·18	7,152·08	695	671·06	641·70	555·47	2,539	2,441·29
Cochin-Kanayannur...	5,473	5,570.35	5,585·34	5,787·35	593	540·28	514·42	475·86	3,883	3,836·03
Cranganur ...	6,961	7,006·86	7,171·82	7,465·89	2,523	2,470·83	2,318·26	2,022·91	516	522·31
Mukundapuram ...	6,547	6,649·82	6,794·91	7,177·72	505	489·39	483·28	420·53	2,887	2,802·46
Trichur ...	7,012	7,116·41	7.223·26	7,373·32	331	339·41	339·18	261·62	2,638	2,513·30
Talapilli ...	7,566	7,670·75	7,808·49	8,012·80	1,083	961·24	877·71	741·29	1,388	1,346·79
Chittur ...	8,407	8,480·16	8,745·19	8,881·64	796	804·14	769·00	685·06	532	484·32

DISTRICT AND NATURAL DIVISION "WEST COAST" MADRAS STATE.	POPULATION WHO ARE													
	Christians.		Animists.				Jews.				Others.			
	1891	1881	1911	1901	1891	1881	1911	1901	1891	1881	1911	1901	1891	1881
	12	13	14	15	16	17	18	19	20	21	22	23	24	25
Cochin State ...	2,404·61	2,271·68	46	47·99	56·71 *	...	13	14·00	15·79	20·81	1·07	...	...	...
Cochin-Kanayannur...	3,849·53	3,672·62	6	9·02	...	...	40	44·11	50·68	64·17	5·07	...	...	...
Cranganur ...	509·92	511·70	...	...	...	...	...	...	...	...	...	...	...	...
Mukundapuram ...	2,715·63	2,892·81	55	52·15	...	...	6	6.51	6·17	...	...	...	...	...
Trichur ...	2,437·56	2,365·06	19	30·87	...	...	0·11	...	...	...	0·29	...	...	...
Talapilli ...	1,318·80	1,245·91	13	21·22	...	...	...	...	...	...	0·06	...	...	...
Chittur ...	485·75	483·30	255	231·38	...	...	...	...	...	...	...	...	...	...

* Figures for the taluks are not available.

SUBSIDIARY TABLE III.

Christians. Number and variations.

DISTRICT AND NATURAL DIVISION "WEST COAST" MADRAS STATE.	ACTUAL NUMBER OF CHRISTIANS IN				VARIATION PER CENT			
	1911	1901	1891	1881	1901—1911	1891—1901	1881—1891	1881—1911
1	2	3	4	5	6	7	8	9
Cochin State. ...	2 33,092	1,98 239	1,73,881	1,36,361	17·58	14·04	27·47	70·93
Cochin-Kanayannur ...	1,02,834	90,179	79,922	65,595	14·03	12·83	21·84	56·77
Cranganur ...	1,713	1,522	1,426	1,072	12·54	6·73	33·02	59·79
Mukundapuram ...	55,990	45,353	39,564	27,568	23 45	14·63	43·51	103·09
Trichur ...	44,775	36.469	31,434	24,761	22 77	16·01	26·94	80·82
Talapilli ...	22,927	20,379	17,658	14,093	12·50	15·40	25·29	62·68
Chittur ...	4,853	4,337	3,827	3,272	11·89	13·32	16·96	48 31

SUBSIDIARY TABLE IV.

Races and Sects of Christians (actual numbers.)

Sect	European		Anglo-Indian		Native		Armenian		Total		Variation + or —
	Male	Female	Male	Female	Male	Female	Male	Female	1911	1901	
1	2	3	4	5	6	7	8	9	10	11	12
Anglican Communion ..	21	15	31	35	743	778	..	..	**1,623**	1,939	—316
Baptist ...	..	..	6	9	18	17	..	..	**44**	45	—1
Congregationalist ..	..	..	..	..	77	90	..	..	**167**	1	+166
Lutheran ..	1	..	10	3	64	57	..	..	**135**	52	+83
Methodist ..	..	..	2	4	..	..	..	..	**6**	..	+6
Minor Protestant Denominations ..	..	..	..	..	19	17	..	..	**36**	28	+8
Presbyterian ..	1	..	..	..	..	..	..	..	**1**	5	—4
Protestants (unsectarian and unspecified) ..	..	..	..	..	142	207	..	..	**349**	..	+349
Roman Catholic ...	33	5	1,192	1,100	49,003	46,894	..	..	**97,787**	79,221	+18,566
Syrian (Roman) ..	..	..	..	..	50,271	49,895	..	..	**100,166**	90,142	+10,024
Do (Jacobite) ...	..	..	..	..	9,904	10,121	..	..	**20,025**	17,408	+2,617
Do. (Reformed) ...	..	..	..	..	291	305	..	..	**596**	514	+82
Do. (Chaldean) ...	..	..	..	..	6,017	6,138	2	..	**12,157**	8,884	+3,273
Total ..	**56**	**20**	**1,241**	**1,205**	**116,549**	**114,019**	**2**	..	**233,092**	**198,239**	**+34,853**

SUBSIDIARY TABLE V.

Distribution of Christians per mille (a) races by sect and (b) sects by race.

Sect	Races distributed by sect					Sects distributed by race				
	European	Anglo-Indian	Native	Armenian	Total	European	Anglo-Indian	Native	Armenian	Total
1	2	3	4	5	6	7	8	9	10	11
Anglican Communion ..	474	27	6·60	..	**6·963**	22·181	40·666	937·153	..	**1,000**
Baptist ...	..	4	·15	..	**·189**	..	204·500	795·500	..	**1,000**
Congregationalist ..	..	..	·72	..	**·717**	..	..	1,000·000	..	**1,000**
Lutheran ...	18	5	·52	..	**·579**	7·400	96·300	896·300	..	**1,000**
Methodist ..	..	2	..	..	**·026**	...	1,000·000	..	..	**1,000**
Minor Protestant Denominations ..	..	..	·16	..	**·155**	..	..	1,000·000	..	**1,000**
Presbyterian ...	13	..	..	...	**·004**	1,000·000	..	..	..	**1,000**
Protestants (unsectarian and unspecified) ..	..	..	1·51	..	**1·497**	..	..	1,000·000	..	**1,000**
Roman Catholic ..	500	962	413·75	..	**419·521**	·389	24·052	975·559	..	**1,000**
Syrian (Roman) ..	..	..	434·48	..	**429·727**	..	..	1,000·000	..	**1,000**
Do. (Jacobite) ..	..	..	86·85	..	**85·910**	..	..	1,000·000	..	**1,000**
Do. (Reformed) ..	..	..	2·59	..	**2·557**	..	..	1,000·000	..	**1,000**
Do. (Chaldean) ..	..	..	52·72	1,000	**52·155**	..	..	999·335	165	**1,000**
Total ...	**1,000**	**1,000**	**1,000**	**1,000**	**1,000**	**·326**	**10·494**	**989·172**	**·008**	**1,000**

SUBSIDIARY TABLE VI.

Religions of Urban and Rural Population.

Natural Division (West coast)	Number per 10,000 of Urban population who are					Number per 10,000 of Rural population who are				
	Hindu	Musalman	Animist	Christian	Others	Hindu	Musalman	Animist	Christian	Others
1	2	3	4	5	6	7	8	9	10	11
Cochin State ..	**5.775**	**941**	..	**3,189**	**95**	**6.833**	**662**	**52**	**2,450**	**3**
Cochin-Kanayannur...	5,227	1,396	..	3,167	210	5,529	408	7	4,049	7
Cranganur ...	..	..	..	..	..	6,961	2.523	..	516	..
Mukundapuram ..	5,678	604	..	3,718	..	6,589	500	57	2,848	6
Trichur ..	5,153	453	..	4,391	3	7,311·80	311·00	22·00	2,354·80	·40
Talapilli ..	3,275	54	..	6,671	..	7,793·70	1,084·79	13·77	1,107·68	·06
Chittur ..	9,007	896	..	97	..	8,242	769	338	651	..

CHAPTER V.

AGE.

Age statistics where to be found.

47. The age statistics of the people are given in Imperial Table VII along with those of sex and civil condition, while Subsidiary Table I gives the exact ages of 100,000 Hindus and as many Christians of each sex and the other subsidiary tables at the end of this chapter give the main facts of the subject in proportional forms.

Accuracy of the returns.

48. The age returns in their raw state are far from being accurate. A great many of the people, especially among non-Christians, do not know their ages at all, while a still greater number do not know them accurately. When questioned by enumerators therefore, the latter give their approximate ages and the former make a wild guess at them. In a steadily growing population, like that of Cochin, which is not materially affected by famine or migration, the number of persons under one year old should ordinarily be larger than the number of those who are of any other age, the numbers in the succeeding ages decreasing gradually as the ages advance and deaths thin their ranks, but in Subsidiary Table I the largest number of person occurs at the age of 30, and the next largest at the age of 12 in the case of males and 25 in the case of females. This table also shows the preference of the people for ages which are multiples of five, the even multiples being more in favour than the odd. The other ages for which the people of Cochin show special preference are 12, 16, 18 and 28. Similar peculiarities are noticeable in the age returns throughout India. The errors arising from the preference given to certain numbers as shown above are removed by experts by subjecting the statistics to one or other of the various processes of smoothing before they examine them for practical purposes. A well known actuary is examining the age statistics for the main Provinces of India, and it is hardly worthwhile therefore to subject to any such processes the statistics for a small State like Cochin, as, owing to the limited extent of the field of investigation, it would be unsafe to draw any important inferences from them. It may however be pointed out that the inaccuracies noticed above almost disappear when the ages of the population are grouped into quinquennial periods, the numbers in the different quinquennial totals steadily decreasing as the ages advance, with one exception, namely, that of females between 60 and 65 years of age, who number more than those between 55 and 60. This exception may be due to the tendency of old women in India to make themselves out older than they really are, but in all other respects the gradation is uniform, and this uniformity is common among the followers of the main religions—Hindus, Christians and Musalmans.

Age statistics by religion.

49. Subsidiary Table III gives the proportion of each sex in each religion who are found at each of the periods. The proportion of children not only under five years of age but also between 5 and 10 and 10 and 15 is highest among Musalmans and Christians and lowest among Animists. The low proportion of children among Animists is no doubt due to the greater danger to which they are exposed and the less care which they receive than the generality of Hindu, Musalman and Christian children. But it is not clear why there should be a higher proportion of children among Musalmans and Christians than among Hindus. The same peculiarity was observed in the Madras Presidency in 1901, and the Madras Census Report for that year has attempted the following explanation:—"Hindu women are more

universally married than either Musalman or Christian women, the percentages of the females in each religion who are married being 42, 40 and 39, respectively, and this is in favour of the fecundity of the Hindu community, but, on the other hand, the early age at which the women of this religion marry, when compared with those of the other two, is probably inimical to the production of large families. In balancing the opposing forces which tend in favour of and against the fecundity of the followers of the three different religions, it is further necessary to take into consideration the facts that Musalmans and Christians eat meat, while many Hindus do not, and that they allow the re-marriage of widows while some of the Hindus forbid it." So far as Cochin is concerned, neither our figures nor our social conditions support this explanation. Hindu women here are less universally married than Musalman and Christian women, the number of females per mille in each religion who are married being 402, 407 and 419 respectively, and as regards the eating of meat and the re-marrying of widows, the prohibition obtains only among a very small minority of Hindus in this State. Of those above the age of 20, the proportion is the highest among Hindus and lowest among Animists. This more rapid decline of Musalmans and Christians as compared with Hindus, as they advance in age, is as inexplicable as their greater prolificness disclosed by the figures.

Age statistics by caste.

50. The different castes present a variety of features in regard to their age distribution, but it is not worthwhile to examine the figures minutely as the divergences, at least in some of the cases, may be due to the greater or less accuracy of the returns. It may however be stated broadly on the authority of subsidiary Table IV that the lower castes are more prolific than the higher, but that a greater proportion of the latter live to adult and old age than the former.

SUBSIDIARY TABLE I.

Age distribution of 100,000 of each sex by annual periods.

AGE.	MALE.			FEMALE.		
	Hindu.	Christian.	Both Religions.	Hindu.	Christian.	Both Religions.
1	2	3	4	5	6	7
0	3,469	3,578	7,047	3,428	3,690	7,118
1	2,794	2,998	5,792	2,718	3,079	5,797
2	2,950	3,255	6,205	2,870	3,378	6,248
3	2,584	2,886	5,470	2,626	2,932	5,558
4	2,557	2,760	5,317	2,416	2,756	5,172
5	2,915	3,258	6,173	2,726	3,183	5,909
6	2,516	2,664	5,180	2,810	2,621	4,931
7	2,537	2,761	5,298	2,478	2,921	5,394
8	2,914	3,041	5,955	2,574	2,889	5,463
9	1,889	1,998	3,887	1,883	2,168	4,051
10	3,297	3,207	6,504	3,034	3,201	6,235
11	1,384	1,505	2,889	1,372	1,616	2,988
12	3,895	3,647	7,542	3,208	3,120	6,328
13	1,468	1,928	3,396	1,525	1,327	3,352
14	2,394	2,596	4,990	2,359	2,490	4,849
15	2,503	2,262	4,765	2,291	2,050	4,341
16	2,696	2,576	5,272	2,503	2,328	4,831
17	1,098	1,257	2,355	1,247	1,222	2,469
18	2,821	2,807	5,628	3,198	3,058	6,256
19	843	966	1,809	887	918	1,755
20	3,292	2,948	6,240	4,122	3,681	7,803
21	902	900	1,802	878	933	1,811
22	2,315	2,351	4,666	2,407	2,498	4,905
23	1,006	1,001	2,007	929	967	1,896
24	1,574	1,689	3,263	1,662	1,819	3,481
25	3,281	2,799	6,080	3,968	3,585	7,553
26	1,303	1,312	2,615	1,212	1,263	2,475
27	843	923	1,766	844	917	1,761
28	2,399	2,476	4,875	2,528	2,595	5,123
29	552	597	1,149	486	472	958
30	4,210	3,641	7,851	4,750	4,051	8,801
31	406	443	849	336	321	657
32	1,539	1,515	3,054	1,317	1,321	2,638
33	650	758	1,408	515	546	1,061
34	608	664	1,362	557	495	1,052
35	3,281	3,138	6,419	3,167	2,975	6,142
36	987	980	1,967	810	736	1,546
37	463	483	946	385	384	769
38	1,644	1,611	3,255	1,333	1,207	2,540
39	344	382	726	280	256	536
40	3,734	3,272	7,006	3,948	3,307	7,250
41	246	255	501	187	199	386
42	774	861	1,635	614	624	1,238
43	331	295	626	251	266	517
44	333	308	641	272	246	518
45	2,244	2,102	4,346	2,148	2,055	4,203
46	428	390	818	340	292	632
47	270	257	527	217	205	422
48	859	824	1,683	775	705	1,480
49	222	210	432	185	155	340
50	2,333	1,903	4,236	2,892	2,379	5,271
51	180	205	385	152	123	275
52	407	437	844	362	365	727
53	203	205	408	163	141	304
54	247	215	462	221	183	404
55	1,185	1,185	2,270	1,258	1,235	2,493
56	319	329	648	264	233	497
57	172	161	333	139	133	272
58	369	374	743	382	307	689
59	132	127	259	126	74	200
60	1,371	1,180	2,554	1,946	1,622	3,568
61	122	95	217	118	94	207
62	217	211	428	228	186	414
63	126	115	241	118	88	206
64	110	105	245	121	88	209
65	505	488	993	594	528	1,122
66	127	121	248	114	65	179
67	95	82	177	75	69	144
68	137	131	268	165	145	310
69	43	42	85	47	40	87
70	410	345	755	670	587	1,257
71	37	25	62	28	35	63
72	64	91	155	71	61	132
73	41	36	77	27	27	54
74	83	34	67	33	27	60

SUBSIDIARY TABLE I.

Age distribution of 100,000 of each sex by annual periods.—Continued.

AGE.	MALE.			FEMALE.		
	Hindu.	Christian.	Both religions.	Hindu.	Christian.	Both religions.
1	2	3	4	5	6	7
75	161	155	**316**	226	37	**463**
76	88	42	**80**	35	33	**68**
77	20	27	**47**	20	25	**45**
78	33	38	**71**	50	41	**91**
79	9	9	**18**	11	9	**20**
80	118	92	**210**	189	154	**343**
81	6	4	**10**	8	4	**12**
82	13	18	**31**	12	21	**33**
83	5	13	**18**	6	5	**11**
84	13	5	**18**	12	5	**17**
85	24	34	**58**	39	47	**86**
86	10	8	**18**	14	10	**24**
87	2	5	**7**	7	5	**12**
88	5	10	**15**	7	7	**14**
89	2	...	**2**	2	4	**6**
90	9	7	**16**	6	23	**49**
91	1	1	**2**	...	1	**1**
92	1	1	**2**	1	...	**1**
93	...	...	...	1	...	**1**
94	...	...	...	...	...	...
95	3	3	**6**	4	4	**8**
96	1	1	**2**	2	3	**5**
97	...	...	...	...	3	**3**
98	3	...	**3**	1	...	**1**
99	...	...	...	1	...	**1**
100	1	...	1	1	...	**1**
101	...	...	...	...	...	...
102	...	...	...	...	...	...
103	...	...	...	...	1	**1**
104	...	...	...	...	...	...
105	...	...	...	...	2	**2**
Total ...	100,000	100,000	**200 000**	100,000	100,000	**200,000**

SUBSIDIARY TABLE II.

Age distribution of 10,000 of each sex in 1911 and 1901.

AGE PERIOD	1911		1901	
	Males	**Females**	Males	Females
1	2	3	4	5
0— 5 ...	**1,469**	**1,460**	1,366·5	1,403·1
5—10 ...	**1,301**	**1,232**	1,385·6	1,389·7
10—15 ...	**1,257**	**1,175**	1,321·6	1,225 9
15—20 ...	**993**	**995**	970·2	979·2
20—25 ...	**904**	**1,002**	885·5	974·8
25—30 ...	**829**	**899**	865·2	909·9
30—35 ...	**789**	**727**	747·8	719·1
35—40 ...	**667**	**583**	639·2	555·2
40—45 ...	**532**	**510**	549·2	583·1
45—50 ...	**393**	**355**	363·8	344·7
50—55 ...	**325**	**360**	338·2	369 5
55—60 ...	**210**	**208**	193·2	183·6
60 and over ...	**381**	**473**	373·4	460·9
Not stated ...	...	...	1 1	1·3
Total ...	**10,000**	**10,000**	**10,000**	**10,000**

SUBSIDIARY TABLE III.

Age distribution of 10,000 of each sex in each main religion

AGE	HINDU		MUSALMAN		CHRISTIAN		ANIMIST		JEW	
	Male	Female	Male	Female	Male	Female	Male	Female	Male	Female
1	2	3	4	5	6	7	8	9	10	11
0—5 ...	1,4 5	1,406	1,509	1,555	1,548	1,588	1 45	1,487	1,471	1,176
5—10 ...	1,2	1,197	1,323	1,345	1,372	1,378	1,288	1,132	1,086	1,076
10—15 ...	1,2 9	1,150	1,317	1,244	1,288	1,226	1,143	1,132	1,033	1,076
15—20 ...	996	1,007	997	1,037	987	958	863	888	911	993
20—40 ...	3,169	3,246	3,136	3,199	3,062	3,102	3,296	3,727	2,837	3,411
40—60 ...	1,494	1,489	1,384	1,270	1,386	1,323	1,697	1,366	2,032	1,606
60 and over ...	395	503	334	350	357	430	348	268	630	662
Total ...	10,000	10,000	10,000	10,000	10,000	10,000	10,000	10,000	10,000	10,000

SUBSIDIARY TABLE IV.

Age distribution of 1,000 of each sex in certain castes.

CASTE.	MALES. NUMBER PER MILLE AGED					FEMALES. NUMBER PER MILLE AGED				
	0 — 5	5 —12	12—15	15—40	40 and over	0 — 5	5 —12	12—15	15—40	40 and over
1	2	3	4	5	6	7	8	9	10	11
HINDU.										
Ambalavasi ...	124	164	74	420	218	124	147	65	409	255
Arayan ...	153	163	71	500	113	146	166	69	440	189
Brahman, Malayali	94	130	60	433	283	107	182	58	411	292
Do. Tamil ...	137	183	77	402	201	152	177	60	392	219
Do. Konkani ...	92	146	55	465	242	121	166	52	426	235
Do. Others ...	62	75	73	542	248	130	143	75	428	224
Total Brahmans ...	114	159	68	431	228	136	165	58	405	236
Chakkan ...	126	170	426	71	207	133	160	73	414	220
Devangan ...	100	144	59	463	234	90	138	97	457	218
Iluvan ...	150	178	82	412	178	147	172	77	427	177
Kadupattan ...	142	169	79	428	182	140	146	78	417	224
Kaikolan ...	1 7	169	75	410	239	117	158	64	422	239
Kammalan ...	151	179	78	409	183	146	162	73	434	185
Kanakkan ...	155	181	84	410	170	159	175	98	411	162
Kaniyan ...	149	182	74	403	192	127	154	94	418	207
Kshatriya, Malayali	127	186	59	393	235	129	155	85	397	234
Do. Paradesi ...	92	125	69	452	262	106	215	40	420	219
Kudumi Chetti ...	124	164	67	454	191	134	139	56	409	202
Kusavan ...	151	156	70	415	208	148	167	64	440	181
Nayar ...	142	168	79	429	182	131	152	67	423	227
Ottanaikan ...	120	156	61	435	228	110	48	77	434	231
Pandaran ...	137	159	93	418	193	145	182	79	387	207
Panan ...	117	178	78	435	192	138	142	62	453	205
Panditattan ...	123	158	83	430	206	133	181	66	421	190
Parayan ...	146	171	71	409	203	147	186	69	407	191
Pulayan ...	157	180	77	388	198	150	170	70	423	187
Valan ...	143	156	72	434	195	157	165	63	420	195
Velan ...	144	166	74	421	195	147	162	69	421	201
Velakkattalavan ...	124	191	71	446	168	129	148	58	435	230
Vellalan ...	123	154	88	421	214	111	161	68	419	241
Veluttedan ...	137	171	77	414	201	132	145	70	431	222
Vettuvan ...	168	165	82	407	178	169	178	70	406	177
MUSALMAN.										
Jonakan ...	157	170	83	411	170	160	188	78	423	156
Ravuttan ...	132	184	88	421	175	137	182	74	425	182
CHRISTIAN.										
Anglo-Indian ...	167	199	77	376	181	143	168	77	439	173
European ...	36	18	...	625	321	100	50	...	550	300
Native Christian ...	155	183	83	405	174	158	186	75	406	175
ANIMIST.										
Malayan ...	133	167	74	426	200	147	147	75	478	158
JEW ...	147	147	65	375	266	118	141	74	440	227

SUBSIDIARY TABLE V.

Proportion of children under 10 and of persons over 50 to those aged 15—40; also of married females aged 15—40 per 100 females.

District and natural division West Coast "Madras State"	Proportion of children both sexes per 100						Proportion of persons over 50 per 100 aged 15—40						Number of married females aged 15—40 per 100 females of all ages		
	Persons aged 15—40			Married females aged 15-40			1911		1901		1891				
	1911	1901	1891	1911	1901	891	Male	Female	Male	Female	Male	Female	1911	1901	1891
1	2	3	4	5	6	7	8	9	10	11	12	13	14	15	16
Cochin State ...	**65·7**	66·6	66·5	**170·2**	179·1	157·2	**22·2**	**24·7**	22·0	24·5	22·5	24·1	**32·1**	30·6	35·1

SUBSIDIARY TABLE VI.

Variation in population at certain age-periods.

District and Natural Division West Coast Madras State"	Period	Variation per cent in Population (increase +. decrease —).					
		All ages	0—10	10—15	15—40	40—60	60 and over
1	2	3	4	5	6	7	8
Cochin State ...	**1901—1911**	**+ 13·06**	**+ 12·79**	**+ 7·91**	**+ 14·36**	**+ 13·72**	**+ 15·78**
	1891—1901	+ 12·32	+ 11·87	+ 18·45	+ 11·63	+ 11·08	+ 9·06
	1881—1891	+ 20·42					

NOTE:—From the figures as given in the report of 1881 information as regards the variation in different age periods cannot be furnished.

SUBSIDIARY TABLE VII.

Reported birth rate by sex and natural divisions.

Year	Number of births per 1000 of total population — Cochin State		
	Persons	Males	Females
1	2	3	4
1901	**6·4**	6·6	6·3
1902	**7·1**	7·0	7·2
1903	**8·5**	8·4	8·5
1904	**9·1**	9·3	8·0
1905	**9·8**	...	...
1906	**10·2**	...	...
1907	**10·9**	...	...
1908	**9·7**	9·8	9·5
1909	**19·1**	19·3	18·8
1910	**19·4**	20·2	18·6
Total	**110·2**	...	...

NOTE:—Separate figures by sex for the years 1905 to 1907 are not available.

SUBSIDIARY TABLE VIII

Reported death rate by sex and natural divisions.

Year	Number of deaths per 1000 of total population		
	Cochin State		
	Persons	Males	Females
1	2	3	4
1901	7·9	9·0	6·8
1902	9·0	10·3	7·7
1903	9·6	10·5	8·6
1904	8·8	9·7	7·9
1905	10·4	...	...
1906	9·8	...	...
1907	15·9	...	...
1908	14·7	...	..
1909	13·2	...	...
1910	13·4	...	..
Total	112·7	...	...

NOTE:—Separate figures by sex are not available from the year 1905 onwards.

SUBSIDIARY TABLE IX.

Reported deaths from certain diseases per mille of the population.

Cochin State			Cochin State		
Year	Actual number of deaths	Ratio per mille	Year	Actual number of deaths	Ratio per mille
1	2	3	1	2	3
Cholera			Fever		
1901	824	1·0	1901	1,936	2·3
1902	786	·9	1902	2,216	2·7
1903	1 088	1·3	1903	2,605	3·2
1904	88	·04	1904	2,930	3·6
1905	...	...	1905	3,105	3·8
1906	...	..	1906	3,462	4·2
1907	2,672	3·2	1907	4,172	5·1
1908	1,923	2·3	1908	3,338	4·1
1909	227	·2	1909	3,750	4·6
1910 (Small-pox and Cholera together)	724	·9	1910	...	...
Small-pox			Dysentery and Diarrhœa		
1901	890	1·0			
1902	1,574	1·9	1901	961	1·1
1903	877	·4	1902	950	1·1
1904	150	·1	1903	1,320	1·6
1905	...	...	1904	1,204	1·4
			1905	1,537	1·8
1906	...	...			
1907	...	...	1906	1,338	1·6
1908	572	·7	1907	2,853	3·5
1909	579	·7	1908	3,038	3·7
1910 (Small-pox and Cholera together)	724	·8	1909	1,880	2·3
			1910	...	...

NOTE:—Figures by sex are not available as also for the columns left blank.

CHAPTER VI.

PROPORTION OF SEXES.

Preponderance of males over females.

51. According to the recent Census there were 1,007 females for every 1,000 males, as against 1,004 in 1901, 998 in 1891 and 989 in 1881. This gradual increase in the relative strength of females disclosed by the successive Censuses is observed in most of the Districts of the Madras Presidency and in the Presidency as a whole, but in most of the other Provinces and States in India males still outnumber females, though successive Censuses showed some improvement in the relative strength of the latter. In view of the preponderance of females over males in most European countries, continental critics of the Census of India are inclined to attribute the deficiency of females to omissions in the Census records. Whether this view is correct or not in regard to other Provinces and States, there can be no doubt of its correctness as regards Cochin and Southern India generally. When the first Censuses were taken, the object of the Census was not understood—was even misunderstood—by the people, and owing to the general disposition of the people of India to conceal the number of females and to the tendency of our enumerators to consider their inclusion or exclusion a matter of no importance, large numbers of females were omitted from the Census records. With the gradually increasing accuracy of the returns, successive Censuses have enhanced the proportion of females, till in 1901 they outnumbered the males and still more so in 1911. This result, which in its way affords collateral testimony to the comparative accuracy of the enumeration, was anticipated in the last two Census Reports of this State.

Proportion of sexes by taluks.

52. As in 1891 and 1901, the preponderance of females over males is observed only in the four northern taluks, while in Cochin-Kanayannur and Cranganur males still continue to outnumber females. Further, while the relative strength of females is found to increase with every decade in the former, a decrease is observed, on the other hand, in the latter. As pointed out in the Report for 1901, this preponderance in Cochin-Kanayannur may probably be due to the existence there of a large number of temporary male residents for business purposes, especially in Mattancheri, Ernakulam and Tripunittura and in their neighbourhood, several of whom have left their families behind in their own homes. But in the case of Cranganur I cannot think of any explanation for the deficiency of females.

Proportion of sexes by religion.

53. It will be seen from Subsidiary Table II that females preponderate over males among Hindus and Jews, and males over females among Christians, Musalmans and Animists. No explanation can be offered for the deficiency of females among Christians and Muhammadans, except that they have suffered most by short counting at the previous Censuses, a supposition to which the figures given in the margin lend some support. Females however outnumber males in the taluks of Trichur, Talapilli and Chittur among Christians and in the two latter taluks among Musalmans.

Females to 1,000 males.

	1891.	*1911.*
Christians	972	978
Musalmans	885	951

Proportion of the sexes by caste.

54. Subsidiary Table III gives the proportion of the sexes among the more important castes found in the State. It will be seen from it that females preponderate over males among most of the indigenous castes, except among Nambudiris, Kshatriyas, Ambalavasis, Valans, Arayans, Kaniyans, Panans and Kanakkans. The deficiency

of females among Nambudiris may be due to the custom obtaining among them of only the eldest son marrying within the caste and to the prevalence of polygamy, but it is not clear why there is such a deficiency among the others. The highest proportion of females is found among Vettuvans (1,159) and Velutte-dans (1,128) and the lowest among Arayans (903).

Age and sex.

55. As the age and sex statistics of European countries show a preponderance of males over females up to the age of 15 and of females over males above that age, it has been generalised that more boys are born into the world than girls, but fewer survive to adult ages. In the Census Report of 1901 this generalisation was shown to be inapplicable to Cochin, as according to the Census returns of that year females outnumbered males below the age of 5. The present Census has shown however that the generalisation is, as a matter of fact, as applicable to Cochin as to other countries. It will be seen from Subsidiary Tables II and III that during the three first quinquennial periods males outnumber females, but between 15 and 40 there are more females than males, after which period the proportion turns in favour of males till they reach the sixtieth year, and then females once more begin to preponderate. Thus more boys than girls are born into the world of Cochin as well, but fewer survive to adult age. After the age of 40 there appears to be more morality among females, though, of those who survive to the age of 60, a greater proportion of women live to old age. The returns show the existence of five centenarians in Cochin at the time of the Census, of whom four are females and one a male.

SUBSIDIARY TABLE I

General proportions of the sexes by natural divisions and districts.

Districts and Natural Divisions "West coast" Madras States	Number of Females to 1000 Males							
	1911		1901		1891		1881	
	Actual population	Natural population	Actual population	Natural population	Actual population	Natural population	Actual population	Natural population
1	2	3	4	5	6	7	8	9
Cochin State ...	1,007	997	1,004	996	998	992	989	*

* Not available.

SUBSIDIARY TABLE II.

Number of females per 1000 males at different age periods by religions at each of the last three Censuses.

Age	All religions 1891	All religions 1901	All religions 1911	Hindus 1891	Hindus 1901	Hindus 1911	Musalmans 1891	Musalmans 1901	Musalmans 1911
0—1	1,129	1,062	1,011	1,160	1,029	1,0[illegible]8	1,058	1,022	1,009
1—2	1,052	1,007	996	1,045	1,006	997	1,119	1,048	945
2—3	1,056	1,051	1,001	1,060	1,061	998	1,088	947	987
3—4	1,065	1,086	1,080	1,082	1,049	1,042	980	1,017	1,048
4—5	1,058	1,026	966	1,058	1,055	969	996	970	914
Total 0—5	1,070	1,081	1,001	1,080	1,041	1,004	1,045	999	981
5—10	967	971	969	959	970	964	942	992	967
10—15	908	981	942	908	987	951	871	924	899
15—20	1,000	1,018	1,011	1,027	1,029	1,087	1,018	1,006	959
20—25	1,135	1,105	1,116	1,139	1,108	1,128	1,127	1,064	1,079
25—30	1,070	1,056	1,093	1,069	1,072	1,106	1,127	1,014	1,058
Total 0—30	1,016	1,010	1,012	1,021	1,017	1,021	1,006	993	985
30—40	921	928	883	936	930	959	901	902	850
40—50	901	965	942	921	997	970	887	852	841
50—60	1,004	1,045	1,069	1,08[illegible]	1,074	1,111	901	894	931
60 and over	1,202	1,239	1,252	1,268	1,317	1,305	1,041	1,053	996
Total 30 and over	961	992	898	986	1,022	1,083	897	902	876
Total all ages Actual population	998	1,004	1,067	1,003	1,019	1,026	885	965	951
Total all ages Natural population	992	996	997	...	...	...	...	...	...

Age	Christians 1891	Christians 1901	Christians 1911	Animists 1891	Animists 1901	Animists 1911	Jews 1891	Jews 1901	Jews 1911	Others 1891	Others 1901	Others 1911
0—1	1,059	1,048	1,009		1,018	692	1,700	759	1,000			
1—2	1,050	998	1,004		1,441	1,52	1,000	1,222	818			
2—3	1,041	1,049	1,0[illegible]8		1,848	1,204	846	1,250	545			
3—4	1,043	1004	994		1,098	1,309	1,067	1,400	1,143			
4—5	1,081	968	977		1,206	812	647	1,125	800			
Total 0—5	1,054	1,011	1,000		1,192	1,066	1,000	1,160	846			2,500 [illegible]
5—10	998	965	9[illegible]2		973	847	1,227	1,198	1,048			1,833
10—15	910	921	981		831	955	842	1,032	1,101			357
15—20	919	971	949		1,140	938	888	1,000	1,154			500
20—25	1,127	1,113	1,069		1,593	1,444	1,160	1,239	1,587			545
25—30	1,083	1,022	1 066		1,072	1,118	1,064	1,075	1,856			643
Total 0—30	1,005	992	993	...	1,085	1,045	1,017	1,108	1,179	...	...	673
30—40	879	884	862		890	687	1,111	1,000	855			778
40—50	858	918	898		525	717	1,086	902	890			59
50—60	934	998	995		1,000	813	674	1,400	744			
60 and over	1,062	1,067	1,178		849	743	1,116	925	1,111			1,000
Total 30 and over	908	934	939		774	821	1,019	1,023	885			436
Total all ages Actual population	972	974	978		977	964	1,018	1,075	1,059			568
Total all ages Natural population	..	...	...		...	...	...	...	...			...

SUBSIDIARY TABLE III.

Number of females per 1000 males for certain selected castes.

CASTE	NUMBER OF FEMALES PER 1000 MALES						
	All ages	0—5	5—12	12—15	15—20	20—40	40 and over
1	2	3	4	5	6	7	8
HINDU ...							
Ambalavasi ...	996	996	894	872	932	981	1,168
Arayan ...	908	857	863	882	849	1,298	1,512
Brahman, Malayali ...	986	1,066	946	908	1,102	889	966
do Tamil ...	982	1,085	902	726	823	941	1,017
do Konkani ...	861	1,183	984	818	848	773	882
do others ...	467	984	893	479	861	870	422
Total Brahmans ...	891	1,057	927	758	848	884	928
Chakkan ...	896	943	846	924	825	885	952
Devangan ...	997	890	959	1,629	969	990	981
Iluvan ...	1,027	1,005	988	972	1,113	1,052	1,022
Kadupattan ...	1,025	1,016	884	952	1,006	996	1,256
Kaikolan ...	1,049	1,144	979	894	1,111	1,070	1,052
Kammalan ...	1,022	990	927	960	1,056	1,091	1,034
Kanakkan ...	986	1,010	955	1,097	1,182	985	989
Kaniyan ...	998	851	845	1,266	1,159	1,002	1,074
Kshatriya, Malayali ..	986	1,000	821	1,488	880	1,038	983
Do Paradesi ...	898	1,086	1,553	524	1,227	759	750
Kudumi Chetti ...	903	980	769	759	1,059	899	950
Kusavan ...	945	928	1,011	859	902	1,082	822
Nayar ...	1,064	978	965	908	1,015	1,060	1,828
Ottanaikan ...	1,058	970	1,005	1,838	1,189	1,085	1,071
Pandaran ...	970	1,028	1,114	824	865	909	1,041
Panan ...	946	1,115	756	744	795	1,055	1,014
Panditattan ...	880	897	958	658	822	810	801
Parayan ...	1,019	1,025	1,106	990	1,025	1,011	961
Pulayan ...	1,068	1,019	1,008	961	1,143	1,168	1,001
Valan ...	935	1,026	987	817	916	900	937
Velan ...	1,029	1,058	1,001	959	998	1,088	1,061
Velakkattalavan ...	1,014	1,050	787	885	1,011	982	1,888
Vellalan ...	965	868	1,004	749	878	988	1,087
Veluttedan ...	1,128	1,092	956	1,016	1,000	1,234	1,241
Vettuvan ...	1,159	1,164	1,249	995	1,242	1,182	1,152
MUSALMAN ...							
Jonakan ...	959	978	979	893	1,002	988	888
Ravuttan ...	955	995	941	810	978	962	991
CHRISTIAN ...							
Anglo Indian ...	972	831	822	979	970	1,197	924
European ...	857	1,000	1,000	...	...	879	838
Native Christian ...	978	1,002	993	881	949	969	984
ANIMIST ...							
Malayan ...	928	1,024	803	957	958	1,012	780
JEW ...	1,058	845	1,012	1,216	1,154	1,272	901

SUBSIDIARY TABLE IV.

Actual number of births and deaths reported for each sex during the periods 1896—1900 and 1901—1910.

YEAR	Number of births			Number of deaths			Difference between columns 2 and 3. Excess of latter over former +, defect —	Difference between columns 5 and 6. Excess of latter over former +, defect —	Difference between columns 4 and 7. Excess of former over latter +, defect —	Number of female births per 1000 male births	Number of female deaths per 1000 male deaths
	Male	Female	Total	Male	Female	Total					
1	2	3	4	5	6	7	8	9	10	11	12
1896 ...	3,818	3,538	7,351	3,207	2,613	5,820	— 275	— 594	+ 1,531	928	815
1897 ...	6,016	4,917	10,933	5,182	4,203	9,385	— 1,099	— 979	+ 1,548	817	811
1898 ...	2,843	2,743	5,586	4,793	4,049	8,842	— 100	— 744	— 3,256	965	845
1899 ...	2,731	2,627	5,358	2,811	2,137	4,948	— 104	— 674	+ 410	962	760
1900 ...	3,042	3,039	6,081	3,159	2,630	5,789	— 3	— 529	+ 292	999	833
Total 1896–1900 ...	18,445	16,864	35,309	19,152	15,632	34,784	— 1,581	— 3,520	+ 525	914	816
1901 ...	2,693	2,574	5,267	3,671	2,775	6,446	— 119	— 896	— 1,179	956	756
1902 ...	2,846	2,941	5,787	4,191	3,163	7,354	+ 95	— 1,028	— 1,567	1,033	755
1903 ...	3,440	3,492	6,932	4,286	3,521	7,807	+ 52	— 765	— 875	1,015	821
1904 ...	3,787	3,632	7,419	3,965	3,228	7,193	— 155	— 737	+ 226	959	814
1905 ...	...	...	7,975	...	...	8,455	...	...	— 480	...	...
1906 ...	...	...	8,845	...	...	8,020	...	...	+ 825	...	...
1907 ...	...	...	8,885	...	...	12,960	...	...	— 4,075	...	...
1908 ...	3,998	3,881	7,879	...	...	12,005	— 117	...	— 4,126	971	...
1909 ...	7,846	7,667	15,513	...	...	10,738	— 179	...	+ 4,775	977	...
1910 ...	8,210	7,574	15,784	...	...	10,946	— 636	...	+ 4,838	923	...
Total 1901–1910 ...	...	...	89,786	...	...	91,924	...	...	— 2,138	...	...

NOTE:—Figures for the years prior to 1896 are not available, since the registration of births and deaths was introduced only in 1896. Figures for the columns left blank are also not available.

CHAPTER VII.

CIVIL CONDITION.

Introductory.

56. Imperial Table VII gives the statistics of civil condition by age, sex and religion, that is, the number of males and females among the adherents of different religions who are married, unmarried or widowed in certain age periods, and Imperial Table XIV gives similar statistics by slightly differing age periods for certain selected castes and races. The Subsidiary Tables at the end of this Chapter give the same statistics in proportional and condensed forms.

Accuracy of the returns.

57. It is not an easy matter to obtain thoroughly accurate returns of civil condition, especially on this coast. The question "Are you married", which the enumerator is required to ask every person enumerated, means in Malayalam "Have you ever been married", and both the widowed and the married would therefore answer such a question in the affirmative. Whether the wife or husband is living or dead has to be brought out by further questioning of an inoffensive nature, the question "Is your wife (or husband) alive" being an ill-omened and therefore offensive one. Further, a large proportion of the people of Cochin follow the *Marumakkattayam* law, and among them all girls go through two forms of marriage—the *Talikettu* and the *Sambandham.* The former is only what the Census Commissioner calls a mock marriage, but the vernacular word for marriage is only used in connection with that ceremony, while the *Sambandham* or cloth-giving ceremony, which is the real marriage, is not called by that name. To ensure that the *Sambandham* alone should be treated as marriage for Census purposes, written and oral instructions of a minute and elaborate nature were given to the Supervisors and Enumerators. That errors on this account were thereby reduced to a minimum is shown by the facts, among others, that, though hundreds of Nayar girls below the age of five have gone through the ceremony of *Talikettu*, not a single one among them has been returned as married, and that the proportion of married males among Namburis is as high as that among other Brahmans, though the majority of them are married only in the sense that they have formed *Sambandham* alliance with Nayar or Ambalavasi women.

Main features of the statistics.

58. The most striking features in the statistics of civil condition in India are the universality of marriage, the early age at which it takes place and the great preponderance of widows over widowers. These features are sufficiently prominent in Cochin, but not to the same extent as elsewhere in India. Nearly 20 per cent. of the population of the State follow the *Marumakkattayam* law of succession, and among them marriage is not compulsory from a religious point of view as it is among several other classes of Hindus. Child marriage in the form of an irrevocable betrothal, which is customary elsewhere, is unknown among them, and the re-marriage of widows is not prohibited. In these latter respects Iluvans, Kammalans, and other indigenous castes, though governed by *Makkattayam* law, follow the lead of Nayars, while Christians and Muhammadans, who form about a third of the population, generally marry their girls only after they attain puberty and do not of course prohibit the re-marriage of widows. The Nambudiris are the only indigenous people among whom widow marriage is prohibited, but child marriage is altogether unknown among them. Religious compulsion to marry, the obligation to marry girls before the attainment of puberty and the prohibition of the

re-marriage of widows, which are so characteristic of the majority of the Indian population, are in force here only among the Tamil, Konkani and other foreign Brahmans.

59. Full descriptions of the several kinds of marriage customs observed by the various castes and tribes here are given in Mr. L. K. Ananthakrishna Iyer's *Cochin Tribes and Castes* and in the Report on the Census of 1901. It is therefore unnecessary to go over the same ground again here. It may however be mentioned here that polyandry does not exist in Cochin and that polygamy is very rare. Polyandry of the fraternal type was once common among the Kammalans, and that of the maternal type among the Nayars, but now both have altogether died out. Polygamy is still common among the Nambudiri Brahmans, among whom the eldest son alone is allowed to marry in the same caste, and the consequent dearth of bridegrooms among them renders polygamy unavoidable.

General remarks.

60. The common belief enjoined by the Hindu religion that a man must beget a son to rescue him from hell by performing his funeral ceremonies chiefly accounts for the universality of marriage. The fashion thus set by the Brahmans is followed not only by the lower classes of Hindus but also by the Christians and Muhammedans of these parts, though they are not bound by any such doctrine. Further, whether or not a man is able to maintain his wife and children is a consideration which is never taken into account, as it is in European countries, in connection with marriage. The consequence is that unmarried adults are very few among males and fewer still among females. It will be seen from Subsidiary Table II that 59 per cent. of the males between the ages 15 and 40 and 83 per cent. of those above 40 are married, while the proportions of married females at the same age periods are 76 and 39 per cent. respectively. But in England and Wales so many as 41 per cent. of the males and 39 per cent. of the females above the age of 15 are unmarried, while in Cochin only 16 per cent. of the males and nearly 6 per cent. of the females of the same age remain in that condition. Though the excessively married character of the people, as compared with those of the west, is evident from these figures, marriage is not, for the reasons already given, quite so universal here as it is in most other parts of India. In the Madras Presidency, for instance, unmarried males and females above the age of 15 form only 25 and 5 per cent. respectively of the population above that age. Again, while 1 per cent of the boys and 9 per cent. of the girls under 15 are married or widowed in the Madras Presidency, only ·07 of the former and 1·1 per cent. of the latter are in that condition in Cochin. The adherents of different religions do not show any marked differences in this respect. The number married among a thousand males is 397 among Hindus, 411 among Christians and 391 among Musalmans, the proportions for females being 402, 419 and 407 respectively. Similar proportions for the most important castes and races are given in Subsidiary Table V, from which it will be seen that the lowest proportion of married is found among the followers of *Marumakkattayam* and the highest among non-indigenous castes.

Universality of marriage.

61. In regard to early marriage also the same peculiarity is noticeable in Cochin. The religious injunction requiring the marriage of girls before they attain puberty operates only among a small section of the population, mainly non-indigenous Brahmans. Among the rest of the people girls are never married before they attain their twelfth year, the average age, when all sections of the population including Christians and Muhammadans are taken together, being about 14. In the case of males the average age is about 20. Though these ages are quite early when compared with those at which marriage takes place in European countries, they are noticeably late when compared with most other parts of India. Thus, while in England and Wales

Early marriage.

not even one male or female in a thousand under the age of fifteen is married or widowed, in Cochin 5 males and 88 females between the ages of ten and fifteen are married and two females widowed, though no male and only three females between five and ten are married. On the other hand, in the Madras Presidency five males and twenty-five females in the same number under the age of ten and 31 males and 230 females between the ages of ten and fifteen are married and ·1 male and one female under ten and one male and eight females between ten and fifteen are widowed. The different religious communities of the State present somewhat different features in regard to early marriage. Christian males generally marry earlier and Christian females later than their Hindu brothers and sisters, while in the case of Muhammadans both males and females marry later than Hindus or Christians. In a thousand of each sex between the ages of ten and fifteen in each religion the number married is shown in the margin. The Jews of Cochin generally marry later than the followers of other religions, no Jew male under fifteen and only thirty-one females between ten and fifteen in a thousand of each sex in that age period are married. In this respect the various castes present marked differences. Of a thousand girls of the ages between five and twelve, 120 are married among Kudumi Chettis, 85 among Tamil Brahmans, 52 among Konkani Brahmans and 34 among foreign Kshatriyas—all non-indigenous castes—while among the indigenous castes, the proportion is much smaller, the Iluvans, Kadupattans and Valans having only three girls each married in a thousand of that age period, and Nayars, Pulayans and Velans only four each. Considerably over a hundred males in a thousand between the ages of twelve and twenty are married among Devangans, Tamil Brahmans, Kudumi Chettis and Kusavans, while considerably less than 30 of the same age period are married among Nayars, Malayali Kshatriyas, Iluvans and Ambalavasis. Early marriage of males obtains comparatively to a large extent among some of the lower castes, the proportion of married men between 12 and 20 in a thousand being as high as 508 among Arayans, 186 among Valans and 151 among Parayans.

	Males	Females
Hindus	4	94
Musalmans	2	73
Christians	8	78
Animists	4	82
Jews	...	31

Widows and widowers.

62. The third noticeable feature of the Indian population in regard to civil condition is the great preponderance of widows over widowers. In Cochin re-marriage of widows is prohibited only among a small proportion of the population, and yet the proportion of widows to widowers is much higher here than in European countries. This is partly due to the greater disparity between the ages of husbands and wives than in Europe and partly to the fact that widows above a certain age are less inclined than widowers to re-enter into the bonds of matrimony. There are 422 widowers for every hundred widows, while in England and Wales there are only 231, but on the other hand there are in the Madras Presidency as many as 506 widows to every hundred widowers. The Jews have the lowest proportion (264 widowers to 100 widows) and next in order come the Christians (337), the Animists (362), the Hindus (448) and the Musalmans (478). The different castes do not present many differences in this respect, except that as a rule the proportion of widows is comparatively low among the lower castes and high among the higher castes.

SUBSIDIARY TABLE I.

Distribution by civil condition of 1000 of each sex, religion and main age period at each of the last four censuses.

Religion, Sex and Age	Unmarried				Married				Widowed			
	1911	1901	1891	1881	1911	1901	1891	1881	1911	1901	1891	1881
1	2	3	4	5	6	7	8	9	10	11	12	13
ALL RELIGIONS												
Males												
0—5 ...	**147**	137	138	..	...	...	...	...	...	...	...	...
5—10 ...	**130**	138	135	...	...	...	...	...	...	...	...	...
10—15 ...	**125**	131	125	...	**1**	1	2	...	...	...	...	...
15—20 ...	**89**	88	80	...	**10**	9	14	...	...	...	...	...
20—40 ...	**67**	79	51	...	**235**	225	260	...	**10**	10	5	...
40—60 ...	**8**	5	5	...	**127**	123	135	...	**16**	16	11	...
60 and over ...	**1**	1	1	...	**26**	25	28	...	**12**	12	10	
All ages ...	**562**	**579**	**535**	...	**400**	**383**	**439**	...	**38**	**36**	**26**	...
Females												
0—5 ..	**146**	140	147	...	...	...	...	...	...	...	...	...
5—10 ...	**125**	134	129	...	...	...	2	...	...	...	...	...
10—15 ...	**107**	118	98	...	**10**	10	17	...	...	...	...	...
15—20 ...	**40**	42	81	...	**57**	54	68	...	**3**	2	1	...
20—40 ...	**15**	24	13	...	**264**	258	288	..	**42**	39	23	...
40—60 ...	**2**	8	5	...	**69**	65	80	...	**73**	75	56	...
60 and over ...	...	...	2	...	**7**	5	9	...	**40**	41	36	...
All ages ..	**435**	**456**	**425**	...	**407**	**387**	**459**	...	**158**	**157**	**116**	...
HINDU												
Males												
0—5 ...	**143**	138	134	...	...	...	...	...	...	...	...	...
5—10 ...	**127**	136	132	...	...	...	...	...	...	...	...	...
10—15 ...	**123**	129	122	...	...	1	2	...	...	...	...	...
15—20 ...	**91**	88	81	...	**9**	8	13	...	...	...	...	...
20—40 ...	**74**	89	57	...	**231**	218	261	...	**12**	11	5	...
40—60 ...	**4**	7	5	...	**130**	125	137	...	**16**	16	11	...
60 and over ...	**1**	1	1	...	**27**	26	29	...	**12**	12	10	...
All ages ..	**563**	**583**	**532**	...	**397**	**378**	**442**	...	**40**	**39**	**26**	...
Females												
0—5 ...	**140**	136	142	...	...	...	1	...	...	...	...	...
5—10 ...	**119**	130	123	...	...	...	3	...	...	...	...	...
10—15 ...	**104**	109	91	...	**12**	10	19	...	...	...	...	...
15—20 ...	**42**	44	34	.	**56**	52	64	...	**3**	2	1	...
20—40 ...	**16**	28	14	...	**260**	247	291	...	**49**	44	28	...
40—60 ...	**2**	3	5	...	**68**	65	83	...	**79**	80	57	...
60 and over ...	...	...	2	...	**6**	6	9	...	**44**	44	38	...
All ages ...	**423**	**450**	**411**	...	**402**	**380**	**470**	...	**175**	**170**	**119**	...
CHRISTIAN												
Males												
0—5 ...	**156**	142	145	...	...	...	...	...	...	...	...	...
5—10 ...	**137**	144	142	...	...	...	...	...	...	...	...	...
10—15 ...	**128**	137	132	...	**1**	1	2	...	...	...	...	...
15—20 ...	**63**	85	76	...	**15**	14	19	...	...	...	...	...
20—40 ...	**46**	50	35	...	**252**	245	260	...	**7**	8	5	...
40—60 ...	**3**	8	3	...	**119**	117	127	...	**17**	17	13	...
60 and over ...	**1**	1	1	...	**24**	23	27	...	**12**	13	13	...
All ages	**553**	**562**	**534**	...	**411**	**400**	**435**	...	**36**	**38**	**31**	...
Females												
0—5 ...	**158**	146	147	...	..	...	...	...	...	...	...	...
5—10 ...	**137**	141	146	...	...	...	1	...	...	...	...	...
10—15 ...	**113**	120	115	...	**10**	9	12	...	...	...	...	...
15—20 ...	**35**	38	31	...	**60**	59	59	...	**1**	1	...	...
20—40 ..	**13**	14	9	...	**271**	269	280	...	**25**	28	20	...
40—60 ...	**2**	2	4	...	**70**	68	74	...	**60**	65	52	...
60 and over ...	**1**	...	2	...	**8**	6	8	...	**35**	34	32	...
All ages ...	**459**	**461**	**454**	...	**419**	**411**	**434**	...	**122**	**128**	**124**	...

Figures as given in the census report of 1881 cannot be thus reduced.

SUBSIDIARY TABLE I.

Distribution by civil condition of 1,000 of each sex, religion and main age period at each of the last four censuses.—Continued.

Religion, Sex and Age	Unmarried				Married				Widowed			
	1911	1901	1891	1881	1911	1901	1891	1881	1911	1901	1891	1881
1	2	3	4	5	6	7	8	9	10	11	12	13
MUSALMAN												
Males												
0—5 ...	151	148	151	...	...	...	...	...	...	...	...	...
5—10 ...	132	138	142	...	...	...	...	...	...	...	..	...
10—15 ...	132	139	129	...	...	1	1	...	...	...	...	...
15—20 ...	92	90	82	...	7	5	10	...	...	...	...	...
20—40 ...	74	80	53	...	232	219	247	...	8	9	3	...
40—60 ...	2	3	8	...	127	126	189	...	10	10	6	...
60 and over ...	...	...	1	...	25	25	27	...	8	7	7	...
All ages ...	583	598	561	...	391	376	424	...	26	25	16	...
Females												
0—5 ...	155	153	162	...	...	...	...	...	...	...	...	...
5—10 ...	134	142	137	...	...	...	1	...	...	...	...	...
10—15 ...	115	127	106	...	9	7	9	...	...	...	...	...
15—20 ...	41	41	37	...	61	55	58	..	3	3	1	...
20—40 ...	13	19	16	...	258	259	279	...	39	35	26	...
40—60 ...	2	2	6	...	68	60	69	...	62	62	55	...
60 and over ...	...	...	2	...	6	4	5	...	29	31	31	...
All ages ..	460	484	466	...	407	385	421	...	133	131	113	...
ANIMIST												
Males												
0—5 ...	134	135	...	...	...	...	...	...	...	...	...	...
5—10 ...	129	149	...	...	...	..	...	...	...	...	...	...
10—15 ...	114	128	...	...	...	1	..	...	...	...	...	...
15—20 ...	81	70	...	...	8	9	...	...	...	1	...	...
20—40 ...	60	49	...	...	251	257	...	...	8	18	...	...
40—60 ...	2	4	...	...	154	189	...	...	14	18	...	...
60 and over ...	...	...	...	...	28	22	...	...	7	5	...	...
All ages ..	520	535	...	...	451	428	...	...	29	37	...	...
Females												
0—5 ...	148	165	...	...	...	...	...	...	...	...	...	...
5—10 ...	113	148	...	...	...	1	...	...	...	...	...	...
10—15 ...	104	108	...	...	9	6	...	...	...	1	...	...
15—20 ...	34	41	...	...	58	51	...	...	1	1	...	...
20—40 ...	17	28	...	...	321	289	...	...	35	35	...	...
40—60 ...	1	2	...	...	62	51	...	...	54	55	...	...
60 and over ...	1	...	...	...	7	4	...	...	20	19	...	...
All ages ..	418	487	...	...	472	462	...	...	110	111	...	...
JEW												
Males												
0—5 ...	147	108	113	...	...	...	...	...	...	...	...	...
5—10 ...	109	113	116	...	...	...	...	...	...	...	...	...
10—15 ...	103	115	101	...	...	...	...	...	...	...	...	...
15—20 ...	86	117	116	...	8	...	...	...	...	...	...	...
20—40 ...	107	119	101	...	166	171	191	...	11	9	7	...
40—60 ...	12	...	8	...	165	150	156	...	25	26	16	...
60 and over ...	2	1	...	...	44	60	65	...	17	11	10	...
All ages ..	566	573	555	...	380	381	412	...	54	46	33	...
Females												
0—5 ...	117	114	111	...	...	...	...	...	...	...	...	...
5—10 ...	108	126	139	...	...	..	2	...	...	...	...	...
10—15 ..	104	107	80	...	3	3	3	...	...	...	...	...
15—20 ...	58	46	52	..	40	59	42	...	2	3	1	...
20—40 ...	51	24	15	...	261	248	292	...	28	31	19	...
40—60 ...	2	1	2	...	108	98	104	...	51	82	54	...
60 and over ...	2	...	2	...	10	9	28	...	55	54	54	...
All ages ..	442	418	401	...	422	412	471	...	136	170	123	...

SUBSIDIARY TABLE I.

Distribution by civil condition of 1,000 of each sex, religion and main age period at each of the last four censuses.—Continued.

Religion, Sex and Age.	Unmarried				Married				Widowed			
	1911	1901	1891	1881	1911	1901	1891	1881	1911	1901	1891	1881
1	2	3	4	5	6	7	8	9	10	11	12	13
OTHERS												
Males												
0—5 ...	23	250	...	...	...	...	..	...	...	...	...	...
5—10 ...	35	...	...	...	...	...	...	..	...	...	...	...
10—15 ...	149	...	...	...	11	...	...	...	...	...	...	...
15—20 ...	57	...	...	...	...	...	...	...	...	...	...	...
20—40 ...	81	250	...	...	379	250	...	...	34	...	...	...
40—60 ...	...	250	...	...	184	...	...	...	23	...	...	...
60 and over ...	...	...	...	...	12	...	...	...	12	...	...	...
All ages ..	345	750	...	...	586	250	...	...	69	...	...	...
Females												
0—5 ...	102	...	...	...	...	...	...	...	...	...	...	...
5—10 ...	82	...	...	...	...	...	...	...	...	...	...	...
10—15 ...	41	...	...	...	61	...	...	...	...	...	...	...
15—20 ...	...	...	...	...	82	1,000	...	...	...	...	...	...
20—40 ...	...	...	...	...	530	...	...	...	61	...	...	...
40—60 ...	...	...	...	...	...	...	...	...	20	..	...	...
60 and over ...	...	...	...	...	...	...	...	..	21	...	...	...
All ages ..	225	...	...	...	673	1,000	...	...	102	...	...	...

Others include Jains, Parsis and Brahmos for 1911, whereas for 1901 it represents Jains.

SUBSIDIARY TABLE II.

Distribution by civil condition of 1,000 of each sex at certain ages in each religion and natural division.

Religion and Natural Division (West Coast, Madras State)	Males.																	
	All ages			0—5			5—10			10—15			15—40			40 and over		
	Unmarried.	Married.	Widowed.	Unmarried.	Married.	Widowed.	Unmarried.	Married.	Widowed.	Unmarried.	Married.	Widowed.	Unmarried.	Married.	Widowed.	Unmarried.	Married.	Widowed.
1	2	8	4	5	6	7	8	9	10	11	12	13	14	15	16	17	18	19
Cochin State																		
All Religions ...	562	400	38	1,000	...	...	1,000	...	...	995	5	...	377	597	26	22	881	147
Hindu ...	563	397	40	1,000	...	...	1,000	...	...	996	4	...	396	574	30	28	830	147
Musalman ...	583	391	23	1,000	...	...	1,000	...	...	998	2	...	402	577	21	11	886	103
Christian ...	553	411	35	1,000	...	...	999	1	..	992	8	...	321	661	18	21	818	161
Animist ...	520	451	29	1,000	...	...	1,000	...	...	996	4	...	336	644	20	9	890	101
Jew ...	566	380	54	1,000	...	...	1,000	...	...	1,000	...	...	514	458	28	53	783	164
Jain ...	350	578	72	1,000	...	...	1,000	...	...	929	71	...	239	696	65	...	883	167
Others ...	230	750	...	...	..	...	...	...	...	...	...	...	500	500	...	...	1,000	...

II. Distribution by civil condition of 1,000 of each sex at certain ages in each religion and natural division.—Continued.

Religion and Natural Division (West Coast, Madras State)	Females.																	
	All ages			0—5			5—10			10—15			15—40			40 and over		
	Unmarried.	Married.	Widowed.	Unmarried.	Married.	Widowed.	Unmarried.	Married.	Widowed.	Unmarried.	Married.	Widowed.	Unmarried.	Married.	Widowed.	Unmarried.	Married.	Widowed.
1	2	3	4	5	6	7	8	9	10	11	12	13	14	15	16	17	18	19
Cochin State.																		
All Religions ...	435	407	158	1,000	...	...	997	3	...	910	88	2	131	763	106	11	394	595
Hindu ...	423	402	175	1,000	...	...	997	3	...	903	94	3	136	742	122	9	375	616
Musalman ...	460	407	133	1,000	...	...	1,000	...	...	924	73	3	127	776	97	12	425	563
Christian ...	459	419	122	1,000	...	...	996	4	...	921	78	1	118	815	67	14	445	541
Animist ...	418	472	110	1,000	...	...	1,000	...	...	918	82	..	110	811	79	12	540	448
Jew ...	442	422	136	1,000	...	...	1,000	...	...	969	31	...	248	684	68	15	518	467
Jain ...	239	652	109	1,000	...	...	1,000	...	...	400	600	...	...	900	100	...	...	1,000
Others ...	...	1,000	...	...	...	...	...	...	...	...	...	...	...	1,000	...	...	...	...

SUBSIDIARY TABLE III.

Distribution by main age periods and civil condition of 10,000 of each sex and religion.

Religion and Age	Males			Females		
	Unmarried	Married	Widowed	Unmarried	Married	Widowed
1	2	3	4	5	6	7
All Religions ...						
0—10 ...	2,769	1	...	2,709	8	...
10—15 ..	1,250	6	...	1,069	103	3
15—40 ...	1,560	2,466	107	551	3,208	448
40 and over ...	40	1,530	271	20	752	1,184
HINDU ...						
0—10 ...	2,708	...	...	2,599	3	...
10—15 ...	1,284	5	...	1,039	108	3
15—40 ...	1,650	2,393	122	579	3,160	517
40 and over ...	44	1,567	277	19	746	[illegible],227
MUSALMAN ...						
0—10 ...	2,831	...	...	2,900	...	...
10—15 ...	1,317	...	...	1,150	90	4
15—40 ...	1,661	2,385	88	536	3,287	413
40 and over ...	19	1,528	176	19	688	918
CHRISTIAN ...						
0—10 ...	2,919	1	...	2,957	4	...
10—15 ...	1,278	10	...	1,180	95	1
15—40 ...	1,801	2,674	73	479	3,310	271
40 and over ...	37	1,427	280	25	779	949
ANIMIST ...						
0—10 ...	2,633	...	...	2,619	...	...
10—15 ...	1,137	5	...	1,089	93	...
15—40 ..	1,406	2,689	85	507	3,742	866
40 and over ...	19	1,819	207	19	883	732
JEW ...						
0—10 ...	2,557	...	...	2,252	...	...
10—15 ...	1,033	...	...	1,048	33	...
15—40 ...	1,927	1,716	105	1,093	3,018	298
40 and over ...	140	2,084	438	83	1,175	1,060
OTHERS ...						
0—10 ...	575	...	...	1,887	...	...
10—15 ...	1,494	115	...	408	612	...
15 - 40 ...	1,870	3,793	345	...	6,128	612
40 and over ...	...	1,954	845	...	...	408

SUBSIDIARY TABLE IV.

Proportion of the sexes by civil condition at certain ages for religions and natural divisions.

Natural Division and Religion. (West Coast. Madras State)	Number of Females per 1,000 Males														
	All Ages			0—10			10—15			15—40			40 and over		
	Unmarried	Married	Widowed	Unmarried	Married	Widowed	Unmarried	Married	Widowed	Unmarried	Married	Widowed	Unmarried	Married	Widowed
1	2	3	4	5	6	7	8	9	10	11	12	13	14	15	16
Province															
Cochin State															
All Religions ...	780	1,024	4,222	985	6,333	...	862	16,322	26,000	856	1,311	4,215	510	495	4,215
Hindu ...	771	1,039	4,481	984	11,750	...	863	21,209	34,000	860	1,354	4,389	442	488	4,532
Musalman ...	752	989	4,788	974	...	...	832	31,222	...	307	1,311	4,503	968	430	4,931
Christian ...	811	996	3,377	991	3,500	...	865	8,948	7,500	360	1,210	3,618	654	584	3,311
Animist ...	776	1,007	3,629	959	...	...	880	19,000	...	348	1,341	4,167	1,000	468	3,409
Jew ...	827	1,175	2,645	931	...	...	1,068	...	...	600	1,857	3,000	250	597	2,560
Jain ...	879	625	833	1,800	...	...	154	3,000	...	...	844	1,000	...	...	667
Others † ...	...	1,000	...	...	...	...	...	...	...	...	3,000	...	...	...	...

† Others include Parsis and Brahmos.

SUBSIDIARY TABLE V.

Distribution by civil condition of 1000 of each sex at certain ages for selected castes.

Caste and Locality	DISTRIBUTION OF 1000 MALES OF EACH AGE BY CIVIL CONDITION																	
	All ages			0—5			5—12			12—20			20—40			40 and over		
	Unmarried	Married	Widowed	Unmarried	Married	Widowed	Unmarried	Married	Widowed	Unmarried	Married	Widowed	Unmarried	Married	Widowed	Unmarried	Married	Widowed
1	2	3	4	5	6	7	8	9	10	11	12	13	14	15	16	17	18	19
COCHIN STATE.																		
Hindu.																		
Ambalavasi ...	604	345	51	1,000	...	...	1,000	...	...	974	26	...	408	549	43	59	767	174
Arayan ...	556	402	42	1,000	...	...	998	2	...	491	508	1	307	644	49	25	707	268
Brahman, Malayali ...	516	457	27	1,000	...	...	1,000	...	...	961	39	...	345	637	18	118	810	72
do Tamil ...	513	453	34	1,000	...	...	1,000	...	...	855	145	...	118	863	19	17	844	139
do Konkani ...	479	479	42	1,000	...	...	996	4	...	918	77	5	245	733	22	39	827	134
do Others ...	450	505	45	1,000	...	...	1,000	...	...	906	94	...	307	666	27	92	775	133
Total Brahmans ...	502	463	35	1,000	...	...	999	1	...	889	110	1	209	771	20	50	828	122
Chakkan ...	569	390	41	1,000	...	...	1,000	...	...	953	42	5	321	654	25	17	830	153
Devangan ...	432	525	43	1,000	...	...	1,000	...	...	828	172	...	130	853	17	12	832	156
Iluvan ...	560	406	34	1,000	...	...	1,000	...	...	971	27	2	180	788	32	12	854	134
Kadupattan ...	555	405	40	1,000	...	...	1,000	...	...	965	34	1	211	744	45	8	856	136
Kaikolan ...	498	445	57	1,000	...	...	1,000	...	...	936	61	3	165	785	50	19	808	173
Kammalan ...	566	406	28	1,000	...	...	999	1	...	956	41	3	204	772	24	13	877	110
Kanakkan ...	548	409	43	1,000	...	...	1,000	...	...	932	63	5	159	799	42	8	826	166
Kaniyan ...	583	387	30	1,000	...	...	1,000	...	...	969	31	...	250	719	31	96	798	106
Kshatriya, Malayali ...	603	313	84	1,000	...	...	1,000	...	...	963	12	25	437	444	119	41	767	192
do Paradesi ...	518	407	75	1,000	...	...	1,000	...	...	953	47	...	336	604	60	150	650	200
Kudumi chetti ...	503	464	33	1,000	...	...	999	1	...	884	115	1	176	793	31	55	834	111
Kusavan ...	498	463	39	1,000	...	...	1,000	...	...	864	129	7	142	829	29	18	843	139
Nayar ...	630	322	48	1,000	...	...	1,000	...	...	972	17	11	402	552	46	43	774	183
Ottanaikan ...	479	468	53	1,000	...	...	1,000	...	...	945	40	15	173	769	58	22	843	135
Pandaran ...	550	411	39	1,000	...	...	997	3	...	943	55	2	191	781	28	19	824	157
Panan ...	543	417	40	1,000	...	...	1,000	...	...	948	52	...	197	763	40	7	850	143
Panditattan ...	565	400	35	1,000	...	...	1,000	...	...	987	13	...	315	663	22	11	856	133
Parayan ...	505	448	47	1,000	...	...	1 000	...	...	840	151	9	166	786	48	11	843	146
Pulayan ...	541	419	41	1,000	...	...	999	1	...	930	66	4	159	799	42	13	846	141
Valan ...	505	447	48	1,000	...	...	998	2	...	812	186	2	200	752	48	19	821	160
Velan ...	522	437	41	1,000	...	...	996	4	...	907	92	1	162	797	41	20	837	143
Velakkattalavan ...	596	355	49	1,000	...	...	1,000	...	...	955	45	...	313	632	55	22	802	176
Vellalan ...	558	404	38	1,000	...	...	1,000	...	...	974	26	...	293	665	42	20	864	116
Veluttedan ...	561	396	43	1,000	...	...	1,000	...	...	940	53	7	262	700	38	19	834	147
Vettuvan ...	545	414	41	1,000	...	...	1,000	...	...	925	70	5	166	801	33	9	823	168
Musalman.																		
Jonakan ...	585	388	27	1,000	...	...	1,000	...	...	957	40	3	284	737	29	11	883	106
Ravuttan ...	581	399	20	1,000	...	...	1,000	...	...	963	37	...	283	747	20	7	914	79
Christian.																		
Anglo Indian ...	650	325	25	1,000	...	...	1,000	...	...	987	13	...	334	651	15	76	809	115
European ...	732	268	...	1,000	...	...	1,000	...	...	1,000	...	...	793	207	...	500	500	...
Native Christian ...	552	412	36	1,000	...	...	998	2	...	911	88	1	150	827	23	20	819	161
Animist.																		
Malayan ...	528	441	31	1,000	...	...	1,000	...	...	948	52	...	201	766	33	15	887	98
Jew. ...	566	380	54	1,000	...	...	1,000	...	...	966	34	...	377	586	37	53	783	164

SUBSIDIARY TABLE V.

Distribution by civil condition of 1000 of each sex at certain ages for selected castes.

Caste and Locality	DISTRIBUTION OF 1000 FEMALES OF EACH AGE BY CIVIL CONDITION.																	
	All ages			0—5			5—12			12—20			20—40			40 and over		
	Unmarried	Married	Widowed	Unmarried	Married	Widowed	Unmarried	Married	Widowed	Unmarried	Married	Widowed	Unmarried	Married	Widowed	Unmarried	Married	Widowed
	20	21	22	23	24	25	26	27	28	29	30	31	32	33	34	35	36	37
COCHIN STATE.																		
Hindu.																		
Ambalavasi ...	367	401	232	1,000	...	...	995	5	...	523	447	30	88	766	201	4	351	645
Arayan ...	419	451	130	1,000	...	...	992	8	...	609	378	13	35	895	70	9	437	554
Brahman, Malayali ...	383	387	230	1,000	...	...	998	2	...	713	281	6	93	787	120	16	329	655
do Tamil ...	328	499	173	1,000	...	...	915	85	...	58	912	30	...	870	130	...	386	614
do Konkani ...	292	467	241	1,000	...	...	947	52	1	48	910	42	16	794	190	5	258	737
do Others ...	297	481	222	1,000	...	...	990	10	...	200	800	...	18	800	182	...	295	705
Total Brahmans ...	326	470	204	1,000	...	...	935	65	...	188	785	27	22	833	145	5	340	655
Chakkan ...	390	404	206	1,000	...	...	994	6	...	527	431	42	22	811	167	9	326	665
Devangan ...	313	518	169	1,000	...	...	969	31	...	429	567	4	7	859	134	...	445	555
Iluvan ...	460	391	149	1,000	...	...	997	3	...	680	305	15	56	814	130	9	405	586
Kadupattan ...	409	395	196	1,000	...	...	997	3	...	625	366	9	41	815	144	12	324	664
Kaikolan ...	354	440	206	1,000	...	...	994	6	...	441	551	8	12	838	150	4	339	657
Kammalan ...	456	393	151	1,000	...	...	995	5	...	684	307	9	76	803	121	12	394	594
Kanakkan ...	493	388	119	1,000	...	...	1,000	...	...	718	266	16	53	859	88	2	450	548
Kaniyan ...	447	383	170	1,000	...	...	996	4	...	756	231	13	62	783	155	6	424	570
Kshatriya, Malayali ...	377	444	179	1,000	...	...	987	13	...	471	494	35	45	872	83	...	373	627
do Paradesi ...	358	478	164	1,000	...	...	966	34	...	263	658	79	23	886	91	...	433	567
Kudumi chetti ...	273	501	226	1,000	...	...	880	120	...	54	912	34	15	776	209	7	269	724
Kusavan ...	401	494	105	1,000	...	...	993	7	...	500	485	15	21	921	58	19	527	454
Nayar ...	404	368	228	1,000	...	...	996	4	...	601	369	30	56	726	218	10	316	674
Ottanaikan ...	360	431	209	1,000	...	...	991	9	...	556	432	12	30	843	127	...	293	707
Pandaran ...	429	387	184	1,000	...	...	982	18	...	523	462	15	36	780	184	8	373	619
Panan ...	399	433	168	1,000	...	...	990	10	...	641	327	32	52	821	127	4	424	572
Panditattan ...	402	421	177	1,000	...	...	990	10	...	508	486	6	25	812	163	...	383	617
Parayan ...	446	425	129	1,000	...	...	998	1	1	585	401	14	39	865	96	53	444	503
Pulayan ...	438	419	143	1,000	...	...	996	4	...	617	368	15	45	840	115	9	441	550
Valan ...	419	441	140	1,000	...	...	997	3	...	520	461	19	39	840	121	22	478	500
Velan ...	425	420	155	1,000	...	...	996	4	...	612	370	18	45	847	108	7	414	579
Velakkattalavan ...	398	375	227	1,000	...	...	992	8	...	500	482	18	73	719	208	21	301	678
Vellalan ...	382	377	241	1,000	...	...	996	4	...	638	345	17	26	766	208	8	287	705
Veluttedan ...	390	391	219	1,000	...	...	992	8	...	598	378	24	51	766	183	3	307	690
Vettuvan ...	465	414	121	1,000	...	...	996	4	...	647	342	11	86	833	81	6	465	529
Musalman.																		
Jonakan ...	469	406	125	1,000	...	...	996	4	...	615	367	18	44	850	106	11	428	561
Ravuttan ...	423	395	182	1,000	...	...	997	3	...	505	478	17	26	775	199	5	350	645
Christian.																		
Anglo Indian ...	510	370	120	1,000	...	...	1,000	...	...	742	258	...	157	756	87	58	413	529
European ...	350	600	50	1,000	...	...	1,000	...	...	...	...	...	364	636	...	...	833	167
Native Christian ...	459	419	122	1,000	...	...	992	8	...	589	405	6	41	875	84	14	445	541
Animist.																		
Malayan ...	417	474	109	1,000	...	...	1,000	...	...	589	396	15	52	858	90	16	524	460
Jew. ...	442	422	136	1,000	...	...	988	12	...	752	238	10	150	767	83	15	518	467

CHAPTER VIII.

EDUCATION.

63. Statistics of education by religion and age will be found in Imperial Table VIII and of education by selected castes and races in Imperial Table IX, while in the Subsidiary Tables at the end of this Chapter the more important facts to be gathered from these figures are exhibited in proportional forms. As in 1901 the population was divided in respect of education into two main categories of literate and illiterate, and not into three categories—learning, literate and illiterate—as in 1881 and 1891. In 1901 a record was made of the vernacular languages in which each person was literate, but on the present occasion the language was not recorded in Cochin, as the collection of this information was declared to be optional. Such information will serve no practical purpose in a State like Cochin, where over 95 per cent. of the population are literate in the same language. In Census phraseology literacy connotes nothing more than ability to read and write. In the instructions issued to the census officers, therefore, it was laid down that a person should be regarded as literate if he could write a letter to a friend and read the answer to it, but not otherwise. In the case of students the Census staff was instructed that, as a rule, those who have passed the primary standard should be returned as literate and those that have passed the lower secondary standard in English should be returned as literate in English.

Introductory.

64. In point of literacy in this limited sense Cochin stands ahead of all the Districts and States in Southern India, save the exceptional District of Madras, the educational centre of Southern India. The number of persons able to read and write according to the Census returns was 139,083, of whom 111,146 were males and 27,937 females. In other words, in every 1,000 of the total population 151 were literate—243 in every 1,000 males and 61 in an equal number of females. In every 1,000 of the population only 149 are literate in Travancore, 112 in Tanjore, 111 in Malabar, 75 in the Presidency, 101 in Baroda and 63 in Mysore, while the proportion for the Madras city is 279. Proportional figures for males and females for these Districts and States are given in the margin for comparison. It will seen from it that Travancore is ahead of Cochin in point of male literacy, but this order is reversed in the case of female literacy. Notwithstanding the introduction of compulsory free education, Baroda is still considerably behind Cochin and Travancore in the proportion of literacy.

General literacy.

No. of literates in 1,000	*Males.*	*Females.*
Cochin	243	61
Travancore	248	50
Malabar	190	35
Tanjore	218	15
Madras City	421	129
Presidency	139	13
Baroda	175	20
Mysore	112	12

65. Almost all the Tables give the figures for literacy by four age periods—namely, 0—10, 10—15, 15—20, and 20 and over, the first three of these corresponding roughly to the stages of primary, secondary and higher education. The most prominent feature of these figures is the great disparity between the number of literate males and that of literate females. For every 100 literate males in the State there are only 25 literate females. This disparity exists in all the age periods, and is due mainly to the low position assigned to women by the Hindu and Muhammadan religions. The

Literacy by sex and age.

disparity, though sufficiently prominent, is considerably less among Christians as will be seen from the statement in the margin. The number of literates in a 1,000 males and an equal number of females of the age period 10 to 15 is 197 and 86 respectively, as against 168 and 59 in 1901, the numbers at the next age period being 303 and 104, against 282 and 77, and at the final stage (20 and over) 367 and 73, against 343 and 56. Thus, there has been a noticeable increase in literacy during the past decade at all age periods and in both sexes.

	No. of female to 100 male literates.
Hindus	21
Muhammadans	4
Christians	35

Literacy by religion.

66. There is comparatively a larger proportion of literates among Christians than among the followers of any other religion. The Jews come next and are followed by the Hindus, while the Muhammadans come last. There is only one Animist in the State who is able to read and write. The high proportion of literates among Christians is due to the influence of the native clergy and to the existence of primary schools attached to all the churches. In these schools reading, writing and certain scripture lessons are taught, and the vicars in charge of them use their influence with their congregations to send their children to these schools. Some of these schools have made considerable progress in recent years, and have been brought into the list of schools aided by Government. In point however of secondary and collegiate education, the Christians have not made as much progress as the Hindus. The percentage of literacy among Hindus would be far higher than among native Christians but for the backwardness of the lower castes, who form about one-half of the Hindu population. The Muhammadans also have schools attached to most of their mosques, but reading and writing are not taught in many of them. The children are simply made to learn a few texts from the Koran by heart. In point of literacy among females also the Christians stand ahead of the rest of the population, 11 per cent. of their females being able to read and write, as against 6·7 per cent. among Hindus and ·7 per cent. among Muhammadans.

Literacy of selected castes.

67. The various castes, tribes and races present considerable differences in regard to the degree of literacy obtaining among them. The actual figures will be found in Imperial Table IX, while Subsidiary Table VI gives them in proportional forms in the case of the more important castes. It will be seen from this that the high caste Hindus of the State are among the most literate classes in India. Illiteracy is almost unknown among Brahman, Kshatriya and Ambalavasi males, as also among high class Nayars. The most literate among the lower castes are the Kaniyans, who are by profession astrologers and village school masters, and after them come the Kammalans, or artisans, who find the three R's a useful acquisition for their profession. The Kusavans, Pulayans, Parayans, Vettuvans and Malayans are the most illiterate castes, having only 8, 5, 2, 3, and ·4 respectively in a thousand among them who are able to read and write. In regard to the degrees of female literacy the several castes present still greater divergences. While 49 per cent. of the females among Malayali Kshatriyas and 25 per cent. among Ambalavasis and 20 per cent. among Malayali Brahmans are literate, only 15 per cent. of the females among Tamil Brahmans, 4 per cent. among Konkani Brahmans and 5 per cent. among other Kshatriyas are able to read and write. In point of female literacy also, the Kaniyans stand comparatively high, 19 per cent. of their females being able to read and write. Among the Devangans, Kanakkans, Kudumi Chettis, Kusavans, Otta Naikans, Vettuvans and Ravuttans, only less than 5 in a thousand are literate, while no female among Parayans, Pulayans and Malayans is able to read and write.

Literacy in English.

68. English education has made marked progress during the last two decades. The number of persons able to read and write English have risen from 1,064 in 1891 to 4,884 in 1901 and 10,512 in 1911: in other words, while only 26 in ten thousand males and 3 in an equal number of females were able to read and write English in 1891, the proportion has risen to 199 males and 31 females in ten thousand in 1911. The figures for some Districts and States are given in the margin for comparison. It will be seen from it that in point of English literacy also Cochin stands ahead of all the Districts and States in Southern India except Madras. The progress of English education is most marked among Tamil Brahmans, Malayali Kshatriyas, Nayars and Native Christians. The Namburis, who stand so high in general literacy, lag wofully behind their Tamil brethren in point of English education, only 7 in a thousand among them being able to read and write English, as against 134 among the latter. English education has not yet touched the castes already referred to as being backward in general literacy, and also some castes which are not so backward in that respect, *viz*, Kadupattans, Kammalans, Kaniyans, Velans, Velakkattalavans and Veluttedans. Knowledge of English has not spread among females to anything like the extent to which it has spread among males, the proportion of literate males to literate females being 111 to 28, while that of males literate in English to females literate in English is 91 to 14. The Brahmans are especially backward in this respect, as only 8 in a thousand females are literate in English, as against 151 males in the same number. Among several castes there is hardly a single woman who has any knowledge of English. Among these may be mentioned, besides the backward classes already referred to, the Namburi Brahmans, Chakkans, Devangans, Kaikolans, Kammalans, Kaniyans, other Kshatriyas, Pandarans, Panditattans, Velans, Velakkattalavans, Veluttedans, Jonakans and Ravuttans. The Native Christians have not made as much progress in English education as one would have expected from them, only 18·6 in a thousand males and 4·5 in an equal number of females being able to read and write English.

No. of literate in English in 1,000.

	Males.	Females.
Cochin	20	8·1
Travancore	13	2·0
Malabar	12	1·7
Tanjore	10	0·7
Madras	180	34·3
Presidency	12	1·3
Baroda	9	0·5
Mysore	18	1·1

Literacy among Christians by sect.

69. Protestant missionaries appear to be under the impression that the comparatively high proportion of literates among Native Christians is due to the diffusion of education through their own agency among the Protestants converted by them. It will be seen from the figures given in the margin that, though there is a higher proportion of literates both in English and in the vernacular among the Protestants, their removal from the total number of Christians will not materially affect the position of the whole Christians in regard to literacy. It has also to be remembered that the Protestants form only one per cent. of the Christians of Cochin. In regard to the other sects the proportion of literates is pretty much the same among them all. Romo-Syrians have a slight advantage in general literacy and Roman Catholics in English literacy.

	No. of literates in 1000.			*No. of English literates in 1000.*		
	Persons.	*Males.*	*Females.*	*Persons.*	*Males.*	*Females.*
Roman Catholics ...	210	305	110	12	19	4·4
Romo-Syrians ...	214	316	112	10	16	4·1
Other Syrians ...	210	315	106	10	17	4·4
Protestants ...	250	379	132	74	123	30·0

Progress of Education.

70. The comparatively high percentage of literate persons in the State is not the result of modern administration. Literacy according to the Census standard was as widespread among the people many decades ago as it is now. Most of the well-to-do families had their family tutors, whose occupation was generally

hereditary, and the children of the poorer families in the neighbourhood were sent to them for such instruction as they stood in need of and for which they had to pay next to nothing. In rural parts each village had its *Eluttacchan*, or hereditary village school master, who received the pupils in his own house and accepted such payments as the means of their parents admitted of. These masters taught the children (boys and girls being taught together) reading and writing, the multiplication table and the recitation of Sanskrit hymns, and in some rare instances Sanskrit poetry, drama and rhetoric were also taught. As children of all standards were taught promiscuously by a single teacher, their progress was necessarily slow; five to ten years were required for the acquisition of these rudiments of knowledge. The Government took steps for the first time only in 1890 to diffuse elementary education, when the old village schools began to disappear. They have now ceased to exist altogether in towns, while in rural parts their number has decreased immensely in recent years. The immediate effect of this change was a retrogression in literacy, the growth of primary schools of the modern type not having kept pace with the decay of the old indigenous schools. The measures taken however during the last decade for the extension of elementary education have, besides making up for the disappearance of the old schools, also provided a more useful and efficient system of education for the masses. Subsidiary Table V bears out the truth of this remark. The number of literate persons decreased considerably between 1891 and 1901, but it has risen since the latter year, until in 1911 it has become as high as it was in 1891.

Statistics of the Educational department.

71. Subsidiary Table VII gives the numbers of institutions and pupils according to the returns of the Educational department. It must however be remarked that the returns of 1901 and 1911 include, while those of 1891 exclude, a large number of schools which have not received the recognition of the department and of which a good many belonged to the old indigenous type. Even after making allowance for this, the progress made during the last two decades has been considerable. To take only institutions maintained or aided by Government, their number has increased from 107 in 1891 to 318 in 1911, the number of pupils attending them having risen from 7,635 to 36,117. The expenditure on the department rose from 77 thousand rupees in 1891 to 99 thousand in 1901 and 278 thousand in 1911. The main results of the University examinations are given in Subsidiary Table VIII, but they are not complete, as Cochin boys have to go to Madras and other places to study for their degrees in arts, law, medicine and engineering. Statistics of Cochin students who have taken these degrees are not available.

Books and newspapers.

72. As there is no provision for the compulsory registration of books newly published, exact statistics of literary production in Cochin are not available. The number and circulation of newspapers and magazines published in the State are given in Subsidiary Table IX. It will be seen from it that all the periodicals published here are in the vernacular of the State, none being in English.

SUBSIDIARY TABLE I.

Education by age, sex and religion.

RELIGION	NUMBER PER MILLE WHO ARE LITERATE											Number per mille who are illiterate			Number per mille who are literate in English		
	All ages			0—10		10—15		15—20		20 & over							
	Total	Male	Female	Male	Female	Male	Female	Male	Female	Male	Female	Total	Male	Female	Total	Male	Female
1	2	3	4	5	6	7	8	9	10	11	12	13	14	15	16	17	18
All Religions ...	**151**	243	61	19	11	197	86	308	104	367	73	**849**	757	859	**11**	20	3
Hindu ...	**136**	228	47	17	8	181	63	282	80	342	56	**864**	772	953	**12**	21	2
Musalman ...	**74**	138	7	4	1	63	7	146	9	234	9	**926**	862	993	**2**	4	...
Christian ...	**215**	314	114	30	22	277	169	404	201	478	139	**785**	686	886	**14**	21	6
European ...	**947**	964	900	333	333	...	...	1,000	...	1,000	1,000	**53**	36	100	**947**	964	900
Anglo Indian ...	**428**	508	352	82	61	522	458	697	548	746	442	**572**	497	648	**182**	195	169
Armenian ...	**1,000**	1,000	...	...	...	...	...	...	...	...	...	...	...	...	**1,000**	1,000	...
Native Christian ...	**212**	312	111	29	21	274	166	400	197	475	135	**788**	688	889	**12**	19	5
Jew ...	**197**	315	86	7	7	169	62	404	183	471	105	**803**	685	914	**83**	53	15
Jain ...	**674**	867	43	...	...	786	...	800	...	966	71	**426**	133	957	**78**	120	...

NOTE:—Of the 5 Parsis (3 males and 2 females) 4 (3 males and 1 female) are literate in English and all of them are literate in vernacular and are over 20 years of age.

The 2 Brahmos are literate both in vernacular and English and are over 20 years of age.

There is only one person among the Animists who is literate. He is over 20 years of age and is literate only in vernacular.

SUBSIDIARY TABLE II.

Education by age, sex and locality.

District and Natural Division "West Coast, Madras State"	NUMBER PER MILLE WHO ARE LITERATE										
	All ages			0—10		10—15		15—20		20 and over	
	Total	Male	Female	Male	Female	Male	Female	Male	Female	Male	Female
1	2	3	4	5	6	7	8	9	10	11	12
Cochin State ...	151	243	61	19	11	197	86	308	104	367	73

SUBSIDIARY TABLE III.

Education by religion, sex and locality.

District and Natural Division "West Coast, Madras State"	NUMBER PER MILLE WHO ARE LITERATE											
	Hindu		Jain		Musalman		Christian		Animist		Jew	
	Male	Female	Male	Female	Male	Female	Male	Female	Male	Female	Male	Female
1	2	3	4	5	6	7	8	9	10	11	12	13
Cochin State ...	228	47	867	43	138	7	314	114	...	...	315	86

NOTE:—There is only one person (male) who is literate among the Animists.

SUBSIDIARY TABLE IV.

English education by age, sex and locality.

District and Natural Division " West Coast, Madras State "	Literate in English per 10000.													
	1911										1901		1891	
	0—10		10—15		15—20		20 and over		All ages		All ages		All ages	
	Male	Female	Male	Female	Male	Female	Male	Female	Male	Female	Male	Female	Male	Female
1	2	3	4	5	6	7	8	9	10	11	12	13	14	15
Cochin State ...	6	4	207	57	475	81	249	29	190	31	108	12	26	3

SUBSIDIARY TABLE V.

Progress of education since 1881.

District and Natural Division "West Coast, Madras State"	Number of literate per mille															
	All ages								15—20				20 and over			
	Male				Female				Male		Female		Male		Female	
	1911	1901	1891	1881	1911	1901	1891	1881	1911	1901	1911	1901	1911	1901	1911	1901
1	2	3	4	5	6	7	8	9	10	11	12	13	14	15	16	17
Cochin State ...	243	224	246	...	61	45	39	...	303	282	104	77	367	343	73	56

Note.—Out of a population of 600,278, there were 10,752 persons returned as literate in 1881. Figures by sex are not available.

SUBSIDIARY TABLE VI.

Education by caste.

CASTE		NUMBER PER 1,000 WHO ARE LITERATE.						NUMBER PER 10,000 WHO ARE LITERATE IN ENGLISH.					
		1911			1901			1911			1901		
		Persons	Males	Females	Persons	Males	Females	Persons	Males	Females	Persons	Males	Females
1		2	3	4	5	6	7	8	9	10	11	12	13
Hindu.	...												
Ambalavasi	...	401	550	250	401	608	253	420	708	131	188	331	50
Arayan	...	107	189	15	...	...	...	6	4	9	...	...	...
Brahman, Malayali	...	423	633	208	472	695	227	73	140	...	34	66	...
do Tamil	...	425	684	150	397	689	80	1,3[illegible]2	2,479	122	830	1,574	25
do Konkani	...	2[illegible]0	502	44	241	443	17	400	703	48	100	299	6
do others	...	354	498	77	401	563	61	361	489	65	369	524	40
Total Brahman	...	391	621	133	376	625	95	839	1,515	80	488	907	16
Chakkan	...	131	215	39	...	...	...	38	72	...	...	...	...
Devangan	...	77	153	1	...	...	...	4	9	...	...	...	...
Iluvan	...	82	154	12	66	126	7	14	27	1	4	9	...
Kadupattan	...	105	196	17	103	188	20	15	28	8	7	14	...
Kaikolan	...	91	178	7	...	...	...	2[illegible]	60	...	...	...	...
Kammalan	...	107	208	9	102	202	6	3	5	...	2	3	...
Kanakkan	...	19	35	2	...	...	...	4	5	3	...	...	...
Kaniyan	...	372	551	193	...	...	...	9	18	...	...	...	...
Kshatriya, Malayali	...	609	724	492	466	615	319	1,163	2,074	238	618	1,171	67
do Paradesi	...	2[illegible]6	479	51	235	382	12	449	852	...	247	410	...
Kudumi chotti	...	45	84	2	22	41	1	6	11	...	3	5	...
Kusavan	...	8	14	1	...	...	...	...	...	...	...	...	...
Nayar	...	271	413	137	266	425	118	246	434	69	108	209	14
Otta Naikan	...	19	34	5	...	...	...	...	...	...	...	...	...
Panan	...	77	121	30	...	...	...	...	...	...	...	...	...
Pandaran	...	57	104	9	...	...	...	8	16	...	...	...	...
Panditattan	...	154	271	13	...	...	...	23	52	...	...	...	...
Parayan	...	2	4	...	...	...	...	...	...	...	...	...	...
Pulayan	...	5	9	...	4	8	...	...	1	...	...	...	...
Valan	...	106	192	14	64	117	6	10	20	...	1	2	...
Velan	...	1[illegible]9	231	10	...	...	...	5	11	...	...	..	...
Velakkatalavan	...	110	195	27	...	...	...	9	18	...	...	...	...
Vellalan	...	156	281	26	...	..	...	2[illegible]2	384	13	...	...	...
Veluttedan	...	101	188	24	...	...	...	9	19	...	...	...	...
Vettuvan	...	3	6	1	...	...	...	...	...	...	...	...	...
Musalman.	...												
Jonakan	...	65	123	6	62	118	5	10	19	...	2	4	...
Ravuttan	...	73	140	4	...	...	...	21	42	...	...	...	...
Christian.	...												
Anglo Indian	...	428	503	352	343	412	278	1,[illegible]23	1,950	1,693	2,062	2,297	1,838
European	...	947	964	900	836	795	938	9,474	9,643	9,000	7,818	7,436	8,750
Native Christian	...	2[illegible]2	312	111	172	270	61	116	183	45	59	96	21
Animist.	...												
Malayan	...	0·4	0·8	...	...	...	...	...	...	...	...	...	...
Jew.	...	197	315	86	207	376	51	332	525	149	132	274	...

Note.—Figures for 1901 wherever available have been shown in this table.

SUBSIDIARY TABLE VII.

Number of institutions and pupils according to the returns of the Educational Department.

Class of Institution	1911		1901		1891 (2)		
	Number of		Number of		Number of		
	Institutions	Scholars	Institutions	Scholars	Institutions		Scholars
1	2	3	4	5	6		7
Second Grade Colleges ...	1	182	1	57	Second Grade College	1 ...	455
High Schools ...	13	1,246	8	804	High School	1 ...	373
Lower Secondary Schools ...	21	2,646	19	1,696	Anglo Vernacular Schools	26 ...	2,062
Primary Schools ...	969	46,550	875	29,189	Vernacular Schools	76 ...	4,683
Special Schools ...	11	698	(1) 386	7,904	Palace Schools	2 ...	25
					Hebrew School	1 ...	37
Total ...	1,015	51,363	1,289	39,600		107 ...	7,635

1) Includes schools where the Koran, music etc. are taught.
2) Classification of schools was different in 1891.

SUBSIDIARY TABLE VIII.

Main results of University examinations.

Examination	1911		1901		1891	
	Candidates	Passed	Candidates	Passed	Candidates	Passed
1	2	3	4	5	6	7
Entrance Examination ...	378	102	133	41	27	16
F. A. or Intermediate Examination ...	55	27	17	11	13	7

SUBSIDIARY TABLE IX.

Number and circulation of newspapers, etc.

Language	Class of newspaper (Daily weekly, etc.)	1911		1901		1891	
		No.	Circulation	No.	Circulation	No.	Circulation.
1	2	3	4	5	6	7	8
Malayalam ...	Weekly	3	2,675				
Do. ...	Bi-monthly	1	280				
Do. ...	Monthly	7	5,200				
Malayalam and Sanskrit ...	Monthly	1	600				
Malayalam ...	Once in 2 months	1	320				
Total ...		13	9,075				

SUBSIDIARY TABLE X.

Education of Christians by sex.

RACE	LITERATE			LITERATE IN ENGLISH		
	Persons	Males	Females	Persons	Males	Females
Total Christians ...	50,086	36,990	13,096	3,198	2,460	738
European and allied races including Armenian	74	56	18	74	56	18
Anglo-Indian ...	1,048	631	424	446	242	204
Native Christian ...	48,964	36,310	12,654	2,678	2,162	516
Roman Catholics ...	20,093	14,969	5,124	1,142	937	205
Romo-Syrians ...	557	403	154	166	131	35
Other Syrians ...	6,882	5,116	1,766	348	275	73
Protestants ...	21,432	15,822	5,610	1,022	819	203

CHAPTER IX.

LANGUAGE.

Introductory.

73. Statistics of the parent tongue of the people will be found in Imperial Table X, in which the languages are arranged under three main heads, namely, (a) vernaculars of India, which have sub-divided into (1) the vernacular of the State and (2) vernaculars foreign to the State; (b) vernaculars of non-Indian Asiatic countries; and (c) European languages. In subsidiary Table I these languages are arranged in families, sub-families and groups according to Dr. Grierson's scheme of classification, while in subsidiary Table II the main facts are given in proportional and condensed forms. The return of parent tongue is on the whole accurate, as there is no want of precision in the popular language nomenclature of the State, and as 97 per cent. of the population have returned one or another of the best known Dravidian languages as their parent tongue. It cannot however be said that the returns are altogether free from error, since 27 Jews and three Roman Catholic native priests have returned Hebrew and Latin respectively as their parent tongue. But such erroneous returns are few and far between.

Malayalam.

74. Malayalam is the vernacular and the official language of the State, and is spoken by over 89 per cent. of the population. It is the mother tongue of as much as 96 per cent. of the people in Mukundapuram and Trichur, 93 per cent. in Talapilli, 91 in Cranganur and 89 in Cochin-Kanayannur, but only 55 per cent. have returned it in Chittur. Chittur is the centre of the Tamil Brahmans in the State, and the eastern portion of the Taluk is peopled mostly by comparatively recent immigrants from Coimbatore, whose home language is Tamil, while the great majority of the Konkani Brahmans and their Sudras, Kudumi Chettis, whose parent tongue is the Konkani dialect of Mahratti, reside in the Cochin-Kanayannur Taluk. Hence the smaller proportion of Malayalam-speaking people in these Taluks. Most of the literate people, however, who have returned Tamil and Konkani as their parent tongue, are literate not in these languages but in Malayalam. Except in a few isolated castes, elementary education is imparted entirely through the medium of Malayalam throughout the State. Malayalam is more akin to Tamil than any other member of the Dravidian group of languages. The large admixture of Sanskrit words and the absence of verbal inflections to denote person, gender and number mainly differentiate it from Tamil. Though the stem of the language is Dravidian, its vocabulary is largely Sanskrit, partly distorted but mostly in its pure form. In point of literature Malayalam is poorer than Kanarese and considerably more so than Tamil and Telugu. Malayalam is the most localised of the Dravidian languages, being practically confined to Travancore, Cochin, Malabar and part of South-Canara, and is the mother tongue of 6,755,940 persons in Southern India, or 765,899 more than in 1901.

Tamil.

75. Tamil is the mother tongue of 55,231 persons, or 6 per cent. of the State population, and is the most widely prevalent language next to Malayalam. For the reasons given in the preceding paragraph, nearly 34 per cent. of the people of Chittur have returned Tamil as their home language, while it is the parent tongue of considerably less than 5 per cent. of the people in other Taluks.

Other Dravidian languages.

76. Telugu is the parent tongue of 1·2 per cent. of the State population, Kanarese of ·4 per cent. and Tulu of ·06 per cent. The great majority of the Telugu and the Kanarese speaking people (Kaikolans, Otta Naickans and Devangans) are found in the Chittur and Talapilli Taluks, while those who speak Tulu (Embrans or Tulu Brahmans) are found mostly in Cochin-Kanayannur.

Other Indian languages.

77. Of the other Indian languages returned as mother tongue, the Konkani dialect of Mahratti is spoken by 2·3 per cent. of the population, and the rest only by ·5 per cent. Of the latter Gujaratti and Kacchi are returned by 1,060 and 352 respectively, mostly merchants and traders from the Bombay side, who are confined almost entirely to Mattancheri and its neighbourhood, Hindustani by 2,234 persons, chiefly Musalmans other than Mappilas and Ravuttans, and Mahratti by 1,061, mostly high class Konkani Brahmans who think it more honourable to call their mother tongue Mahratti rather than Konkani.

Non-Indian languages.

78. Only 821 persons have returned non-Indian languages as their parent tongue, though as many as eleven such languages have been so turned amongst them. Arabic is returned by Arab traders and pedlars, whose mother tongue is really Arabic, but the return of Hebrew as mother tongue is of doubtful accuracy. The local Jews, both White and Black, speak Malayalam in their homes, but a few among them have some knowledge of Hebrew, and they were apparently so proud of the fact that they returned it as their home speech, as did three Native Christian priests, who returned Latin as their mother tongue. Though, according to Imperial Table XIII, there were 2,522 Europeans and Anglo-Indians, only 679 have returned Eurepean languages as their parent tongue. It is clear from this that the majority of Anglo-Indians have returned Malayalam as their home speech, which is actually the case. The number of English-speaking men has risen from 347 in 1901 to 412 in 1911, while the Portuguese speaking persons have fallen from 407 to 237. The Verapoly Mission has of late been recruited almost entirely from Spain: hence the return of Spanish and Basque by 21 persons.

Caste and language.

79. In most cases the caste, as given in Table XIII, indicates the language of its members. A statement showing how the strength of Table X (language) stands as compared with that of XIII (caste) in regard to the main languages returned is given in the margin. It will be seen from it that the strength of the one closely approximates to that of the other, which shows that the language return is generally accurate.

	Strength as per Table X	*Table XIII*
Malayalam	820,129	819,080
Tamil	55,231	54,868
Telugu	11,224	11,305
Konkani	21,153	21,983

Literary activity.

80. Malayalam is the only vernacular in which any literature is produced in this State. A short but full account of Malayalam literature is given in the report for 1901: it is superfluous to repeat it here. There is considerable literary activity going on still, but both in regard to quality and in regard to quantity the literary output of the last decade falls short of that of the preceding one. As there is no provision for the regular registration of books either in Cochin or in Travancore, correct statistics of literary production are not available.

SUBSIDIARY TABLE I.

Distribution of total population by language.

Family	Group	Language	Dialect	Total number of speakers 1911	Total number of speakers 1901	Number per mille of the population of the State	Where chiefly spoken
1	2	3	4	5	6	7	8
		LANGUAGES OF INDIA					
Indo-European (Aryan sub family)	Southern	Marathi ...	Marathi ...	1.061	926	1·2	
			Goanese ...	11	...	...	
			Konkani ...	21.153	19,207	23·0	
	Western	Gujarati ..	Gujarati ...	1.060	695	1·1	
			Kachchi ...	362	402	0·4	
		Western Hindi...	Hindi ...	121	83	·1	
			Urdu ...	13	...	...	
			Hindustani ...	2 234	2,481	2·4	
	Eastern	Bengali ...	Bengali ...	2	2	...	
Dravidian		Canarese ...		4.152	4,180	4·5	
		Malayalam ...		820,129	715,847	893·8	
		Tamil ...		55,231	54,171	60·2	
		Telugu ...		11,224	12.676	12·2	
		Tulu ...		546	657	0·6	
		LANGUAGES FOREIGN TO INDIA					
Indo-European	Western	Persian ...		2	...	...	
		French ...		2	1	...	
	Romance	Latin ...		3	...	...	
		Portuguese ...		237	407	·3	
		Spanish ...	Spanish ...	16	1	...	
			Basque ...	5	...	...	
	Teutonic	English ...		412	347	·4	
		German ...		4	...	...	
Semetic	Northern Branch	Hebrew ...		27	10	...	
		Syriac ...		2	4	...	
	Southern Branch	Arabic ...		111	17	0·1	

SUBSIDIARY TABLE II.

Distribution by language of the population of each district.

Taluks	NUMBER PER 10,000 OF POPULATION SPEAKING.						
	Malayalam	Tamil	Konkani	Telugu	Canarese	Hindustani	Other languages
1	2	3	4	5	6	7	8
Cochin-Kanayannur ...	8,988	259	643	6	10	24	120
Cranganur ...	9,150	341	495	...	...	5	9
Mukundapuram ...	9,609	222	115	26	4	10	15
Trichur ...	9,605	277	16	58	4	25	14
Talapilli ...	9,803	446	...	149	90	9	3
Chittur ...	5,483	3,383	...	778	245	89	22
Mean for the State ...	8,933	602	280	122	45	24	44

CHAPTER X.

INFIRMITIES.

81. Imperial Table XII-Part I gives the statistics of infirmities by age, and Table XII-Part II, their distribution by Taluks, while Table XII-A shows the extent to which each of the castes, tribes and races is afflicted with them. The Subsidiary Tables at the end of this Chapter exhibit the main facts in the usual proportional and condensed forms. As on previous occasions, only four kinds of infirmities were recorded at the present Census, *viz.*, insanity, deaf-mutism by birth, total blindness and corrosive leprosy.

Introductory.

82. Of all the particulars gathered at the Census, the return of infirmities is the least liable to freedom from error. Errors of omission as well as commission are very likely to occur in returning infirmities. A feeling of delicacy prevents enumerators from minutely questioning heads of families regarding cases of infirmities like insanity and leprosy, while there is a tendency on the part of the latter to prevent such mental and bodily afflictions from being brought on record. In the case of children suspected of insanity, of deaf-mutism, or even of leprosy, most parents hesitate to return them as afflicted as long as there is the least possibility of persuading themselves that its existence is still open to doubt. Further, the great majority of the people do not know the distinction between idiocy and insanity and between lupus and leprosy, and consequently persons suffering from only idiocy or lupus may very probably have been returned as insanes or lepers. Again, according to the instructions to enumerators, only those persons should be shown as deaf-mutes who were deaf and dumb from birth, but it appears very probable from the returns that persons who appeared to be hard of hearing in their advancing years were also returned as such. The figures are thus liable both to over-statement and to under-statement.

Accuracy of the returns.

83. Such as they are, the numbers returned as afflicted are shown in the margin, as compared with those so returned at the previous Census. The numbers afflicted in a hundred thousand of the population at each of these Censuses is also given for purposes of comparison.

Numbers and proportion of the afflicted.

Actual numbers

	Insane	*Deaf-mute*	*Blind*	*Lepers.*
1881	108	235	281	148
1891	218	307	863	330
1901	197	549	886	334
1911	293	381	1,185	461

Numbers in 100,000 who are

	Insane	*Deaf-mute*	*Blind*	*Lepers.*
1881	17	39	47	25
1891	29	55	109	48
1901	24	68	109	41
1911	32	86	129	50

In view of the partial unreliability of the figures, it will probably be hazarduous to draw any inferences from these comparative statements. If the figures are to be believed, all the infirmities have been on the increase except deaf-mutism, which shows a great decrease since 1901. These variations are not capable of any satisfactroy explanation. The figures for 1911 probably represent the actual state of things more approximately than those of the previous Censuses. Of the blind, two males are also insane, two males and a female are also deaf-mutes, and one male is also a leper.

84. The distribution of infirmities by Taluk is shown in the margin, the figures within brackets being the number in 100,000 of the population. There appear to be no clear inferences

Local distribution.

deducible from the territorial distribution of any of them, except leprosy. In regard to the latter, the figures confirm the impression produced by local observation, *viz*., that leprosy prevails more largely on the sea-board than in any other part of the State, the sea-board taluk, Cochin-Kanayannur, accounting for nearly half the number of lepers in the State. Chittur, the driest taluk, has proportionately the least number. In urban areas there are 73 insanes, of whom Trichur, where there is a Lunatic Asylum, accounts for 22, Mattancheri for 12 and Ernakulam for 11. Of the 30 deaf-mutes in towns, 7 are found in Irinjalakuda and 6 each in Ernakulam and Trichur. Trichur accounts for 50, Mattancheri for 22 and Irinjalakuda for 18 of the 135 blind persons found in towns, and of the 40 lepers, 19 are found in Mattancheri and 9 in Ernakulam. There are no deaf-mutes in Tripunittura, Tattamangalam and Nemmara, and no lepers in Kunnamkulam, Chittur and Nemmara.

	Insane	*Deaf-mutes*	*Blind*	*Lepers*
Cochin-Kanayannur	95 (36)	105 (40)	251 (94)	223 (84)
Cranganur	4 (12)	4 (12)	16 (48)	15 (45)
Mukundapuram	51 (26)	74 (38)	228 (116)	76 (39)
Trichur	61 (36)	62 (36)	292 (172)	51 (30)
Talapilli	50 (30)	66 (40)	307 (186)	73 (44)
Chittur	32 (35)	20 (22)	91 (99)	23 (25)

Infirmities by sex.

85. There is a considerable preponderance of males over females in the number afflicted, as will be seen from the statement in the margin. In the case of insanity and blindness one would naturally expect this preponderance. Some of the more important causes assigned for insanity are the excessive use of alcohol, opium and ganja, and constant strain and continued worry to the mental faculties. The opium and ganja habit does not prevail in the State to any large extent, while the alcohol habit, though prevalent, is not anything so wide spread as in western countries. There are proportionately ten times as many insane persons in England and Wales as there are in Cochin. Such as they are, however, these habits prevail more largely among males than among females. Blindness is generally ascribed, among other causes, to diseases caused by constant exposure to the heat and glare of the tropical sun and the dust blown by the hot winds. As the males engage themselves in out-door work more largely than females, the preponderance of the blind among the former is but natural. No such explanation can be given for their preponderance among deaf-mutes and lepers. It is probably due to the short return of females suffering from deaf-mutism and leprosy, as they are more prone to hide these afflictions from the public than the males.

Number of females to 100 males afflicted.

Insane	88
Deaf-mute	86
Blind	94
Leper	39

Infirmities by age.

86. It will be seen from Subsidiary Table II that there are proportionately a much larger number of insanes in the quinquennial periods between 20 and 45. This is the period of life in which people are most tempted to take to the habits already referred to as predisposing them to insanity. As insane people succumb more easily in the struggle for existence, the number of lunatics above the age of 45 is naturally much smaller in proportion. The largest proportion of deaf-mutes is found in the quinquennia between 5 and 30. As only those who were born such were to be returned as deaf-mutes, there ought to be a larger number of them in the first quinquennium, but as already pointed out, parents hesitate to enter children as deaf-mutes so long as they possibly can pursuade themselves and try to persuade others that the existence of the infirmity is open to doubt. The comparatively small proportion of deaf-mutes after the age of 35 is to be ascribed to the same cause as in the case of insanity. The number of the blind increases with each of the advancing age periods with one or two exceptions, for except in the case of those who are born blind, the predisposing causes operate more strongly as people advance in years. Leprosy also is found more commonly in middle age than in childhood or old age.

Inherited leprosy generally manifests itself in childhood or youth, and seldom in infancy, while very few lepers live to old age.

Infirmities by caste, race, etc.

87. The several castes, tribes and races present a variety of features in regard to the proportion of the afflicted, but no explanation can be given for this variety. There is comparatively, for instance, a large proportion of afflicted among Ambalavasis and a small one among Kudumi Chettis, but the former are an intelligent and clean-living people, while the latter are not. There are no insanes and lepers among Malayali Kshatriyas, who belong to the best type of people on the West Coast, but these infirmities are not found also among Pandarans, Panans and Velakkattalavans, who are far behind that type. The largest proportion of insanes is found among Kavundans, Ambalavasis, Konkani Brahmans and Kaniyans, while there are few or none among Kusavans, Panans, Pandarans, Parayans and Pulayans. Deaf-mutism is most prevalent among Brahmans other than Malayali, Tamil or Konkani, and among Kusavans, Vaisyans, Pandarans and Malayali Kshatriyas, and least among Konkani Brahmans, Vettuvans, Pulayans, and Kudumi Chettis. The highest proportion of blind people is found among Kavundans, Malayali Brahmans, Kadupattans, Malayali Kshatriyas, Velakkattalavans, Vaisyans, Pandarans and Ambalavasis, and the lowest among Kanakkans, Kudumi Chettis and Konkani Brahmans. There is proportionately a large number of lepers among Vadukans, Kavundans, Vaisyans, Velans, Anglo-Indians and Jews, and a small number among other Brahmans, Devangans, Kaikolans, Malayali Kshatriyas, Kusavans, Pandarans, Velakkattalavans, Vettuvans, Ravuttans and Malayali Brahmans.

SUBSIDIARY TABLE I.

Number afflicted per 100,000 of the population at each of the last four censuses.

District and Natural Division (Cochin State) Taluks	Insane								Deaf-mute							
	Male				Female				Male				Female			
	1911	1901	1891	1881	1911	1901	1891	1881	1911	1901	1891	1881	1911	1901	1891	1881
1	2	3	4	5	6	7	8	9	10	11	12	13	14	15	16	17
Cochin State ...	**34**	**27**	**32**	**21**	**30**	**23**	**27**	**13**	**39**	**77**	**66**	**41**	**38**	**60**	**43**	**37**
Cochin-Kanayannur ...	**40**		36	26	**32**		26	17	**39**		58	45	**41**		34	29
Cranganur ...	**6**		43	9	**18**		43	...	**18**		21	9	**6**		29	...
Mukundapuram ...	**23**		25	14	**30**		27	2	**46**		95	22	**31**		41	23
Trichur ...	**44**		38	19	**28**		31	17	**41**		70	52	**32**		45	30
Talapilli ...	**30**		27	27	**31**		13	23	**45**		59	58	**35**		63	67
Chittur ...	**42**		31	18	**30**		37	3	**18**		57	39	**25**		42	52

District and Natural Division (Cochin State) Taluks	Blind								Lepers							
	Male				Female				Male				Female			
	1911	1901	1891	1881	1911	1901	1891	1881	1911	1901	1891	1881	1911	1901	1891	1881
	18	19	20	21	22	23	24	25	26	27	28	29	30	31	32	33
Cochin State ...	**133**	**118**	**133**	**50**	**125**	**107**	**105**	**43**	**73**	**57**	**66**	**27**	**28**	**25**	**31**	**23**
Cochin-Kanayannur ...	**108**		88	45	81		55	38	**123**		106	31	**43**		29	22
Cranganur ...	**71**		113	19	24		101	48	**59**		128	9	**31**		22	10
Mukundapuram ...	**119**		125	39	117		107	33	**52**		74	33	**27**		47	32
Trichur ...	**163**		191	37	161		149	40	**42**		23	23	**19**		26	23
Talapilli ...	**175**		177	104	196		126	74	**66**		40	30	**24**		29	28
Chittur ...	**93**		114	24	102		124	26	**35**		26	9	**15**		20	6

Talukwar figures for 1901 are not available.

SUBSIDIARY TABLE II.

Distribution of the infirm by age per 10,000 of each sex.

AGE	INSANE						DEAF-MUTE	
	Male			Female			Male	
	1911	1901	1891	1911	1901	1891	1911	1901
1	2	3	4	5	6	7	8	9
0—5 ...	...	...	...	**73**	..	...	**281**	160
5—10 ...	**64**	182	256	**73**	426	208	**1,011**	1,090
10—15 ...	**192**	273	256	**73**	218	208	**1.461**	1,442
15—20 ...	**518**	909	342	**365**	582	417	**1,578**	1,250
20—25 ...	**1,090**	1,182	598	**1,022**	852	1,042	**899**	1,282
25—30 ...	**1,538**	1,182	1,453	**511**	1,276	1,042	**1.461**	1,058
30—35 ...	**1,2 8**	1,454	1,881	**1,606**	1,276	1,771	**730**	897
35—40 ...	**1,731**	1,182	1,111	**584**	957	1,354	**674**	705
40—45 ...	**1,218**	1,001	1,453	**1,460**	1,489	1.771	**552**	385
45—50 ...	**769**	864	...	**1,387**	532	..	**449**	417
50—55 ...	**513**	727	1,197	**949**	745	1,354	**281**	449
55—60 ...	**885**	727	...	**687**	213	...	**225**	288
60 and over ...	**769**	727	684	**1,241**	1,489	833	**398**	557
			* 769					
Total ...	10,000	10,000	10,000	10,000	10,000	10.000	10.000	10.000

AGE	DEAF-MUTE—*contd.*				BLIND		
	Male—*cont.*	Female			Male		
	1891	1911	1901	1891	1911	1901	1891
	10	11	12	13	14	15	16
0—5 ...	167	**467**	244	127	**246**	197	124
5—10 ...	1,000	**654**	1,097	956	**640**	482	600
10—15 ...	917	**1,111**	1,219	764	**590**	592	787
15—20 ...	1,458	**1,488**	1.504	1.788	**678**	724	668
20—25 ...	1,088	**1,488**	732	1,083	**476**	614	973
25—30 ...	875	**1,488**	1,098	1,210	**755**	768	1,035
30—35 ...	1,042	**784**	1,220	701	**808**	855	849
35—40 ...	708	**588**	569	637	**903**	680	849
40—45 ...	1,042	**528**	691	956	**755**	724	1.387
45—50 ...	...	**458**	406	...	**427**	789	...
50—55 ...	833	**523**	366	573	**772**	1,009	1,077
55—60 ...	...	**65**	...	...	**608**	526	...
60 and over ...	875	**523**	854	1,210	**2 250**	2,040	1,656
Total ...	10,000	1,0000	10.000	10,000	10,000	10,000	10,000

AGE	BLIND—*contd.*			LEPERS					
	Female			Male			Female		
	1911	1901	1891	1911	1901	1891	1911	1901	1891
	17	18	19	20	21	22	23	24	25
0—5 ...	**243**	206	105	...	43	42	**77**	97	90
5—10 ...	**382**	549	368	**30**	178	42	**155**	388	90
10—15 ...	**434**	458	558	**211**	808	377	**543**	388	451
15—20 ...	**573**	549	684	**753**	606	335	**543**	971	991
20—25 ...	**607**	847	870	**964**	438	711	**698**	1,262	541
25—30 ...	**781**	709	790	**753**	1,420	1,088	**1,085**	1,262	1,171
30—35 ...	**799**	664	895	**1,144**	952	1,255	**1,395**	777	1,171
35—40 ...	**660**	801	789	**1,236**	1,C82	1,171	**1,473**	680	811
40—45 ...	**881**	824	947	**1,265**	1,212	2,385	**1,085**	874	2,342
45—50 ...	**573**	549	...	**934**	953	...	**698**	485	90
50—55 ...	**955**	778	1,894	**954**	779	1,297	**698**	1,068	991
55—60 ...	**642**	595	...	**904**	909	...	**698**	583	...
60 and over ...	**2,500**	2,471	2,605	**848**	1,126	1,297	**852**	1,165	1,261
Total ...	10,000	10,000	10,000	10,000	10,000	10,000	10,000	10.000	10,000

* Not stated.

SUBSIDIARY TABLE III.

Number afflicted per 100,000 persons of each age period and number of females afflicted per 1,000 males.

AGE	Number afflicted per 100,000								Number of females afflicted per 1,000 males			
	Insane		Deaf-mute		Blind		Lepers		Insane	Deaf-mute	Blind	Lepers
	Male	Female	Male	Female	Male	Female	Male	Female				
1	2	3	4	5	6	7	8	9	10	11	12	13
0—5	...	1	7	10	22	21	...	1	...	1,400	933	...
5—10	2	2	30	17	66	38	2	3	1,000	556	564	2,000
10—15	5	2	45	31	73	46	12	13	333	654	595	1.000
15—20	18	11	62	48	90	72	55	15	625	786	805	280
20—25	41	30	39	48	70	76	77	19	824	1,375	1.207	281
25—30	68	17	69	53	121	109	66	34	292	846	978	560
30—35	56	66	38	36	145	137	112	54	1,158	923	989	474
35—40	88	30	89	33	180	141	131	71	296	750	691	468
40—45	78	85	41	34	189	209	173	60	1,058	800	1.065	333
45—50	67	116	44	48	144	202	172	55	1,583	875	1,269	290
50—55	54	78	34	48	317	332	216	54	1,625	1.600	1,170	281
55—60	62	94	42	10	385	386	312	94	1,500	250	1,000	300
60 and over	69	78	40	37	787	660	161	50	1,417	1,143	1,051	398
All ages	**34**	**30**	**39**	**33**	**133**	**125**	**78**	**28**	**878**	**860**	**946**	**889**

SUBSIDIARY TABLE IV.

Number afflicted per 100,000 persons and number of females afflicted per 1,000 males among selected castes, tribes or races.

CASTE	NUMBER AFFLICTED PER 100,000								NUMBER OF FEMALES AFFLICTED PER 1,000 MALES			
	Insane		Deaf-mute		Blind		Lepers		Insane	Deaf-mute	Blind	Lepers
	Male	Female	Male	Female	Male	Female	Male	Female				
1	2	3	4	5	6	7	8	9	10	11	12	13
HINDU												
Ambalavasi ...	230	51	51	26	153	205	26	...	222	500	1,333	..
Arayan ...	80	88	...	...	80	177	80	88	1,000	...	2,000	1,000
Brahman, Malayali	117	31	59	31	822	188	29	...	250	500	545	...
Do Tamil ...	61	33	20	33	123	186	71	22	500	1,500	1,417	286
Do Konkani	197	51	...	...	87	76	44	...	222	...	750	...
Do Others	100	...	...	427	200	...	...	...	...	...	...	...
Chetti ...	48	40	...	...	96	119	...	119	1,000		1,500	...
Devangan ...	...	171	85	171	170	85	...	...	...	2,000	500	...
Iluvan ...	28	26	41	34	134	108	79	21	931	857	826	272
Kadupattan ...	42	28	42	41	254	235	99	55	667	1,000	944	571
Kaikolan ...	50	47	...	95	99	142	...	...	1,000	...	1,500	...
Kammalan ...	29	57	47	57	128	97	64	46	2,000	1,250	810	727
Kanakkan ...	79	27	...	...	26	80	79	107	333	...	3,000	1,333
Kaniyan ...	123	62	...	62	62	123	62	62	500	...	2,000	1,000
Kavundan ...	385	...	...	...	385	174	193	...	...	...	500	...
Kshatriya, Malayali	...	...	196	...	196	198	...	...	...	...	1,000	...
Kudumi Chetti ...	15	34	15	17	62	51	92	68	2,000	1,000	750	667
Kusavan ...	...	...	109	115	164	115	...	...	...	1,000	667	...
Nayar ...	36	27	22	30	191	232	54	27	810	1,462	1,295	531
Otta Naikkan ...	...	69	73	...	73	207	73	...	...	...	3,000	...
Panan ...	...	...	...	...	...	283	67	71	...	...	...	1,000
Pandaran ...	...	...	53	109	265	164	...	...	...	2,000	600	...
Parayan ...	...	24	73	...	97	300	48	166	...	...	3,250	3,500
Pulayan ...	8	5	14	29	85	96	99	53	667	2,200	1,200	571
Vadukan ...	...	...	...	...	207	391	828	...	...	...	2,000	...
Vaisyan ...	...	...	290	...	1,159	1,064	290	...	...	...	750	...
Valan ...	...	26	99	26	124	26	49	...	...	250	200	...
Velan ...	44	63	65	42	131	148	152	85	1,500	667	1,167	571
Velakkattalavan ...	...	...	...	...	493	248	...	...	...	...	500	...
Vellalan ...	65	...	65	34	65	67	65	...	...	500	1,000	...
Veluttedan ...	...	...	63	56	252	112	63	...	...	1,000	500	...
Vettuvan ...	...	35	...	...	123	106	...	...	...	...	1,000	...
Others ...	47	9	28	27	66	36	56	18	200	1,000	571	333
MUSALMAN												
Jonakan ...	19	44	57	52	133	75	69	24	2,200	867	543	333
Ravuttan ...	...	24	70	...	139	73	23	...	...	...	500	...
Others ...	...	...	...	...	47	...	47	...	...	...	...	...
CHRISTIAN												
Anglo-Indian ...	81	83	...	...	...	83	322	...	1,000	...	...	...
European ...	...	...	...	...	...	...	...	...	...	...	...	...
Native Christian ...	32	35	49	32	122	96	77	18	1,081	632	775	222
Animist	...	...	94	...	47	244	...	94	...	...	5,000	...
Jew ...	350	...	...	...	...	166	175	...	...	...	...	...

CHAPTER XI.

CASTE, TRIBE AND RACE.

Caste Tables.

88. Imperial Table XIII gives the names of the castes returned and the strength of each. Selected castes are dealt with in four other Tables also, viz., IX (Education), XII—A (Infirmities), XIV (Civil condition) and XVI (Occupation). As the statistics contained in the last four are discussed in the corresponding Chapters, the present Chapter deals only with the figures in Table XIII. These figures relate only to the main castes, as the instructions did not require the return of the sub-castes of the enumerated, as they did in 1891. In some cases sub-castes were returned by the enumerators notwithstanding the instructions to the contrary, but in the final Table they have been incorporated with the main castes to which they respectively belong.

Accuracy of the return.

89. The instructions, both written and oral, which were given to the Supervisors and Enumerators, were so minute and exhaustive that the returns on the whole have proved extremely satisfactory. The entry of sub-castes in some cases, though superfluous, has not materially affected the accuracy of the returns. In a few cases, relating mainly to the floating population, the generic name Sudra was returned as the caste of the enumerated, and slight mistakes may have been made in the entries relating to some non-indigenous castes that are little known in this State, but the number of such returns is extremely small.

Scope of the Chapter.

90. In the *Cochin Tribes and Castes* the subject is treated exhaustively by Mr. L. K. Ananthakrishna Iyer, who was specially deputed by the Darbar to make an Ethnographical Survey of the State. It is also dealt with at length, though less minutely, in the Census Report for 1901. I do not therefore propose to go over the same ground again. This Chapter will consequently confine itself to certain general observations on the castes indigenous to Cochin. No attempt will be made to theorise on the origin of the caste system or that of the Cochin peoples, nor to describe the ceremonies and customs of the various castes in the State. A glossary is given at the end of this Chapter, in which will be found the names of the castes mentioned in Table XIII, with brief notes on their traditional occupations, sub-divisions, customs, present condition, etc.

Classification of castes.

91. In 1891 the castes were classified on the basis of their reputed or traditional occupations with certain modifications. As this classification was found to be unsatisfactory for the reason, among others, that it grouped together the most discordant elements under the same class, a classification by social precedence was prescribed in its place in 1901. The discussions to which the latter led appear to have aroused a great deal of ill-feeling between rival castes, and the Census Commissioner for India has therefore laid down that on the present occasion the question of social precedence need not be re-opened. But so far however as the castes indigenous to Cochin are concerned, the position of each caste on the social ladder is more or less well understood and defined, and its consideration is not likely to engender jealousy or ill-feeling. In Imperial Table XIII castes are arranged alphabetically, and in Subsidiary Table I they are classified according to their traditional occupations, as was done in 1891.

Social precedence.

92. Inter-marriage, inter-dining and pollution by touch or proximity are the tests by which caste status is determined in Cochin. The meals prepared by persons belonging to higher castes can be partaken of by those belonging to the lower ones, but the converse is strictly prohibited, especially in the case of females. A high class Nambudiri male may eat the food cooked by low class Nambudiris, and even by Tirumulpads, but their females cannot. Similarly Nayar males can partake of the meals prepared by any Nayar without distinction of sub-caste; but a female belonging to a higher sub-caste cannot eat the food prepared by one belonging to a lower. All Nayar females can eat together in the same room; but those of higher sub-castes may not sit in the same row for the purpose with those of a lower one. Similar rules are observed also among the lower castes. Inter-marriage also is generally governed by the same rules as those of inter-dining. A Nambudiri female can of course be married only in her own class, but a Nambudiri male can form *Sambandham* union in any caste below his, but not below that of Nayars. As a rule, women belonging to the Nayar and intermediate castes may marry only where they eat, that is, with equals and superiors, but these rules are not so strictly observed in these days as formerly, especially by the Nayars. Pollution is another element for caste differentiation, and there are some features of it which are peculiar to this part of India. A Nambudiri is polluted by the touch of any one below him in the social scale, while Kammalans and the castes below them pollute him, if they approach within a prescribed radius. Similarly, the members of any other castes are polluted by the touch or approach, as the case may be, of the castes below them. Kammalans, Iluvans and Panans cause atmospheric pollution to the higher castes within a radius of 24 Malabar feet (about 19 English feet). The castes below them cause similar pollution from a still greater distance, the length increasing with the fall in the social status. A classification of castes based on these considerations is given on pages 181-2 of the Cochin Census Report for 1901.

Caste rules and restrictions.

93. Caste rules and restrictions are in some respects more rigid and severe among the Malayalis than among most other classes in India. The rules regarding pollution by touch or proximity, which has already been referred to, are strictly enforced. Such pollution can be removed only by complete immersion in water either in a tank or a river. Besides this pollution, there is what may be called ceremonial pollution. A death or birth in a family causes such pollution to all members of the family in all its branches, and a similar pollution is also entailed on women during their monthly periods and after delivery. The duration of the ceremonial pollution varies according to the status of the different castes, the highest having the shortest period, but in the case of monthly periods, the duration is three days uniformly. Pollution of all kinds, however acquired, can be removed only by complete immersion in water. In the case of death pollution and women's special pollutions, certain purificatory ceremonies, besides immersion in water, are necessary to remove the taint. Similar ceremonies are also required if a Brahman or a Kshatriya is touched by members of castes below them when under death, monthly or delivery pollution. Again, the extreme penalty of formal excommunication is enforced here more regularly and rigidly than elsewhere in serious cases of violation of caste rules. The member of any main caste partaking of the meals prepared by one of a lower caste; any member of a twice born caste eating flesh or fish or drinking intoxicating liquor; a Nayar or a member of any higher caste having sexual connection with a female of any caste below that of Nayars; a male member of any caste having similar connection with a woman of any higher main caste; the non-observance of ceremonial pollution and the non-performance of funeral rites; these are some of the offences punishable with formal excommunication, and such offences are seldom overlooked. Similar offences, if committed between members of sub-castes, are treated as minor ones, and punishment in such cases

is a fine, or expulsion from the *enangu* or *tara* association, the nature of which is explained below. The eating of flesh and fish and the use of distilled or fermented liquors are prohibited only in the case of Brahmans, Kshatriyas and Ambalavasis, while in the case of Nayars and those below them beef is the only prohibited article of food. The re-marriage of widows is prohibited only among the Brahmans, while the marriage of girls before puberty is not enforced among any of the Malayali castes.

Caste government.

94. The caste rules and restrictions, such as those mentioned in the preceding paragraph, are enforced by the *enangu* and *tara* associations in the case of minor offences and by the *Vaidikans* and the ruler of the State in the case of more serious ones. *Enangu* is the association of a number of families belonging to the same sub-caste in a village, formed for the purpose of rendering mutual assistance and of dealing with social disputes and minor caste offences. On the occasion of a death, marriage or other occurrence in a family, the members of the other associated families look after all the details of the necessary arrangements, and also undertake the catering for the feasts; and the *enangans*, as the members of the associated families are called, act as bridegrooms when *tali* marriages are performed. The elders of the families on such occasions settle all social disputes and dispose of minor caste offences. The punishment generally awarded for such offences is suspension from the *enangu* pending their expiation by the payment of a fine or other penalty. The fines thus realised are paid into the funds of the village temple. The *enangu* system does not exist in several of the villages, especially in the south. Where it does not exist and where the *enangu* association fails to take action, members of other castes and sub-castes intervene and take cognizance of the offence. The leading men of the various castes in a village are associated together for purposes of this kind, and this is what is meant by the *tara* association. The procedure adopted in all cases is the same as that adopted by the *enangu* association, and the punishment for the breach of caste rules is suspension from the privileges of the village community, such as the services of the village barber, washerman, Chitikan (purifier for pollution), etc. In more important cases the matter is reported to the Vaidikan or His Highness the Raja, according to the seriousness of the offence, and action is taken according to their orders. No order of complete excommunication can be passed except by, or under the sanction of, His Highness.

The present condition of caste.

95. The caste system still continues to reign supreme over the Hindu community of Cochin, but signs of disintegration have begun to make themselves visible on all sides, more especially in towns. Among the more important forces that are working towards the relaxation of caste rules are English education, the public school system, the railways and the enactment of equal laws for all, and their impartial administration without distinction of caste or creed. English education has given a new turn to the ideas and aspirations of the people, and is working a change in the national frame of mind, which has hitherto accepted all that exists among the Hindus as divinely ordained and consequently as being beyond question or investigation. Public schools and railways are open to all castes and creeds, and high castes and low are thrown together there, where it is impossible for a casteman to preserve that aloofness which he maintains in his own village, or to purify himself as often as he should, or to be as particular as he should be in regard to what he eats and drinks. Equal laws and their impartial administration have considerably affected the supremacy of one caste over another in some respects, and are leading the people to question why there should be such supremacy in other respects as well. A Nayar could in the good old days take into his own hands the punishment of a Pulaya who polluted him by approaching

within the prohibited distance, but he can no longer do it with impunity. This leads him to ask himself why he should accept without question the mandates of the Brahman as he used to do formerly. Traditional occupation was another force making for caste exclusiveness and caste preservation. But the advent of railways and the introduction of machinery have made it impossible for many to confine themselves to their traditional occupations. Many of the old village industries have become unprofitable, while a great and growing demand is springing up for labour in mills, plantations and workshops. Numbers of people are therefore deserting their traditional means of livelihood in favour of new and more profitable vocations, and a man's caste is no longer, as it once was, a fairly certain index to his occupation. Again, the organisations which take cognizance of minor caste offences have also begun to undergo disintegration. Respect for the authority of elders, which is essential for the maintenance of the *enangu* and *tara* organisations, is very much on the decline in the altered political and social conditions of these days, and these organisations have therefore almost entirely disappeared from towns and are gradually disappearing from villages also. It must however be admitted that the great majority of the people, especially in the villages, are still as particular as ever they were in regard to caste observances. But the influence of the small but powerful minority, who are bidding a lingering farewell to them, is surely, if slowly, permeating the masses. This minority honour caste rules nowadays more by their breach than by their observance, especially when they are away from home, although in their own homes the fear of giving offence to their more orthodox relatives and friends leads them to make a show of observing the established rules and proprieties. In return for this show their lapses elsewhere are tacitly condoned. While disintegration is thus in progress now, certain relaxations permissible in the old days have ceased to be in operation. In the case of caste offences meriting excommunication, Sudras and persons inferior to them in caste could be saved from that penalty by the Raja of Cochin by presenting to them with his own hands a *kindi* or vessel of water to drink. A Tamil Sudra could be made a Nayar, and any one could be raised to a superior sub-caste by the same means. This has however become obsolete in these days.

Caste among Christians and Muhammedans.

96. Caste as a socio-religious institution is of course not observed by the Christians and Muhammedans of Cochin. But the caste prejudices which influence their Hindu brethren in their social and domestic relations obtain to some extent among some sections of both Christians and Muhammedans. The Syrians of the present day, who claim their descent from high caste Hindus converted by St. Thomas, will not even in these days inter-marry—some of them even refuse to inter-dine—with later converts from the lower castes. Similarly, a Muhammedan Mappila, who claims descent from a high caste Hindu, will not allow the descendant of a low caste convert to marry his daughter. The Catholics of the Chittur Taluk, who are mostly Tamil Sudras recently converted, have even returned themselves as Vellalans, Kavundans, etc., under "Caste" and Christians under "Religion".

Comparison with 1901.

97. The Hindus as a whole have increased by 11 per cent. during the last decade, but some of the castes have increased at a rate considerably more than this, and some others at a much less rate, as will be seen from Subsidiary Table II. No explanation can be offered for such differences in the rates of increase in the case of some of the castes, such, for instance, as the Ambalavasis, Kallasaris, Kanakkans, Kaniyans, Otta Naikans, Panans, Pandarans, Velakkattalavans, Vellalans, Veluttedans, Vettuvans, Malayans, and Jews. The abnormal increases in other cases are capable of explanation more or less satisfactory. Arayans have increased by 17 per cent.

and Valans only by three. The former is considered a more honourable designation, and consequently Valans in comparatively easy circumstances appear to have returned themselves as Arayans. The low rate of increase among Nambudiris and other Malayali Brahmans is due to the fact that the eldest sons alone marry in their own caste. Extinction of families is no unusual occurrence among them on account of this rule. The increase among Tamil and Konkani Brahmans appears to have been due to the additions received from other Districts and States. Chakkans are also known as Vaniyans, a name by which Konkani Vaisyans too are known. The great care taken in the Tabulation office to differentiate the two by reference to their home language—Tamil in the case of the former and Konkani in that of the latter—accounts for the apparent increase among Chakkans. Chetti is only a cognomen and not a caste name, and many Kudumis appear to have returned themselves as Chettis at the previous Censuses. Hence the decrease in their number. Tattans (Malayali gold-smiths) have increased and Pandi Tattans (Tamil gold-smiths) have decreased at a very abnormal rate. This variation is only apparent, as it is due merely to the greater care taken to differentiate them. The large decrease among Parayans and the increase among Pulayans appear to be explicable in the same way, as both are sometimes called Valliyals in ordinary parlance.

SUBSIDIARY TABLE I.

Castes classified according to their traditional occupations.

Group and Caste	Strength
1	2
LAND HOLDERS (134)	122,800
Kshatriya, Malayali	1,015
Do Others	579
Nayars	121,206
CULTIVATORS (97)	88,088
Agamudaiyan	148
Kavundan	1,095
Parayan	8,340
Parayan, Tamil	16
Muttariyan	70
Pulayan	72,787
Puluvan	188
Vellalan	6,044
LABOURERS (13)	12,871
Kudumi Chetti	12,871
FOREST AND HILL TRIBES (5)	4,177
Eravalan	503
Kadan	447
Kurumban	9
Malayan	2,461
Nayati	220
Ullatan	537
FISHERMEN, BOATMEN, PALKI BEARERS, ETC. (23)	21,015
Arayan	4,766
Kanakkan	7,527
Mukkuvan	323
Pondan	70
Valan	7,827
Valluvan	502
HUNTERS AND FOWLERS (6)	5,300
Boya	39
Vettuvan	5,261
PRIESTS AND DEVOTEES (39)	35,674
Embran	943
Gauda Brahman	151
Konkani do	8,522
Elayad	859
Muttad	238
Nambudiri	5,520
Tamil Brahman	18,923
Other Brahmans	376
Bairagi	142
TEMPLE SERVANTS (8)	7,804
Adikal	24
Chakkiyar	46
Chakkiyar Nambiyar	70
Chengazhi Nambiyar	183
Kallattu Kurup	115
Marar	1,574
Nambiyassan	1,640

Group and Caste	Strength
3	4
Pisharodi	1,237
Puthuval	354
Thiyyattunni	5
Variyar	2,556
BARDS AND ASTROLOGERS (4)	3,244
Kaniyan	3,244
MUSICIANS, SINGERS, DANCERS, MIMICS AND JUGGLERS (8)	2,902
Panan	2,902
TRADERS AND PEDLARS (7)	6,460
Baniya	186
Bhattia	11
Chetti	4,606
Komatti	30
Kavara	537
Vaniyan	1,090
BARBERS (5)	4,872
Ambattan	1,101
Velakkattalavan	3,271
WASHERMEN (14)	12,800
Vannan	97
Velan	9,822
Veluthedan	3,881
WEAVERS (9)	8,163
Chaliyan	1,693
Devangan	2,349
Kaikolan	4,121
CARPENTERS (19)	17,779
Marasari	17,779
MASONS (4)	4,046
Kallasari	3,101
Kallan	945
POTTERS (4)	3,557
Kusavan	3,557
BLACKSMITHS (8)	7,156
Kollan	7,156
GOLD AND SILVER SMITHS (7)	6,765
Tattan	4,309
Panditattan	2,456
BRASS AND COPPER SMITHS (1)	1,263
Kannan	185
Moosari	1,078

Group and Caste	Strength
5	6
CONFECTIONERS AND GRAIN PARCHERS (4)	3,715
Pandaram	3,715
TODDY DRAWERS AND DISTILLERS (227)	208,539
Iluvan	208,453
Shanan	86
OIL PRESSERS (2)	2,101
Chakkan	2,101
LEATHER WORKERS (2)	1,874
Chakkiliyan	739
Tolkollan	1,135
EARTH, SALT, ETC., WORKERS AND QUARRIERS (19)	17,138
Kadupattan	14,323
Ottannikan	2,815
OTHERS (336)	308,407
Andi	331
Dasi	367
Idaiyan	310
Kakkalan	682
Kammalan Tamil	151
Kurukkal	258
Manayar	361
Manuppan	116
Mudaliyar	732
Naidu	995
Nambidi	424
Nanjanattu Pillai	236
Pulluvan	110
Samantan	110
Sudra unspecified	140
Tarakan	713
Tottiyan	195
Vadukan	994
Vaisyan	627
Valachetti	329
Vilkurup	1,433
Anglo Indian	2,446
European	76
Native Christian	280,568
Arab	137
Jonakan	51,469
Kachchi	484
Pathan	1,899
Ravuttan	8,430
Saiyad	242
Sheik	416
Sunni	560
Black Jew	983
White Jew	192
Jain	129
Others	762

Note.—The number given within brackets indicates the proportion per mille to the total population of the State.

SUBSIDIARY TABLE II.

Variation in Caste, Tribe, etc., since 1881.

CASTE, TRIBE OR RACE	PERSONS				PERCENTAGE OF VARIATION INCREASE + DECREASE—			NET VARIATION
	1911	1901	1891	1881	1901—1911	1891—1901	1881—1891	1881—1911
1	2	3	4	5	6	7	8	9
HINDU.	615,708	554,255	501,544	429,824	+ 11	+ 10·5	+ 16·8	+ 186,884
Ambalavasi ...	7,804	7,483	7,143	...	+ 4 3	+ 4·7	...	+ 661
Variyar ...	2 556	2,209	2,011	...	+ 15 7	+ 9·8	...	+ 545
Arayan ...	4,766	4,081	3,093	...	+ 16·8	+ 31·9	...	+ 1673
Brahman ...	35.532	31,244	26,233	22,110	+ 13 7	+ 19·1	+ 18·6	+ 13,422
Konkani Brahman ...	8,522	7,250	6,086	7,277	+ 17·5	+ 19·1	— 16·3	+ 1,245
Malayali do ...	6,617	6,407	5,982	5,003	+ 3 3	+ 7·1	+ 19·5	+ 1,614
(Nambudiri) ...	5,520	5,290	5,002	4,256	+ 4 3	+ 5·7	+ 17·5	+ 1,264
Tamil do ...	18,923	16,017	12,201	10,577	+ 18·1	+ 31·2	+ 15·3	+ 8,346
Chakkan ...	2,101	1,525	1,068	...	+ 37·8	+ 42·8	...	+ 1,033
Chetti ...	4 606	5,143	10,060	...	— 10·4	— 48·8	...	— 5,454
Devangan ...	2 349	3,557	2,033	...	— 33·9	+ 74·9	...	+ 316
Iluvan ...	208,453	185,464	169,972	...	+ 12·4	+ 9·1	...	+ 38,481
Kadupattan ...	14.323	13,063	11,796	...	+ 9 6	+ 10·7	...	+ 2,527
Kaikolan ...	4,121	3,616	3,645	...	+ 13 9	— ·8	...	+ 476
Kammalan ...	34.558	29,809	26,956	...	+ 15·9	+ 10·5	...	+ 7,602
Kallasari ...	3,101	2,328	1,210	...	+ 33 2	+ 92·3	...	+ 1,891
Kollan ...	7,156	6,407	6,545	...	+ 11·7	— 2·1	...	+ 611
Marasari ...	17,779	15,533	14,538	...	+ 14·4	+ 6·8	...	+ 3.241
Tattan ...	4 309	3,554	3,179	...	+ 21·2	+ 11·7	...	+ 1,130
Kanakkan ...	7.527	5,917	9,926	...	+ 27·2	— 40·3	...	— 2,399
Kaniyan ...	3 244	2,547	2,522	...	+ 27·4	+ ·9	...	+ 722
Kshatriya ...	1.594	1,539	1,218	740	+ 3·5	+ 26·3	+ 64·6	+ 854
Kshatriya, Malayali..	1,015	892	803	...	+ 13 8	+ 11	...	+ 712
Kudumi Chetti ...	12,371	10,843	10,158	...	+ 14·1	+ 6·7	...	+ 2,213
Kusavan ...	3.557	3,231	2,168	...	+ 10	+ 49	...	+ 1,389
Nayar ...	121.206	111,837	101,691	...	+ 8 3	+ 9·9	...	+ 19,515
Otta Naikan (Odde) ...	2 815	2,066	2,719	...	+ 36·2	— 24	...	+ 96
Panan ...	2 902	2,781	2,398	...	+ 4 3	+ 15·9	...	+ 504
Pandaran ...	3.715	2,735	2,841	...	+ 35·8	+ 3·7	...	+ 874
Panditattan ...	2 456	3,648	1,423	...	— 32·6	+ 156·3	...	+ 1,033
Parayan ...	8 340	8,841	6,245	...	— 5 6	+ 41·5	...	+ 2,095
Pulayan ...	72.787	59,810	51,251	...	+ 21·6	+ 16·7	...	+ 21,536
Valan ...	7.827	7.564	6,157	...	+ 3 4	+ 22·8	...	+ 1,670
Velakkattalavan ...	3,271	2,761	2,299	...	+ 18·4	+ 20·1	...	+ 972
Velan ...	9 322	8,243	7,084	...	+ 13·1	+ 16·3	...	+ 2,238
Vellalan ...	6 044	8,242	2,868	...	— 25·6	+ 187·3	...	+ 3,176
Veluttedan ...	3 381	3,152	2,989	...	+ 7·2	+ 5·4	...	+ 392
Vettuvan ...	5 251	6,349	747	...	— 17·1	+ 749·9	...	+ 4,514
CHRISTIAN.	233,092	198,239	173,891	136,361	+ 17 5	+ 14	+ 27·4	+ 96,731
Anglo Indian ...	2,446	4,033	270	346	— 39 3	+ 1,393·7	+ 21·9	+ 2,100
European ...	76	55	38	23	+ 38·1	+ 44·7	+ 65·2	+ 53
Native Christian ...	230.568	194,151	173,523	135,992	+ 18·7	+ 11·8	+ 27·6	+ 94,576
MUSALMAN.	63 822	54,492	46,389	33,344	+ 17·1	+ 17·4	+ 39·1	+ 30,478
Jonakan ...	51,469	43,604	36,308	...	+ 18	+ 19·8	...	+ 15,076
Pathan ...	1,893	2,109	2,291	...	— 9·9	— 7·9	...	— 392
Ravuttan ...	8,430	8,160	6,486	...	+ 3·3	+ 25·8	...	+ 1,944
ANIMIST.	4.177	3,897	4,027	...	+ 7·1	— 3·2	...	+ 150
Malayan ...	2,461	2,631	3,094	...	— 6·4	— 14·9	...	— 633
JEW.	1,175	1,137	1,142	1,249	+ 3·3	— ·4	— 8·5	— 74
Black Jew ...	983	957	...	...	+ 2·7	...	...	...
White Jew ...	192	180	...	...	+ 6·6	...	...	...

Note:—Net variation in periods 1881—1911 has been given in all cases wherever available, while in other cases the figures given in indicate the net variation in the period 1891—1911.

GLOSSARY OF CASTES, TRIBES AND RACES.

(Those included in Table XIII.)

Note.—1. Names printed in antique type as **Ambalavasi** *are those of castes indigenous to Cochin, and names printed in capitals are those of non-indigenous castes.*

2. Indigenous castes marked with an asterisk follow the Marumakkattayam system of marriage and inheritance, and the rest Makkattayam.

3. In the case of indigenous castes where the period of pollution is not mentioned, it is to be assumed to be fifteen days, and where it is not mentioned how their women are called, it is to be understood that the usual feminine affix has only to be added to the male names.

4. The figures entered after each name show the total strength of the caste.

* **Adikal** (24).—A class of Ambalavasis. They are said to have been Brahmans originally, but were degraded for having officiated as priests in Bhadrakali temples and made offerings of flesh and liquor. They wear the holy thread, officiate as priests in minor temples and do other temple services. They follow Makkattayam, and their pollution period is ten days. Their women are called Adiyammas.

AGAMUDAIYAN (148).—A Tamil cultivating caste. They are found only in the easternmost villages of the Chittur Taluk.

* **Ambalavasi** (7,804).—The word means temple-resident, and is the generic name of a group of castes whose hereditary occupation is temple service. They are mostly either degraded Brahmans or the offspring of hypergamy. The castes to which this name is applied in Cochin are the Adikal, Chakkiyar, Chakkiyar Nambiyar, Chengazhi Nambiyar, Kallattu Kurup, Marar, Nambiyassan, Pisharodi, Puduval, Thiyyattunni and Variyar. These castes will be found treated separately in alphabetical order. They follow the Marumakkattayam law, all except Thiyyattunnis and Nambiyassans; the former follow the Makkattayam system, while among the latter some follow the one system and the rest the other. Marars eat the food cooked by other Ambalavasis, and Pisharodi and Variyar males dine with each other. With these exceptions there is no inter-dining or inter-marriage between the several sections of Ambalavasis. The majority of Ambalavasis still follow their hereditary occupation, but many among them now are land-holders, Government servants, medical and legal practitioners and school masters.

AMBATTAN (1,101).—Tamil barber caste.

ANDI (331).—Tamil beggars who are recruited from all classes of Sudras.

ANGLO-INDIAN (2,446).—The name now officially given to Europeans of mixed Indian descent, hitherto known as Eurasians. The great majority of the Eurasians of Cochin are however of Portuguese and Dutch descent and there is nothing "Anglo" about them.

ARAB (137).—A Musalman territorial name.

ARASUPALLI (62).—It is not known whether they are the Telugu Pallis or the Kanarese Arasus. The latter are supposed to be related to the ruling family of Mysore.

* ARAYAN (4,766).—They are fishermen and boatmen like the Valans, but while the latter fish only in the backwaters and lagoons, the former engage themselves in sea fishing. They are therefore also called Kadalarayans (or sea Arayans). Their approach within 32 feet of high caste Hindus will pollute the latter. Though Arayans and Valans are of equal status in the eyes of other castes, they neither inter-marry nor inter-dine with each other. They observe birth and death pollution only for eleven days. Amukkuvans, who are a sub-caste of Arayans, are their priests as well as those of Valans.

ARMENIAN (2).—A Christian territorial name.

BAIRAGIS (142).—Upper Indian ascetics and devotees. They constantly move from one place of pilgrimage to another and live on alms.

BANIYA (186).—Vaisya immigrants from the Bombay Presidency residing chiefly in Mattancheri and its neighbourhood for trade.

BHATIYA (11).—A Bombay trading caste residing chiefly in Mattancheri for trade.

BLACK JEW (983).—One of the two divisions of local Jews. They are considered the offspring of mixed unions or converts from the lower classes of Hindus. They themselves claim, however, that they were the first settlers on this coast, the White Jews being later immigrants, and that the darkness of their complexion was due chiefly to their long residence in the tropics.

BORA. (46).—Musalman converts from the Bombay side. They are the only Shiyas in Cochin.

BOYA (39).—A Shikari tribe in the Deccan Districts, who subsist on game and forest produce.

BRAHMAN (35,532).—In Table XIII Brahmans are classified by the parent tongues returned by them. The classes are Embran, Gouda, Konkani, Malayali, Tamil and others. Malayali Brahmans are again divided into Nambudiris, Elayads and Muttads. The reader is referred to the notes given under the respective heads.

CHAKKAN (2,101).—A Tamil caste of oil pressers locally called by this name, *Chakku* meaning an oil mill. Elsewhere they are called Vaniyans. Though they wear the sacred thread, their touch pollutes Nayars and the higher castes, and they are also not allowed access to the Brahmanical temples. The reason for this seems to be that Manu has for some unknown reasons classed oil pressing as a low occupation. A class of Tamil Brahmans officiate as their priests.

CHAKKILIYAN (739).—A Telugu caste of leather workers.

* **Chakkiyar** (46).—A class of Ambalavasis. They are the offspring of adulterous Nambudiri women born after the commencement of their guilt but before its discovery and their expulsion from caste. Boys so born, who have already been invested with the sacred thread, become Chakkiyars, and those who have not been so invested become Chakkiyar Nambiyars, the girls joining either caste indifferently. Their females are called Illodammas, and those of Chakkiyar Nambiyars, Nangiyars. The traditional occupation of the Chakkiyar is the *kuttu*, or the recitation of passages from the Puranas, with commentaries interspersed with witty allusions to current

events and to the members of the audience. The Nambiyar accompanies the performance on a metal drum called *Mishavu* and the Nangiyar keeps time with a cymbal. The Nangiyars also perform on occasions another kind of *kuttu*, which is a pantomimic performance on the Chakkiyar's stage. This stage is a consecrated one built within the premises of important temples. The Chakkiyar wears the holy thread, but the Nambiyar does not. The former may marry a Nangiyar, while the latter cannot marry an Illodamma. Their pollution period is eleven days.

* **Chakkiyar Nambiyar** (70).—*See* Chakkiyar above.

***Chaliyan** (1,693).—A Malayali caste of cotton weavers. They are considered as a low class of Sudras, but are not allowed access to the Brahmanical temples. Their touch pollutes Nayars and those above them. Most of them follow Marumakkattayam, and to a great extent resemble the Nayars in their customs and usages, but some among them follow Makkattayam. They have their own temples, in which their barbers officiate as priests. They are the only indigenous people that live in streets, which probably points to the fact of their being comparatively recent settlers from the East Coast.

*CHENGAZHI NAMBIYAR (188).—A class of Ambalavasis. They wear the sacred thread, and resemble Nambiyassans in their customs and usages, except that they all follow Marumakkattayam.

CHETTI (4,606).—This is a titular or occupational term, meaning trader, and not the name of a caste. The members of several Tamil and Telugu castes tack this title on to their names to denote, though not in all cases, that trade is their occupation.

CHUNNAMBOTTAN (15).—A Telugu caste of people who deal in *Chunnam*.

DASI (367).—Devadasis attached to the Konkani temples in Cochin-Kanayannur Taluk, and recruited mainly from Konkani Sudras. They speak the Konkani dialect.

DEVANGAN (2,349).—A weaving caste found only in the Chittur Taluk and the eastern portion of the Talapilli Taluk, more commonly known here as Chetans. They are immigrants from Mysore, and speak Kanarese. They wear the holy thread, and Chetti is their agnomen. A number of them seem to have been classed under Chetti in the caste table.

Elayad. (859).—A class of Malayali Brahmans who have suffered social degradation for having officiated at the funeral rites of the Nayars, which is now their hereditary occupation. In regard to marriage, inheritance, pollution, etc., they closely follow the usages of Nambudiris. Their women are called Elormas.

EMBRAN (943).—Tulu Brahman immigrants from South Canara. They are treated on a footing of equality by the Nambudiris, who however will not inter-marry with them. They are mostly employed as officiating priests in the temples of the State.

ERAVALAN (508).—A Tamil speaking forest tribe, immigrants from Coimbatore. In Cochin they are mostly agricultural labourers in the plains.

EUROPEAN (76).—A territorial name.

GAUDA. (151).—A class of Brahman mendicants wandering from place to place. They speak Telugu, and it is not clear why they are called Gaudas.

HANAVI. (26).—A Musalman sect.

IDAIYAN. (310).—The great shepherd caste of the Tamil country.

Iluvan. (208,453).—They are called also Chogans in Cochin, and correspond to the Tiyyans of British Malabar and the Shanans of the Tamil Districts. They are believed to have immigrated from Ceylon and introduced the cultivation of the cocoanut palm. Cocoanut growing and toddy drawing are still their hereditary occupation, but as they are numerically the strongest caste in Cochin, a great many of them have taken to other occupations, chiefly agriculture. The Iluvans in Cochin-Kanayannur follow Marumakkattayam and those in the rest of the State Makkattayam. Among the former divorce and widow marriage are allowed. The headmen of the Iluvans are called Tandans, and are appointed to that position by the ruler of the State. They are to perform certain specified functions, and are entitled to fees, at marriage and other ceremonies. Kavutiyans or Vattis are their priests and barbers, and form a distinct sub-caste inferior to them in status. Iluvans pollute Nayars and the higher castes by approach within 24 Malabar feet.

Jonakan. (51,469).—Malayalam-speaking Muhammadans, also called Mappilas or Jonaka Mappilas, to distinguish them from Native Christians, who are locally known as Nasrani (Nazarene) Mappilas. They are the descendants of the offspring of mixed unions or converts from the lower classes of Hindus. They are all Sunis, and polygamy prevails among them. They are mostly poor, and very backward in point of education.

KACCHI. (184).—A class of Musalmans, more commonly known as Kacchi Memons. They are so called here as they come from Cutch and its neighbouring Districts.

Kadan. (447).—A hill tribe confined to the Nelliampatis and Parambikolam, from which other hill tribes are excluded. They are a short, muscular people, of a deep black colour, with thick lips and curly hair, and speak a *patois* more akin to Malayalam than to Tamil. They are good trackers and tree climbers, and are useful in the collection of minor forest produce. During the working season they live on the rice supplied by forest contractors, and at other times on such animals as they are able to trap and on wild yams and other forest produce.

Kadupattan. (14,323).—Low class Malayali Sudras, popularly supposed to have been the descendants of Pattar Brahmans degraded for having eaten *kadu*, a kind of fish. Like Brahmans they observe pollution only for ten days, but they are not allowed access to Brahmanical temples. There is a peculiarity in their system of inheritance, *viz.*, that in the absence of sons the father's property does not descend to his daughters, but to his nearest male relatives. Kadupattans are also called Eluthacchans, and in former times they were largely employed as village school masters. The manufacture and sale of salt were among their chief occupations, when salt was not a Sirkar monopoly. They are now chiefly engaged in agriculture and general labour.

KAIKOLAN. (4,121).—A caste of Tamil weavers found only in Chittur and Talapilli taluks. Some of them speak Malayalam, and wear their tuft in front like the Nayars. Most of them still follow their hereditary occupation.

KAKKALAN. (682).—A gipsy tribe, whose males are tailors, mat makers, jugglers and snake charmers, and whose females are professional beggars and palmists. They speak a corrupt Tamil. They are called Kuravans in the northern taluks.

KALLAN. (945).—A Tamil caste of workers in granite. They wear the sacred thread, and are not distinguishable from Pandi Tattans (Tamil goldsmiths) in any respect except their occupation. They are not allowed access to Brahmanical temples in Cochin.

KALLAR. (18).—A Tamil caste of evil reputation. The term means a thief.

Kallasari. (3,101).—A division of Kammalans, who are masons by occupation. They work only in laterite. See Kammalan.

* **Kallattu Kurup.** (115).—The lowest division of Ambalavasis.

Kammalan. (34,558).—The artisan class, divided into a number of endogamous sub-castes—Marasari (carpenter), Kallasari (mason), Musari (brazier), Kollan (blacksmith), Tattan (goldsmith) and Tolkollan (leather-worker). As their services are much in requisition and as they earn better wages than unskilled labourers, they are still engaged in their hereditary occupations. The first five groups are socially on a par with each other. They all inter-dine, but do not inter-marry. But the Tolkollans are considered inferior in status to the rest, and cannot touch them without causing pollution, probably on account of their work in leather, which in its raw state is considered impure. Polyandry of the fraternal type was prevalent among them, several brothers marrying one wife and the children being treated as common to all. This practice is however fast dying out, if it has not already done so. The Kurups, who form a sub-caste among them, are their priests as well as barbers, and officiate at their marriage and funeral ceremonies. The Kammalans pollute the Nayars and the higher castes by approach within 24 feet.

Kammalan, Tamil. (151).—The artisan classes of the Tamil country, who are like those referred to immediately above, but take a higher position in the social scale than the Kammalans of the west coast.

Kanakkan. (7,527).—A class of fishermen and boatmen, who pollute the higher castes by approach within a radius of 48 feet. They are also engaged in agriculture and general labour. They are a very poor class, and very backward in point of education.

Kaniyan. (3,244).—Also called Kanisan. They are professional astrologers, whose services are in constant requisition for casting horoscopes and for fixing propitious hours for marriage and other ceremonies. Many among them are employed as village school masters. They are the most literate and, at the same time, the most unsophisticated among the polluting castes. Their pollution distance is 24 feet.

KANNADIYAN. (23).—A Kanarese caste of shepherds and cattle breeders.

KANNAN. (185).—A division of Tamil Kammalans, the members of which do braziers' work.

KAVARA. (537).—A Telugu caste of basket makers.

KAVUNDAN. (1,095).—A title of Kongu Vellalas.

Kavutiyan. (814).—*See* Iluvan.

KOLLAN. (7,156).—A class of Kammalans, who are hereditary blacksmiths. They are called Karuvans in the northern taluks. *See* Kammalan.

KOMATTI. (80).—A Telugu speaking trading class.

KONKANI BRAHMAN. (8,522).—A branch of the Saraswat sub-division of Pancha Gaudas. They are so called because they are immigrants from Konkan. They speak the Konkani dialect of Mahratti, and are found only in the southern taluks. They are Vaishnavites, and have well-endowed temples of their own in the State. The Nambudiris and other Brahmans will not treat them as Brahmans; not only will they not inter-dine with them, but they will not even allow them access to their temples and tanks. The Konkanis return the compliment by refraining from dining with other Brahmans and by refusing them admission to their temples. By occupation they are mostly traders and shop-keepers, but there are landholders also among them.

***Kshatriya** (1,594).—Kshatriyas are grouped under four classes in the caste Table, *viz.*, Malayali (1,015), Rajput (34), Raju (67), and others (478). These last consist of those who returned themselves as Kshatriyas unspecified. The Malayali Kshatriyas are known as either Tampurans, Tampans or Tirumulpads: this is a sub-division not by caste but by position. The Tampurans are members of ruling families, while Tampans are those who were once ruling chiefs but have since lost their political power. All the rest are Tirumulpads. Their women are called Tampurattis, Tampattis and Nambashtaris respectively. Brahman males partake of the meals prepared by them. In their personal habits, observances and ceremonies they are very like the Nambudiris, who act as their priests in all ceremonies. They observe pollution for eleven days, follow the Marumakkathayam law of succession, and have two marriages like the Nayars, the *Tali* and the *Sambandham*.

KUDUMI CHETTI (12,371).—Konkani Sudras, who serve Konkani Brahmans as their domestic servants, live in their midst and speak their language. They are among the most illiterate classes of the population, but for capacity for continued hard work they are unrivalled. They are employed in all kinds of unskilled labour, and they are also good boatmen. Their headman styled Muppan, who is appointed by the ruler of the State, directs all their social concerns, while Konkani Brahmans officiate as their priests.

***Kurukkal** (258).—A sub-division of Nayars, who take part in the worship of non-Aryan tutelary deities in village temples called *Kavus*.

KURUMBAN (9).—A Kanarese speaking hill tribe.

Kurup (29).—A title of Nayars and other castes. Also a sub-caste of Kammalans. The latter are the priests as well as the barbers of Kammalans.

KUSAVAN (3,557).—Tamil potters.

MAHARATTI (56).—A linguistic term rather than the name of a distinct caste.

Malayali Brahman (6,617).—*See* Elayad, Muttad and Nambudiri.

* **Malayali Kshatriya** (1015).—*See* Kshatriya.

Malayan (2,461).—A hill tribe found chiefly in the Kodasseri and Palapilli forests. They do not differ much in appearance and habits from the Kadans, except that they are less wild and less averse to manual labour than the latter. Besides collecting minor forest produce like the Kadans, they make good bamboo mats and baskets. They are also good trackers and tree climbers.

***Manayar** (361).—A sub-division of Nayars consisting originally of 24 families and generally known therefore as Irupattinalu Manayar.

MANUPPAN (116).—A class of Tamil Sudras.

***Marar** (1,574).—A division of Ambalavasis, who are temple musicians. They eat the food cooked by the other Ambalavasis, but none of the latter will partake of the meals prepared by them.

Marasari (17,779).—A class of Kammalans, who are carpenters by occupation. *See* Kammalan.

MUDALIYAR (732).—A title of Vellalans and other Tamil Sudras and not the name of a caste.

Mukkuvan (323).—A caste of fishermen and boatmen found chiefly on the sea coast. They are said to have immigrated from Ceylon along with the Iluvans. *See* Valan.

Musari (1,078).—A division of Kammalans, whose hereditary occupation is work in bell-metal. *See* Kammalan.

Muttad (238).—Malayali Brahmans who are said to have suffered social degradation for having tattooed their body with figures representing the weapons of Siva and for partaking of offerings made to that god. They perform some of the duties in the temples which Ambalavasis perform and are therefore considered by some to belong to the latter class, but they also carry the idols when taken out in procession, which no Ambalavasi is entitled to do, and, like the Elayads, they follow the usages of Nambudiris. Their women are called Manayammas, who are ghoshas like the Nambudiri women.

MUTTIRIYAN (70).—A Tamil caste of cultivators and village watchmen.

NAIDU (995).—A title used by Balijas and other Telugu castes.

***Nambidi** (424).—An intermediate caste between Nambudiris and Nayars. They are said to be the descendants of certain Brahmans who were degraded for assassinating one of the Perumals. They wear the sacred thread, and observe pollution only for ten days like the Brahmans, and Nambudiris officiate as priests in all their ceremonies. Their women are called Manolpads. Nambidi is also the title of some Nayar aristocrats.

Nambi Kurup (13).—The same as Nambiyassan.

Nambiyassan (1,640).—A class of Ambalavasis. Pushpakan is the generic name of this class, the particular local names being Nambiyassan, Nambiyar and Unni. Their duty is the collecting of flowers and making garlands for decorating idols, while their women, who are called Pushpanis or Brahmanis, sing certain songs in Bhadrakali temples and at the *tali* marriage ceremonies of Nayars and others. Among them some follow Makkattayam and others Marumakkattayam. They are the only Ambalavasis, except Chakkiyars, Thiyyattunnis and Chengazhi Nambiyars, who wear the sacred thread. Their pollution period is ten days.

Nambudiri (5,520).—The Brahmans of Kerala. They follow the Makkattayam system of marriage and inheritance, but as a rule only the eldest sons marry in their own caste, while the other members form Sambandham union with Kshatriya, Ambalavasi and Nayar women. Their women are gosha and are called Antarjanams or Akattammars (in-doors ladies). They generally marry after puberty, and their chastity is jealously guarded. The Nambudiris are divided, on the basis of certain sacerdotal rights and privileges enjoyed by them, into ten social groups. The highest class enjoy all the ten privileges, the next only nine and so on. The first six groups have the privilege of studying the Vedas, while the last four have not. The Vedic Nambudiris again are divided into three groups, of which the Adhyans occupy the highest position, the Asyans, the intermediate, and the Samanyans, the lowest. The Asyans are entitled to perform *Yagams* or sacrifices, and the Samanyans are not, while the Adhyans are above it. Among Vedic Nambudiris some are hereditary Tantris, who are the highest temple priests and whose authority is final in all matters of temple ritual, Vadhyans, who preside over the Yogams and Vedic schools at Trichur and Tirunavaya, Vaidikans, who decide all matters relating to caste, and Smartans, who preside over caste tribunals. The non-Vedic Nambudiris also are divided into various groups. Among them are the Mussads or Ashtavaidyans, whose hereditary occupation is the study and practice of medicine, the Sastrangakars, or more correctly Kshatrangakars (military Brahmans), who are believed to be the descendants of the Brahmans who were engaged in military service in former days, and the Graminis, who were engaged in administering *gramams* or Namburi colonies. All the Nambudiris are divided, like other Brahmans, into exogamous *gotras*. Their pollution period is ten days.

NANJANATTU PILLAI (236).—Tamil Vellalas long domiciled in the country and therefore partaking of the character of the Nayars to some extent. The men wear the fore-tuft, and dress themselves like the Nayars, while the women's dress looks more like that of Vellala women. They follow a system of marriage and inheritance, which is partly Tamil and partly Malayali. The *tali* marriage is the regular marriage, but divorce is freely permitted. Divorced women and widows cannot marry, but can form *Sambandham* alliance with men of their own caste. The sons are entitled to inherit a fourth of their father's property, while the rest goes to his sister's children. Nanjanattu Pillais and Nayars do not inter-marry or inter-dine with each other, at least in Cochin.

NATIVE CHRISTIAN (230,568).—*See* paragraphs 41 and 42 of the report.

***Nayar** (121,206).—Once a military class of people, who, with the Nambudiris and Ambalavasis, form the most characteristic section of the people of Cochin. Their martial spirit however has during a century of unbroken peace died out, but its traces still remain in some of their titles, games, etc. They are however making considerable advance in other respects. English education has made considerable progress among them, and they are found in all the literate walks of life in large numbers. The great majority of the Nayars however are petty farmers and agricultural labourers, though there are several land-holders and substantial farmers among them. Domestic servants in well-to-do caste Hindu families are almost entirely recruited from this caste. The Nayars are divided into a number of sub-castes, most of which are known by different names in British Malabar, Cochin and Travancore. The highest sub-caste, for instance, is known as Kiriyam in Malabar, while in Cochin it is generally called Vellayma. Next comes the Sudra Nayar, who is attached to Nambudiri and Kshatriya houses for certain services, religious and domestic: if attached to the former, he is called Illattu Nayar and, if to the latter, Swarupattil Nayar. Charna Nayars are attendants on Rajas and chiefs, but the sub-caste is not indigenous to Cochin. Pallichans are the palanquin bearers of Brahmans and Rajas, and Vattekadans are oil mongers for temples and Nambudiri houses. Odattu Nayars tile temple buildings, and Anduru Nayars make earthen vessels for the temples, while Attikurussi Nayars or Chitikans act as purifiers and quasi priests to the other Nayars. These are the main sub-divisions, but there are shades of differences within each sub-caste which are too numerous and too subtle to be dealt with here. Every Nayar has a title affixed to his name, which is conferred upon him by the Raja as a hereditary or personal distinction, while those who have received no title affix the title Nayar to their names. The title does not indicate one's position in the caste heirarchy, as the Raja can confer any of these titles without reference to the sub-caste of the recipients. Acchan, Karta, Kaimal and Mannadiyar are among the titles of nobility, while Panikkar, Kurup and Kuruppal are the titles of those who maintain *Kalaris*, or military gymnasia, as a hereditary profession. Menon is the title which was in the old days generally conferred on the Nayars who followed literate occupations and which is now most in use among the middle classes. It is the only title now conferred by the Raja as a personal distinction, but in these days many Nayars assume it without any such formality.

Nayadi (220).—An animistic tribe living in the outskirts of the jungles. Begging, watching crops in the plains, beating for game in the jungles and collecting forest produce are their chief occupations. They are the laziest and the most uncleanly people in the State, and eat the most dirty reptiles and vermins. Their approach within 72 feet will pollute caste Hindus. Even Pulayans and Parayans are polluted by their approach.

ODIYA (65).—An Uriya speaking race and not a distinct caste.

OTTA NAIKAN, OR ODDE (2,815).—Telugu tank diggers and earth workers. They are among the most illiterate classes in Cochin, but for earth work they are unrivalled. They are probably the most law abiding people in the State: the Cochin prisons have never had a single member of this caste as an inmate.

PALLI (5).—A Tamil caste claiming Kshatriya origin, which claim is not generally accepted.

Panan (2,902).—A polluting caste whose hereditary occupation is sorcery and exorcism. Some of them still exercise that profession, but the great majority of them are agriculturists and umbrella makers. Fraternal polyandry once prevailed among them. Their pollution distance is 24 feet.

PANDARAN (3,715).—A caste of Tamil priests and beggars. The Pandarans who have long been domiciled in Cochin are however neither priests nor beggars. Most of them are engaged in making *pappadams*, the crisp pulse cakes much affected by the Malayalis. The men have their tuft in front and dress like the Nayars, while the women dress like Tamil Sudras. Their home language here is Malayalam.

PANDITATTAN (2,456).—Tamil goldsmith caste. They wear the sacred thread, but are not allowed access to Brahmanical temples and public tanks in Cochin. Their touch will pollute the Nayars and the higher castes.

Paravan (28).—A polluting caste akin to Kaniyans and Panans. Their occupation is shell collecting, lime burning, etc.

Parayan (8,340).—An agricultural labourer caste, the lowest in the social scale. They pollute the higher castes by approach within 72 feet. Many among them live by making mats and baskets and practising witchcraft. As magicians they are much feared, especially by the lower classes. Their principal cult is the *odi*, the patron goddess of which is Nili of Kalladikod. They are the only caste in Cochin that eat beef. The Tamil Parayans are superior to them in status.

PATHAN (1,899).—Musalmans of Afghan descent. The name is also assumed by many who have no right to it. Here they are employed chiefly in subordinate Government service, especially as peons and constables.

***Pisharodi** (1,237).—A division of Ambalavasis. They make garlands for idols and do other menial services in temples. Their women are called Pisharasyars. They are said to be the descendants of a Brahman novice who, when about to be ordained a *sanyasi*, ran away after he was divested of the holy thread but before his head was completely shaved. In memory of this they are buried like sanyasis in a sitting position and the grave filled with salt and paddy. They inter-dine with Variyars, but not with any other division of Ambalavasis. Their pollution period is 12 days.

PONDAN (70).—A sub-caste of Idaiyan. They are palanquin bearers to the Raja of Cochin.

Pulayan (72,787).—Aggrestic serfs emancipated in 1854. They are also called Cherumans. They are all engaged in field labour—ploughing, sowing, crop-watching and reaping—and are paid in kind. They are all poor and illiterate, and live in the confines of paddy flats in miserable huts. They pollute the higher castes by approach within 64 feet. Parayans pollute them by touch, and Nayadis, Vettuvans, Ullatans, etc., by approach.

Pulluvan (110).—A polluting caste of professional beggars. They also sing in serpant groves to the accompaniment of a quaint musical instrument called *Pulluvakkudam*.

PULUVAN (188).—A Tamil cultivating caste.

***Puduval** (854).—A division of Ambalavasis, who are stewards of temples. They do not dine or inter-marry with other Ambalavasis, nor the latter (except Marars) with them. Their women are called Putuvalasyars.

RAJPUT (34).—A Kshatriya caste from Upper India.

RAJU (67).—They are said to be the descendants of a military section of Kapu and other Telugu castes.

RAVUTTAN (8,430).—Native Muhammadans, like Jonaka Mappilas, who are the descendants of mixed unions or converts from the lower classes. They are immigrants from the east coast, and speak Tamil. They are mostly petty shop-keepers.

REDDI (27).—Another name for Kapus, the great cultivating caste of the Telugu country.

SAIYID (242).—A Musalman tribe from Upper India. They are regarded as the direct descendants of the Prophet, and are therefore the highest sect of Musalmans.

***Samantan** (110).—This caste is not indigenous to Cochin, and those who have returned themselves as Samantans are either natives of British Malabar or are Nayar aristocrats who have of late begun to like to be considered to be superior to the ordinary Nayars in caste. Samantans are said to have sprung from the union of Kshatriya males and Nayar females. Like the Kshatriyas, they observe pollution for 11 days, but do not wear the sacred thread.

SHABI (91).—A Musalman sect.

SHANAN (86).—A Tamil toddy drawing caste corresponding to the Iluvans of the west coast.

SHEIK (416).—A Musalman tribe from Upper India. They are the descendants of the first three Caliphs, or successors of the Prophet, and are therefore second only to the Saiyids in racial purity and social precedence.

SUNNI (560).—A Musalman sect and not the name of a tribe or race.

TAMIL BRAHMAN (18,923).—They are locally known as Pattars, and are more numerous in the State than the Nambudiris. They are immigrants from the neighbouring Tamil Districts and settled in the State at different periods. They retain the customs and the usages of the east coast, but many among them, especially the earlier immigrants, have by their contact with the Malayalis for centuries made some change in their manners and customs, such as the wearing of *mundus* by many of their males, the observance of pollution by touch, approach, &c. By their intelligence, education and enterprise they have attained a prominent position everywhere. They are employed in all grades of Government service, and are conspicuous in all the learned professions. A good many of them are traders, money-lenders, land-holders and farmers, while the poorer among them are engaged in domestic service. They have rendered their personal service indispensable to all the princely and aristocratic families, where large numbers of them are employed in various capacities, especially as cooks. They are as good Brahmanas as the highest class of Nambudiris from a spiritual point of view, but the latter will not admit such equality. Nambudiri women, for instance, will not take the meals cooked by Pattar Brahmans, nor will the men allow them to take part in their religious ceremonies. They are also not allowed access to the inner shrines of Nambudiri temples, nor to touch the Nambudiris when engaged in their devotions and ceremonies.

Tarakan (713).—A trading class of Tamil Sudras, who settled on this side of the Palghat gap to act as trade medium between the Malayalam and Tamil countries, Tarakan meaning literally a broker. They gradually adopted the customs and usages of the Nayars except in regard to marriage and inheritance, and have in recent years been practically assimilated with them.

Tattan (4,309).—A division of Kammalans who are gold and silver-smiths. *See* Kammalan.

Thiyyattunni (5).—A division of Ambalavasis, whose occupation is the performance of ceremonies in Bhagavati temples called *Tiyyattam*, in which they paint the image of the goddess on the floor and chant certain propitiatory songs, especially to check the spread of small-pox. They are also called Tiyyattu Nambiyars. Some among them follow Makkattayam and others Marumakkattayam. Their pollution period is ten days. Their women are called Pushpinis or Brahmanis.

Tolkollan (1,185).—A division of Kammalans, who work in leather. *See* Kammalan.

TOTTIYAN (195).—A Telugu cultivating caste.

Ullatan (587).—A hill tribe living in the outskirts of jungles. They are chiefly engaged in felling trees, in scooping out logs for boats and in agricultural labour. Their approach pollutes Pulayans and Parayans.

VADUKAN (994).—Means simply a Telugu speaking man, and therefore is not the name of a caste. Balijas, Kapus, &c., are often called by this name in Tamil and Malayalam countries.

VAISYAN (627).—The third of Manu's four castes. There are no Vaisyans among Malayalis. Those who have been so returned are mostly Komattis, who are a Telugu speaking people, and Baniyas a Gujaratti speaking people from Bombay.

Valan (7,827).—A caste of fishermen and boatmen. The fishermen and boatmen of this coast are divided into four endogamous groups, *viz*., Sankhan, Bharatan, Amukkuvan and Mukkuvan. Of these, Arayan belongs to the first group, and Valans to the second. Amukkuvans, who form a sub-caste of Arayans, are the priests of Valans and as well as of Arayans. Among the Valans again there are four exogamous divisions called *Illoms*. They are Alayakad, Ennalu, Vaisyagiriyam and Vazhapilli. Each division has its own headman, called Arayar, who is appointed by the Raja. Under each headman there are subordinate social heads called Ponambans, who are appointed by the Arayar himself. The Valans have the exclusive privilege of fishing in the backwaters and rowing His Highness' escort snake boats. Their pollution distance is 32 feet.

VALACHETTI (320).—Gazalu Balijas, who are engaged in making and selling glass bangles, are known by this name in Tamil and Malayalam countries, *vala* meaning a bangle.

VALLUVAN (502).—A Tamil caste of priests to Parayans. They consider themselves superior to Parayans and will not dine or inter-marry with them.

VANIYAN (1,090).—Konkani Vaisyans. They wear the sacred thread, and resemble Konkani Brahmans in their habits. They have their own priests, who are called Panditans. They are mostly petty traders. These Vaniyans are to be distinguished from Chakkans, who are also called by that name. Their pollution period is twelve days.

VANNAN (97).—Tamil washerman.

•**Variyar** (2,556).—The most numerous division of Ambalavasis. Their hereditary occupation is making flower garlands for idols and sweeping temple premises. They inter-dine with Pisharodis, but with no other division of Ambalavasis. Their women are called Varasyars, and their pollution period is 12 days. The Variyars are the most progressive among Ambalavasis in point of English education.

•**Velakkattalavan** (3,271).—Low caste Sudras, who are hereditary barbers to the Nayars and the higher castes. They are like the Nayars in their customs and usages, but are not allowed access to Brahmanical temples and public tanks. They inter-dine but not inter-marry with Veluttedans. Unlike the Nayars and other low class Sudras, Velakkattalavans observe birth and death pollution only for ten days, and Brahmans give them holy water for purification after pollution. Their touch pollutes Nayars and those above them.

Velan (9,322).—Washermen to the higher polluting castes, whose services are also required by Nayar and other caste women for purification after delivery and monthly periods. There are several herbalists and exorcists among them. Plucking cocoanuts is one of their chief occupations in the south. Their pollution distance is 32 feet.

VELLALAN (6,044).—The great cultivating caste of the Tamil countries and the highest division among the Tamil Sudras. The great majority of Vellalans in Cochin belong to the eastern villages of the Chittur Taluk bordering Coimbatore.

* **Veluttedan** (3,381).—Low caste Sudras, who are hereditary washermen to the Nayars and the higher castes. They are like the Velakkattalavans in all respects except in regard to the period of pollution.

Vettuvan (5,961).—Emancipated agricultural serfs, who live mainly in the outskirts of the jungles. They are, as their name implies, hunters by occupation. The great majority of them however are now agricultural labourers and collectors of forest produce. Vettuvans and Pulayans pollute each other by approach. Their pollution distance is 72 feet.

Vilkurup (1,438).—The same caste as Tolkollans. Some of them were in the old days engaged in making bows and arrows : hence the name.

VIRASAIVAN (28).—The same as Lingayats, a sect of Hindu reformers who denied the sacerdotal authority of the Brahmans.

WHITE JEW (192).—One of the two divisions of the local Jews. They are considered the only Jews here of pure and unmixed origin. They preserve their racial purity and light complexion to a remarkable extent, notwithstanding their being here for many centuries.

CHAPTER XII.

OCCUPATION.

98. The statistics of occupation or means of livelihood of the people will be found in Imperial Tables XV and XVI. The former Table is divided into four parts-(A) Agricultural statistics; (B) Subsidiary occupations of agriculturists—actual workers only; (D) Distribution of occupation by religion; and (E) Statistics of industries collected at the special Industrial Census referred to in paragraph 5. Part C, which is intended to show certain mixed traditional occupations, has not been prepared for this State, as such cases are extremely rare here. Table XVI gives the occupations of certain selected castes, tribes or races. The main facts contained in these Tables are given in the Subsidiary Tables at the end of this Chapter in condensed and proportional forms. These will enable the reader to appreciate the facts more readily than the actual figures themselves.

Introductory.

99. The scheme of classification adopted on the present occasion differs considerably from that of 1901. It is more logically arranged, more elastic and much less elaborate than the previous ones. All occupations or means of livelihood are now divided into four classes and sub-divided into twelve sub-classes, as against eight and twenty-four respectively in 1901. These are again split up into 55 orders, as against 79 at the previous Census, and each order is further sub-divided into 170 groups, as against 520. The greater elasticity of the scheme enables it to be used in countries at all stages of industrial development and economic differentiation. It has the further merit of being the scheme recommended by the International Statistical Institute for general adoption. Indian occupational statistics can therefore be compared hereafter with more exactitude and intelligibility with those of other countries. Some of the main principles followed in classifying the occupation returns may be briefly stated here. In Table XV-A, a person is classed according to his principal occupation, while his subsidiary occupation is also given, if it is agriculture and not otherwise. If his principal occupation is agriculture, his subsidiary occupation, if there is any, is given, whatever it may be, in Part B. Only those Government servants are shown in sub-class 7 who are engaged in general administration, including the administration of justice. Members of the medical, legal and other similar services are classed under special heads provided for these occupations. The actual occupation and not the source from which the remuneration comes is what is taken into account. It is otherwise in Table XV-E, which is based on the special industrial schedule. In this the industry is what is looked to and not the actual occupation of individual employes. A blacksmith employed in an oil mill, for instance, is treated here only as a mill hand, but in the general occupation Table, on the other hand, he is classed under group 41 as worker in iron, while only the persons directly concerned with the mill industry, including clerks and menials, are classed under it.

Scheme of classification.

To suit the conditions of the State a few additions were made to the groups of occupations with the sanction of the Census Commissioner for India. Group 1—Income from agricultural land—is split up into (a) non-cultivating land owners and (b) cultivating land-owners, and group 2—Ordinary cultivators—into non-cultivating tenants and cultivating tenants. Anchal or Cochin postal service is shown separately as group 105 (a), and group 145—Service of Native and Foreign States—is sub-divided into (a) chiefs and their families, (b) officers and servants of chiefs and their families, (c) Sirkar officers, (d) clerical establishment, (e) menials unspecified and (f) service of States other than Cochin. Similarly, group 146—Municipal service—is split up into (a) and (b) to show clerical and menial establishments separately.

Accuracy of the return.

100. All possible attempts were made to ensure accuracy in the return of occupations. The instructions to the Enumerators on the covers of the enumeration books and to the Supervisors in the "Manual" regarding the filling up of the three columns—one for the principal occupation of actual workers, the second for their subsidiary occupation, if any, and the third for the occupation of those who do not actually follow any calling themselves but depend upon others for their livelihood—were supplemented by a circular of instructions, in which the attention of the Supervisors and Enumerators was specially called to those points where they were most likely to make mistakes. Further, in the classes I held in different centres for the instruction of Supervisors I devoted a considerable portion of my time to explaining as minutely and accurately as I could how these three columns were to be filled up. Notwithstanding all this care and trouble, it cannot be said that all errors have been eliminated, but the returns may be accepted as on the whole fairly representing the distribution of the means of livelihood of the people. A careful examination of hundreds of schedule books and of the tabulation registers has satisfied me that the Enumerators have in almost all cases correctly drawn the line between workers and dependents and that, where entries have been made in definite terms, there is no reason to doubt their accuracy. But the number of entries in vague terms is unfortunately large, over 7 per cent. of the population having been returned as supported by insufficiently described occupations. Errors in compilation have been minimised as much as possible by the careful checking of the entries in slips and by employing the very best hands in the office for sorting and compiling the occupation entries. The great simplicity of the new scheme of classification and the elaborate Index furnished by the Census Commissioner have also largely contributed to the minimising of errors in compilation. The results obtained may therefore be considered to be on the whole satisfactory. The explanations given below in dealing with the statistics will bear out the truth of this remark. A few general facts may however be referred to here. Any one who knows the State also knows that a much larger number of females than males are engaged in making cocoanut fibre, baskets and mats, in rice pounding, washing, sweeping and selling sweet-meats, and this fact is confirmed by the returns, as will be seen from a reference to Subsidiary Table VI. Again, women are not returned as toddy drawers, boatmen, cart-drivers, palki bearers, railway, postal and anchal employes, village accountants, lawyers, etc., and it is well known that women have not yet begun to aspire to these positions in Cochin. These facts may be taken as affording some testimony to the accuracy of the returns.

General distribution of population by occupation.

101. The four classes into which occupations are divided are the production of raw materials, the preparation and supply of material substances, public administration and the liberal arts, and miscellaneous. The first class includes not only the agricultural population but also those maintained by forestry, fishing and hunting, and the extraction of minerals. The second class consists of industrial and commercial population including those engaged in transport, and the third consists of the public force, those engaged in public administration or pursuing legal, medical and other professions and liberal arts, and persons living on their income. Domestic service, insufficiently described occupations and unproductive means of livelihood make up the class "Miscellaneous". Agriculture supports just one-half of the population, industries 21 per cent., commerce 13·6 per cent. and professions

3·3 per cent. Agriculture is thus the predominent occupation of the people, as in other parts of India, but it does not exhaust the resources of the State to the same extent as it does elsewhere, as will be seen from the figures given in the margin.* Travancore alone has a smaller proportion of agricultural population than Cochin, but the proportion of population supported by industry and commerce is also smaller there. † This comparative preponderance of industrial population in these two States is due not to the infertility of the soil or its unsuitability to agriculture but to certain natural advantages possessed by them, which have diverted a larger proportion of people than in most other parts of India from agriculture to industrial occupations. Among these may be mentioned the existence of a large extent of backwaters and canals teeming with fish life and providing occupation to a large number of fishermen, fish-curers and dealers, and boat and bargemen; of valuable forests covering nearly one-half of the States and providing employment to numbers of wood cutters, sawyers, carpenters and collectors of forest produce; and of facilities for the cultivation of the cocoanut palm, the raw produce of which affords scope for important and extensive industries, such as toddy drawing, jaggery making, arrack distilling, oil pressing, coir making, etc. The industries connected with these three support 3·4, 4·2 and 9 per cent. respectively of the population in Cochin.

PERCENTAGE TO THE POPULATION.

	Agriculture.	*Industry and Commerce.*	*Professions.*
Cochin ...	50·4	34·6	3·8
Travancore ...	47·2	28·5	2·5
Malabar ...	60·7	30·1	3·0
Madras Presidency..	70·0	21·3	3·2
India ...	65·2	16·9	1·7

102. The agricultural population consists of cultivating and non-cultivating land-holders, cultivating and non-cultivating tenants, agents, managers etc. of landed estates, farm servants and field labourers, growers of special products, and breeders, keepers, etc. of farm stock. The strength of each section is given in the margin as compared with that of 1901. The total number supported by agriculture is 465,185, of whom nearly 39 per cent. are workers and the rest dependents, as against 412,256 in 1901 (44 per cent. workers and 55 per cent. dependents). The increase in the agricultural population has thus been almost at the same rate as that of the total population, *viz.*, about 13 per cent. Taking the sub-divisions of the agricultural population into consideration, there was an enormous increase in land owners, both cultivating and non-cultivating, and a similar decrease in non-cultivating tenants. This was due to the granting of occupancy right to the holders of Government lands since the Census of 1901. Owners of such lands who returned themselves as tenants in that year have rightly returned themselves as land owners at the present Census. The decrease in the number of field labourers appears to be due to the fact that a number of them returned themselves as general labourers, the number of the latter being 60,017, as against 41,781 in 1901. Irrigation on an extensive scale does not exist in the State except in the Chittur Taluk, where the Government anicuts, with their main and branch channels, 53 and 76 miles respectively in length, serve an area of nearly 18,000

Agricultural population.

	1911.	*1901.*
Non-cultivating land owners	14,667	7,518
Cultivating land owners	47,476	6,566
Non-cultivating tenants	2,818	10,195
Cultivating tenants	206,509	181,877
Agents, managers, etc., of landed estates	1,507	2,336
Farm servants and field labourers	167,466	178,280
Growers of special products	23,196	25,074
Farm stock breeders, keepers, etc.	1,940	4,871

* The figures given for Travancore and India are those of 1901.

† In Travancore 15 per cent of the population were returned under general labour, while the percentage for Cochin is only 6. A good many of the former were very likely agricultural labourers.

acres. The irrigation department employed 275 hands on the Census day, of whom two (an upper subordinate and a contractor) were Europeans, and the rest Indians.

Industrial population.

103. The industrial population comes next in numerical strength and importance. In every thousand of the population 209 are engaged in industrial pursuits, of whom 97 are actual workers and the rest dependents. The industries in which more than one per cent. of the population are employed are connected with textiles, wood, metals, food, dress and the toilet, and buildings. The numbers supported by these industries are given in the margin, together with the figures for 1901.

	1911	*1901.*
Textiles	46,825	39,684
Wood	43,232	30,598
Metals	9,277	8,590
Food	40,211	48,253
Dress and the toilet	18,438	17,718
Building	19,632	8,524

The textile industries are chiefly cotton weaving and cocoanut fibre making. The former as a cottage industry has received a great impetus during the last ten or fifteen years owing to the patronage of the well-to-do people of Cochin, who had hitherto gone in for cloths manufactured in Tinnevelly. Numbers of Native Christians, Muhammadan Mappilas and Iluvans have taken to it besides the hereditary weavers, Chaliyans, Chetans and Kaikolans. A weaving factory worked by steam power was also brought into existence recently. The making of cocoanut fibre and yarn has proved a paying occupation, especially to women in the intervals of household work. The systematic exploitation of the forests, which began about twelve years ago, accounts for the large increase in the number of people employed in industries connected with wood. Of those supported by food industries, 58 per cent. are toddy drawers and 38 per cent. rice pounders and huskers. The decrease in the number employed in the former is due to the more systematic administration of the Abkari revenue introduced in recent years, and in the latter to the establishment of a few rice hulling mills worked by steam power. The population supported by industries of dress and the toilet consist mainly of tailors, (3,954) and hereditary washermen (8,701) and barbers (5,405). The increase in metal and building industries seems to be due to the improvement in the standard of living. People have begun to live in better houses than formerly and to use metal utensils in the place of ordinary earthen ones.

While the above six orders of industry support 18·7 per cent. of the population, the remaining 8 support only 2·8 per cent. Order 7—hides, skin and hard materials— is almost wholly represented by makers of leather articles, order 10—ceramics—by potters and brick and tile makers, and order 11—chemical products—by the manufacturers of oils, chiefly cocoanut oil. Furniture industries (order 14) maintain only 132 persons, and the construction of the means of transport (order 16) only 66, while the production and transmission of physical forces supports only a single individual. Nearly 92 per cent. of those engaged in industries of luxury and those pertaining to literature and the arts and sciences (order 18) are workers in precious stones or metals, and gilders. This craze of ornaments and jewellery is characteristic of the people of Cochin as those of the rest of India.

Special Industrial Census.

104. The results of the special Census of factories, plantations, etc. in which at least 20 persons were employed, are embodied in Imperial Table XV--E. There were 65 such concerns on the Census day, employing 5,434 males and 968 females. Of these, about one-half are employed in rubber plantations, of which there are six. Rubber is a growing industry in Cochin, and new plantations have been open out since the Census. Coffee on the other hand is a declining industry. Ten years ago over two thousand persons used to be employed on the coffee estates, but the number has now dwindled into about a thousand. As the Census was taken at the close of the working season, only 425 males and 218 females have been returned as employees in them. The cocoanut oil mills, of which there are nine, are doing good work,

turning out, as they do, oil to the approximate value of sixty lakhs of rupees a year. The fifteen brick and tile factories not only manufacture all the bricks and tiles required for the State, but also meet the demand in the southern parts of Malabar and the northern taluks of Travancore. All the rubber plantations shown in the table, about half the coffee estates, the cask making and fisheries factories, the saw mills and one of the iron works are run by European capitalists, while the rest are owned by Indians. Of the 211 men employed in direction, supervision and clerical work, 36 are Europeans and Anglo Indians and the rest Indians, and of the 1,311 skilled workmen, only 18 are Europeans and Anglo Indians. As many as 521 boys and 227 girls under the age of 14 are employed in these establishments. For fuller information regarding these and other industries the reader is referred to my Report on the Industrial Survey of Cochin and Chapter VI of my Cochin State Manual.

Commercial population.

105. The existence of an excellent harbour with plenty of good roads and internal waterways and also a railway running right across the State has made Cochin a place of considerable commercial importance. The commercial population of the State, including those engaged in transport, forms 13·6 per cent. of the total population, while the percentages for Travancore, Malabar and the Madras Presidency are only 2·6, 12·2 and 8 respectively. The chief articles of trade are given in the margin, together with the number of persons supported by their sale in 1911 and 1901. The largest number employed is in other trade in food stuffs. Of these, 25 per cent. are grocers and sellers of vegetable oil, salt and other condiments, 23 per cent. are grain and pulse dealers, 20 per cent. are fish dealers, and 19 per cent. are cardamom, betel-leaf, vegetable fruit and arecanut sellers. Hotels, cafes, restaurants, etc. support the next largest number. Of these, 64 per cent. are vendors of wine, liquors, aerated waters, etc., and 36 per cent. are owners and managers of hotels, cook-shops, etc. and their employees. The former have decreased by about a third during the decade, owing to the greater restrictions placed on the sale of liquor, while the latter have increased nearly sixfold in strength, which is due to the establishment of coffee shops in all parts of the State in recent years. The decrease in trade in textiles appears to be due to the fact that many of the local weavers are also sellers and that as such they are shown under textile industry. The same remark applies to the decrease in trade in pottery and building materials. Bankers and money lenders have also increased largely in recent years, which has had the beneficial effect of lowering the rate of interest by about 50 per cent. during the last 10 or 15 years.

	1911	*1901*
Trade in textiles	5,646	6,897
Hotels, cafes, restaurants, etc	9,690	10,047
Other trade in food stuffs	59,578	58,763
Banks, establishments of credit, etc.	4,424	3,022

Transport.

106. A comparatively large number of persons are employed in connection with transport by water owing to the extensive waterways possessed by the State. The number has however decreased since the last census owing to the introduction of the railway. The increase in cart traffic on the feeder roads on account of the introduction of the railway has considerably enhanced the number of persons employed in transport by road. Subsidiary table IX, of which an abstract is given in the margin, gives the number of persons employed on the census day on railways, etc. The figures were furnished by the departments concerned.

	Europeans & Anglo Indians	*Indians*
Railway	8	305
Postal Department	1	95
Telegraph Department.	3	25
Cochin Forest Tramway.	17	369
Cochin Anchal Department...		181

107. The professional population consists of those engaged in public administration and the pursuit of the liberal arts, namely, religion, law, medicine, instruction, and letters and arts and sciences. They form 4·6 per cent. of the total population. Public administration, including the army and the police, and religion support the largest number, 11,785 and 10,648 respectively. Among the latter, Ambalavasis, or those who perform non-priestly functions in temples, predominate, while the rest are mainly Brahmans and Native Christians. Instruction claims the next largest number (7,417), as might be expected in a State where literacy is so prevalent. Medicine supports 4,088 persons and law 2,163. Of the former, the majority of the workers are imperics and quacks, nearly one half of them being Velans and Iluvans, while the latter are entirely the product of modern administration. Among those supported by letters, arts and sciences, the majority of the workers are astrologers, singers and actors. It must be remembered in this connection that census statistics are no respecters of persons. They allow bishops and burial ground keepers, high priests and temple sweepers, monks and mendicants equally to claim religion as their profession. They bracket barristers and High Court vakils with muktyars and petition writers, doctors of medicine and surgery with barber midwives, and literary and musical geniuses with Pulluva singers in serpent groves.

Professional population.

108. The number of persons who do not belong to any of the above classes forms 8·2 per cent. of the population. Nearly 80 per cent. of these are supported by labour otherwise unspecified, and a little over 7 per cent. by domestic service. A good many among the former are probably agricultural labourers, while the strength of the latter is undoubtedly understated, as some enumerators appear to have returned domestic servants as dependents, and entered the occupations of their masters against their names in column 11 of the schedule. The remaining 13 per cent. consists mainly of clerks, accountants, etc. in unspecified offices and shops (5,148), proprietors (other than of agricultural lands), fund and scholarship holders, and pensioners (1129), and beggars, vagrants and prostitutes (2,390). The population dealt with in this paragraph would have been considerably less, if enumerators had taken more care and used more intelligence in filling up the occupation columns.

Other classes of occupations.

109. Besides the agricultural population referred to in paragraph 102, 7,982 persons (6,422 males and 1,560 females) among those engaged in other pursuits have returned agriculture as their subsidiary occupation. They are all workers, and the groups of occupation to each of which over 200 of them belong are shown in the margin. Of these, the first—herdsmen and shepherds—have already been included among the agricultural population, and the last—general labourers—are probably in fact agricultural labourers. Basket makers and rice pounders work in the field when agricultural labour is brisk, especially during the harvest season, while the rest are mostly non-cultivating tenants. Those who belong to the other groups than those mentioned in the margin form only a third of the total number.

Partial agriculturists.

Group of occupation.	*Partial agriculturists* Males.	Females.
12. Herdsmen, shepherds, etc.	1,895	65
25. Workers in cocoanut and other fibres	65	211
36. Sawyers, carpenters, etc.	239	3
37. Basket makers, etc.	130	325
56. Rice pounders	25	300
65. Toddy drawers	581	—
72. Barbers	177	28
117. Grocers, sellers of vegetable oil, etc.	313	5
121. Grain and pulse dealers	168	187
167. General labourers	875	145

Subsidiary occupation of agriculturists.

110. Of the actual workers among the agricultural population, who number 1,16,097 males and 62,274 females, 15,804 persons have returned subsidiary occupations. But 2,773 of these have returned as such some group of agricultural occupation other than their own; land owners, for instance, who are also tenants have returned the latter as their subsidiary occupation and *vice versa*. The remaining 13,031 agriculturists (10,429) males and 2,602 females) are also engaged in non-agricultural pursuits, of which the most favourite ones are mentioned in the margin. A comparison of this marginal statement with that given in the preceding paragraph shows that, if agriculturists have a special preference for certain non-agricultural occupations, it is generally those who pursue these same occupations that favour agriculture. Of the agriculturists who have returned subsidiary occupations, nearly 45 per cent are cultivating tenants, 34 per cent are field labourers, and 12 per cent are cultivating tenants.

Subsidiary occupations of Agriculturists.	*Number engaged.* Males	Females
25. Cocoanut and other fibre makers	388	439
37. Basket makers	351	493
58. Manufacturers of vegetable oil	280	20
56. Rice pounders	42	625
65. Toddy drawers	961	2
99. Cart owners, drinkers, etc.	393	..
106. Bankers and money lenders	583	99
116. Fish dealers	285	103
117. Grocers, sellers of vegetable oil, etc.	391	75
120. Betel-leaf, vegetable, etc., sellers	955	25
121. Grain and pulse dealers	249	40
135. Unspecified shopkeepers	639	24
167. General labourers	1,369	400
Others	3,543	325

Actual workers and dependents.

111. Of the total population, 375,513, or 41 per cent., are actual workers, and the rest dependents. Of the former again, only 127,266 or 34 per cent. are women. Deducting from the number of dependents 363,252 persons below the age of 15 and 58,427 above 55, who may be considered too young or too old to work, we find 120,918 or 13 per cent. of the population eating the bread of idleness. But these latter are almost all women. In the Madras Presidency the percentage of actual workers is as high as 53 per cent, as against 41 in Cochin, which shows that here a larger proportion of the young and the old can afford to eat the bread of idleness than elsewhere in Southern India.

Occupation of females

112. In a few groups of occupations the work is comparatively light and the remuneration not adequate for male workers. In six of these, as shown in the margin, female workers greatly preponderate over males, and two-thirds of the female workers are engaged in these. Trade in food stuffs and liquor, domestic service and cotton weaving employ another 8 per cent. of them, though males preponderate in these occupations. Ten per cent. of them have interest in land as owners or tenants, and about half per cent. are bankers and money lenders. They carry on these two occupations mainly through agents or servants. Only 15 per cent. of the females are engaged in all the other occupations put together. There are several occupations from which women are practically shut out, such, for instance, as forestry, work in wood, metals and precious stones, toddy drawing, masonry, boating and fishing, cart driving, railway and postal service, army, police and public administration, law, and letters, arts and sciences except music.

	Males.	*Females.*
Field labourers	46,626	47,674
Fibre making	7,821	17,417
Baskets, etc. making	8,801	5,571
Rice pounding	688	9,102
Washing and cleaning	1,885	3,647
Sweeping and scavenging	115	1,519

Caste and occupation.

113. Imperial Table XVI gives the occupations of certain selected castes and subsidiary Table VIII gives an abstract of it in proportional figures. It will be seen from these that the lines of caste and of occupation do not now enclose identical spaces as they once did, and that,

though the association between them is still kept up to a considerable extent, the altered conditions of modern times are sweeping away many old hindrances to a free choice of occupation. Toddy-drawing and selling is the hereditary occupation of Iluvans, but there are ten Iluvan workers for every one toddy drawer required for the State. The remaining nine-tenths of the Iluvans must live, and they therefore take to other occupations such as cultivation, fibre making, trade, general labour, etc. The Brahmans are still priests and clerks, but some of them are cultivating tenants, police constables and domestic servants, while educated Nayars compete with them in every literate employment; but no one in these days scoffs at the former or resents the latter. The inner barriers however have not yet been broken through by the new waves of innovation, and in the case of the castes, noted in the margin the majority are still engaged in their hereditary occupations. In the case of several other castes, though the majority are not engaged in their hereditary occupations, the majority engaged in those occupations belong to the respective castes. Only a tenth of the Iluvans are toddy drawers and sellers, but the great majority of toddy drawers are still Iluvans. Similarly, though only a small proportion of Brahmans are priests, almost all the Hindu priests are Brahmans.

Caste	*No. of workers*	*No. engaged in hereditary occupation*
Ambalavasi (temple servant)	2,954	1,659
Arayan (fisherman)	2,641	1,728
Chakkan (oil presser)	973	599
Devangan and Kaikolan (weavers)	2,928	2,278
Kammalan (artisan)	12,113	11,014
Kanakkan (boatman and agricultural labourer)	3,974	2,727
Kusavan (potter)	2,063	1,859
Parayan (agricultural labourer and basket maker)	5,184	4,905
Pulayan (agricultural labourer)	44,085	41091
Valan (boatman and fisherman)	4,220	3,265
Velan (barber and priest)	5,027	3,610
Velakkattalavan (barber)	1,538	1,283
Veluttedan (washerman)	2,076	1,891

Distribution of occupations by caste.

114. It will be interesting to examine how the main occupations are distributed among the several castes and races. The most important fact disclosed by such examination is the catholicity of native Christians in the choice of occupation, unhampered as they are by hereditary prejudices and predilections. There is hardly any branch of work in which they do not take a more or less prominent part. Of the agricultural population, 26 per cent. are Iluvans, chiefly field labourers, 23 per cent. Pulayans, all labourers, 18 per cent. native Christians and 15 per cent. Nayars, mainly cultivating tenants and field labourers. A third of those engaged in forestry are Iluvans, chiefly wood cutters and firewood collectors and a tenth Malayans, collectors of minor produce, while the rest are mainly Nayars, native Christians and Jonakans. Of fishermen, 29 per cent. are native Christians, while Arayans, Valans and Kanakkans form 27, 26 and 9 per cent. respectively.

As regards industries, 56 per cent. of those who work in hides and leather are Tolkollans, the rest being mostly Chakkiliyans, native Christians and Parayans. Of those engaged in textile industries, 38 per cent. are Iluvans and 33 per cent. native Christians, both making cocoanut fibre, while only 5 per cent. are Kaikolans and 3 per cent. Devangans, both being cotton weavers. About 35 per cent. of workers in wood are Marasaris (carpenters), 17 per cent. native Christians (sawyers and carpenters), 17 per cent. Parayans (basket makers) and 11 per cent. Iluvans (sawyers and basket makers). Of metal workers, 71 per cent. are Musaris, Kollans, and Tattans, and 13 per cent. native Christians. In every hundred potters and brick and tile makers, 85 are Kusavans and 8 native Christians, and in an equal number of manufacturers of vegetable oils, 58 are native Christians, 27 Chakkans and 14 Iluvans. Food industries employ in every hundred 55 Iluvans (mainly in toddy drawing), and 20 native Christians and 12

Nayars (chiefly in rice pounding). Of those employed in industries of dress and the toilet, 36 and 20 per cent. respectively are Velans and Veluttedans (washermen), 13 and 5 per cent. are Velakkattalavans and Kavutiyans (barbers), and 7 per cent. are native Christians. Industries of luxury employ in every hundred 78 Tattans (Malayalam and Tamil) as jewellers, and 13 native Christians mainly as gilders, printers and book binders.

Many of the above industries are the hereditary occupations of certain castes, the members of which still preponderate in them. But no branch of trade is the hereditary occupation of any caste in Cochin, and consequently any one who has a turn and the means for it takes to it without distinction of caste or creed. Of every 100 persons employed in transport work, over 8 are Kanakkans and Valans (transport by water), 13 and 10 respectively are Iluvans and Odda Naikans, the former mainly and the latter wholly engaged in road work, 35, 10 and 6 respectively are native Christians, Jonakans and Nayars (transport work of all kinds). Of bankers, money lenders and brokers, 43 per cent. are Tamil Brahmans, 26 per cent. Nayars, and 7 per cent. native Christians, and of dealers in textiles, 40 per cent. are native Christians, 14 per cent. Tamil Brahmans, 12 per cent. Iluvans and 11 per cent. Ravuttans. Native Christians partly and Iluvans wholly deal in cocoanut fibre, and the rest in cotton fabrics. In every hundred engaged in keeping hotels, restaurants, etc., 58 are Iluvans, mainly vendors of toddy and arrack, 13, 9 and 7 respectively are Tamil Brahmans, native Christians and Nayars, and of those engaged in other trade in food-stuffs, 30 per cent. are native Christians, 17 per cent. Jonakans, 11 per cent. Iluvans, 6 per cent. Valans, 5 per cent. Pandarans, and 4 per cent. each Nayars, Konkani Brahmans and Ravuttans. In every hundred unspecified shopkeepers, 67 are native Christians, 18 Konkani Brahmans, and 4 each Tamil Brahmans, Kudumi Chettis and Jonakans. The other trades are not numerously represented.

In public administration and the liberal arts the higher castes naturally predominate. The army and the police are practically monopolised by Nayars, and public administration by Nayars (61 per cent.), Tamil Brahmans (16 per cent.), and native Christians (6 per cent). To put it in another form, only 5 per cent. of the Nayars and ·3 per cent. of the native Christians are engaged in public administration, while 12 per cent. of the Tamil Brahmans and 48 per cent. of the Malayali Kshatriyas are so employed. Brahmans and Ambalavasis form 37½ per cent. each of the religious profession, and native Christians 12 per cent., and of lawyers and their clerks, 50 per cent. are Nayars and 14 per cent. each Tamil Brahmans and native Christians, while the medical profession consists of 24 Velans, 20 native Christians, 18 Iluvans and 9 Nayars in every hundred. The teaching profession is represented in almost all castes, 29 per cent. being Nayars, 20 per cent. native Christians, 16 per cent. Tamil Brahmans and 8 per cent. Kaniyans, and of the representatives of letters, arts and sciences, 24 per cent. are Nayars, 16 per cent. Kaniyans (astrologers), 12 per cent. Ambalavasis (temple musicians) and 9 per cent. native Christians.

Of domestic servants, cooks, etc., 42 per cent. are Nayars, 14 per cent native Christians and 7 per cent. Iluvans, and in every hundred of general labourers, 37 are Iluvans, 33 native Christians and about 6 each Nayars, Jonakans and Kudumi Chettis. About 35 per cent. of beggars, vagrants and prostitutes are native Christians, 17 per cent. Iluvans and 12 per cent. Pandarans.

SUBSIDIARY TABLE I.

General distribution by occupation.

CLASS, SUB-CLASS AND ORDER.	NUMBER PER 10,000 OF TOTAL POPULATION.		PERCENTAGE IN EACH CLASS, SUB-CLASS AND ORDER OF		PERCENTAGE OF DEPENDANTS TO ACTUAL WORKERS
	Persons supported	Actual workers	Actual workers	Dependants	
1	2	3	4	5	6
A. PRODUCTION OF RAW MATERIALS.	**5,271**	**2,051**	**39**	**61**	**157**
I. EXPLOITATION OF THE SURFACE OF THE EARTH.	5,271	2,051	39	61	157
(1) Pasture and Agriculture ...	5,126	1,982	39	61	159
(2) Fishing and hunting ...	145	69	48	52	110
II. EXTRACTION OF MINERALS ...	...	...	...	100	...
(3) Mines ...	...	...	...	100	...
(4) Quarries of hard rocks ...	...	...	...	...	...
(5) Salt, etc. ...	...	...	...	...	...
B. PREPARATION AND SUPPLY OF MATERIAL SUBSTANCES ..	**3,446**	**1,484**	**43**	**57**	**132**
III. INDUSTRY ..	2,092	976	47	53	114
(6) Textiles ...	510	305	60	40	67
(7) Hides, skins and hard materials from the animal kingdom ...	13	5	38	62	160
(8) Wood ...	471	198	42	58	137
(9) Metals ...	101	34	34	66	196
(10) Ceramics ...	46	24	52	48	92
(11) Chemical products properly so called and analogous..	46	15	34	66	198
(12) Food industries ...	438	191	44	56	129
(13) Industries of dress and the toilet ...	201	109	54	46	85
(14) Furniture industries ...	1	1	28	72	257
(15) Building industries ...	147	49	33	67	199
(16) Construction of means of transport ..	1	...	38	62	164
(17) Production and transmission of physical forces (heat, light, electricity, motive power, etc.) ...	...	...	100	...	...
(18) Industries of luxury and those pertaining to literature and the arts and sciences ...	85	27	32	68	212
(19) Industries concerned with refuse matter ...	32	18	55	45	83
IV. TRANSPORT ...	205	83	41	59	147
(20) Transport by water ...	74	32	43	57	132
(21) Do road ...	109	42	39	61	159
(22) Do rail ...	14	6	44	56	128
(23) Post office, Telegraph and Telephone services ...	8	3	38	62	166
V. TRADE ...	1,149	425	37	63	171
(24) Banks, establishments of credit, exchange and insurance ...	48	16	33	67	207
(25) Brokerage, commission and export ...	3	1	35	65	187
(26) Trade in textiles ...	61	21	34	66	197
(27) Trade in skins, leather and furs ...	6	2	26	74	280
(28) Do wood ...	14	4	31	69	225
(29) Do metals ...	3	1	24	76	312
(30) Do pottery ...	2	1	28	72	262
(31) Do chemical products ...	9	3	36	64	175

SUBSIDIARY TABLE I.—*Cont.*

General distribution by occupation.

CLASS, SUB-CLASS AND ORDER.	NUMBER PER 10,000 OR TOTAL POPULATION. Persons supported	NUMBER PER 10,000 OR TOTAL POPULATION. Actual workers	PERCENTAGE IN EACH CLASS SUB-CLASS AND ORDER OF Actual workers	PERCENTAGE IN EACH CLASS SUB-CLASS AND ORDER OF Deputation	PERCENTAGE OF DEPENDENTS TO ACTUAL WORKERS
1	2	3	4	5	6
(32) Hotels, cafes, restaurants, etc. ...	106	41	39	61	158
(33) Other trade in food stuffs ...	649	252	39	61	158
(34) Trade in clothing and toilet articles ...	4	2	46	54	118
(35) Trade in furniture ...	17	7	43	57	131
(36) Do building materials.	17	6	38	62	163
(37) Do means of transport	9	4	44	56	130
(38) Do fuel ...	22	10	44	56	125
(39) Do articles of luxury and those pertaining to letters and the arts and sciences ...	12	3	27	73	271
(40) Trade in refuse matter ...	1	...	43	57	135
(41) Trade of other sorts ...	166	51	31	69	226
C. PUBLIC ADMINISTRATION AND LIBERAL ARTS ..	**474**	**173**	**36**	**64**	**174**
VI. PUBLIC FORCE ...	19	8	40	60	149
(42) Army ...	6	3	43	57	133
(43) Navy ...	...	...	...	...	...
(44) Police ...	13	5	39	61	157
VII. PUBLIC ADMINISTRATION ...	110	41	37	63	169
(45) Public administration ..	110	41	37	63	169
VIII. PROFESSION AND LIBERAL ARTS ...	333	120	36	64	176
(46) Religion ...	116	48	42	58	141
(47) Law ...	24	6	27	73	301
(48) Medicine ...	53	16	30	70	231
(49) Instruction ...	81	28	35	65	186
(50) Letters and arts and sciences ...	59	22	37	63	174
IX. PERSONS LIVING ON THEIR INCOME	12	4	30	70	230
(51) Persons living principally on their income ...	12	4	30	70	230
D. MISCELLANEOUS ..	**809**	**382**	**47**	**53**	**112**
X. DOMESTIC SERVICE ...	61	42	69	31	44
(52) Domestic service ...	61	42	69	31	44
XI. INSUFFICIENTLY DESCRIBED OCCUPATIONS ...	721	320	44	56	126
(53) General terms which do not indicate a definite occupation ...	721	320	44	56	126
XII. UNPRODUCTIVE ...	28	20	74	26	35
(54) Inmates of jails, asylums and hospitals ...	2	1	73	27	37
(55) Beggars, vagrants, prostitutes ...	26	19	74	26	35
Total ..	10,000	4,090	41	59	144

SUBSIDIARY TABLE II.

Distribution by occupation in Natural Divisions.

Occupation	Number per mille of total population supported in the "Cochin State"	Occupation	Number per mille of total population supported in the "Cochin State"
1	2	1	2
A. PRODUCTION OF RAW MATERIALS ...	527	IV. Transport ...	21
I. Exploitation of the surface of the earth ...	527	V. Trade ...	115
Agriculture ...	504	Trade in food stuffs ..	76
Pasture ...	2	Trade in textiles ...	6
Fishing and hunting ...	15	Other trades ...	33
Others ...	6	C. PUBLIC ADMINISTRATION AND LIBERAL ARTS ...	47
II. Extraction of minerals ...	...	VI. Public force ...	2
B. PREPARATION AND SUPPLY OF MATERIAL SUBSTANCES...	345	VII. Public administration ...	11
III. Industry ...	209	VIII. Professions and liberal arts ...	33
Textile industries ...	51	IX. Persons living on their income ..	1
Wood industries ...	47	D. MISCELLANEOUS ...	81
Metal industries ...	10	X. Domestic Service ...	6
Food industries ...	44	XI. Insufficiently described occupations ...	72
Industries of dress and the toilet .	20	XII. Unproductive ...	3
Other industries ...	37		

SUBSIDIARY TABLE III.

Distribution of the agricultural industrial, commercial and professional population in Natural Divisions and Districts.

District and Natural Division 'West coast' 'Madras States'	Agriculture				Industry (including mines)			
	Population supported by agriculture	Proportion of agricultural population per 1,000 of district population	Percentage on agricultural population of		Population supported by industry	Proportion of industrial population per 1,000 of district population	Percentage on industrial population of	
			Actual workers	Dependants			Actual workers	Dependants
1	2	3	4	5	6	7	8	9
Cochin State ...	468,074	504	39	61	192,057	209	47	53

District and Natural Division 'West coast' 'Madras States'	Commerce				Professions				Other Occupations			
	Population supported by commerce	Proportion of commercial population per 1,000 of district population	Percentage on commercial population of		Population supported by profession	Proportion of professional population per 1,000 of district population	Percentage on professional population of		Population supported by other occupations	Proportion of population who follow other occupations per 1,000 of district population	Percentage on population who follow other occupations of	
			Actual workers	Dependants			Actual workers	Dependants			Actual workers	Dependants
	10	11	12	13	14	15	16	17	18	19	20	21
Cochin State ...	124,857	136	37	63	30,564	33	36	64	108,053	118	46	54

SUBSIDIARY TABLE IV.

Occupations combined with agriculture (where agriculture is the subsidiary occupation)

Occupation	Number per mille who are partially agriculturists (Cochin State)	Occupation	Number per mille who are partially agriculturists (Cochin State)
1	2	1	2
A. PRODUCTION OF RAW MATERIALS ...	956	V. Trade ...	39
		Trade in food stuffs ...	87
		Trade in textiles ...	71
I. Exploitation of the surface of the earth ...	956	Other trades ...	39
Pasture ...	941		
Fishing and hunting ...	17	C. PUBLIC ADMINISTRATION AND LIBERAL ARTS ...	46
Others ...	72		
II. Extraction of minerals ...	...	VI. Public force ...	9
		VII. Public Administration ...	43
B. PREPARATION AND SUPPLY OF MATERIAL SUBSTANCES.	32	VIII. Professions and liberal arts ...	47
		IX. Persons living on their income...	94
III. Industry ...	29	D. MISCELLANEOUS ...	·33
Textile industries	11		
Wood industries ...	38	X. Domestic service ...	10
Metal industries ..	20	XI. Insufficiently described occupations ...	38
Food industries ...	54		
Industries of dress and the toilet .	27	XII. Unproductive ..	7
Other industries ...	22		
IV. Transport ...	33	Total ...	496

SUBSIDIARY TABLE V.

Occupation combined with agriculture (where agriculture is the principal occupation).

Land lords (rent receivers)		Cultivators (rent payers)		Farm servants and field labourers	
Subsidiary occupation	Number per 10,000 who follow it	Subsidiary occupation	Number per 10,000 who follow it	Subsidiary occupation	Number per 10,000 who follow it
1	2	3	4	5	6
Total	1768	Total	1252	Total	507
Non-cultivating land-owners	6	Non-cultivating land-owners	2	Cultivating land-owners	1
Cultivating land-owners	8	Cultivating land-owners	10	Cultivating tenants	16
Cultivating tenants	192	Agents, managers of landed estates, clerks, rent collectors, etc.	18	Tea, coffee, rubber, etc., plantations	1
Agents, managers of landed estates, clerks, rent collectors, etc.	29	Farm servants and agricultural coolies	74	Fruit, flower, vegetable, betel, vine, arecanut, etc., growers	7
Farm servants and agricultural coolies	16	Tea, coffee, rubber, etc., planters	7	Wood cutters	15
Tea, Coffee, rubber, etc., plantations	3	Fruit, flower, vegetable, betel, vine, arecanut, etc., growers	170	Herdsmen, shepherds, etc., goatherds	3
Fruit, flower, vegetable, betel, vine, arecanut, etc., growers	94	Wood cutters	9	Fishing	20
Fishing.	26	Fishing	6	Fibres such as cocoanut, etc.	66
Fibres such as cocoanut, etc.	17	Fibres such as cocoanut, etc.	27	Sawyers, carpenters, etc.	3
Sawyers, carpenters, etc.	6	Sawyers, carpenters, etc.	16	Basket-makers and other industries of woody material	84
Basket makers and other industries of woody material.	4	Basket makers and other industries of woody material	6	Potters and earthern pipe makers	1
Manufacture and refining of vegetable oil	44	Potters and earthern pipe makers	4	Manufacture and refining of vegetable oil	2
Rice pounders, and huskers and flour grinders	8	Manufacture and refining of vegetable oil	36	Rice pounders and huskers and flour grinders	52
Toddy drawers	10	Rice pounders and huskers and flour grinders	16	Grain parchers	1
Tailors	3	Grain parchers	7	Toddy drawers	29
Washing, cleaning, etc.	15	Toddy drawers	109	Tailors	1
Barbers, hair dressers, etc.	10	Tailors	5	Barbers, hair dressers, etc.	1
Stone and marble workers, masons and brick layers	3	Washing, cleaning, etc.	17	Stone and marble workers, masons and brick layers	5
Boat-owners, boatmen and towmen	8	Barbers, hair dressers, etc.	12	Boat-owners, boatmen and towmen	8
Cart-owners, drivers, coachmen, etc.	23	Stone and marble workers, masons and brick layers	12	Cart-owners, drivers, coachmen, etc.	2
Porters and messengers	6	Boat-owners, boatmen and towmen	13	Porters and messengers	2
Bank managers and money lenders	239	Cart-owners, drivers, coachmen, etc.	56	Bank managers and money lenders	1
Trade in piece goods, wool, cotton, silk, etc.	43	Porters and messengers	3	Trade in piece goods, wool, cotton, silk, etc.	1
Trade in wood (not firewood)	12	Bank managers and money lenders	41	Trade in wood (not firewood)	1
Vendors of wine, liquors, aerated waters, etc.	15	Trade in piece goods, wool, cotton, silk, etc.	9	Vendors of wine, liquors, aerated waters, etc.	2
Fish dealers	29	Trade in wood (not firewood)	4	Fish dealers	14
Grocers and sellers of vegetable oil, salt and other condiments	59	Vendors of wine, liquors, aerated waters, etc.	27	Grocers and sellers of vegetable oil, salt and other condiments	3
Sellers of milk, butter, ghee, etc.	9	Fish dealers	31	Sellers of sweet meats, sugar, gur and molasses	3
Sellers of sweet meats, sugar, gur and molasses	3	Grocers and sellers of vegetable oil, salt and other condiments	41	Cardamom, betel leaf, vegetables, fruits and arecanut sellers	1
Cardamom, betel leaf, vegetables, fruits and arecanut sellers	134	Sellers of milk, butter, ghee, etc.	9	Grain and pulse dealers	2
Grain and pulse dealers	61	Sellers of sweet meats, sugar, gur and molasses	8	Dealers and hirers of cattle, etc.	1
Tobacco, opium, ganja, etc. sellers	10	Cardamom, betel leaf, vegetables, fruits and arecanut sellers	109	Shop-keepers otherwise unspecified	3
Dealers and hirers of cattle, etc.	3	Grain and pulse dealers	28	Conjurors, fortune tellers	2
Shop-keepers otherwise unspecified	128	Tobacco, opium, ganja, etc., sellers	4	Temple, burial or burning ground service	1
Conjurors and fortune tellers	5	Dealers and hirers of cattle, etc.	5	Medical practitioners of all kinds	1
Sirkar officers of all kinds	21	Shop-keepers otherwise unspecified	73	Music composers, singers, etc.	3
Village officials and servants	29	Conjurors and fortune tellers	4	Cooks, water carriers, etc.	6
Priests, ministers, etc.	19	Sirkar officers of all kinds	3	Labourers and workmen otherwise unspecified	124
Temple, burial or burning ground service	82	Village officials and servants	12	Other occupations	18
Medical practitioners of all kinds	56	Priests, ministers, etc.	3		
Professors and teachers of all kinds	53	Temple, burial or burning ground service	13		
Authors, photographers, artists, etc.	9	Medical practitioners of all kinds	23		
Music composers, singers, etc.	17	Professors and teachers of all kinds	13		
Proprietors (other than of agricultural land), pensioners	41	Authors, photographers, artists, etc.	6		
Cooks, water carriers	5	Musiccomposers, singers, etc.	9		
Cashiers, accountants, etc.	49	Proprietors (other than of agricultural land), pensioners	5		
Labourers and workmen otherwise unspecified	14	Cooks, water carriers	3		
Other occupations	97	Cashiers, accountants, etc.	7		
		Labourers and workmen otherwise unspecified	89		
		Other occupations	41		

SUBSIDIARY TABLE VI.

Occupation of females by sub-classes, and selected orders and groups.

Group No.	Occupation.	Number of Actual Workers.		Number of females per 1,000 males.
		Males.	Females.	
1	2	3	4	5
	I. EXPLOITATION OF THE SURFACE OF THE EARTH ...	124,717	68,602	510
	(1) Pasture and Agriculture ...	119,343	62,641	525
1	Income from rent of agricultural land	12,045	2.308	192
2	Ordinary cultivators ...	50,285	10.906	217
4	Farm servants and field labourers ...	47,527	47.846	1,007
5	Tea, coffee, cinchona, rubber and indigo plantations ...	1,204	437	363
6	Fruit, flower, vegetable, betel, vine, arecanut etc., growers. ...	4,506	772	171
8	Wood cutters ; firewood, lac, catechu, rubber, etc , collectors and charcoal burners ...	1,513	299	198
12	Herdsmen, shepherds, goatherds, etc.	1,400	56	40
	(2) Fishing and hunting ...	5,374	961	179
14	Fishing ...	5,354	961	179
	II. EXTRACTION OF MINERALS	...	...	...
	III. INDUSTRY ...	47,088	42,556	904
	6. Textiles ...	9,381	18,632	1,986
22	Cotton spinning, sizing and weaving	2,083	1,094	525
25	Other fibres (cocoanut, aloes, flax, hemp, straw, etc.) ...	7,021	17,417	2,481
	8. Wood ...	12,459	5,761	462
36	Sawyers, carpenters, turners and joiners ...	9,158	190	21
37	Basket makers and other industries of woody material including leaves ...	3,301	5.571	1,688
	9. Metals ...	2,755	360	131
41	Workers in iron and makers of implements and tools principally or exclusively of iron ...	2,115	288	136
	10. Ceramics ...	1,271	914	719
47	Potters and earthern pipe and bowel makers ...	1,121	814	726
	11. Chemical products properly so called and analogous ...	1,042	365	350
53	Manufacture and refining of vegetable and mineral oils ...	986	365	370
	12. Food Industries ...	8,058	9,508	1,180
56	Rice pounders and huskers and flour grinders ...	688	9,102	13,230
65	Toddy drawers ...	6,985	..	...
	13. Industries of dress and the toilet	4,910	5,049	1,028
68	Tailors, milliners, dress makers, and darners, embroiderers on linen ...	1,303	588	451
71	Washing, cleaning and dyeing ...	1,855	3.647	1,966
72	Barbers, hair dressers and wig makers	1,669	783	469
	15. Building industries ...	4,180	352	84
78	Stone and marble workers, masons and bricklayers ...	3,661	152	42
	18. Industries of luxury and those pertaining to literature and the arts and sciences ...	2,449	48	20
80	Workers in precious stones and metals, enamellers, imitation jewellery makers, gilders, etc. ...	2,169	45	21
	19. Industries concerned with refuse matter ...	115	1,519	13,209
93	Sweepers, scavengers, dust and sweeping contractors ...	115	1,519	13.209
	IV. TRANSPORT ...	7,282	357	49
	20. Transport by water ...	2,911	10	3
97	Boat owners, boatmen and towmen ...	2,658	1	...
	21. Transport by road ...	3,527	346	98
99	Cart owners and drivers, coachmen, stable boys, tramway, mail carriage, etc., managers and employees (excluding private servants) ...	2,698	8	3
	V. TRADE ...	29,505	9,402	321
	24. Banks, establishments of credit, exchange and insurance ...	844	595	705
106	Bank managers, money lenders, exchange and insurance agents, money changers and brokers and their employees ...	844	595	705
	26. Trade in textiles ...	1,812	86	47
108	Trade in piece goods, wool, cotton, silk, hair and other textiles ...	1,812	86	47

SUBSIDIARY TABLE VI.—*Cont.*

Occupation of females by sub-classes, and selected orders and groups.

Group No.	Occupation.	Number of Actual Workers.		Number of females per 1,000 males.
		Males.	Females.	
1	2	3	4	5
	32. Hotels, restaurants, cafes, etc....	2,346	1,411	601
114	Vendors of wine, liquors, aerated waters, etc. ...	1,336	1,061	794
115	Owners and managers of hotels, cook-shops, sarais, etc., and their employees. ...	1,010	350	347
	33. Other trade in food stuffs ...	16,761	6,362	380
116	Fish dealers ...	2,895	1,483	512
117	Grocers and sellers of vegetable oil, salt and other condiments ...	4,805	557	116
119	Sellers of sweet meats, sugar, gur and molasses ...	891	921	1,030
120	Cardamom, betel leaf, vegetables, fruit and arecanut sellers ...	3,262	847	260
121	Grain and pulse dealers ...	3,812	2,015	529
	41. Trade of other sorts ...	4,234	436	103
135	Shop keepers otherwise unspecified ...	3,929	416	106
	VI. PUBLIC FORCE ...	700	...	...
	VII. PUBLIC ADMINISTRATION	3,507	224	64
	45. Public administration ...	3,507	224	64
145	Service of Native and Foreign States	2,772	214	77
	VIII. PROFESSIONS AND LIBERAL ARTS	9,457	1,616	171
	46. Religion ...	3,484	938	269
151	Temple, burial or burning ground service, pilgrim conductors, circumcisers ...	2,164	779	360
	48. Medicine ...	1,280	195	152
154	Medical practitioners of all kinds including dentists, oculists and veterinary surgeons ...	1,203	55	46
	49. Instruction ...	2,289	308	35
156	Professors and teachers of all kinds and clerks and servants connected with education ...	2,289	308	135
	50. Letters and arts and sciences ...	1,819	175	96
160	Music composers and masters, players on all kinds of musical instruments (not military), singers, actors, dancers....	1,151	172	149
	IX. PERSONS LIVING ON THEIR INCOME ...	326	16	49
	X. DOMESTIC SERVICE ...	2,351	1,516	645
	52. Domestic service ...	2,351	1,516	645
162	Cooks, water carriers, door keepers, watchmen and other indoor servants ...	2,073	1,510	728
	XI. INSUFFICIENTLY DESCRIBED OCCUPATIONS ...	22,306	7,045	316
	53. General terms which do not indicate a definite occupation ...	22,306	7,045	316
165	Cashiers, accountants, book keepers, clerks and other employees in unspecified offices, warehouses and shops ...	1,600	125	78
167	Labourers and workmen otherwise unspecified ...	20,187	6,920	339
	XII. UNPRODUCTIVE ...	1,008	872	865
	55. Beggars, vagrants, prostitutes,...	900	865	961
169	Beggars, vagrants, procurers, prostitutes, receivers of stolen goods, cattle poisoners ...	900	865	961

SUBSIDIARY TABLE VII.

Selected occupations 1911 *and* 1901.

Group No.	Occupation	Population supported in 1911	Population supported in 1901	Percentage of variation
1	2	3	4	5
	SUB CLASS I.—Exploitation of the surface of the Earth ...	483,904	433,883	+ 12
	Order 1.—Pasture and Agriculture. ...	**470.607**	**421 290**	+ 12
1	Income from rent of agricultural land ...	62.143	14.084	+ 341
2	Ordinary cultivators ...	208.822	192.072	+ 9
3	Agents, managers of landed estates (not planters), clerks, rent collectors, etc. ...	1,507	1.966	— 23
4	Farm servants and field labourers ...	167,406	178,280	— 6
5	Tea, coffee, cinchona, rubber and indigo plantations. ...	3,319	1,934	+ 72
6	Fruit, flower, vegetable, betel, vine, arecanut, etc., growers ...	19,877	23,140	— 14
8	Wood cutters, firewood, lac, catechu, rubber, etc., collectors and charcoal burners ...	4.775	4.771	...
9	Cattle and buffalo breeders and keepers ...	190	221	— 14
10	Sheep, goat and pig breeders ...	65	113	— 42
11	Breeders of other animals (horses, mules, camels, asses, etc). ...	2	281	— 99
12	Herdsmen, shepherds, goatherds, etc. ...	1,683	4,058	— 58
	Order 2.—Fishing and hunting.	**13 297**	**12,593**	+ 6
14	Fishing ...	13,261	12,580	+ 5
15	Hunting ...	36	13	+ 177
	SUB CLASS II.—Extraction of minerals. ...	6	3	+ 100
	Order 3.—Mines. ...	**6**	**3**	+ **100**
	SUB CLASS III.—Industry ...	192,051	172,002	+ 12
	Order 6.—Textiles. ...	**46.823**	**39,684**	+ **18**
22	Cotton spinning, sizing and weaving ...	6,626	6,243	+ 6
24	Rope, twine and string ...	684	...	...
25	Other fibres (cocoanut, aloes, flax, hemp, straw, etc.) ...	39.510	33,415	+ 18
29	Persons occupied with feathers	4	...	...
30	Dyeing, bleaching, printing, preparation and sponging of textiles ...	1	26	— 96
	Order 7.—Hides, skins and hard materials from the Animal kingdom. ...	**1,179**	**272**	+ **33**
32	Tanners, curriers, leather dressers, etc. ...	1	268	— 100
33	Makers of leather articles such as trunks, water bags, etc. ...	1,177	...	...
35	Bone, ivory, horn, shell, etc., workers ...	1	4	— 75
	Order 8.—Wood. ...	**43 232**	**30 598**	+ **41**
36	Sawyers, carpenters, turners and joiners, etc. ...	30,217	21,369	+ 41
37	Basket makers and other industries of wood material including leaves ...	13,015	9,229	+ 41
	Order 9.—Metals. ...	**9 277**	**8,590**	+ **8**
41	Workers in iron and makers of implements and tools, principally or exclusively of iron ...	7,843	6.714	+ 9
42	Workers in brass, copper and bell metal ...	1,425	1,513	+ 6
	Order 10.—Ceramics. ...	**4,198**	**3 512**	+ **19**
47	Potters and earthernpipe and bowl makers ...	3,400	1,772	+ 92
	Order 11.—Chemical products properly so called and analogous ...	4,193	**7,093**	— **41**
53	Manufacture and refining of vegetable and mineral oils ...	3,936	6,873	— 43
	Order 12.—Food Industries. ...	**40 211**	**48 253**	— **17**
56	Rice pounders and huskers and flour grinders ...	15,230	19,530	— 22
57	Bakers and biscuit makers ...	176	98	+ 80
58	Grain parchers etc. ...	224	28	+ 700
59	Butchers ...	467	454	+ 3
60	Fish curers ...	8	...	...
62	Makers of sugar, molasses and gur ...	479	204	+ 53
63	Sweet meat makers, preparers of jam and condiments, etc. ...	15	...	...
64	Brewers and distillers ...	5	77	— 94
65	Toddy drawers ...	23,303	27,593	— 16

SUBSIDIARY TABLE VII. *Cont.*

Selected occupations, 1911 and 1901.

GROUP NO.	OCCUPATION	POPULATION SUPPORTED IN 1911	POPULATION SUPPORTED IN 1901	PERCENTAGE OF VARIATION
1	2	3	4	5
	Order 13.—Industries of dress and the toilet ...	**18,488**	**17,718**	**+ 4**
68	Tailors, milliners, dressmakers and darners, embroiderers on linen	3,954	3,640	+ 9
69	Shoe, boot and sandal makers ...	99	940	— 89
71	Washing, cleaning and dyeing ...	8,701	7,788	+ 12
72	Barbers, hair dressers, and wigmakers ...	6,405	4,367	+ 24
	Order 14.—Furniture Industries. ..	**182**	**42**	**+ 214**
	Order 15.—Building Industries. ..	**13,882**	**8,524**	**+ 89**
77	Excavators, plint builders and well sinkers ...	20	90	— 350
78	Stone and marble workers, masons and bricklayers ...	11,842	7,006	+ 50
79	Others (thatchers, building contractors, house painters, tilers plumbers, locksmiths, etc.) ...	1,129	224	+ 404
	Order 16.—Construction of means of transport ...	**66**	**168**	**— 60**
	Order 17.—Production and transmission of physical forces (heat, light, electricity, motive power, etc.) ...	**1**	..	...
	Order 18.—Industries of luxury and those pertaining to literature and the arts and sciences ...	**7,765**	**6,683**	**+ 16**
89	Workers, in precious stones and metals, enamellers, imitation jewellery makers, gilders, etc. ...	7,145	6,115	+ 17
	Makers of bangles, rosaries, bead and other neck laces, spangles, lingams, and sacred threads ...	82	78	— 59
	Order 19.—Industries concerned with refuse matter ...	**2,985**	**868**	**232**
93	Sweepers, scavengers, dust and sweeping contractors ...	2,985	868	+ 232
	SUB CLASS IV.—Transport ...	18,856	18,250	+ 3
	Order 20.—Transport by water. ...	**6,778**	**10,221**	**— 34**
95	Shipowners and their employees, ship brokers, ships' officers, engineers, mariners, firemen ...	408	2	+ 20,300
96	Persons employed on the maintenance of streams, rivers and canals (including construction) ...	18	2,305	— 99
97	Boatowners, and boatmen and towmen ...	6,347	7,914	— 20
	Order 21.—Transport by road. ...	**10,060**	**7,010**	**+ 43**
98	Persons employed on the construction and maintenance of roads and bridges ...	1,458	2,287	— 36
99	Cartowners and drivers, coachmen, stable boys, tramway, mail-carriage, etc., managers and employees (excluding private servants) ...	7,568	4,569	+ 66
100	Palki, etc., bearers and owners ...	31	94	— 67
102	Porters and messengers ...	993	60	+ 1,555
	Order 22.—Transport by rail. ...	**1,301**	**491**	**+ 165**
103	Railway employees of all kinds other than ordinary labourers ...	1,287	491	+ 162
104	Labourers employed on railway construction ...	14	...	..
	Order 23.—Post office, Telegraph and Telephone services. ...	**732**	**528**	**+ 39**
105	Post office, Telegraph and Telephone services (including Anchal service) ...	732	528	+ 39
	SUB CLASS V.—Trade. ...	105,501	90,186	+ 17
	Order 24.—Banks, establishments of credit, exchange and insurance ...	**4,424**	**3,022**	**+ 46**
106	Bank managers, money lenders, exchange and insurance agents money changers and brokers, and their employees ...	4,424	3,022	+ 46
	Order 25.—Brokerage, commission and export ...	**255**	**320**	**— 20**
107	Brokers, commission agents, commercial travellers, warehouse owners and employees ...	255	320	— 20

SUBSIDIARY TABLE VII.—*Cont.*

Selected occupations 1911 *and* 1901.

GROUP No.	OCCUPATION	POPULATION SUPPORTED IN 1911	POPULATION SUPPORTED IN 1901	PERCENTAGE OF VARIATION
1	2	3	4	5
	Order 26.—Trade in textiles. ...	**5,646**	**6,877**	**— 18**
108	Trade in piece goods, wool, cotton, silk, hair and other textiles ...	5,646	6,877	— 18
	Order 27.—Trade in skins, leather and furs ...	**544**	**295**	**+ 84**
109	Trade in skins, leather, furs, feathers, horn, etc. ...	544	295	+ 84
	Order 28.—Trade in wood ...	**1,305**	**1,245**	**+ 5**
110	Trade in wood (not firewood), cork, bark, etc. ...	1,305	1,245	+ 5
	Order 29.—Trade in metals ...	**321**	...	...
	Order 30.—Trade in pottery ...	**217**	**1,420**	**— 85**
112	Trade in pottery ...	217	1,420	— 85
	Order 31.—Trade in chemical products ...	**842**	**77**	**+ 994**
113	Trade in chemical products (drugs, dyes, paints, petroleum, explosives, etc.) ...	842	77	+ 994
	Order 32.—Hotels, cafes, restaurants, etc. ...	**9,690**	**10,047**	**— 4**
114	Vendors of wine, liquors, aerated waters, etc. ...	6,203	9,440	— 34
115	Owners and managers of hotels, cookshops, sarais, etc., and their employees ...	3,487	607	+ 474
	Order 33.—Other trade in food stuffs ...	**69,5?3**	**68,763**	**+ 1**
116	Fish dealers ...	11,342	9,948	+ 19
117	Grocers and sellers of vegetable, oil, salt and other condiments ...	14,742	21,252	— 31
118	Sellers of milk, butter, ghee, poultry, eggs, etc. ...	1,625	1,311	+ 24
119	Sellers of sweet-meats, sugar, gur and molasses ...	9,842	8,164	+ 21
120	Cardamom, betel-leaf, vegetables, fruit and arecanut sellers ...	11,317	12,222	— 7
121	Grain and pulse dealers ...	13,813	9,182	+ 51
122	Tobacco, opium, ganja, etc. sellers ...	1,340	945	+ 42
123	Dealers in sheep, goats and pigs ...	459	100	+ 359
124	Dealers in hay, grass and fodder ...	563	689	— 18
	Order 34.—Trade in clothing and toilet articles ...	**335**	**930**	**— 64**
125	Trade in readymade clothing and other articles of dress and the toilet (hats, umbrellas, socks, ready-made shoes, perfumes, etc.) ...	336	930	— 64
	Order 35.—Trade in furniture ...	**1,537**	**896**	**+ 72**
127	Trade in hardware, cooking utensils, porcelain, crockery, glassware, bottles, articles for gardening, the cellar, etc. ...	592	551	+ 7
	Order 36.—Trade in building materials ...	**1,585**	**3,210**	**— 51**
128	Trade in building materials (stones, bricks, plaster, cement, sand, tiles, thatch, etc.) ...	1,585	3,210	— 51
	Order 37.—Trade in means of transport ...	**797**	**299**	**+ 167**
129	Dealers and hirers of elephants, camels, horses, cattle, asses, mules, etc., sellers (not makers) of carriages, saddlery, etc. ...	797	299	+ 167
	Order 38.—Trade in fuel ...	**2,043**	**904**	**+ 126**
130	Dealers in fire-wood, charcoal, coal, cowdung, etc. ...	2,043	904	+ 126
	Order 39.—Trade in articles of luxury and those pertaining to letters and the arts and sciences ...	**1,1?8**	**945**	**+ 18**
131	Dealers in precious stones, jewellery (real and imitation) clocks, optical instruments, etc. ...	642	792	+ 8
132	Dealers in common bangles, bead necklaces, fans, small articles toys, hunting and fishing tackle, flowers, etc. ...	346	193	+ 80
	Order 40.—Trade in refuse matter ...	**84**	...	...

SUBSIDIARY TABLE VII.—*Cont.*

Selected occupations 1911 *and* 1901.

Group No.	Occupation	Population supported in 1911	Population supported in 1901	Percentage of variation
1	2	3	4	5
	Order 41.—Trade of other sorts ...	**15,214**	**936**	**+ 1,525**
135	Shop-Keepers otherwise unspecified ...	14,450	776	+ 1,762
138	Other trades (including farmers of pounds, tolls and markets) ...	166	145	+ 14
	SUB CLASS VI.—Public Force ...	1,740	763	+ 128
	Order 42.—Army ...	**576**	**700**	**— 18**
140	Army (Native States) ...	576	700	— 18
	Order 44.—Police ...	**1,164**	**63**	**+ 1,747**
142	Police ...	1,164	63	+ 1,747
	SUB CLASS VII.—Public Administration ...	10,045	8,648	+ 16
	Order 45.—Public Administration ...	**10,045**	**8,648**	**+ 16**
144	Service of the State (British) ...	71	22	+ 223
145	Service of Native and Foreign States ...	8,355	8,513	— 2
146	Municipal and other local (not village) service ...	400	113	+ 254
147	Village officials and servants other than watchmen ...	1,219	...	...
	SUB CLASS VIII.—Professions and liberal arts ...	30,564	24,960	+ 22
	Order 46.—Religion ...	**10,648**	**9,785**	**+ 9**
148	Priests, ministers, etc. ...	2,699	3,367	— 20
149	Religious mendicants, inmates of monasteries, etc. ...	155	155	...
150	Catechists, readers, church and mission service ...	1,332	235	+ 467
151	Temple, burial or burning ground service, pilgrim conductors, circumcisers ...	6,462	6,029	+ 7
	Order 47.—Law ...	**2,163**	**1,106**	**+ 96**
152	Lawyers of all kinds, including Kazis, law agents and mukhtiars.	1,157	954	+ 21
153	Lawyers' clerks, petition writers, etc. ...	1,006	152	+ 562
	Order 48.—Medicine ...	**4,881**	**3,770**	**+ 29**
154	Medical practitioners of all kinds including dentists, oculists and veterinary surgeons ...	4,451	3,493	+ 27
155	Midwives, vaccinators, compounders, nurses, masseurs, etc. ...	430	277	+ 55
	Order 49.—Instruction ...	**7,417**	**4,810**	**+ 54**
156	Professors and teachers of all kinds, and clerks and servants connected with education ...	7,417	4,810	+ 54
	Order 50.—Letters and arts and sciences ...	**5,456**	**5,489**	**— 1**
159	Others (authors, photographers, artists, sculptors, astronomers meteorologists, botanists, astrologers, etc. ...	1,708	1,221	+ 40
160	Music composers and masters, players on all kinds of musical instruments (not military), singers, actors and dancers ...	3,061	2,626	+ 17
	SUB CLASS IX.—Persons living on their income ...	1,129	3,622	— 69
	Order 51.—Persons living principally on their income ...	**1,129**	**3,622**	**— 69**
161	Proprietors (other than of agricultural land) fund and scholarship holders and pensioners ...	1,129	3,622	— 69
	SUB CLASS X.—Domestic service ...	5,573	7,698	— 38
	Order 52.—Domestic service ...	**5,573**	**7,698**	**— 38**
162	Cooks, water carriers, door keepers, watchmen and other indoor servants ...	5,061	7,392	— 30
163	Private grooms, coachmen, dog boys, etc. ...	512	306	+ 67
	SUB CLASS XI.—Insufficiently described occupations ...	66,192	48,674	+ 36
	Order 53.—General terms which do not indicate a definite occupation ...	**66,192**	**48,674**	**+ 36**

SUBSIDIARY TABLE VII.—*Cont.*

Selected occupations 1911 and 1901.

Group No.	Occupation	Population supported in 1911	Population supported in 1901	Percentage of variation
1	2	3	4	5
164	Manufacturers, businessmen and contractors otherwise unspecified	956	399	+ 140
165	Cashiers, accountants, book keepers, clerks and other employees in unspecified offices, warehouses and shops ...	5,148	3,457	+ 49
167	Labourers and workmen otherwise unspecified ...	60,068	44,818	+ 34
	SUB-CLASS XII.—Unproductive ...	2,547	3,336	— 24
	Order 54.—Inmates of jails, asylums and hospitals...	**157**	**297**	**— 47**
168	Inmates of jails, asylums and hospitals ...	157	297	— 47
	Order 55.—Beggars, vagrants, prostitutes ...	**2,390**	**3,039**	**— 21**
169	Beggars, vagrants, procurers, prostitutes, receivers of stolen goods, cattle poisoners ...	2,390	3,039	— 21

SUBSIDIARY TABLE VIII.

Occupations of selected castes.

Caste and occupation	Number per 1000 workers engaged on each occupation	Number of female workers per 100 males
1	2	3
Hindu.		
Ambalavasi—		
Ordinary cultivation ...	183	21
Public administration ...	27	...
Religion ...	562	72
Instruction ...	21	40
Letters and arts and sciences ...	83	...
Other occupations ...	124	50
Arayan—		
Fishing and hunting ...	651	50
Textiles	155	1,178
Trade in food stuffs ...	100	2
Other occupations ...	94	35
Brahman, Malayali.—		
Ordinary cultivation ...	618	6
Religion ...	264	2
Instruction ...	44	...
Other occupations ...	74	9
Brahman, Tamil—		
Ordinary cultivation ...	202	10
Banks, establishment of credit exchange and insurance ...	125	49
Trade in textiles ..	52	...
Hotels, cafes, restaurants, etc. ...	95	16
Other trade in food stuffs ...	75	45
Trade of other sorts ...	34	...
Public administration ..	117	...
Religion ...	73	...
Law ...	15	...
Instruction ...	80	...
Letters and arts and sciences ...	19	...
Other occupations ...	113	6
Brahman, Konkani—		
Ordinary cultivation ...	84	11
Trade in food stuffs ...	290	23
Trade of other sorts ..	260	...
Religion ...	94	3
Domestic service ..	68	9
Other occupations ...	209	8
Brahman, Others.—		
Hotels, cafes and restaurants ...	51	...
Religion ...	648	...
Domestic service ...	103	2
Other occupations ...	198	13
Chakkan.—		
Ordinary cultivation ...	58	65
Chemical products properly so called and analogous ...	388	86
Trade in food stuffs ...	330	8
Other occupations ...	224	28
Devangan.—		
Ordinary cultivation ...	106	53
Textile industries ...	743	42
Other occupations ...	151	105
Iluvan.—		
Ordinary cultivation ...	496	62
Growers of special products and market gardening ...	20	26
Textile industries ...	118	271
Wood industries ...	22	135
Food industries ...	109	86
Hotels, cafes and restaurants ...	24	99
Other trade in food stuffs ...	28	32
Other occupations ...	183	27
Kadupattan.—		
Ordinary cultivation ...	649	52
Food industries ...	61	617
Other occupations ...	290	42
Kaikolan—		
Ordinary cultivation ...	157	20
Textile industries ...	750	66
Other occupations ..	93	76
Kammalan.—		
Ordinary cultivation ...	46	353
Wood industries ...	529	24
Metal industries ...	185	4

SUBSIDIARY TABLE VIII.—*Cont.*

Occupation of selected castes.

Caste and occupation	Number per 1000 workers engaged on each occupation	Number of female workers per 100 males
1	2	3
Building industries	72	7
Industries of luxury and those pertaining to literature and the arts and sciences	102	4
Other occupations	66	125
Kanakkan.—		
Ordinary cultivation	292	122
Fishing and hunting	115	4
Textile industries	151	1,775
Wood do	110	4,767
Transport by water	87	...
Other occupations	245	16
Kaniyan—		
Ordinary cultivation	177	40
Wood industries	49	44
Instruction	190	10
Letters and arts and sciences	300	4
Other occupations	284	62
Kshatriya, Malayali—		
Ordinary cultivation	198	13
Public administration	484	6
Other occupations	318	13
Kshatriya, Others.—		
Trade in food stuffs	85	12
Trade of other sorts	118	9
Domestic service	127	8
Other occupations	670	16
Kudumi Chetti—		
Ordinary cultivation	412	23
Food industries	120	1,441
Other occupations	468	31
Kusavan.—		
Ceramics	901	68
Other occupations	99	82
Nayar.—		
Ordinary cultivation	626	38
Growers of special products and market gardening	27	41
Food industries	51	3,371
Industries concerned with refuse matter	27	2,911
Public administration	56	10
Domestic service	40	35
Other occupations	173	25
Otta Naikkan.—		
Ordinary cultivation	273	122
Transport by road	434	69
Other occupations	293	77
Pandaran—		
Ordinary cultivation	138	31
Trade in food stuffs	573	69
Other occupations	289	69
Panan.—		
Ordinary cultivation	142	168
Wood industries	525	81
Building industries	131	3
Other occupations	202	49
Pandi Tattan.—		
Industries of luxury and those pertaining to literature and the arts and sciences	828	...
Other occupations	172	135
Parayan—		
Ordinary cultivation	326	89
Wood industries	614	64
Other occupations	60	25
Pulayan.—		
Ordinary cultivation	930	93
Textile industries	23	33,638
Other occupations	47	82
Valan.—		
Fishing and hunting	391	...
Textile industries	177	192
Transport by water	63	...
Trade in food stuffs	320	690
Other occupations	49	32
Velan.—		
Industries of dress and the toilet	703	172
Medicine	67	...
Other occupations	230	216
Velakkattalavan.—		
Ordinary cultivation	94	40
Industries of dress and the toilet	834	52
Medicine	43	6,600
Other occupations	29	83
Vellalan.—		
Ordinary cultivation	548	54
Trade in food stuffs	136	300
Other occupations	316	23
Veluttedan.—		
Ordinary cultivation	78	18
Industries of dress and the toilet	911	125
Other occupations	11	28
Vettuvan.—		
Ordinary cultivation	833	100
Other occupations	167	132
Musalman.		
Jonakan.—		
Ordinary cultivation	316	58
Textile industries	73	529
Trade in food stuffs	236	12
Other occupations	375	22
Ravuttan.—		
Ordinary cultivation	334	79
Transport by road	78	...
Trade in food stuffs	257	18
Other occupations	331	57
Christian.		
Anglo-Indian.—		
Ordinary cultivation	89	42
Textile industries	108	447
Wood industries	229	3
Metal industries	82	...
Industries of dress and the toilet	117	173
Transport by rail	35	...
Letters and arts and sciences	69	2
Other occupations	271	25
European.—		
Growers of special products and market gardening	192	...
Public administration	77	...
Religion	558	16
Other occupations	173	...
Native Christian.—		
Ordinary cultivation	369	30
Growers of special products and market gardening	28	13
Fishing and hunting	23	7
Textile industries	115	146
Wood industries	38	5
Food industries	43	766
Building industries	15	1
Transport by water	17	1
Trade in food stuffs	85	31
Trade of other sorts	31	15
Other occupations	236	23
Animist.		
Malayan.—		
Ordinary cultivation	576	87
Growers of special products and market gardening	67	...
Forestry	195	59
Other occupations	162	91
Jew.—		...
Ordinary cultivation	50	
Industries of dress and the toilet	180	2,600
Hotels, cafes and restaurants	40	...
Other trade in food stuffs	426	27
Trade of other sorts	62	5
Other occupations	242	15

SUBSIDIARY TABLE IX.

Number of persons employed on the 16th March on Railways and in the Irrigation, Post Office and Telegraph Departments.

Class of persons employed.	Europeans and Anglo-Indians.	Indians.	Remarks.
Railways.			
TOTAL PERSONS EMPLOYED.	9	305	
Persons directly employed.			
Officers	...	1	
Subordinates drawing more than Rs. 75 per mensem ...	2	...	
Do from Rs. 20 to 75 do ...	6	26	
Do under Rs. 20 do ...	1	229	
Persons indirectly employed.			
Contractors	...	33 *	
Contractors' regular employees	...	3	
Coolies	...	13	
Irrigation Department.			
TOTAL PERSONS EMPLOYED.	2	275	
Persons directly employed.			
Officers	1	3	
Upper subordinates	...	4	
Lower ,, ...	...	7	
Clerks	...	...	
Peons and other servants...	..	26	
Coolies	...	68	
Persons indirectly employed.			
Contractors	1	28	
Contractors' regular employees	...	7	
Coolies	...	132	
Postal Department.			
TOTAL.	1	96	
Supervising Officers	...	1	
Post Masters	1	7	
Miscellaneous Agents	...	18	
Clerks	...	6	
Postmen, etc.	...	39	
Road Establishment	...	18	
Railway mail service :—			
Supervising officers	...	...	
Clerks and Sorters	...	..	
Mail guards, etc.	...	...	
Combined offices :—			
Signallers	...	...	
Messengers etc.	...	6	
Telegraph Department.			
TOTAL	3	25	
Administrative Establishment	...	...	
Signalling ,, ...	3	7	
Clerks	...	2	
Skilled labour	..	...	
Unskilled labour	...	...	
Messengers, etc.	...	16	
Cochin Forest Tramway.			
TOTAL	17	369	
Persons directly employed.			
Officers	2	...	
Subordinates drawing more than Rs. 75 per mensem ...	2	2	
,, from Rs. 20 to 75 per mensem ...	12	38	
,, under Rs. 20 do ...	1	271	
Persons indirectly employed.			
Contractors	...	6	
Contractors' regular employees	...	2	
Coolies	...	50	
Cochin Anchal Department.			
TOTAL	...	181	
Supervising officers	...	1	
Anchal Masters	...	45	
Miscellaneous Agents	...	2	
Clerks	...	12	
Postmen and other servants	...	84	
Road Establishment	...	37	

PART II.

IMPERIAL TABLES.

TABLE I.

AREA, HOUSES AND POPULATION.

Since the census of 1901, the Taluks of Cochin and Kanayannur were amalgamated, but without any re-distribution of territory.

TABLE I.

Area, Houses and Population.

Taluks.	Area in square miles.	Towns.	Villages.	Occupied Houses.			Population.								
							Persons.			Males.			Females.		
				Total.	In Towns.	In Villages.	Total.	Urban.	Rural.	Total.	Urban.	Rural.	Total.	Urban.	Rural.
1	2	3	4	5	6	7	8	9	10	11	12	13	14	15	16
Cochin State.	1,361	9	273	163,286	17,744	145,542*	918,110	108,952	809,158	457,342	57,236	400,106	460,768	52,716	408,052
Cochin-Kanayannur	143	3	37	48,094	7,901	40,193	264,828	49,679	215,149	136,622	27,271	109,351	128,206	22,408	105,798
Cranganur	19	...	5	6,111	...	6,111	33,193	...	33,193	16,856	...	16,856	16,337	...	16,337
Mukundapuram	418	1	60	34,097	1,404	32,693	193,930	8,699	185,231	96,143	4,402	91,741	97,787	4,297	93,490
Trichur	225	1	72	28,502	3,628	24,874	169,756	23,574	146,182	83,520	12,089	71,431	86,236	11,485	74,751
Talapilli	271	1	74	28,414	1,426	26,988	165,114	8,336	156,778	80,126	4,064	76,062	84,988	4,272	80,716
Chittur	285	3	35	18,068	3,385	14,683	91,289	19,664	71,625	44,075	9,410	34,665	47,214	10,254	36,960

* This includes houses in Reserved Forests which are outside the Village area.

TABLE II.

VARIATION IN POPULATION SINCE 1875.

The first systematic census of the State was taken in 1875, and not in 1872 as in British India.

TABLE II

Variation in Population since 1875.

TABLE II.

Variation in Population since 1875.

TALUKS.	PERSONS					MALES.					FEMALES.					VARIATION, INCREASE (+) DECREASE (—)				NET VARIATION IN PERIOD 1875-1911 INCREASE (+) DECREASE (—)
	1911	1901	1891	1881	1875	1911	1901	1891	1881	1875	1911	1901	1891	1881	1875	1901 to 1911	1891 to 1901	1881 to 1891	1875 to 1881	
1	2	3	4	5	6	7	8	9	10	11	12	13	14	15	16	17	18	19	20	21
Cochin State ..	**918,110**	**812,025**	**722,906**	**600,278**	**601,114**	**457,342**	**405,200**	**361,904**	**301,815**	**302,873**	460,768	**406,825**	**361,002**	**298,463**	**298,741**	**+106,085**	**+ 89,119**	**+122,628**	**— 836**	**+316,996**
Cochin-Kanayannur ...	**264,828**	235,084	207,615	178,605	187,584	**136,622**	121,016	106,850	91,466	95,678	**128,206**	114,068	100,765	87,139	91,706	+ **29,744**	+27,469	+ 29,010	— 8,979	+ **77,244**
Cranganur ...	**33,198**	29,140	27,965	20,950	20,397	**16,866**	14,710	14,111	10,634	10,759	**16,337**	14,430	13,854	10,316	9,638	+ **4,058**	+ 1,175	+ 7,015	+ 553	+ **12,796**
Mukundapuram ..	**193,930**	161,833	145,690	115,212	114,974	**96,143**	80,335	72,814	58,351	57,606	**97,787**	81,498	72,876	56,861	57,368	+ **32,097**	+ 16,143	+ 30,478	+ 288	+ **78,956**
Trichur ...	**169,756**	145,104	128,957	104,695	101,742	**83,520**	71,647	63,980	51,766	50,430	**86,236**	73,457	64,977	52,929	51,312	+ **24,652**	+ 16,147	+ 24,262	+ 2,953	+ **68,014**
Talapilli ...	**165,114**	151,815	133,894	113,114	110,465	**80,126**	73,886	65,719	56,528	55,073	**84,988**	77,429	68,175	56,586	55,392	+ **13,299**	+ 17,421	+ 20,780	+ 2,649	+ **54,649**
Chittur ..	**91,289**	89,549	78,785	67,702	65,952	**44,075**	43,606	38,430	33,070	32,627	**47,214**	45,943	40,355	34,632	33,325	+ **1,740**	+ 10,764	+ 11,083	+ 1,750	+ **25,337**

TABLE III.

TOWNS AND VILLAGES CLASSIFIED BY POPULATION.

The State was surveyed cadastrally since the census of 1901, and split up into 278 survey villages, more or less uniform in size. Before the survey, it was divided into 652 *Desams* varying very much in extent.

TABLE III.

COCHIN STATE. IMPERIAL SERIES.

Towns and Villages classified by Population.

TALUKS.	Total number of inhabited Towns.	Total number of inhabited Villages.	Population.	UNDER 500. Number	UNDER 500. Population	500—1000. Number	500—1000. Population	1000—2000. Number	1000—2000. Population	2000—5000. Number	2000—5000. Population	5000—10000. Number	5000—10000. Population	10000-20000. Number	10000-20000. Population	20000-50000. Number	20000-50000. Population	Encampments Boat and Railway Population Unclassed. Population	Remarks
1	2	3	4	5	6	7	8	9	10	11	12	13	14	15	16	17	18	19	20
Cochin State.	9	273	918,110	9	2,578	24	18,480	78	117,272	130	412,645	30	208,541	8	92,709	3	68,277	2,618	
Cochin-Kanayannur ..	3	37	264,828	1	400	2	1,601	4	7,232	12	44,112	12	84,135	7	82,645	2	44,708	..	
Cranganur	...	5	38,193	..	..	..	..	..	..	1	2,739	3	20,390	1	10,064	..	..	..	
Mukundapuram ..	1	60	198,980	..	..	3	2,527	12	18,562	39	127,712	7	43,845	..	..	..	..	1,284	
Trichur	1	72	169,786	6	1,579	6	4,807	31	46,228	28	87,715	1	5,858	..	..	1	28,574	..	
Talapilli	1	74	165,114	..	..	10	7,633	26	38,240	37	105,715	2	13,526	..	..	..	..	..	
Chittur	3	25	91,239	2	594	3	1,912	5	7,010	13	44,652	5	35,792	..	..	..	..	1,329	

TABLE IV.

TOWNS CLASSIFIED BY POPULATION, WITH VARIATION SINCE 1875.

Urban population was separately censused for the first time in 1891. The figures given in columns 7 and 8 are only approximate.

Tripunittura and Nemmara were for the first time treated as towns in 1911.

TABLE IV.

COCHIN STATE. IMPERIAL SERIES.

Towns classified by population, with variation since 1875.

TOWN.	TALUK.	MUNICIPALITY, SUBURBS, CANTONMENTS, ETC.	POPULATION.					VARIATION INCREASE (+) DECREASE (—).				Variation in period 1875 to 1911 Increase (+) Decrease (—).	MALES.			FEMALES.		
			1911.	1901.	1891.	1881.	1875.	1901 to 1911.	1891 to 1901.	1881 to 1891.	1875 to 1881.		1911.	1901.	1891	1911	1901.	1891.
1	2	3	4	5	6	7	8	9	10	11	12	13	14	15	16	17	18	19
Cochin State..			**109,952**	**87,478**	**78,666**	**68,682**	**59,924**	**+22,474**	**+13,813**	**+9,983**	**+3,758**	**+50,028**	**57,236**	**46,389**	**37,757**	**52,716**	**42,089**	**35,908**
Trichur ...	Trichur ...	Municipality	**23,874**	15,585	12,945	10,822	11,109	+7,989	+2,640	+2,123	— 287	**+12,465**	**12,089**	7,932	6,592	**11,485**	7,653	6,353
Mattancheri ...	Cochin-Kanayanur ...	Do.	**23,508**	20,061	17,254	14,624	13,775	+3,447	+2,807	+2,620	+ 859	**+ 9,733**	**12,625**	10,687	9,028	**10,883**	9,374	8,226
Ernakulam ...	Cochin-Kanayanur ...	Do.	**21,195**	21,901	17,870	15,467	14,038	— 706	+4,031	+2,403	+1,429	**+7,157**	**11,944**	12,205	9,529	**9,251**	9,696	8,341
Irinjalakuda ...	Mukundapuram ...	...	**8,699**	8,420	7,334	6,606	5,204	+ 279	+1,086	+ 728	+1,402	**+ 3,495**	**4,402**	4,198	3,723	**4,297**	4,227	3,611
Chittur ...	Chittur ...	...	**8,528**	8,095	7,496	6,698	6,509	+ 433	+ 599	+ 798	+ 189	**+ 2,019**	**4,078**	3,897	3,575	**4,450**	4,198	3,921
Kunnamkulam...	Talapilli ...	...	**8,336**	7,194	5,632	4,988	4,399	+1,142	+1,562	+ 644	+ 589	**+ 3,937**	**4,064**	3,438	2,741	**4,272**	3,696	2,891
Tattamangalam..	Chittur ...	...	**6,178**	6,222	5,134	4,467	4,890	— 44	+1,088	+ 667	— 423	**+1,288**	**2,932**	2,977	2,569	**3,246**	3,245	2,565
Tripunittura ...	Cochin-Kanayannur .	...	**4,976**	...	...	...	...	+4,976	...	...	...	**+ 4,976**	**2,702**	...	...	**2,274**	...	...
Nemmara ...	Chittur ...	...	**4,958**	...	...	...	...	+4,958	...	...	...	**+ 4,958**	**2,400**	...	...	**2,558**	...	...

TABLE V.

TOWNS ARRANGED TERRITORIALLY WITH POPULATION BY RELIGION.

TABLE V.

Towns arranged territorially with Population by Religion.

TOWN	TALUK	POPULATION			HINDU			CHRISTIAN			MUSALMAN			JEW			PARSI			JAIN		
		Persons	Males	Females	Persons	Males	Females	Persons	Males	Females	Persons	Males	Females	Persons	Males	Females	Persons	Males	Females	Persons	Males	Females
1	2	3	4	5	6	7	8	9	10	11	12	13	14	15	16	17	18	19	20	21	22	23
Cochin State		**109,952**	**57,236**	**52,716**	**63,497**	**33,237**	**30,260**	**35,067**	**17,880**	**17,187**	**10,337**	**5,541**	**4,796**	**918**	**443**	**475**	**5**	**3**	**2**	**128**	**82**	**46**
Mattancheri ...	Cochin-Kanayannur ...	23,508	12,625	10,883	10,927	5,928	4,999	6,143	3,330	2,813	5,883	3,092	2,791	428	194	234	...	...	...	127	81	46
Ernakulam ...	do ...	21,195	11,944	9,251	11,165	6,521	4,644	8,593	4,561	4,032	948	613	335	488	248	240	...	...	...	1	1	...
Tripunithura $ ...	do ...	4,976	2,702	2,274	3,877	2,121	1,756	995	518	477	104	63	41	...	...	...	...	...	...	...	...	...
Irinjalakuda ...	Mukundapuram ...	8,699	4,402	4,297	4,939	2,510	2,429	3,234	1,626	1,608	526	266	260	...	...	...	...	...	...	...	...	...
Trichur ...	Trichur ...	23,574	12,089	11,485	12,147	6,346	5,801	10,351	5,153	5,198	1,069	586	483	2	1	1	5	3	2	...	...	...
Kunnankulam ...	Talapilli ...	8,336	4,061	4,272	2,730	1,387	1,343	5,561	2,646	2,915	45	31	14	...	...	...	...	...	...	...	...	...
Chittur ...	Chittur ...	8,528	4,078	4,450	8,248	3,943	4,305	125	61	64	155	74	81	...	...	...	...	...	...	..	...	...
Tattamangalam ...	do ...	6,178	2,932	3,246	4,788	2,239	2,549	34	18	16	1,356	675	681	...	...	...	...	...	...	...	...	...
Nemmara $ ...	do ...	4,958	2,400	2,558	4,676	2,242	2,434	31	17	14	251	141	110	...	...	...	...	...	...	...	...	...

These were treated as towns for the first time in 1911.

TABLE V.
Towns arranged territorially with Population by Religion.

TABLE VI.

RELIGION.

COCHIN STATE.

TABLE VI.

RELIGION.

IMPERIAL SERIES.

Name of Taluk.	Population.			Hindu.			Musalman.			Christian.			Animist.			Jew.			Parsi.			Brahmo.			Jain.		
	Persons.	Males.	Females.	Persons.	Males.	Females.	Persons.	Males.	Females.	Persons.	Males.	Females.	Persons.	Males.	Females.	Persons.	Males.	Females	Persons.	Males.	Females.	Persons.	Males.	Females.	Persons.	Males.	Females.
1	2	3	4	5	6	7	8	9	10	11	12	13	14	15	16	17	18	19	20	21	22	23	24	25	26	27	28
Cochin State..	**918,110**	**457,342**	**460,768**	**615,708**	**304,002**	**311,706**	**63,822**	**32,707**	**31,115**	**233,092**	**117,848**	**115,244**	**4,177**	**2,127**	**2,050**	**1,175**	**571**	**604**	**5**	**3**	**2**	**2**	**1**	**1**	**129**	**83**	**46**
Cochin-Kanayannur ...	**264,828**	136,622	128,206	**144,927**	74,807	70,120	**15,715**	8,374	7,341	**102,834**	52,771	50,063	**159**	73	86	**1,063**	514	549	...	...	...	2	1	1	**128**	82	46
Cranganur ...	**33,193**	16,856	16,337	**23,104**	11,659	11,445	**8,376**	4,276	4,100	**1,713**	921	792	...	...	...	...	...	...	...	...	...	...	...	...	...	...	...
Mukundapuram..	**193,930**	96,143	97,787	**125,978**	62,145	64,833	**9,791**	5,130	4,661	**55,990**	28,272	27,718	**1,061**	540	521	**110**	56	54	...	...	...	...	...	...	...	...	...
Trichur ...	**169,756**	83,520	86,236	**119,083**	58,389	60,694	**5,618**	2,881	2,737	**44,775**	22,130	22,645	**323**	166	157	**2**	1	1	5	3	2	...	...	...	...	...	...
Talapilli ...	**165,114**	80,126	84,988	**124,918**	60,189	64,729	**17,052**	8,442	8,610	**22,927**	11,372	11,555	**216**	122	94	...	...	...	...	...	...	...	...	...	1	1	...
Chittur ...	**91,289**	44,075	47,214	**76,748**	36,863	39,885	**7,270**	3,604	3,666	**4,853**	2,382	2,471	**2,418**	1,226	1,192	...	...	...	...	...	...	...	...	...	...	...	...

TABLE VII.

ALL RELIGIONS.

Age, Sex and Civil Condition.

Note:—The table for all religions includes 5 Parsis and 2 Brabmos. Their age, sex and civil condition are shown below:—

		Unmarried.		*Married.*		*Widowed.*	
		Male.	Female.	Male.	Female.	Male.	Female.
Parsi ...	25—30 ...	1	...	...	1	...	...
	35—40 ...	...	...	...	1	...	...
	40—45 ...	...	...	1	...	...	...
	45—50 ...	...	...	1	...	...	...
Brahmo ...	30—35 ...	...	...	...	1	...	...
	35—40 ...	...	...	1	...	...	...

TABLE VII.

ALL RELIGIONS.

Age, Sex and Civil Condition.

AGE.	POPULATION.			UNMARRIED.			Married			WIDOWED.		
	Persons	Males	Females	Persons	Males	Females	Persons	Males	Females	Persons	Males	Females
1	2	3	4	5	6	7	8	9	10	11	12	13
0— 1 ...	32 231	16,027	16,204	32 231	16,027	16,204	...	...	...	...	...	...
1— 2 ...	25,944	12,996	12,948	25,944	12,996	12,948	...	...	...	...	...	...
2— 3 ...	27,891	13,986	13,955	27,891	13,936	13,955	...	...	...	...	...	...
3— 4 ...	24,741	12,188	12,553	24,741	12,188	12,553	...	...	...	...	...	...
4— 5 ...	23,665	12,039	11,626	23,665	12,039	11,626	...	...	...	...	...	...
TOTAL 0— 5 ...	134,472	67,186	67,286	134,472	67,186	[illegible],286	...	...	...	...	...	...
5—10 ...	117,171	59,507	57,664	116,987	59,483	[illegible],504	176	24	152	8	...	8
10—15 ...	111,609	57,463	54,146	106,416	57,166	49,250	5 058	292	4,766	135	5	130
15—20 ...	91,327	45,416	45,911	59,039	40,605	1[illegible],434	30 990	4,650	26,340	1,298	161	1,137
20—25 ...	87,538	41,361	46,177	21,530	20,439	[illegible],091	50 291	20,180	30,111	3,717	742	2,975
25—30 ...	79 346	37,919	41,427	8 264	6,717	1,547	65 852	30,119	35,733	5,230	1,083	4,147
30—35 ...	67,275	33,786	33,489	3,287	2,423	864	56,899	29,950	26,949	7,089	1,413	5,676
35—40 ...	57,384	30,517	26,867	1,635	1,163	472	47,503	27,839	19,704	8,186	1,495	6,691
40—45 ...	47,784	24,307	23,477	1,065	711	354	35 835	21,897	13,938	10,684	1,099	9,185
45—50 ...	34,331	17,994	16,337	607	423	184	21 471	15,889	8,585	9,270	1,682	7,588
50—55 ...	31,426	14,849	16,577	451	290	161	18,573	12,518	6,055	12,402	2,011	10,361
55—60 ...	19,186	9,610	9,577	219	149	70	10 775	7,762	3,013	8,2[illegible]2	1,708	6,494
60—65 ...	19,613	8,676	10,937	215	130	85	8,406	6,413	1,993	10,962	2,133	8,859
65—70 ...	8,316	4,050	4,266	86	60	26	3 389	2,821	568	4,841	1,169	3,672
70 and over ...	11 302	4,692	6,610	130	73	57	3 138	2,660	478	8,039	1,959	6,080
TOTAL ...	918,110	457,342	460,768	457,403	257,018	200,385	370,414	183,034	187,380	90 238	17,230	73,008

TABLE VII.

HINDU.

Age, Sex and Civil Condition.

Age	Population			Unmarried			Married			Widowed		
	Persons	Males	Females	Persons	Males	Females	Persons	Males	Females	Persons	Males	Females
1	2	3	4	5	6	7	8	9	10	11	12	13
0—1 ...	21,232	10,547	10,685	21,232	10,547	10,685	...	...	...	...	...	...
1—2 ...	16,964	8,493	8,471	16,964	8,493	8,471	...	...	...	...	...	...
2—3 ...	17,915	8,968	8,947	17,915	8,968	8,947	...	...	...	...	...	...
3—4 ...	16,044	7,857	8,187	16,044	7,857	8,187	...	...	...	...	...	...
4—5 ...	15,306	7,774	7,532	15,306	7,774	7,532	...	...	...	...	...	...
TOTAL 0—5 ...	87,461	43,639	43,822	87,461	43,639	43,822	...	...	...	...	...	...
5—10 ...	75,969	38,672	37,297	75,860	38,664	37,196	102	8	94	7	...	7
10—15 ...	73,496	37,657	35,839	69,872	37,496	32,376	3,519	158	3,361	105	3	102
15—20 ...	61,684	30,281	31,403	40,590	27,520	13,070	20,031	2,639	17,392	1,063	122	941
20—25 ...	58,793	27,629	31,164	17,762	14,767	2,995	38,024	12,280	25,744	3,007	582	2,425
25—30 ...	53,644	25,170	28,171	6,196	5,113	1,083	43,343	19,530	23,813	4,105	827	3,278
30—35 ...	46,115	22,814	23,301	2,467	1,882	585	38,134	19,844	18,290	5,514	1,088	4,426
35—40 ...	39,046	20,426	18,620	1,202	884	318	31,698	18,446	13,252	6,146	1,096	5,050
40—45 ...	32,890	16,170	16,420	751	535	216	24,246	14,763	9,483	7,893	1,172	6,721
45—50 ...	23,655	12,230	11,425	425	308	117	16,551	10,780	5,771	6,680	1,142	5,538
50—55 ...	22,057	10,245	11,812	304	200	104	12,735	8,636	4,099	9,018	1,409	7,609
55—60 ...	13,225	6,466	6,759	149	104	45	7,229	5,251	1,975	5,847	1,108	4,739
60—65 ...	13 886	6,017	7,869	147	94	53	5,681	4,436	1,245	8,058	1,487	6,571
65—70 ...	5 858	2,757	3,101	54	39	15	2,285	1,908	377	3,519	810	2,709
70 and over ...	7,928	3,229	4,699	85	45	37	2,171	1,869	302	5,672	1,312	4,360
TOTAL ...	616,708	301,002	[illegible]	303,323	171,293	132,032	245,749	120,551	125,198	66,364	12,158	54,476

TABLE VII.
HINDU.
Age, Sex and Civil Condition.

TABLE VII.

JAIN.

Age, Sex, and Civil Condition.

AGE	POPULATION			UNMARRIED			MARRIED			WIDOWED		
	Persons	Males	Females	Persons	Males	Females	Persons	Males	Females	Persons	Males	Females
1	2	3	4	5	6	7	8	9	10	11	12	13
0—1 ...	2	...	2	2	...	2	...	...	...	...	...	...
1—2 ...	1	1	...	1	1	...	...	...	...	...	...	...
2—3 ...	2	...	2	2	...	2	...	...	...	...	...	...
3—4 ...	1	1	...	1	1	...	...	...	...	...	...	...
4—5 ...	1	...	1	1	...	1	...	...	...	...	...	...
TOTAL 0—5 ...	7	2	5	7	2	5	...	...	...	...	...	..
5—10 ...	7	3	4	7	3	4	...	...	...	..	...	...
10—15 ...	19	14	5	15	13	2	4	1	3	...	...	...
15—20 ...	9	5	4	5	5	...	4	...	4	...	...	...
20—25 ...	17	11	6	3	3	...	14	8	6	...	...	...
25—30 ...	21	13	8	3	3	...	15	8	7	3	2	1
30—35 ...	15	9	6	...	...	...	14	8	6	1	1	...
35—40 ...	14	8	6	...	...	...	12	8	4	2	...	2
40—45 ...	9	9	...	...	...	...	7	7	...	2	2	...
45—50 ...	7	6	1	...	...	...	6	6	...	1	...	1
50—55 ...	1	1	...	...	...	...	1	1	...	...	...	...
55—60 ...	...	...	...	...	...	...	..	...	...	...	...	...
60—65 ...	1	1	...	...	...	...	1	1	...	...	...	...
65—70 ...	...	...	...	...	...	...	..	...	...	...	...	...
70 and over ...	2	1	1	...	...	...	..	...	...	2	1	1
TOTAL ...	129	83	46	40	29	11	78	48	30	11	6	5

TABLE VII.

COCHIN STATE. IMPERIAL SERIES.

MUSALMAN.

Age, Sex and Civil Condition.

Age	Population.			Unmarried.			Married			Widowed.		
	Persons	Males	Females	Persons	Males	Females	Persons	Males	Females	Persons	Males	Females
1	2	3	4	5	6	7	8	9	10	11	12	13
0—1 ..	**2,326**	1,158	1,168	**2,326**	1,158	1,168	..	..	..	..	..	..
1—2 ..	**1,815**	933	882	**1,815**	933	882	..	..	..	..	..	..
2—3 ..	**2,098**	1,056	1,042	**2 098**	1,056	1,042	..	..	..	..	..	..
3—4 ..	**1,759**	860	899	**1,759**	860	899	..	..	..	..	..	..
4—5 ..	**1,778**	929	849	**1,778**	929	849	..	..	..	..	..	..
TOTAL 0—5 ..	**9,776**	4,936	4,840	**9,776**	4,936	4,840	..	..	..	..	..	..
5—10 ..	**8,509**	4,325	4,184	**8,507**	4,325	4,182	**2**	..	2	..	..	..
10—15 ..	**8.179**	4,308	3,871	**7,876**	4,299	3.577	**290**	9	281	**13**	..	13
15—20 ..	**6,489**	3,262	3,227	**4 279**	3,021	1,258	**2,112**	229	1,883	**98**	12	86
20—25 ..	**6,291**	3,026	3,265	**1,975**	1,720	255	**4,067**	1,255	2,812	**249**	51	198
25—30 ..	**5,461**	2,660	2,801	**599**	516	83	**4,559**	2,076	2,483	**303**	68	235
30—35 ..	**4,682**	2,466	2,216	**177**	131	46	**4,083**	2,261	1,822	**422**	74	348
35—40 ..	**3,776**	2,105	1,671	**71**	44	27	**3,205**	1,978	1,227	**500**	83	417
40—45 ..	**3,331**	1,763	1,568	**60**	26	34	**2,577**	1,656	921	**694**	81	613
45—50 ..	**2,083**	1,177	906	**19**	13	6	**1,589**	1,090	499	**475**	74	401
50—55 ..	**1,992**	1,007	985	**23**	14	9	**1,274**	892	382	**695**	101	594
55—60 ..	**1,071**	579	492	**5**	4	1	**680**	513	167	**386**	62	324
60—65 ..	**1.209**	590	619	**6**	4	2	**611**	476	135	**592**	110	482
65—70 ..	**426**	248	178	**3**	..	3	**211**	192	19	**212**	56	156
70 and over ..	**547**	255	292	**6**	1	5	**179**	162	17	**362**	92	270
TOTAL ..	**63,822**	32,707	31,115	**33,382**	19,054	14,328	**25,439**	12,789	12,650	**5,001**	804	4,137

TABLE VII.
CHRISTIAN.

COCHIN STATE. IMPERIAL SERIES

Age, Sex and Civil Condition.

AGE	POPULATION			UNMARRIED			MARRIED			WIDOWED		
	Persons	Males	Females	Persons	Males	Females	Persons	Males	Females	Persons	Males	Females
1	2	3	4	5	6	7	8	9	10	11	12	13
0—1 ..	8,470	4,217	4,253	8,470	4,217	4,253	..	..	..	..	..	..
1—2 ..	7,081	3,533	3,548	7,081	3,533	3,548	...	..	..	..	..	..
2—3 ..	7,723	3,836	3,887	7,723	3,836	3,887	..	..	..	..	..	..
3—4 ..	6,780	3,401	3,379	6,780	3,401	3,379	..	..	..	..	..	..
4—5 ..	6,428	3,252	3,176	6,428	3,252	3,176	..	..	..	..	..	..
TOTAL 0—5 ..	35,482	18,239	18,243	35,482	18,239	18,243	..	..	..	..	..	..
5—10 ..	32,053	16,171	15,882	31,980	16,155	15,825	72	16	56	1	..	1
10—15 ..	29,316	15,182	14,134	28,076	15,057	13,019	1,223	123	1,100	17	2	15
15—20 ..	22,663	11,628	11,035	13,839	9,838	4,001	8,691	1,763	6,928	133	27	106
20—25 ..	21,880	10,474	11,406	4,625	3,835	790	16,814	6,532	10,282	441	107	334
25—30 ..	19,732	9,553	10,179	1,409	1,036	373	17,524	8,383	9,101	799	184	615
30—35 ..	16,034	8,274	7,760	619	390	229	14,297	7,646	6,651	1,118	238	880
35—40 ..	14,184	7,780	6,404	354	229	125	12,331	7,243	5,088	1,499	308	1,191
40—45 ..	11,230	5,881	5,349	248	144	101	8,734	5,302	3,432	2,248	435	1,813
45—50 ..	8,389	4,457	3,932	159	99	60	6,160	3,902	2,258	2,070	456	1,614
50—55 ..	7,171	3,493	3,678	120	75	45	4,421	2,897	1,524	2,630	521	2,109
55—60 ..	4,789	2,506	2,283	64	40	24	2,791	1,943	848	1,934	523	1,411
60—65 ..	4,404	2,011	2,393	61	32	29	2,052	1,455	597	2,291	524	1,767
65—70 ..	1,993	1,018	975	28	20	8	871	701	170	1,094	297	797
70 and over ..	2,772	1,181	1,591	38	24	14	762	610	152	1,972	547	1,425
TOTAL ..	233,092	117,848	115,244	118,102	65,213	52,889	96,743	48,466	48,277	18,247	4,169	14,078

COCHIN STATE. IMPERIAL SERIES

TABLE VII.

JEW.

Age, Sex and Civil condition.

TABLE V11. JEW. Age, sex and Civil Condition

AGE	POPULATION.			UNMARRIED.			MARRIED.			WIDOWED.		
	Persons	Males	Females	Persons	Males	Females	Persons	Males	Females	Persons	Males	Females
1	2	3	4	5	6	7	8	9	10	11	12	13
0—1 ...	44	22	22	44	22	22	...	...	...	...	...	...
1—2 ...	20	11	9	20	11	9	...	...	...	...	...	...
2—3 ...	34	22	12	34	22	12	...	...	...	...	...	...
3—4 ...	30	14	16	30	14	16	...	...	...	...	...	...
4—5 ...	27	15	12	27	15	12	...	...	...	...	...	...
TOTAL 0—5 ...	155	84	71	155	84	71	...	...	...	...	...	...
5—10 ...	127	62	65	127	62	65	...	...	...	...	...	...
10—15 ...	124	59	65	122	59	63	2	...	2	...	...	...
15—20 ...	112	52	60	84	49	35	27	3	24	1	...	1
20—25 ...	122	43	79	63	38	25	58	5	53	1	...	1
25—30 ...	92	36	56	19	15	4	70	21	49	3	...	3
30—35 ...	75	41	34	8	7	1	59	32	27	8	2	6
35—40 ...	79	42	37	2	1	1	66	37	29	11	4	7
40—45 ...	76	42	34	5	5	...	61	35	26	10	2	8
45—50 ..	62	31	31	1	...	1	48	26	22	13	5	8
50—55 ...	45	21	21	1	1	...	32	21	11	12	2	10
55—60 ...	30	19	11	1	1	...	18	12	6	11	6	5
60—65 ...	34	15	19	...	...	...	17	11	6	17	4	13
65—70 ..	13	8	5	1	1	...	5	5	...	7	2	5
70 and over ...	29	13	16	1	...	1	9	9	...	19	4	15
TOTAL ...	1,175	571	604	590	323	267	472	217	255	118	31	82

COCHIN STATE. IMPERIAL SERIES.

TABLE VII.

ANIMISTIC

Age, Sex and Civil condition.

AGE	POPULATION.			UNMARRIED.			MARRIED.			WIDOWED.		
	Persons	Males	Females	Persons	Males	Females	Persons	Males	Females	Persons	Males	Females
1	2	3	4	5	6	7	8	9	10	11	12	13
0—1 ...	157	83	74	157	83	74	...	...	...	...	...	...
1—2 ...	63	25	38	63	25	38	...	...	...	...	...	...
2—3 ...	119	54	65	119	54	65	...	...	...	...	...	...
3—4 ...	127	55	72	127	55	72	...	...	...	...	...	...
4—5 ...	125	69	56	125	69	56	...	...	...	...	...	...
TOTAL 0—5 ...	591	286	305	591	286	305	...	...	...	...	...	...
5—10 ...	506	274	232	506	274	282	...	...	...	...	...	...
10—15 ...	475	243	232	455	242	213	20	1	19	...	...	...
15—20 ...	370	188	182	242	172	70	125	16	109	3	...	3
20—25 ...	435	178	257	102	76	26	314	100	214	19	2	17
25—30 ...	394	186	208	37	33	4	340	151	189	17	2	15
30—35 ...	353	182	171	16	13	3	311	159	152	26	10	16
35—40 ...	283	155	128	6	5	1	249	146	103	28	4	24
40—45 ...	247	141	106	1	1	...	209	133	76	37	7	30
45—50 ...	153	92	61	3	8	...	119	84	35	31	5	26
50—55 ...	160	79	81	3	...	3	110	71	39	47	8	39
55—60 ...	81	49	32	...	...	...	57	40	17	24	9	15
60—65 ...	79	42	37	1	...	1	44	34	10	34	8	26
65—70 ...	26	19	7	...	...	...	17	15	2	9	4	5
70 and over ...	24	13	11	...	...	...	12	10	2	12	3	9
TOTAL ...	4.177	2,127	2,050	1,938	1,105	858	1,927	960	967	287	62	225

TABLE VIII.

EDUCATION.

NOTE 1:—The table for all religions includes 5 Parsis and 2 Brahmos, whose literacy is shown below:—

Age	Literate		Illiterate		Literate in English.	
	Male	Female	Male	Female	Male	Female.
Parsis—20 and over	3	2	...	...	3	1
Brahmos—20 and over	1	1	...	...	1	1

NOTE 2:—Of the 3,196 (2,458 males and 738 females) Christians literate in English, 72 (54 males and 18 females) are Europeans, 416 (242 males and 204 females) are Anglo-Indians and 2 males are Armenians.

TABLE VIII.

Education by religion and age.

Religion	Age	Population: Total: Persons	Total: Males	Total: Females	Literate: Persons	Literate: Males	Literate: Females	Illiterate: Persons	Illiterate: Males	Illiterate: Females	Literate in English: Persons	Literate in English: Males	Literate in English: Females
1	2	3	4	5	6	7	8	9	10	11	12	13	14
All Religions	0—10 ...	261,643	126,693	124,950	3,844	2,461	1,383	247,799	124,232	123,567	131	78	53
	10—15 ...	111,609	57,463	54,146	15,969	11,309	4,660	95,640	46,154	49,486	1,499	1,192	307
	15—20 ...	91,327	45,416	45,911	18,531	13,755	4,776	72,796	31,661	41,135	2,529	2,158	371
	20 and over ...	463 531	227,770	235,761	100,739	83,621	17,118	362 792	144,149	218,643	6,353	5,679	677
	TOTAL ...	918,110	457 342	460,768	139,083	111,146	27,937	779,027	346,196	432,831	10,512	9,104	1,408
Hindu	0—10 ...	163,430	82,311	81,119	2,045	1,409	636	161,385	80,902	80,483	84	50	34
	10—15 ...	73,496	37,657	35,839	9,054	6,812	2,242	64,442	30,845	33,597	1,039	858	181
	15—20 ...	61,684	30,281	31,403	11,076	8,556	2,520	50,608	21,725	28,883	1,731	1,537	194
	20 and over ...	317,098	153,753	163,345	61,802	52,621	9,181	255,296	101,132	154,164	4,261	4,012	249
	TOTAL ...	615,708	304,002	311,706	83,977	69,398	14,579	531,731	234,604	297,127	7,115	6,457	658
Christian	0—10 ...	68,535	34,410	34,125	1,753	1,017	736	66,782	33,393	33,389	47	28	19
	10—15 ...	29 316	15,182	14,134	6,593	4,204	2,389	22,723	10,978	11,745	441	316	125
	15—20 ...	22,663	11,628	11,035	6,915	4,698	2,217	15,748	6,930	8,818	769	594	175
	20 and over ...	112,578	56,628	55,950	34,825	27,071	7,754	77,753	29,557	48,196	1,941	1,522	119
	TOTAL ...	233,092	117,848	115,244	50,086	36,990	13,096	183,006	80,858	102,148	3,198	2,460	738

TABLE VIII.

Education by religion and age.

TABLE VIII.

Education by religion and age.

Religion	Age	Population: Total: Persons	Total: Males	Total: Females	Literate: Persons	Literate: Males	Literate: Females	Illiterate: Persons	Illiterate: Males	Illiterate: Females	Literate in English: Persons	Literate in English: Males	Literate in English: Females
1	2	3	4	5	6	7	8	9	10	11	12	13	14
Musalman	0—10 ...	18,285	9,261	9,024	44	34	10	18,241	9,227	9,014	...	...	...
	10—15 ...	8,179	4,308	3,871	297	272	25	7,882	4,036	3,846	17	17	...
	15—20 ...	6,489	3,262	3,227	504	476	28	5,985	2,786	3,199	19	19	...
	20 and over ...	30,869	15,876	14,993	3,861	3,719	142	27,008	12,157	14,851	108	107	1
	TOTAL ...	63,822	32,707	31,115	4,706	4,501	205	59,116	28,206	30,910	144	143	1
Animist	0—10 ...	1,097	560	537	...	...	...	1,097	560	537	...	...	...
	10—15 ...	475	243	232	...	...	...	475	243	232	...	...	...
	15—20 ...	370	188	182	...	...	...	370	188	182	...	...	...
	20 and over ...	2,235	1,136	1,099	1	1	...	2,234	1,135	1,099	...	...	...
	TOTAL ...	4,177	2,127	2,050	1	1	...	4,176	2,126	2,050	...	...	...
Jew	0—10 ...	282	146	136	2	1	1	280	145	135	...	...	...
	10—15 ...	124	59	65	14	10	4	110	49	61	1	...	1
	15—20 ...	112	52	60	32	21	11	80	31	49	10	8	2
	20 and over ...	657	314	343	184	148	36	473	166	307	28	22	6
	TOTAL ...	1,175	571	604	232	180	52	943	391	552	39	30	9
Jain	0—10 ...	14	5	9	...	...	...	14	5	9	...	...	...
	10—15 ...	19	14	5	11	11	...	8	3	5	1	1	...
	15—20 ...	9	5	4	4	4	...	5	1	4	...	...	...
	20 and over ...	57	59	28	59	57	2	28	2	26	9	9	...
	TOTAL ...	129	83	46	74	72	2	55	11	44	10	10	...

TABLE IX.

EDUCATION BY SELECTED CASTES, TRIBES OR RACES.

NOTE:— While in Table VIII the whole population is dealt with, this Table deals with only selected castes, tribes and races, the minor ones being left out of account.

TABLE IX.

Education by selected Castes, Tribes or Races.

CASTE, TRIBE OR RACE.	POPULATION. Total Persons	Total Males.	Total Females.	Literate Persons.	Literate Males.	Literate Females.	Illiterate Persons.	Illiterate Males	Illiterate Females.	Literate in English Persons.	Literate in English Males.	Literate in English Females.
1	2	3	4	5	6	7	8	9	10	11	12	13
HINDU:-												
Ambalavasi ...	7.804	3,910	3,894	3,127	2,152	975	4,677	1,758	2,919	328	277	51
Arayan ...	4.766	2,505	2,261	508	473	35	4,238	2.032	2,226	3	1	2
Brahman Malayali ...	6.617	3,418	3,199	2,812	2.164	648	3,805	1,254	2,551	48	48	...
Do. Tamil ...	18,923	9,794	9,129	8,073	6,702	1,371	10.850	3.092	7,758	2,539	2.428	111
Do. Konkani ...	8,622	4,580	3,942	2,472	2,298	174	6,050	2,282	3,768	341	322	19
Do. Others ...	1,470	1.002	468	535	499	36	935	508	432	53	49	4
Chakkan ...	2.101	1,108	993	277	238	39	1,824	870	954	8	8	...
Devanga ...	2 349	1,176	1,173	181	180	1	2,168	996	1,172	1	1	...
Iluvan ...	208,453	102,817	105,636	17.171	15,910	1,261	191,282	86,907	104,375	290	280	10
Kadupattan ...	14 323	7,074	7,249	1,507	1,386	121	12.816	5,688	7,128	22	20	2
Kaikolan ...	4,121	2,011	2,110	373	358	15	3,748	1,653	2,095	12	12	...
Kammalan ...	34.658	17,089	17,469	3,705	3,554	151	30,853	13,535	17,318	9	9	...
Kanakkan ...	7.527	3,790	3,737	141	134	7	7.356	3,656	3,730	3	2	1
Kaniyan ...	3.244	1,624	1,620	1 208	895	312	2,036	729	1,307	3	3	...
Kshatriya, Malayali .	1,015	511	504	618	370	248	397	141	256	118	106	12
Do. Others ...	579	305	274	160	146	14	419	159	260	26	26	...
Kudumi Chetty ...	12 371	6,500	5,871	555	544	11	11,816	5,956	5,860	7	7	...
Kusavan ...	3,557	1,829	1,728	27	26	1	3,530	1,803	1,727	...	...	...
Nayar ...	121.206	58,720	62,486	32,826	24,276	8.550	88,380	34,444	53,936	2,981	2,551	430
Otta Naikkan ...	2.815	1,368	1,447	53	46	7	2.762	1,322	1,440	...	...	...
Panan ...	2,902	1,491	1,411	223	181	42	2,679	1,310	1,369	...	...	...

TABLE IX.

Education by selected Castes, Tribes or Races.

CASTE, TRIBE OR RACE	POPULATION									LITERATE IN ENGLISH		
	TOTAL			LITERATE			ILLITERATE					
	Persons	Males.	Females	Persons	Males	Females	Persons	Males.	Females	Persons	Males	Females
1	2	3	4	5	6	7	8	9	10	11	12	13
Pandaran ...	3,715	1,886	1,829	212	196	16	3,503	1,690	1,818	3	3	...
Pandittattan ...	2,456	1,342	1,114	378	364	14	2,078	978	1,100	7	7	...
Parayan ...	8,340	4,131	4,209	19	17	2	8,321	4,114	4,207	1	1	...
Pulayan ...	72,787	35,284	37,503	346	328	18	72,441	34,956	37,485	2	2	...
Valan ...	7,827	4,046	3,781	827	775	52	7,000	3,271	3,729	8	8	...
Velan ...	9,322	4,595	4,727	1,107	1,060	47	8,215	3,535	4,680	5	5	...
Velakkattalavan ...	3,271	1,624	1,647	360	316	41	2,911	1,308	1,603	3	3	...
Vellalan ...	6,044	3,076	2,968	942	864	78	5,102	2,212	2,890	122	118	4
Veluttedan ...	3,381	1,589	1,794	342	299	43	3,039	1,290	1,749	3	3	...
Vettuvan ...	5,261	2,437	2,821	17	14	3	5,244	2,423	2,821	...	...	...
MUSALMAN:—												
Jonakan ...	51,469	26,274	25,195	3,367	3,223	144	48,102	23,051	25,051	52	51	1
Ravuttan ...	8,430	4,311	1,119	619	602	17	7,811	3,709	4,102	18	18	...
CHRISTIAN:—												
Anglo-Indian ...	2,446	1,241	1,205	1,048	624	424	1,398	617	781	446	242	204
European ...	76	56	20	72	54	18	4	2	2	72	54	18
Native christian ...	230,568	116,519	111,019	48,964	36,310	12,654	181,604	80,239	101,365	2,678	2,162	516
ANIMIST.:—												
Malayan ...	2,461	1,280	1,181	1	1	...	2,460	1,279	1,181	...	...	...
Jew. ...	1,175	571	631	232	180	52	943	391	552	39	30	9

TABLE X.

LANGUAGE.

TABLE X.

Language.

COCHIN STATE — IMPERIAL SERIES.

LANGUAGE.	Persons	Males	Females
1	2	3	4
Cochin State. ...	918,110	457,342	460,768
A. Vernaculars of India. ...	917,289	456,847	460,442
1. VERNACULAR OF THE STATE.			
Malayalam ...	820,129	407,228	412,901
2. VERNACULARS FOREIGN TO THE STATE.	97 160	49,619	47,541
Bengali ...	2	1	1
Gujarati ...	1,060	663	397
Goanese ...	11	11	...
Hindi ...	121	55	66
Hindustani ...	2,234	1,206	1,028
Kachchi ...	352	191	161
Kanarese ...	4,152	2,180	1,972
Konkani ...	21,153	11,226	9,927
Marathi ...	1,061	307	754
Tamil ...	55,231	27,858	27,373
Telugu ...	11,224	5,511	5,713
Tulu ...	546	405	141
Urdu ...	13	5	8
B. Vernaculars of non-Indian Asiatic countries.	142	85	57
Arabic ...	111	70	41
Hebrew ...	27	11	16
Persian ...	2	2	...
Syriac ...	2	2	...
C. European Languages.	679	410	269
Basque ...	5	5	...
English ...	412	243	169
French ...	2	2	...
German ...	4	1	3
Latin ...	3	3	...
Portuguese ...	237	140	97
Spanish ...	16	16	...

TABLE XI.

BIRTH PLACE.

9

TABLE XI.

CCCHIN STATE. IMPERIAL SERIES.

Birth Place.

Birth place	Population		
	Persons	Males	Females
A.—Born in India	918.031	457,281	460,753
I.—Within the State of enumeration—Cochin.	870.844	434.379	436,465
II.—Province and States in India beyond the State of enumeration.	47.190	22,902	24,288
(a) PROVINCE AND STATES ADJACENT TO THE STATE OF ENUMERATION.	45.695	21,863	23,833
I.—British Territory.	30,486	14,941	15,545
Bellary	4	3	1
Chingelput	14	10	4
Coimbatore	3.026	1,391	1,635
Coorg	1	...	1
Cuddupah	12	11	1
Godavari	6	4	2
Guntur	6	2	4
Karnool	16	15	1
Madras	193	107	86
Madura	183	83	100
Malabar	25,342	12,131	13,211
Nellore	2	2	...
Nilgiris	31	20	11
North Arcot	22	16	6
Ramnad	1	1	...
South Canara	500	420	80
Salem	67	40	27
South Arcot	39	16	23
Tanjore	199	119	80
Tinnevelly	653	461	192
Trichinopoly	166	88	78
Vizagapattam	3	1	2
II.—Feudatory States	15,210	6,922	8,288
Travancore	15,207	6,922	8,285
Puddukotai	3	...	3
(b) OTHER PROVINCES AND STATES IN INDIA ...	1,377	934	443
I.—British territory	578	425	153
Bengal (including Orissa)	47	37	10
Bombay (including Aden)	464	339	125
Central Provinces and Berar	12	7	5
North-West Frontier Province	1	1	...
Punjab	3	3	...
United Provinces of Agra and Oudh	51	38	13

TABLE XI. (*Continued*).

COCHIN STATE. IMPERIAL SERIES.

Birth Place.

BIRTH PLACE	POPULATION		
	Persons	Males	Females
II.—Feudatory States	799	509	290
BOMBAY STATES	611	385	226
Cutch	342	204	138
Kathiawar	267	179	88
Rewa Kantha Agency	2	2	...
CENTRAL INDIA AGENCY	33	30	8
Gwalior	4	3	1
Indore	1	...	1
Other States	33	27	6
HYDERABAD	27	16	11
MYSORE	108	73	35
RAJPUTANA	15	5	10
(c) FRENCH AND PORTUGUESE SETTLEMENTS ...	87	81	6
FRENCH SETTLEMENT	11	7	4
Pondicherry	1	1	...
Karikal	3	1	2
Mahe	7	5	2
PORTUGUESE SETTLEMENT.			
Goa	76	74	2
(d) INDIA UNSPECIFIED	30	24	6
B.—Born in other Asiatic Countries	22	17	5
Ceylon	13	11	2
Persia	2	2	...
Strait Settlements and Malaya	4	1	3
Turkey in Asia	3	3	...
C.—Born in Europe	50	42	8
UNITED KINGDOM	20	14	6
England and Wales	18	12	6
Scotland	2	2	...
Belgium	1	1	...
France	2	2	...
Germany	4	2	2
Spain	23	23	...
D.—Born in America			
West Indies	3	2	1
E.—Born in Australia			
New Zealand	1	...	1
Grand Total ..	918,110	457,342	460,768

TABLE XII.

PART I.—INFIRMITIES BY AGE.

„ II.— Do DISTRIBUTION BY TALUKS.

NOTE.—Of the blind, 2 males are also insane, 3 persons (2 males and 1 female) are also deaf-mute, and one male is also a leper.

Persons suffering from more infirmities than one are included under each head.

TABLE XII.

INFIRMITIES.

COCHIN STATE. IMPERIAL SERIES.

Part I.—Distribution by Age.

Age.	Population Afflicted			Insane			Deaf-Mutes			Blind			Lepers		
	Persons	Males	Females	Persons	Males	Females	Persons	Males	Females	Persons	Males	Females	Persons	Males	Females
1	2	3	4	5	6	7	8	9	10	11	12	13	14	15	16
0—1 ...	**4**	2	2	...	...	...	...	...	...	**4**	2	2	...	...	...
1—2 ...	**3**	2	1	...	...	...	...	...	...	**3**	2	1	...	..	...
2—3 ...	**11**	1	10	**1**	...	1	**4**	...	4	**6**	1	5	**1**	...	1
3—4 ...	**10**	8	2	...	...	...	**3**	3	...	**7**	5	2	...	...	...
4—5 ...	**14**	7	7	...	...	...	**5**	2	3	**9**	5	4	...	...	...
TOTAL 0-5 ...	**42**	20	22	**1**	...	1	**12**	5	7	**29**	15	14	**1**	...	1
5—10 ...	**94**	59	35	**2**	1	1	**28**	18	10	**61**	39	22	**3**	1	2
10—15 ...	**128**	78	50	**4**	3	1	**43**	26	17	**67**	42	25	**14**	7	7
15—20 ...	**169**	102	67	**13**	8	5	**50**	28	22	**74**	41	33	**32**	25	7
20—25 ...	**174**	94	80	**31**	17	14	**38**	16	22	**64**	29	35	**41**	32	9
25—30 ...	**208**	120	88	**31**	24	7	**48**	26	22	**91**	46	45	**39**	25	14
30—35 ...	**217**	119	98	**41**	19	22	**25**	13	12	**95**	49	46	**56**	38	18
35—40 ...	**209**	135	74	**35**	27	8	**21**	12	9	**93**	55	38	**60**	41	19
40—45 ...	**207**	116	91	**39**	19	20	**18**	10	8	**95**	46	49	**56**	42	14
45—50 ...	**145**	77	68	**31**	12	19	**15**	8	7	**59**	26	33	**40**	31	9
50—55 ...	**177**	92	85	**21**	8	13	**13**	5	8	**102**	47	55	**41**	32	9
55—60 ...	**133**	77	56	**15**	6	9	**5**	4	1	**74**	37	37	**39**	30	9
60—65 ...	**158**	86	72	**16**	8	8	**8**	2	6	**115**	63	52	**20**	14	6
65—70 ...	**68**	35	33	**3**	...	3	**2**	2	...	**50**	23	27	**13**	10	3
70 and over ...	**135**	60	75	**10**	4	6	**5**	3	2	**116**	51	65	**6**	4	2
TOTAL ...	**2.264**	1,270	994	**293**	156	137	**331**	178	153	**1185**	609	576	**461**	332	129

Part II.—Distribution by Taluks.

Taluk.	Population Afflicted.			Insane.			Deaf-Mutes			Blind			Lepers		
	Persons	Males	Females	Persons	Males	Females	Persons	Males	Females	Persons	Males	Females	Persons	Males	Females
1	2	3	4	5	6	7	8	9	10	11	12	13	14	15	16
Cochin State ...	**2.264**	**1.270**	**994**	**293**	**156**	**137**	**331**	**178**	**153**	**1.185**	**609**	**576**	**461**	**332**	**129**
Cochin-Kanayannur ...	**672**	420	252	**95**	54	41	**105**	53	52	**251**	147	104	**223**	168	55
Cranganur ...	**39**	26	13	**4**	1	3	**4**	3	1	**16**	12	4	**15**	10	5
Mukundapuram ...	**427**	228	199	**51**	22	29	**74**	44	30	**228**	114	114	**76**	50	26
Trichur ...	**466**	259	207	**61**	37	24	**62**	34	28	**292**	153	139	**51**	35	16
Talapilly ...	**494**	252	242	**50**	24	26	**66**	36	30	**307**	140	167	**73**	53	20
Chittur ...	**166**	85	81	**32**	18	14	**20**	8	12	**91**	43	48	**23**	16	7

TABLE XII—A.

INFIRMITIES BY SELECTED CASTES, TRIBES OR RACES.

NOTE.—The following statement exhibits combination of infirmities by Caste, Sex and Age.

Caste.		*Sex.*	*Age.*	*Infirmities.*
Iluvan	...	Female	2	Blind and Deaf-mute.
Iluvan	...	Male	25	Do do
Iluvan	...	Male	73	Blind and Leper
Iluvan	...	Male	75	Blind and Deaf-mute
Nayar	...	Male	60	Blind and Insane
Velan	...	Male	40	Do do

Persons suffering from more infirmities than one are included under each head.

TABLE XII—A.

Infirmities by selected Castes, Tribes or Races.

COCHIN STATE. IMPERIAL SERIES.

CASTE, TRIBE OR RACE	Population dealt with			Insane			Deaf-mute			Blind			Leper		
	Persons	Males	Females	Persons	Males	Females	Persons	Males	Females	Persons	Males	Females	Persons	Males	Females
1	2	3	4	5	6	7	8	9	10	11	12	13	14	15	16
HINDU—	615,708	304,002	311,706	195	111	84	205	101	104	861	424	437	318	217	101
Ambalavasi ...	7,804	3,910	3,894	11	9	2	3	2	1	14	6	8	1	1	...
Arayan ...	4,766	2,505	2,261	4	2	2	...	...	...	6	2	4	4	2	2
Brahman, Malayali...	6,617	3,418	3,199	5	4	1	3	2	1	17	11	6	1	1	...
Do. Tamil ...	18,923	9,794	9,129	9	6	3	5	2	3	29	12	17	9	7	2
Do. Konkani...	8,522	4,580	3,942	11	9	2	...	...	...	7	4	3	2	2	...
Do. Others ...	1,470	1,002	468	1	1	...	2	...	2	2	2	...	...	...	...
Chetti ...	4,606	2,092	2,514	2	1	1	...	...	...	5	2	3	3	...	3
Devangan ...	2 349	1,176	1,173	2	...	2	3	1	2	3	2	1	...	...	...
Iluvan ...	208,453	102,817	105,686	56	29	27	78	42	36	252	138	114	103	81	22
Kadupattan ...	14 323	7,074	7,249	5	3	2	6	3	3	35	18	17	11	7	4
Kaikolan ...	4,121	2,011	2,110	2	1	1	2	...	2	5	2	3	...	..	...
Kanmalan ...	34 558	17,089	17,469	15	5	10	18	8	10	38	21	17	19	11	8
Kanakkan ...	7.527	3,790	3,737	4	3	1	...	...	...	4	1	3	7	3	4
Kaniyan ...	3.244	1,624	1,620	3	2	1	1	...	1	3	1	2	2	1	1
Kavundan ...	1,095	519	576	2	2	...	...	...	...	3	2	1	1	1	...
Kshatriya, Malayali..	1.015	511	504	...	...	...	1	1	...	2	1	1	...	...	...
Kudumi Chetti ...	12 371	6,500	5,871	3	1	2	2	1	1	7	4	3	10	6	4
Kusavan ...	3 557	1,829	1,728	...	...	...	4	2	2	5	3	2	...	...	...
Nayar ...	121,206	58,720	62,486	38	21	17	32	13	19	257	112	145	49	32	17
Ottanaikan ...	2,815	1,368	1,447	1	...	1	1	1	...	4	1	3	1	1	...
Panan ..	2902	1,491	1,411	...	...	...	...	...	...	4	...	4	2	1	1
Pandaran ...	3.715	1,886	1,829	...	...	..	3	1	2	8	5	3	...	...	...
Parayan ...	8 340	4,131	4,209	1	...	1	3	3	...	17	4	13	9	2	7
Pulayan ...	72,787	35,284	37,503	5	3	2	16	5	11	66	30	36	55	35	20
Vadukan ...	994	483	511	...	...	...	...	...	...	3	1	2	4	4	...
Vaisya ...	627	345	282	...	...	...	1	1	...	7	4	3	1	1	...
Valan ...	7,827	4,046	3,781	1	...	1	5	4	1	6	5	1	2	2	...
Velan ...	9,322	4,595	4,727	5	2	3	5	3	2	13	6	7	11	7	4
Velakkattalavan ...	3,271	1,624	1,647	...	...	...	...	...	...	12	8	4	...	...	...
Vellalan ...	6.044	3,076	2,968	2	2	...	3	2	1	4	2	2	2	2	...
Veluttedan ...	3 381	1,589	1,792	...	...	...	2	1	1	6	4	2	1	1	...
Vettuvan ...	5,261	2,437	2,824	1	...	1	...	...	...	6	3	3	...	...	...
Others ...	21,895	10,686	11,209	6	5	1	6	3	3	11	7	4	8	6	2
MUSALMAN—	63,822	32,707	31,115	17	5	12	31	18	13	64	42	22	26	20	6
Jonakan ..	51,469	26,274	25,195	16	5	11	28	15	13	54	35	19	24	18	6
Ravuttan ...	8,430	4.311	4,119	1	...	1	3	3	...	9	6	3	1	1	...
Others ...	3,923	2,122	1,801	...	...	...	...	...	...	1	1	...	1	1	...
CHRISTIAN—	233,090	117,846	115,244	79	38	41	93	57	36	253	142	111	114	94	20
European ...	76	56	20	...	...	...	...	...	...	...	...	...	...	...	...
Anglo Indian ...	2,446	1,241	1,205	2	1	1	...	...	...	1	...	1	4	4	...
Native Christian ...	230,568	116,549	114,019	77	37	40	93	57	36	252	142	110	110	90	20
JEW	1,175	571	604	2	2	...	...	...	...	1	...	1	1	1	...
ANIMIST	4,177	2,127	2,050	...	...	...	2	2	...	6	1	5	2	...	2
Grand Total ...	917,972	457,253	460,719	293	156	137	331	178	153	1185	609	576	461	332	129

TABLE XIII.

CASTE, TRIBE, RACE OR NATIONALITY

NOTE.—Non-indegenous castes with a strength of less than 10 each are lumped together in the Table as "minor castes."

TABLE XIII.

COCHIN STATE. IMPERIAL SERIES.

Caste, Tribe, Race or Nationality.

CASTE.	TOTAL.	MALES.	FEMALES.
HINDU. ...	615,708	304,002	311,706
Agamudaiyan ...	148	74	74
Ambalavasi ...	7,804	3,910	3,894
Adikal ...	24	14	10
Chakkiyar ...	46	19	27
Chakkiyar Nambiyar ...	70	26	44
Chengazhi Nambiyar ...	183	86	97
Kallattu Kurup ...	115	57	58
Marar ...	1,574	832	742
Nambiyassan ...	1,640	866	774
Pisharodi ...	1,237	598	639
Putuval ...	354	169	185
Tiyyattunni ...	5	4	1
Variyar ...	2,556	1,239	1,317
Ambattan ...	1,101	511	590
Andi ...	331	115	216
Arasupalli ...	62	30	82
Arayan ...	4,766	2,505	2,261
Bairagi ...	142	42	100
Baniya ...	186	83	103
Bhattia ...	11	9	2
Boya ...	39	17	22
Brahman ...	35,532	18,794	16,738
Embran ...	943	704	239
Gauda ...	151	77	74
Konkani ...	.8,522	4,580	3,942
Malayali { *Elayad* ...	859	469	390
Malayali { *Muttad* ...	238	134	104
Malayali { *Nambudiri* ...	5,520	2,815	2,705
Tamil ...	18 923	9,794	9,129
Others ...	376	221	155
Chakkan ...	2,101	1,108	993
Chakkiliyan ...	739	383	356
Chaliyan ...	1,693	864	829
Chetti ...	4,606	2,092	2,514
Chunnambottan ...	15	8	7
Dasi ...	367	128	289
Devangan ...	2,349	1,176	1,173
Idaiyan ...	310	150	160
Iluvan ...	208,453	102,817	105,636
Iluvan ...	207,639	102,397	105,242
Kavutiyan ...	814	420	394
Kaduppattan ...	14,323	7,074	7,249
Kaikolan ...	4,121	2,011	2,110
Kakkalan ...	682	323	359
Kallan ...	945	396	549
Kallar ...	18	14	4

TABLE XIII.—(*Continued.*)

COCHIN STATE IMPERIAL SERIES.

Caste, Tribe, Race or Nationality.

CASTE.	TOTAL.	MALES.	FEMALES.
Kammalan	34,558	17,089	17,469
Kallasari	3,101	1,488	1,613
Kollan	7,156	3,490	3,666
Marasari	17,779	8,816	8,963
Moosari	1,078	548	530
Tattan	4,309	2,161	2,148
Tolkollan	1,135	586	549
Kammalan, Tamil	151	70	81
Kanakkan	7,527	3,790	3,737
Kaniyan	3,244	1,624	1,620
Kannadiyan	28	6	17
Kannan	185	99	86
Kavara	537	261	276
Kavundan	1,095	519	576
Komatti	30	19	11
Kshatriya	1,594	816	778
Malayali	1,015	511	504
Rajput	34	15	19
Raju	67	24	43
Others	478	266	212
Kudumi Chetti	12,371	6,500	5,871
Kurukkal	258	119	139
Kurup	29	9	20
Kusavan	3,557	1,829	1,728
Manayar	361	181	180
Manuppan	116	50	66
Mahratti	56	37	19
Mudaliyar	732	365	367
Mukkuvan	323	158	140
Muttiriyan	70	36	34
Naidu	995	469	526
Nayar	121,206	58,720	62,486
Nambi Kurup	18	8	10
Nambidi	424	227	197
Nanjanattu Pillai	283	100	186
Odiya	65	30	35
Ottazhan	50	25	25
Otta Naikan (Odde)	2,815	1,368	1,447
Palli	5	3	2
Panan	2,902	1,491	1,411
Pandaran	3,715	1,886	1,829
Panditattan	2,456	1,342	1,114
Paravan	23	13	10
Parayan	8,340	4,131	4,209
Parayan, Tamil	16	4	12
Pondan	70	39	31
Pulayan	72,787	35,284	37,503
Pulluvan	110	58	52
Puluvan	188	59	129
Reddi	27	6	21
Samantan	110	60	50
Shanan	86	43	43
Sudra unspecified	140	115	25

TABLE XIII.—(*Continued.*)

COCHIN STATE | IMPERIAL SERIES.

Caste, Tribe, Race or Nationality.

CASTE.	TOTAL.	MALES.	FEMALES.
Tarakan	713	329	384
Tottiyan	195	99	96
Vadukan	994	483	511
Vaisya	627	345	282
Valan	7,827	4,046	3,781
Valachetti	329	164	165
Valluvan	502	239	263
Vaniyan	1,090	454	636
Vannan	97	54	43
Velakkattalavan	3 271	1,624	1,647
Velan	9 322	4,595	4,727
Vellala	6,044	3,076	2,968
Veluttedan	3 381	1,589	1,792
Vettuvan	5,261	2,437	2,824
Vilkurup	1,433	660	773
Virasaivan	28	15	13
Minor castes	154	81	73
CHRISTIAN	233,092	117,848	115,244
Anglo Indian	2,446	1,241	1,205
Armenian	2	2	...
European (British subject)	47	30	17
European (others)	29	26	3
Native Christian	230,568	116,549	114,019
MUSALMAN	63,822	32,707	31,115
Arab	137	63	74
Bora	46	31	15
Hanevi	26	11	15
Jonakan	51,469	26,274	25,195
Kachchi	484	273	211
Pathan	1,899	1,013	886
Ravuttan	8,430	4,311	4,119
Shabi	91	48	43
Saiyad	242	122	120
Sheik	416	224	192
Sunni	560	312	248
Others	22	15	7
ANIMIST	4,177	2,127	2 050
Eravalan	503	245	258
Kadan	447	210	237
Kurumban	9	7	2
Malayan	2,461	1,280	1,181
Nayati	220	124	96
Ullatan	537	261	276
JEW	1,175	571	604
Black Jew	983	481	502
White Jew	192	90	102
Jain	129	83	46
Parsi	5	3	2
Brahmo	2	1	1
Grend Total ...	918,110	457 342	430,768

TABLE XIV.

CIVIL CONDITION BY AGE FOR SELECTED CASTES.

NOTE :—This Table like Table IX deals only with certain selected castes and not with the whole population. All main castes over 2,000 in strength and a few others which, though not numerically so strong, are of local importance, are included in this Table.

TABLE XIV.

MALE.

Civil condition by Age for Selected Castes.

COCHIN STATE. IMPERIAL SERIES.

CASTE, TRIBE OR RACE	POPULATION DEALT WITH	UNMARRIED							MARRIED							WIDOWED						
		Total	0—5	5—12	12—15	15—20	20—40	40 and over	Total	0—5	5—12	12—15	15—20	20—40	40 and over	Total	0—5	5—12	12—15	15—20	20—40	40 and over
1	2	3	4	5	6	7	8	9	10	11	12	13	14	15	16	17	18	19	20	21	22	23
HINDU																						
Ambalavasi ..	3,910	2,360	484	642	289	391	504	50	1,849	..	..	..	18	678	658	201	..	..	..	..	53	148
Arayan ..	2,505	1,392	384	408	161	252	180	7	1,007	..	1	17	411	378	200	106	..	..	..	1	29	76
Brahman, Malayali ..	3,418	1,763	320	446	206	264	418	114	1,568	..	..	...	19	762	782	92	..	..	..	..	22	70
Do. Tamil ..	9,794	5,022	1,842	1,791	739	772	345	33	4,442	..	..	16	240	2,528	1,658	330	..	..	..	..	57	273
Do. Konkani ..	4,580	2,194	421	664	251	408	407	43	2,196	..	2	1	54	1,219	919	190	..	..	..	4	37	149
Do. Others ..	1,002	451	62	75	72	82	137	23	506	...	..	1	15	297	193	45	..	..	..	..	12	33
Chakkan ..	1,108	631	140	188	77	107	115	4	432	..	..	2	6	234	190	45	..	..	..	1	9	35
Devangan ..	1,176	508	118	169	68	96	54	3	618	..	..	2	32	355	229	50	..	..	..	..	7	43
Iluvan ..	102,817	57,525	15,389	18,369	8,349	9,335	5,869	214	41,746	...	6	48	450	25,609	15,633	3,546	..	..	1	38	1,042	2,465
Kadupattan ..	7,074	3,927	1,002	1,194	558	675	488	10	2,867	..	..	..	44	1,718	1,105	280	..	..	..	1	108	176
Kaikolan ..	2,011	1,001	215	340	151	184	102	9	895	..	..	..	22	485	388	115	..	..	..	1	81	88
Kammalan ..	17,089	9,663	2,582	3,049	1,327	1,589	1,074	42	6,948	..	2	4	121	4,074	2,742	488	..	..	...	10	128	345
Kanakkan ..	2,790	2,078	589	666	316	287	195	5	1,551	..	...	2	39	979	531	161	..	..	..	3	51	107
Kaniyan ..	1,624	947	242	296	119	131	129	30	628	..	..	1	7	371	249	49	..	..	..	..	16	33
Kshatriya, Malayali ..	511	308	65	95	30	47	66	5	160	..	..	..	1	67	92	43	..	..	..	2	18	23
Do. Paradesi ..	305	158	28	38	21	20	39	12	124	..	..	...	2	70	52	28	..	..	..	..	7	16
Kudumi Chetti ..	6,500	3,272	805	1,062	427	497	418	68	3,017	..	1	9	111	1,857	1,039	211	..	..	..	1	72	138
Kusavan ..	1,829	911	276	285	121	139	83	7	846	..	..	7	82	436	321	72	..	..	..	2	17	53
Nayar ..	58,720	36,966	8,839	9,872	4,631	6,042	7,626	456	18,312	..	..	..	189	10,469	8,254	2,842	..	..	..	19	872	1,951
Ottansikan ..	1,368	655	164	213	88	105	83	7	640	..	..	1	7	369	263	73	..	..	..	3	28	42
Pandaran ..	1,886	1,037	259	298	176	186	111	7	775	..	1	..	21	454	299	74	..	..	..	1	16	57

TABLE XIV.—*Continued.*

MALE.

Civil condition by Age for Selected Castes.

COCHIN STATE. IMPERIAL SERIES.

CASTE, TRIBE OR RACE	POPULATION DEALT WITH	UNMARRIED							MARRIED							WIDOWED						
		Total	0—5	5—12	12—15	15—20	20—40	40 and over	Total	0—5	5—12	12—15	15—20	20—40	40 and over	Total	0—5	5—12	12—15	15—20	20—40	40 and over
1	2	3	4	5	6	7	8	9	10	11	12	13	14	15	16	17	18	19	20	21	22	23
Panan ..	1,491	809	174	266	117	156	94	2	£22	..	..	..	15	364	243	60	..	..	..	..	19	41
Panditattan ..	1,342	753	165	212	111	126	141	3	537		..	..	3	297	237	47	..	..	..	..	10	37
Parayan ..	4,131	2,085	632	708	286	258	222	9	1,853	..	..	5	98	1,048	707	193	...	..	1	5	64	123
Pulayan ..	85,284	19,073	5,540	6,330	2,716	2,712	1,683	92	14,759	..	9	10	378	8,451	5,911	1,452	..	..	1	23	441	987
Valan ..	4,046	2,045	580	680	290	255	275	15	1,808	..	1	..	125	1,035	647	193	..	..	..	1	66	126
Velan ..	4,595	2,400	659	760	337	387	239	18	2,006	..	3	4	69	1,179	751	189	..	..	..	1	60	128
Velakkattalavan ..	1,624	968	202	310	115	164	171	6	577	..	..	..	13	345	219	79	..	..	...	..	31	48
Vellalan ..	3.076	1,716	879	475	269	290	290	13	1,242	..	..	2	13	659	568	118	..	..	..	..	42	76
Veluttedan ..	1,589	892	217	272	123	144	130	6	629	..	..	..	15	347	267	68	..	..	..	2	19	47
Vettuvan ..	2,487	,327	409	402	199	184	129	4	1,009	..	..	..	29	622	358	101	..	..	..	2	26	73
MUSALMAN																						
Jonakan ..	26,274	15,358	4,113	4,713	2,185	2,871	1,927	49	10,195	..	..	5	186	6,068	3,936	721	..	..	..	12	237	472
Ravuttan ..	4,311	2,506	568	796	375	452	310	5	1,719	..	..	3	29	997	690	86	..	...	..	...	26	60
CHRISTIAN																						
Anglo Indian ..	1,241	807	207	247	95	129	112	17	403	..	..	..	3	218	182	31	..	...	..	..	5	26
European ..	56	41	2	1	..	6	23	9	15	..	..	..	..	6	9	..	..	..	..	..	..	..
Native Christian ..	116,549	64,363	18,030	21,327	9,542	9,708	5,354	407	48,048	..	44	95	1,760	29,530	16,619	4,138	..	..	2	27	832	3,277
ANIMIST																						
Malayan ..	1,280	676	170	214	95	107	86	4	565	..	..	..	11	327	227	39	..	..	..	..	14	25
JEW ..	571	323	84	84	87	49	61	8	217	..	..	..	3	95	119	31	..	..	..	..	6	25

TABLE XIV.—*Continued*.

FEMALE.

COCHIN STATE. IMPERIAL SERIES.

Civil condition by Age for Selected Castes.

CASTE, TRIBE OR RACE	POPULATION DEALT WITH	UNMARRIED							MARRIED							WIDOWED						
		Total	0—5	5—12	12—15	15—20	20—40	40 and over	Total	0—5	5—12	12—15	15—20	20—40	40 and over	Total	0—5	5—12	12—15	15—20	20—40	40 and over
1	2	3	4	5		7	8	9	10	11	12	13	14	15	16	17	18	19	20	21	22	23
HINDU																						
Ambalavasi ...	3,894	1,428	482	571	211	120	40	4	1,568	..	8	39	244	928	349	903	...	...	2	17	248	641
Arayan ...	2,261	947	329	350	149	88	27	4	1,019	...	3	8	139	682	187	295	...	...	...	5	53	287
Brahman, Malayali..	8,199	1,226	341	421	174	182	93	15	1,288	...	1	18	127	790	807	785	...	...	...	8	121	611
Do Tamil ...	9,129	2,947	1,389	1,478	80	...	...	...	4,557	...	188	462	797	2,589	771	1,625	...	...	6	36	357	1,226
Do Konkani ...	3,942	1,152	477	621	18	11	20	5	1,889	...	84	183	368	1,021	238	951	...	1	4	21	244	681
Do Others ...	468	139	61	61	8	6	8	...	225	...	6	27	29	132	81	104	...	...	...	...	80	74
Chakkan ...	993	387	132	158	58	80	7	2	401	...	1	14	58	257	71	205	...	...	1	6	58	145
Devangan ...	1,178	367	105	157	90	12	8	...	603	...	5	24	111	354	114	198	...	...	...	1	55	142
Iluvan ...	105,636	48,615	15,460	18,097	7,683	5,352	1,895	178	41,808	...	58	511	5,807	27,861	7,571	15,718	...	5	22	271	4,457	10,958
Kadupattan ...	7,249	2,968	1,018	1,052	465	319	95	19	2,861	...	3	65	394	1,874	525	1,420	...	...	1	11	330	1,078
Kaikolan ..	2,110	748	246	331	118	48	8	2	928	...	2	22	179	554	171	434	...	...	...	3	99	332
Kammalan ...	17,469	7,960	2,555	2,815	1,164	952	486	88	6,864	...	13	112	888	4,624	1,277	2,645	...	1	2	26	695	1,921
Kanakkan ...	8,787	1,842	595	655	828	202	61	1	1,451	...	...	20	176	98	272(?)	444	...	...	1	11	101	381
Kaniyan ...	1,620	725	206	249	145	91	32	2	620	...	1	7	65	.	142	275	...	...	...	4	80	191
Kshatriya, Malayali.	504	190	65	77	32	9	7	...	224	...	1	9	34	186	44	90	...	...	2	1	18	74
Do Paradesi ...	274	98	29	57	8	2	2	...	131	...	2	3	22	78	26	45	...	...	...	8	8	34
Kudumi Chetti ...	5,871	1,601	789	719	80	23	32	8	2,940	..	98	295	595	1,634	318	1,330	...	...	6	27	440	857
Kusavan ...	1,728	694	256	296	84	49	13	6	853	...	2	24	105	557	165	181	...	...	2	2	35	142
Nayar ...	62,486	25,282	8,158	9,488	6,673	2,867	1,118	138	28,010	...	41	507	3,385	14,596	4,481	14,244	...	...	23	291	4,888	9,542
Ottanaikan ...	1,447	521	159	212	88	47	15	...	624	...	2	24	81	419	98	302	...	..	...	3	63	236
Pandaran ...	1,829	784	265	327	112	58	12	3	709	...	6	33	117	412	141	336	...	...	..	5	97	234

TABLE XIV.—*Continued.*

FEMALE.

COCHIN STATE. IMPERIAL SERIES.

Civil condition by Age for Selected Castes.

CASTE, TRIBE OR RACE	POPULATION DEALT WITH	UNMARRIED							MARRIED							WIDOWED						
		Total	0–5	5–12	12–15	15–20	20–40	40 and over	Total	0–5	5–12	12–15	15–20	20–40	40 and over	Total	0–5	5–12	12–15	15–20	20–40	40 and over
1	2	3	4	5	6	7	8	9	10	11	12	13	14	15	16	17	18	19	20	21	22	23
Panan ...	1,411	568	194	199	78	65	26	16	611	...	2	9	64	418	128	287	...	...	...	7	64	166
Panditattan ...	1,114	448	148	200	54	87	9	...	469	...	2	19	68	295	85	197	...	...	...	1	59	137
Parayan ...	4,209	1,876	617	781	259	124	52	43	1,788	...	1	27	285	1,167	358	545	...	1	3	6	180	405
Pulayan ...	37,503	16,444	5,646	6,359	2,355	1,458	560	66	15,705	...	25	259	2,014	10,321	3,086	5,354	...	3	7	85	1,411	3,848
Valan ...	3,781	1,585	595	621	199	106	48	16	1,666	...	2	87	233	1,041	353	580	...	...	1	10	150	369
Velan ...	4,727	2,010	694	761	293	186	69	7	1,986	...	3	32	258	1,299	394	731	...	..	2	12	186	551
Velakkattalavan ..	1,647	655	212	242	80	74	39	8	618	...	2	16	100	386	114	374	...	...	...	5	112	257
Vellalan ...	2,968	1,184	329	475	186	113	25	6	1,119	...	2	17	145	750	205	715	...	...	...	8	204	503
Veluttedan ...	1,792	698	237	258	108	63	31	1	701	...	2	17	91	469	122	398	...	...	...	7	112	274
Vettuvan ...	2,824	1,318	476	501	187	114	32	8	1,170	...	1	10	149	777	233	341	...	...	1	4	71	265
MUSALMAN																						
Jonakan ..	25,195	11,810	4,024	4,597	1,756	1,032	358	43	10,240	...	18	193	1,468	6,875	1,985	3,145	...	1	7	72	856	2,208
Ravuttan ...	4,119	1,740	565	747	243	148	33	4	1,629	...	2	60	310	995	262	750	...	...	8	10	255	482
CHRISTIAN																						
Anglo Indian ..	1,205	614	172	208	86	78	63	12	446	...	...	7	50	303	86	145	...	...	...	...	35	110
European ...	20	7	2	1	...	...	4	...	12	...	...	...	...	7	5	1	...	...	...	...	...	1
Native Christian ...	114,019	52,268	18,069	21,058	7,496	3,928	1,450	272	47,819	...	162	987	6,878	30,902	8,890	13,932	...	7	9	106	2,985	10,825
ANIMIST																						
Malayan ...	1,181	492	174	178	76	43	23	3	560	...	...	13	67	382	98	129	...	...	...	3	40	86
JEW ...	604	267	71	84	44	35	31	2	255	...	1	1	24	158	71	82	...	...	...	1	17	64

TABLE XV.

OCCUPATION OR MEANS OF LIVELIHOOD.

PART A.—GENERAL TABLE.

NOTE.— Table XV is divided, according to the Census Commissioner's scheme, into five parts, A, B, C, D and E. Parts A and D deal with the whole population of the State. Part B shows the subsidiary occupations of the actual workers among the agriculturists only. Part C is intended to show certain mixed traditional occupations, but as such cases are extremely rare in Cochin, this part has not been prepared for the State. Part E gives information regarding industries, which was collected in a special industrial schedule which was filled up by the owners, managers or agents of factories, mills, etc., in which at least 20 persons were employed on the 11th March 1911.

TABLE XV.

Occupation or means of Livelihood.

COCHIN STATE. IMPERIAL SERIES.

PA A. GENERAL TABLE.

CLASS.	SUB-CLASS.	ORDER.	GROUP.	OCCUPATION OR MEANS OF LIVELIHOOD.	TOTAL WORKERS AND DEPENDENTS.	ACTUAL WORKERS. TOTAL. Males.	ACTUAL WORKERS. TOTAL. Females.	PARTIALLY AGRICULTURISTS. Males.	PARTIALLY AGRICULTURISTS. Females.	DEPENDENTS.
1	2	3	4	5	6	7	8	9	10	11
A. PRODUCTION OF RAW MATERIALS.	I. Exploitation of the surface of the earth.	1		**Pasture and Agriculture** ...	**470,607**	**119,343**	**62,641**	**1,522**	**101**	**288,623**
		(a)		ORDINARY CULTIVATION.						
			1	Income from rent of agricultural land—						
			(a)	*Non-cultivating land owners* ...	14,667	2,309	545	...	...	11,813
			(b)	*Cultivating land owners* ...	47,476	9,736	1,763	...	...	35,977
			2	Ordinary cultivators—						
			(a)	*Non-cultivating tenants* ...	2,313	388	155	...	...	1,770
			(b)	*Cultivating tenants* ...	206,509	49,897	10,751	...	...	145,861
			3	Agents, managers of landed estates (not planters), clerks, rent collectors, etc....	1,507	530	5	...	...	972
			4	Farm servants and field labourers—						
			(a)	*Farm servants* ...	2,756	901	172	...	...	1,683
			(b)	*Field labourers and agricultural coolies.*	164,650	46,626	47,674	...	...	70,350
		(b)		GROWERS OF SPECIAL PRODUCTS AND MARKET GARDENING.						
			5	Tea, coffee, cinchona, (rubber) and indigo plantations ...	3,319	1,204	437	...	...	1,678
			6	Fruit, flower, vegetable, betel, vine, arecanut, etc., growers ...	19,877	4,506	772	...	...	14,599
		(c)		FORESTRY.						
			7	Forest officers, Rangers, Guards, etc. ...	647	223	...	5	...	424
			8	Wood cutters; firewood, lac, catechu, rubber, etc., collectors and charcoal burners ...	4,775	1,518	299	97	46	2,963
		(d)		RAISING OF FARM STOCK.						
			9	Cattle and buffalo breeders and keepers.	190	74	10	3	...	106
			10	Sheep, goat and pig breeders ...	65	23	2	20	...	40
			11	Breeders of other animals, (horses, mules, camels, asses, etc.) ...	2	2	...	2	...	...
			12	Herdsmen, shepherds, goatherds, etc. ...	1,683	1,400	56	1,805	55	227
		(e)		RAISING OF SMALL ANIMALS.						
			13	Birds, bees, silkworms, etc. ...	171	11	...	...	...	160
		2		**Fishing and Hunting** ...	**13,297**	**5,374**	**961**	**93**	**14**	**6,362**
			14	Fishing ...	13,261	5,354	961	93	14	6,946
			15	Hunting ...	36	20	...	...	...	16
				Total Sub-Class I ...	**483,904**	**124,717**	**63,602**	**1,615**	**115**	**295,585**
	II. Extraction of minerals.	3		**Mines** ...	**6**	...	...	...	...	**6**
			17	Mines and metallic minerals (gold, iron, manganese, etc.) ...	6	...	...	...	...	6
				Total Sub-Class II ...	**6**	...	...	...	...	**6**
				Total Class A ...	**483,910**	**124,717**	**63,602**	**1,615**	**115**	**295,591**
B. PREPARATION AND SUPPLY OF MATERIAL SUBSTANCES.	III. Industry.	6		**Textiles** ...	**46,823**	**9,381**	**18,632**	**103**	**219**	**18,812**
			22	Cotton spinning, sizing and weaving ...	6,626	2,083	1,094	28	2	3,449
			24	Rope, twine and string ...	684	274	121	9	6	289
			25	Other fibres (cocoanut, aloes, flax, hemp, straw, etc.) ...	39,510	7,021	17,417	65	211	15,072
			29	Persons occupied with feathers ...	4	3	...	1	...	1
			30	Dyeing, bleaching, printing, preparation and sponging of textiles ...	1	...	...	...	...	1

TABLE XV.—*Continued.*

Occupation or means of Livelihood.

COCHIN STATE. IMPERIAL SERIES.

PART A. GENERAL TABLE.

CLASS.	SUB-CLASS.	ORDER.	GROUP.	OCCUPATION OR MEANS OF LIVELIHOOD.	TOTAL WORKERS AND DEPENDENTS.	ACTUAL WORKERS. Total. Males.	Total. Females.	Partially Agriculturists. Males.	Partially Agriculturists. Females.	DEPENDENTS.
1	2	3	4	5	6	7	8	9	10	11
B. Preparation and Supply of Material Substances.	III. Industry.	7		**Hides, Skins and hard materials from the Animal Kingdom** ...	**1,179**	**405**	**48**	**18**	...	**726**
			32	Tanners, curriers, leather dressers, and dyers, etc.	1	1	...	...	...	...
			33	Makers of leather articles, such as trunks, water bags, etc. ...	1,177	403	48	18	...	726
			35	Bone, ivory, horn, shell, etc., workers .	1	1	...	...	...	...
		8		**Wood** ...	**43,232**	**12,459**	**5,761**	**369**	**328**	**23,012**
			36	Sawyers, carpenters, turners and joiners, etc. ...	30,217	9,158	190	239	3	20,869
			37	Basket makers and other industries of woody material including leaves ...	13,015	3,301	5,571	130	325	4,143
		9		**Metals** ...	**9,277**	**2.756**	**360**	**57**	**5**	**6,162**
			39	Plough and agricultural implement makers ...	16	3	...	...	...	13
			41	Other workers in iron and makers of implements and tools, principally or exclusively of iron ...	7,343	2,115	288	54	4	4,940
			42	Workers in brass, copper and bell metal .	1,425	484	72	3	1	869
			43	Workers in other metals (tin, zinc, lead, quicksilver, etc.) ...	491	152	...	...	...	339
			44	Workers in mints, die sinkers, etc. ...	2	1	...	...	...	1
		10		**Ceramics** ..	**4,196**	**1.271**	**914**	**14**	**12**	**2,011**
			45	Makers of glass and crystal ware ...	18	...	8	...	2	5
			46	Makers of porcelain and crockery ...	62	...	3	...	...	59
			47	Potters and earthen pipe and bowl makers ...	3,400	1,121	814	2	10	1,465
			48	Brick and tile makers ...	721	150	89	12	...	482
		11		**Chemical Products properly so called and Analogous** ...	**4,192**	**1,042**	**365**	**6**	**11**	**2,785**
			50	Manufacture of matches and explosive materials ...	254	54	...	...	...	200
			51	Manufacture of aerated and mineral waters ...	1	1	...	...	...	...
			52	Manufacture of dyes, paint and ink ...	1	1	...	...	...	...
			53	Manufacture and refining of vegetable and mineral oils ...	3,936	986	365	6	11	2,585
		12		**Food Industries** ..	**40,211**	**8,058**	**9,508**	**609**	**339**	**22,645**
			56	Rice pounders and huskers and flour grinders ...	15,230	688	9,102	25	300	5,440
			57	Bakers and biscuit makers ...	176	38	17	...	...	121
			58	Grain parchers, etc. ...	224	44	79	1	...	101
			59	Butchers ...	467	83	3	2	...	381
			60	Fish curers ...	8	7	...	...	...	1
			61	Butter, cheese and ghee makers ...	20	3	9	...	...	8
			62	Makers of sugar, molasses and gur ...	479	56	298	...	39	125
			63	Sweetmeat makers, preparers of jam and condiments, etc. ...	15	2	...	...	...	13

TABLE XV.—*Continued.*

Occupation or means of Livelihood.

COCHIN STATE. IMPERIAL SERIES.

PART A. GENERAL TABLE.

CLASS.	SUB-CLASS.	ORDER.	GROUP.	OCCUPATION OR MEANS OF LIVELIHOOD.	TOTAL WORKERS AND DEPENDENTS.	ACTUAL WORKERS. Total. Males.	ACTUAL WORKERS. Total. Females.	ACTUAL WORKERS. Partially Agriculturists. Males.	ACTUAL WORKERS. Partially Agriculturists. Females.	DEPENDENTS.
1	2	3	4	5	6	7	8	9	10	11
B. PREPARATION AND SUPPLY OF MATERIAL SUBSTANCES.	III. Industry.	12		**Food Industries.—contd.**						
			64	Brewers and distillers ...	5	5	...	...	...	...
			65	Toddy drawers ...	23,303	6,985	...	581	...	16,318
			66	Manufacturers of tobacco, opium and ganja ...	284	147	...	...	...	137
		13		**Industries of Dress and the Toilet** ..	**18,438**	**4,910**	**5,049**	**214**	**58**	**8,479**
			67	Hat, cap and turban makers ...	1	...	1	...	...	...
			68	Tailors, milliners, dress makers and darners, embroiderers on linen ...	3,954	1,303	588	25	12	2,063
			69	Shoe, boot and sandal makers ...	99	19	1	...	...	79
			70	Other industries pertaining to dress, gloves, socks, gaiters, belts, buttons, umbrellas, canes, etc. ...	36	...	...	...	...	36
			71	Washing, cleaning and dyeing ...	8,701	1,855	3,647	9	18	3,199
			72	Barbers, hair dressers and wig-makers ...	5,405	1,669	782	177	28	2,954
			73	Other industries connected with the toilet (tattooers, shampooers, bath houses, etc). ...	242	64	30	3	...	148
		14		**Furniture Industries** ..	**132**	**37**	...	**2**	...	**95**
			74	Cabinet makers, carriage painters, etc....	132	37	...	2	...	95
		15		**Building Industries** ..	**13,532**	**4,180**	**352**	**113**	**11**	**9,000**
			76	Lime burners, cement workers ...	541	233	46	3	...	262
			77	Excavators, plinth builders & well sinkers	20	12	...	...	...	8
			78	Stone and marble workers, masons and bricklayers ...	11,842	3,661	152	107	7	8,029
			79	Others (thatchers, building contractors, house painters, tilers, plumbers, locksmiths, etc.) ...	1,129	274	154	3	4	701
		16		**Construction of means of Transport** ..	**66**	**25**	...	...	...	**41**
			80	Cart, carriage, palki, etc., makers and wheelwrights ...	5	3	...	...	...	2
			82	Ship and boat builders ...	61	22	...	...	...	39
		17		**Production and Transmission of Physical Forces (Heat, Light, Electricity, Motive Power, etc.)** ..	**1**	**1**	...	...	...	...
			83	Gas works, electric light and ice factories..	1	1	...	...	...	...
		18		**Industries of Luxury and those pertaining to Literature and the Arts and Sciences** ...	**7,785**	**2,449**	**48**	**66**	**1**	**5,288**
			84	Printers, lithographers, engravers, etc ...	287	128	...	1	...	159
			85	Newspaper and magazine managers and editors, journalists, etc. ...	14	4	...	...	...	10
			86	Book binders and stitchers, envelope makers, etc. ...	157	58	1	...	...	98
			87	Makers of musical instruments ...	9	2	...	...	...	7

TABLE XV.—*Continued.*

Occupation or means of Livelihood.

COCHIN STATE. IMPERIAL SERIES.

PART A. GENERAL TABLE.

CLASS.	SUB-CLASS.	ORDER.	GROUP.	OCCUPATION OR MEANS OF LIVELIHOOD.	TOTAL WORKERS AND DEPENDENTS.	ACTUAL WORKERS. Total. Males	Total. Females	Partially Agriculturists. Males	Partially Agriculturists. Females	DEPENDENTS.
1	2	3	4	5	6	7	8	9	10	11
B. PREPARATION AND SUPPLY OF MATERIAL SUBSTANCES.	III. Industry.	18		**Industries of Luxury and those pertaining to Literature and the Arts and Sciences.—contd.**						
			88	Makers of watches and clocks and optical, photographic and surgical instruments. ...	50	21	...	...	...	29
			89	Workers in precious stones and metals, enamellers, imitation jewellery makers, gilders, etc. ...	7,145	2,169	45	65	1	4,931
			90	Makers of bangles, rosaries, bead and other necklaces, spangles, lingams and sacred threads ...	32	12	2	...	...	18
			91	Toy, kite, cage, fishing tackle, etc., makers, taxidermists, etc. ...	89	55	...	...	...	34
			92	Others, including managers, persons other than performers employed in theatres and other places of public entertainment, employees of public societies, race course service, huntsmen, etc. ...	2	...	...	...	...	2
		19		**Industries concerned with Refuse matter** ..	**2,985**	**115**	**1,519**	**2**	**29**	**1,351**
			93	Sweepers, scavengers, dust and sweeping contractors ...	2,985	115	1,519	2	29	1,351
				Total Sub-Class III ...	**192,061**	**47,088**	**42,556**	**1,573**	**1,013**	**102,407**
	IV. Transport.	20		**Transport by Water** ..	**6,773**	**2,911**	**10**	**123**	...	**3,852**
			95	Ship owners and their employees, ship brokers, ships' officers, engineers, mariners and firemen ...	408	248	9	81	...	151
			96	Persons employed on the maintenance of streams, rivers and canals, (including construction) ...	18	5	...	...	...	13
			97	Boatowners, boatmen and towmen ...	6,347	2,658	1	47	...	3,688
		21		**Transport by Road** ..	**10,050**	**3,527**	**346**	**118**	**4**	**6,177**
			98	Persons employed on the construction and maintenance of roads and bridges .	1,458	596	307	11	4	555
			99	Cart owners and drivers, coachmen, stable boys, tramway, mailcarriage, etc., managers and employees (excluding private servants) ...	7,568	3,698	8	100	...	4,862
			100	Palki, etc., bearers and owners ...	81	12	...	...	...	19
			102	Porters and messengers ...	993	221	31	2	...	741
		22		**Transport by Rail** ...	**1,301**	**569**	**1**	**2**	...	**731**
			103	Railway employees of all kinds other than construction coolies ..	1,287	559	1	1	...	727
			104	Labourers employed on railway construction ...	14	10	...	1	...	4

TABLE XV.—*Continued.*

Occupation or means of Livelihood.

COCHIN STATE. IMPERIAL SERIES.

PART A. GENERAL TABLE.

CLASS.	SUB-CLASS.	ORDER.	GROUP.	OCCUPATION OR MEANS OF LIVELIHOOD.	TOTAL WORKERS AND DEPENDENTS.	ACTUAL WORKERS.				DEPENDENTS.
						TOTAL.		PARTIALLY AGRICULTURISTS.		
						Males.	Females.	Males.	Females.	
1	2	3	4	5	6	7	8	9	10	11
B. PREPARATION AND SUPPLY OF MATERIAL SUBSTANCES.	IV. Transport	23		**Post Office, Telegraph and Telephone Services** ..	**732**	**275**	...	**6**	...	**457**
			105	Post Office, Telegraph and Telephone services ...	415	143	...	1	...	272
			105(a)	Anchal service * ...	317	132	...	5	...	185
				Total Sub-Class IV ..	**18,856**	**7,282**	**357**	**249**	**4**	**11,217**
	V. Trade	24		**Banks, Establishments of Credit Exchange and Insurance** ..	**4,424**	**844**	**595**	**79**	**4**	**2,985**
			106	Bank managers, money lenders, exchange and insurance agents, money changers and brokers and their employees ...	4,424	844	595	79	4	2,985
		25		**Brokerage, Commission and Export** ..	**255**	**85**	**4**	...	...	**166**
			107	Brokers, commission agents, commercial travellers, warehouse owners and employees ...	255	85	4	...	...	166
		26		**Trade in Textiles** ..	**5,646**	**1,812**	**86**	**184**	...	**3,748**
			108	Trade in piece goods, wool, cotton, silk, hair and other textiles ...	5,646	1,812	86	184	...	3,748
		27		**Trade in Skins, Leather, and Furs** ..	**544**	**132**	**11**	**5**	...	**401**
			109	Trade in skins, leather, furs, feathers, horn, etc. ...	544	132	11	5	...	401
		28		**Trade in Wood** ..	**1,305**	**394**	**8**	**24**	**1**	**903**
			110	Trade in wood (not firewood), cork, bark, etc. ...	1,305	394	8	24	1	903
		29		**Trade in Metals** ..	**321**	**71**	**7**	...	...	**243**
			111	Trade in metals, machinery, knife, tool, etc., sellers ...	321	71	7	...	...	243
		30		**Trade in Pottery** ..	**217**	**37**	**23**	**1**	...	**157**
			112	Trade in pottery ...	217	37	23	1	...	157
		31		**Trade in Chemical Products** ..	**842**	**301**	**5**	**3**	...	**536**
			113	Trade in chemical products (drugs, dyes, paints, petroleum, explosives, etc.) ...	842	301	5	3	...	536

* Cochin State Postal Service.

TABLE XV.—*Continued.*

Occupation or means of Livelihood.

COCHIN STATE — IMPERIAL SERIES.

PART A. GENERAL TABLE.

CLASS.	SUB-CLASS.	ORDER.	GROUP.	OCCUPATION OR MEANS OF LIVELIHOOD.	TOTAL WORKERS AND DEPENDENTS.	ACTUAL WORKERS. TOTAL. Males.	ACTUAL WORKERS. TOTAL. Females.	ACTUAL WORKERS. PARTIALLY AGRICULTURISTS. Males.	ACTUAL WORKERS. PARTIALLY AGRICULTURISTS. Females.	DEPENDENTS.
1	2	3	4	5	6	7	8	9	10	11
B. PREPARATION AND SUPPLY OF MATERIAL SUBSTANCES.	V. Trade	32		**Hotels, Cafes, Restaurants, etc.** ..	**9,690**	**2,346**	**1,411**	**57**	**9**	**5,938**
			114	Vendors of wine, liquors, aerated waters, etc. ...	6,203	1,336	1,061	23	5	3,806
			115	Owners and managers of hotels, cook-shops, sarais, etc., and their employees	3,487	1,010	350	34	4	2,127
		33		**Other trade in food stuffs** ..	**59,573**	**16,761**	**6,362**	**715**	**219**	**36,450**
			116	Fish dealers ...	11,842	2,895	1,483	66	5	7,464
			117	Grocers and sellers of vegetable oil, salt and other condiments ...	14,742	4,805	557	313	5	9,380
			118	Sellers of milk, butter, ghee, poultry, eggs, etc. ...	1,625	321	458	9	12	846
			119	Sellers of sweetmeats, sugar, gur and molasses ...	3,842	894	921	5	6	2,027
			120	Cardamom, betel-leaf, vegetables, fruit and areca nut sellers ..	11,347	3,262	847	144	1	7,238
			121	Grain and pulse dealers ...	13,813	3,812	2,015	168	197	7,986
			122	Tobacco, opium, ganja, etc., sellers ...	1,340	434	10	4	1	896
			123	Dealers in sheep, goats and pigs ...	459	148	10	4	...	301
			124	Dealers in hay, grass and fodder ...	563	190	61	2	2	312
		34		**Trade in Clothing and Toilet articles** ..	**336**	**154**	...	**1**	...	**182**
			125	Trade in ready made clothing and other articles of dress and the toilet (hats, umbrellas, socks, ready made shoes, perfumes, etc.) ...	336	154	...	1	...	182
		35		**Trade in furniture** ..	**1,537**	**558**	**108**	**21**	...	**871**
			126	Trade in furniture, carpets, curtains and bedding ...	945	344	101	10	...	500
			127	Trade in hardware, cooking utensils, porcelain, crockery, glassware, bottles, articles for gardening, the cellar, etc....	592	214	7	11	...	371
		36		**Trade in Building Materials** ..	**1,585**	**379**	**223**	**15**	**4**	**983**
			128	Trade in building materials (stones, bricks, plaster, cement, sand, tiles, thatch, etc.) ...	1,585	379	223	15	4	983
		37		**Trade in means of Transport** ..	**797**	**336**	**11**	**11**	...	**450**
			129	Dealers and hirers of elephants, camels, horses, cattle, asses, mules, etc., sellers (not makers) of carriages, saddlery, etc. ...	797	336	11	11	...	450
		38		**Trade in Fuel** ..	**2,043**	**817**	**92**	**24**	**2**	**1,134**
			130	Dealers in firewood, charcoal, coal, cowdung, etc. ...	2,043	817	92	24	2	1,134

TABLE XV. – *Continued.*

COCHIN STATE. **Occupation or means of Livelihood.** IMPERIAL SERIES.

PART A. GENERAL TABLE.

CLASS	SUB-CLASS	ORDER	GROUP	OCCUPATION OR MEANS OF LIVELIHOOD	TOTAL WORKERS AND DEPENDENTS	ACTUAL WORKERS: TOTAL: Males	ACTUAL WORKERS: TOTAL: Females	ACTUAL WORKERS: PARTIALLY AGRICULTURISTS: Males	ACTUAL WORKERS: PARTIALLY AGRICULTURISTS: Females	DEPENDENTS
1	2	3	4	5	6	7	8	9	10	11
B. PREPARATION AND SUPPLY OF MATERIAL SUBSTANCES	V. Trade	39		**Trade in Articles of Luxury and those Pertaining to Letters and the Arts and Sciences** ..	**1,118**	**237**	**64**	**11**	...	**817**
			131	Dealers in precious stones, jewellery (real and imitation) clocks, optical instruments, etc. ...	642	133	26	10	...	483
			132	Dealers in common bangles, bead necklaces, fans, small articles, toys, hunting and fishing tackle, flowers, etc. ...	346	88	38	1	...	220
			133	Publishers, booksellers, stationers, dealers in music, pictures, musical instruments and curiosities. ...	130	16	...	...	...	114
		40		**Trade in Refuse matter** ..	**54**	**7**	**16**	...	**1**	**31**
			134	Dealers in rags, stable refuse, etc. ...	54	7	16	...	1	31
		41		**Trade of other Sorts** ..	**15,214**	**4,234**	**436**	**176**	**12**	**10,544**
			135	Shop-keepers otherwise unspecified ...	14,450	3,929	416	168	12	10,105
			137	Conjurors, acrobats, fortune tellers, reciters, exhibitors of curiosities and wild animals ...	598	260	20	4	...	318
			138	Other trades (including farmers of pounds, tools and markets) ...	166	45	...	4	...	121
				Total Sub-Class V. ..	**105,501**	**29 505**	**9,462**	**1,277**	**232**	**66,534**
				Total Class B. ..	**316,406**	**83 875**	**52,375**	**3 099**	**1,269**	**180.158**
C. PUBLIC ADMINISTRATION AND LIBERAL ARTS.	VI. Public force.	42		**Army** ..	**576**	**247**	...	**1**	...	**329**
			140	Army (Native States) ...	576	247	...	1	...	329
		44		**Police** ..	**1,164**	**453**	...	**5**	...	**711**
			142	Police ...	1,164	453	...	5	..	711
				Total Sub-Class VI ..	**1,740**	**700**	...	**6**	...	**1,040**
	VII. Public Administration.	45		**Public Administration** ..	**10,045**	**3,507**	**224**	**159**	**1**	**6 314**
			144	Service of the State (British) ...	71	40	...	...	...	31
			145	Service of Native and Foreign States ..						
			(a)	*Chiefs and their families* ...	304	85	...	...	...	219
			(b)	*Officers and servants of chiefs and their families* ...	1,473	397	214	16	1	862
			(c)	*Sirkar officers* ...	690	126	...	20	...	564
			(d)	*Clerical establishment* ...	2,477	863	...	43	...	1,614
			(e)	*Menials unspecified* ...	3,377	294	...	33	...	2,083
			(f)	*Service of States other than Cochin* ...	34	7	...	...	...	27
			146	Municipal and other local (not village) service ..						
			(a)	*Municipal service (clerical establishment)* ...	82	24	...	1	...	58
			(b)	*Do. other menials* ...	318	143	10	1	...	165

TABLE XV.—*Continued.*

Occupation or means of Livelihood.

COCHIN TATE. IMPERIAL SERIES.

ART A. GENERAL TABLE.

CLASS	SUB-CLASS	ORDER	GROUP	OCCUPATION OR MEANS OF LIVELIHOOD	TOTAL WORKERS AND DEPENDENTS	ACTUAL WORKERS				DEPENDENTS
						TOTAL		PARTIALLY AGRICULTURISTS		
						Males	Females	Males	Females	
1	2	3	4	5	6	7	8	9	10	11
C. PUBLIC ADMINISTRATION AND LIBERAL ARTS	VII. Public Administration	45		**Public Administration.—contd.**						
			147	Village officials and servants other than watchmen ...	1,219	528	...	45	...	691
				Total Sub-Class VII ..	**10,045**	**3,507**	**224**	**159**	**1**	**6.314**
	VIII. Professions and liberal arts.	46		**Religion** ..	**10.648**	**8.484**	**938**	**200**	**1**	**6.226**
			148	Priests, ministers, etc. ...	2,699	970	13	68	...	1,716
			149	Religious mendicants, inmates of monasteries, etc. ..	155	12	114	...	...	29
			150	Catechists, readers, church and mission service ...	1,332	338	32	19	...	962
			151	Temple, burial or burning ground service, pilgrim conductors, circumcisers ...	6,462	2,164	779	113	1	3,519
		47		**Law** ..	**2,163**	**585**	...	**59**	...	**1,578**
			152	Lawyers of all kinds including kazis, law agents and mukhtiars ...	1,157	223	...	35	...	934
			153	Lawyers' clerks, petition writers, etc...	1.006	362	...	24	...	644
		48		**Medicine** ..	**4,881**	**1.280**	**195**	**79**	**5**	**3,406**
			154	Medical practitioners of all kinds, including dentists, oculists and veterinary surgeons ...	4,451	1,203	55	76	...	3,193
			155	Midwives, vaccinators, compounders, nurses, masseurs, etc. ...	430	77	140	3	5	213
		49		**Instruction** ..	**7.417**	**2.289**	**308**	**119**	**2**	**4.620**
			156	Professors and teachers of all kinds, and clerks and servants connected with education ...	7,417	2,289	308	119	2	4,620
		50		**Letters and Arts and Sciences** ..	**5.455**	**1.819**	**175**	**58**	**1**	**3.461**
			157	Public scribes, stenographers, etc. ...	69	37	...	...	...	32
			158	Architects, surveyors, engineers and their employees ...	617	193	...	3	...	424
			159	Others (authors, photographers, artists, sculptors, astronomers, meteorologists, botanists, astrologers, etc). ...	1,708	438	3	25	...	1,267
			160	Music composers and masters, players on all kinds of musical instruments (not military), singers, actors and dancers ...	3,061	1,151	172	30	1	1,738
				Total Sub-Class VIII ..	**30,564**	**9,457**	**1,616**	**515**	**9**	**19,491**
	IX. Persons living on their income	51		**Persons Living Principally on their income** ..	**1,129**	**326**	**16**	**32**	...	**787**
			161	Proprietors (other than of agricultural land) fund and scholarship holders and pensioners ...	1,129	326	16	32	...	787
				Total Sub-Class IX ..	**1,129**	**326**	**16**	**32**	...	**787**
				Total Class C ...	**43,478**	**18,990**	**1.856**	**712**	**10**	**27.632**

TABLE XV.—*Continued.*

COCHIN STATE. IMPERIAL SERIES.

Occupation or means of Livelihood.

PART A. GENERAL TABLE.

CLASS.	SUB-CLASS.	ORDER.	GROUP.	OCCUPATION OR MEANS OF LIVELIHOOD.	TOTAL WORKERS AND DEPENDENTS.	ACTUAL WORKERS. TOTAL Males	ACTUAL WORKERS. TOTAL Females	PARTIALLY AGRICULTURISTS Males	PARTIALLY AGRICULTURISTS Females	DEPENDENTS.
1	2	3	4	5	6	7	8	9	10	11
D. MISCELLANEOUS.	X. Domestic service	52		**Domestic Service** ..	**5,573**	**2,331**	**1,516**	**23**	**16**	**1,706**
			162	Cooks, water carriers, door keepers, watchmen and other indoor servants	5,061	2,073	1,510	12	16	1,478
			163	Private grooms, coachmen, dog boys, etc.	512	278	6	11	...	228
				Total Sub-Class X ..	**5,573**	**2,331**	**1,516**	**23**	**16**	**1,706**
	XI. Insufficiently described occupations.	53		**General Terms which do not indicate a Definite Occupation** ..	**66,194**	**22,806**	**7,045**	**964**	**145**	**36,843**
			164	Manufacturers, business men and contractors otherwise unspecified ...	956	260	...	5	...	696
			165	Cashiers, accountants, book keepers, clerks and other employees in unspecified offices, warehouses and shops...	5,148	1,600	125	84	...	3,423
			166	Mechanics otherwise unspecified ...	20	9	...	...	...	11
			167	Labourers and workmen otherwise unspecified ...	60,070	20,437	6,920	875	145	32,713
				Total Sub-Class XI ..	**66,194**	**22,806**	**7,045**	**964**	**145**	**36,843**
	XII. Unproductive.	54		**Inmates of Jails, Asylums and Hospitals** ..	**157**	**108**	**7**	**1**	...	**42**
			168	Inmates of jails, asylums and hospitals	157	108	7	1	...	42
		55		**Beggars, Vagrants, Prostitutes** ..	**2,390**	**900**	**865**	**8**	**5**	**625**
			169	Beggars, vagrants, procurers, prostitutes, receivers of stolen goods, cattle poisoners ...	2,390	900	865	8	5	625
				Total Sub-Class XII ..	**2,547**	**1,008**	**872**	**9**	**5**	**667**
				Total Class D ...	**74,314**	**25,665**	**9,433**	**996**	**166**	**39,216**
				Grand Total ...	**918,110**	**248,247**	**127,266**	**6,422**	**1,560**	**542,597**

TABLE XV.

OCCUPATION OR MEANS OF LIVELIHOOD.

Part B.—Subsidiary occupations of Agriculturists—actual workers only.

TABLE XV.

COCHIN STATE. IMPERIAL SERIES.

OCCUPATION OR MEANS OF LIVELIHOOD.

PART B.—Subsidiary occupations of Agriculturists—actual workers only.

Occupation.	Total number of actual workers.		Number of actual workers who returned subsidiary occupations.		Details of subsidiary occupations returned.																					
					Non-cultivating land owners.		Cultivating land owners.		Cultivating tenants.		Agents, managers of landed estates (not planters) clerks, rent collectors, etc.		Farm servants and agricultural coolies.		Tea, coffee, rubber, etc. plantations.		Fruit, flower, vegetable, betel, vine, arecanut, etc., growers.		Wood cutters.		Herdsmen, shepherds and goatherds.		Fishing.		Other fibres (coconut) etc.	
	Males.	Females.	Males.	Females.	Males.	Females.	Males.	Females.	Males.	Females.	Males.	Females.	Males.	Females.	Males.	Females.	Males.	Females.	Males.	Females.	Males.	Females.	Males.	Females.	Males.	Females.
1	2	3	4	5	6	7	8	9	10	11	12	13	14	15	16	17	18	19	20	21	22	23	24	25	26	27
1. (a) Non-cultivating land owners ...	2 809	535	587	45	...	...	3	1	8	...	15	...	1	...	1	...	10	1	...	...	...	...	...	...	...	...
(b) Cultivating land owners ...	9 736	1,768	1,842	113	8	...	...	...	242	26	27	...	21	1	4	...	113	11	...	...	...	...	38	...	24	...
2. (a) Non-cultivating tenants ...	308	166	115	23	...	...	...	...	1	...	5	...	2	...	..	...	6	4	...	...	...	...	...	...	...	...
(b) Cultivating tenants ...	49,897	10,751	7,012	509	13	1	56	3	...	...	102	...	359	91	45	...	998	38	56	...	...	...	37	...	132	32
3. Agents. Managers of landed estates (not planters), clerks, rent collectors, etc. ...	530	5	49	...	3	...	4	...	13	...	...	...	...	...	...	...	5	...	...	...	...	...	...	...	...	...
4. (a) Farm servants ...	901	172	184	9	...	...	...	...	42	...	1	...	...	...	...	...	10	...	3	...	...	...	6	...	5	...
(b) Field labourers and agricultural coolies ...	46 028	47,674	2,641	2,008	...	...	10	...	99	11	...	...	...	...	8	...	44	18	128	13	27	4	180	...	224	401
5. Tea, coffee, cinchona, rubber and indigo plantations ...	1 20	437	18	2	...	...	1	...	...	...	...	...	2	1	...	...	4	...	...	...	1	...	...	...	...	...
6. Fruit, flower, vegetable, betel, vine, arecanut, etc., growers ...	4 800	772	509	108	2	...	58	...	105	4	21	...	61	...	...	...	...	...	1	...	2	...	18	...	3	6
Total ...	1 6 097	62 2.4	12,992	2,812	26	1	132	4	515	41	171	...	446	93	58	...	1,185	67	188	13	30	4	279	...	388	439

OCCUPATION OR MEANS OF LIVELIHOOD.

PART B.—Subsidiary occupations of Agriculturists—actual workers only.

OCCUPATION.	DETAILS OF SUBSIDIARY OCCUPATIONS RETURNED.																													
	Sawyers, carpenters, etc.		Basket makers and other industries of woody material.		Potters and earthen pipe makers.		Manufacture and refining of vegetable oil.		Rice pounders and huskers and flour grinders.		Grain parchers.		Toddy drawers.		Tailors.		Washing, cleaning, etc.		Barbers, hair dressers, etc.		Stone and marble workers, masons and brick layers.		Boat owners, boatmen and towmen.		Cart owners, Drivers, coachmen, etc.		Porters and messengers.		Bank managers and money lenders.	
	Males.	Females.	Males.	Females.	Males.	Females.	Males.	Females.	Males.	Females.	Males.	Females.	Males.	Females.	Males.	Females.	Males.	Females.	Males.	Females.	Males.	Females.	Males.	Females.	Males.	Females.	Males.	Females.	Males.	Females.
1	28	29	30	31	32	33	34	35	36	37	38	39	40	41	42	43	44	45	46	47	48	49	50	51	52	53	54	55	56	57
1. (a) Non-cultivating land owners ..	...	...	2	...	...	...	...	...	1	...	...	...	...	...	1	...	...	...	...	...	...	..	2	...	4	...	2	...	166	28
(b) Cultivating land owners ...	8	...	3	1	...	...	61	2	...	10	...	...	15	...	4	...	14	8	13	1	4	...	10	...	29	...	6	...	110	24
2. (a) Non-cultivating tenants ...	..	...	...	...	...	...	...	...	...	...	...	...	2	...	...	...	...	...	...	...	...	...	...	...	...	...	...	...	25	6
(b) Cultivating tenants ...	90	1	25	13	25	...	204	18	23	77	30	2	664	...	29	...	90	16	68	3	69	3	66	14	341	...	18	...	206	14
3. Agents, managers of landed estates (not planters), clerks, rent collectors, etc.	...	...	...	...	...	...	...	...	...	...	...	...	1	...	...	...	...	...	...	...	...	...	...	...	1	...	...	...	4	...
4. (a) Farm servants ..	6	..	...	1	...	...	9	...	1	5	...	...	47	2	5	...	...	...	...	...	2	...	1	...	3	...	...	...	...	...
(b) Field labourers and agricultural coolies ...	21	...	321	478	6	5	6	...	17	475	5	2	226	...	6	...	3	...	13	1	42	8	72	3	15	...	22	...	4	4
5. Tea, coffee, cinchona, rubber, and indigo plantations ...	...	...	...	...	...	...	...	...	...	1	...	...	...	...	2	...	...	...	...	...	...	...	...	...	...	...	...	...	...	...
6. Fruit, flower, vegetable, betel, vine, arecanut, etc. growers ...	...	...			...	...	...	...	...	57	...	...	6	...	1	...	4	...	1	...	...	...	2	...	...	...	...	...	45	28
Total ...	131	1	51	493	31	5	280	20	42	625	44	4	961	2	48	...	111	24	94	5	117	11	158	17	393	...	48	...	[illegible]	90

COCHIN STATE. IMPERIAL SERIES.

TABLE XV.—*Continued.*

OCCUPATION OR MEANS OF LIVELIHOOD.

PART B.—Subsidiary occupations of Agriculturists—actual workers only.

OCCUPATION.	DETAILS OF SUBSIDIARY OCCUPATIONS RETURNED.																											
	Trade in piece goods, wool, cotton, silk, etc.		Trade in wood (not firewood).		Vendors of wine, liquors, aerated waters, etc.		Fish dealers.		Grocers and sellers of vegetable oil, salt and other condiments.		Sellers of milk, butter, ghee, etc.		Sellers of sweetmeats, sugar, gur and molasses.		Cardamom, betel leaf, vegetables, fruit and arecanut sellers.		Grain and pulse dealers.		Tobacco, opium, ganja, etc., sellers.		Dealers and hirers of cattle, etc.		Shop-keepers otherwise unspecified.		Conjurers and fortune-tellers.		Sirkar officers of all kinds.	
	Males.	Females.	Males.	Females.	Males.	Females.	Males.	Females.	Males.	Females.	Males.	Females.	Males.	Females.	Males.	Females.	Males.	Females.	Males.	Females.	Males.	Females.	Males.	Females.	Males.	Females.	Males.	Females.
1	58	69	60	61	62	63	64	66	66	67	68	60	70	71	72	73	74	75	76	77	78	79	80	81	82	83	84	85
1. (a) Non-cultivating land owners ...	13	...	6	...	...	...	...	...	3	1	...	...	...	1	2	3	11	1	2	...	...	...	12	...	3	...	16	...
(b) Cultivating land owners ...	49	...	11	...	21	...	40	1	77	3	13	...	3	1	185	3	61	15	12	...	4	...	169	3	4	...	14	...
2. (a) Non-cultivating tenants ...	2	...	2	...	1	...	...	...	18	...	...	...	...	...	...	...	12	...	...	...	...	...	1	...	...	...	1	...
(b) Cultivating tenants ...	51	1	20	...	148	16	181	7	228	3	56	...	43	6	652	13	150	9	25	...	31	...	427	17	22	2	19	...
3. Agents, managers of landed estates (not planters) clerks, rent collectors, etc. ...	...	...	...	...	...	...	...	...	...	...	...	...	...	...	2	...	1	...	...	...	...	...	...	...	...	...	...	...
4. (a) Farm servants ...	...	...	...	...	4	...	2	...	2	...	...	...	...	...	3	...	1	1	...	...	...	...	7	...	...	...	...	...
(b) Field labourers and agricultural coolies ...	5	...	5	...	8	8	41	95	28	...	1	...	7	19	4	6	6	14	1	...	5	...	13	4	11	6	...	...
5. Tea, coffee, cinchona, rubber, and indigo plantations ...	...	...	...	...	...	...	...	...	...	...	...	...	...	...	...	...	...	...	...	...	...	...	...	...	...	...	...	...
6. Fruit, flower, vegetable, betel, vine, arecanut, etc., growers ...	...	...	...	...	1	...	21	...	35	...	...	...	1	...	107	...	7	...	...	...	...	...	10	...	18	...	...	...
Total ...	120	1	44	...	183	24	285	103	391	7	70	...	54	27	955	25	249	40	40	...	40	...	639	24	58	8	50	...

TABLE XV.—*Continued.*

OCCUPATION OR MEANS OF LIVELIHOOD.

PART B.—Subsidiary occupations of Agriculturists—actual workers only.

OCCUPATION.	DETAILS OF SUBSIDIARY OCCUPATIONS RETURNED.																							
	Village officials and servants.		Priests, ministers, etc.		Temple, burial or burning ground service.		Medical practitioners of all kinds.		Professors and teachers of all kinds.		Authors, photographers, artists, etc.		Music composers, singers, etc.		Proprietors (other than of agricultural land), pensioners.		Cooks, water-carriers.		Cashiers, accountants, etc.		Labourers and workmen otherwise unspecified.		Other occupations.	
	Males.	Females.	Males.	Females.	Males.	Females.	Males.	Females.	Males.	Females.	Males.	Females.	Males.	Females.	Males.	Females.	Males.	Females.	Males.	Females.	Males.	Females.	Males.	Females.
1	86	87	88	89	90	91	92	93	94	95	96	97	98	99	100	101	102	103	104	105	106	107	108	109
1. (a) Non-cultivating land owners ...	19	...	20	...	64	14	14	...	24	...	4	...	4	...	25	...	4	...	14	...	1	...	40	...
(b) Cultivating land owners ...	23	...	7	...	37	2	67	...	52	...	9	...	20	...	34	...	3	...	56	...	19	...	98	1
2 (a) Non-cultivating tenants ...	4	...	3	...	14	10	...	...	3	...	...	...	2	...	2	1	1	...	4	...	...	...	4	2
(b) Cultivating tenants ...	67	...	13	...	53	5	141	...	78	...	37	...	51	...	30	...	13	1	37	...	453	83	227	20
3. Agents, managers of landed estates (not planters) clerks, rent collectors, etc. ...	...	...	...	...	2	...	1	...	...	...	...	...	5	...	2	...	...	...	...	...	...	...	...	...
4. (a) Farm servants ...	1	...	...	...	2	...	...	...	1	...	...	...	1	...	...	...	...	...	...	...	12	...	7	...
(b) Field labourers and agricultural coolies ...	2	...	...	...	3	1	11	...	1	...	...	...	10	13	...	...	17	45	1	...	862	308	101	66
5. Tea, coffee, cinchona, rubber, and indigo plantations ...	...	...	...	...	...	...	...	...	...	...	...	...	...	...	...	...	...	...	...	...	3	...	...	...
6. Fruit, flower, vegetable, betel vine, arecanut, etc., growers ...	4	...	...	...	6	4	18	...	2	...	2	...	...	...	...	...	...	...	...	...	19	9	15	...
Total ...	120	...	43	...	181	36	252	...	161	...	52	...	93	13	93	1	38	46	112	...	1,369	400	492	99

TABLE XV.

OCCUPATION OR MEANS OF LIVELIHOOD.

PART D—Distribution by Religion.

TABLE XV.

Occupation or means of Livelihood.

COCHIN STATE. IMPERIAL SERIES.

PART D. DISTRIBUTION BY RELIGION.

CLASS.	SUB-CLASS.	ORDER.	GROUP.	OCCUPATION OR MEANS OF LIVELIHOOD.	TOTAL NUMBER OF WORKERS AND DEPENDENTS.	DISTRIBUTION BY RELIGION.				
						Hindu.	Musalman.	Christian.	Animist.	Others.
1	2	3	4	5	6	7	8	9	10	11
A. PRODUCTION OF RAW MATERIALS.	I. Exploitation of the surface of the earth.	1		**Pasture and Agriculture** ...	470,607	334,956	26,121	105,940	3,485	106
		(a)		ORDINARY CULTIVATION.						
			1	Income from rent of agricultural land—						
			(a)	*Non-cultivating land owners* ...	14,667	13,731	211	724	...	1
			(b)	*Cultivating land owners* ...	47,476	29,341	2,444	15,650	...	41
			2	Ordinary cultivators—						
			(a)	*Non-cultivating tenants* ...	2,313	2,125	16	172	...	...
			(b)	*Cultivating tenants* ...	206,509	128,712	13,299	64,880	76	42
			3	Agents, managers of landed estates (not planters), clerks, rent collectors, etc....	1,507	1,308	14	185	...	...
			4	Farm servants and field labourers—						
			(a)	*Farm servants* ...	2,756	1,694	135	900	27	...
			(b)	*Field labourers and agricultural coolies.*	164,650	139,941	6,620	15,967	2,122	...
		(b)		GROWERS OF SPECIAL PRODUCTS AND MARKET GARDENING.						
			5	Tea, coffee, cinchona, (rubber) and indigo plantations ...	3,319	2,203	252	739	125	...
			6	Fruit, flower, vegetable, betel, vine, arecanut, etc., growers ...	19,877	10,917	2,506	6,424	8	22
		(c)		FORESTRY.						
			7	Forest officers, Rangers, Guards, etc. ...	647	561	36	49	1	...
			8	Wood cutters ; firewood, lac, catechu, rubber, etc., collectors and charcoal burners ...	4,775	2,850	465	480	980	...
		(d)		RAISING OF FARM STOCK.						
			9	Cattle and buffalo breeders and keepers.	190	175	...	15	...	...
			10	Sheep, goat and pig breeders ...	65	65	...	...	...	...
			11	Breeders of other animals, (horses, mules, camels, asses, etc.) ...	2	2	...	...	...	...
			12	Herdsmen, shepherds, goatherds, etc. ...	1,688	1,328	123	86	140	...
		(e)		RAISING OF SMALL ANIMALS.						
			13	Birds, bees, silkworms, etc. ...	171	2	...	169	...	...
		2		**Fishing and Hunting** ...	13,297	7,984	407	4,906	...	...
			14	Fishing ...	13,261	7,968	407	4,886	...	...
			15	Hunting ...	36	16	...	20	...	...
				Total Sub-Class I ...	483,904	342 939	26,528	110,846	3,485	106
	II. Extraction of minerals.	3		**Mines** ...	6	6	...	...	...	...
			17	Mines and metallic minerals (gold, iron, manganese, etc.) ...	6	6	...	...	...	...
				Total Sub-Class II ...	6	6	...	...	...	...
				Total Class A ...	483,910	342,945	26,528	110,846	3,485	106
B. PREPARATION AND SUPPLY OF MATERIAL SUBSTANCES.	III. Industry.	6		**Textiles** ...	46,825	25,251	1,909	19,533	129	3
			22	Cotton spinning, sizing and weaving ...	6,626	6,101	298	227	...	...
			24	Rope, twine and string ...	684	546	6	...	129	3
			25	Other fibres (cocoanut, aloes, flax, hemp, straw, etc.) ...	39,510	18,599	1,605	19,306	...	...
			29	Persons occupied with feathers ...	4	4	...	...	...	...
			30	Dyeing, bleaching, printing, preparation and sponging of textiles ...	1	1	...	...	...	...

TABLE XV.—*Continued.*

Occupation or means of Livelihood.

COCHIN STATE. IMPERIAL SERIES.

PART D. DISTRIBUTION BY RELIGION.

CLASS.	SUB-CLASS.	ORDER.	GROUP.	OCCUPATION OR MEANS OF LIVELIHOOD.	TOTAL NUMBER OF WORKERS AND DEPENDENTS.	DISTRIBUTION BY RELIGION.				
						Hindu.	Musalman.	Christian.	Animist.	Others.
1	2	3	4	5	6	7	8	9	10	11
B. PREPARATION AND SUPPLY OF MATERIAL SUBSTANCES.	III. Industry.	7		**Hides, Skins and hard materials from the Animal Kingdom** ...	**1,179**	**1,033**	...	**146**	...	...
			32	Tanners, curriers, leather dressers, and dyers, etc. ...	1	1	...	...	...	...
			33	Makers of leather articles, such as trunks, water bags, etc. ...	1,177	1,031	...	146	...	...
			35	Bone, ivory, horn, shell, etc., workers.	1	1	...	...	...	...
		8		**Wood** ...	**43,232**	**30,626**	**1,784**	**10,812**	**10**	...
			36	Sawyers, carpenters, turners and joiners, etc. ...	30,217	18,942	1,364	9,906	5	...
			37	Basket makers and other industries of woody material including leaves ...	13,015	11,684	420	906	5	...
		9		**Metals** ...	**9,277**	**7,693**	**155**	**1,429**	...	...
			39	Plough and agricultural implement makers ...	16	16	...	...	...	...
			41	Other workers in iron and makers of implements and tools, principally or exclusively of iron ...	7,343	6,480	14	849	...	...
			42	Workers in brass, copper and bell metal.	1,425	1,141	...	284	...	...
			43	Workers in other metals (tin, zinc, lead, quicksilver, etc.) ...	491	56	141	294	...	...
			44	Workers in mints, die sinkers, etc. ...	2	...	...	2	...	...
		10		**Ceramics** ..	**4,196**	**3,417**	**21**	**758**	...	...
			45	Makers of glass and crystal ware ...	13	13	...	...	...	...
			46	Makers of porcelain and crockery ...	62	...	...	62	...	...
			47	Potters and earthen pipe and bowl makers ...	3,400	3,214	...	186	...	...
			48	Brick and tile makers ...	721	190	21	510	...	...
		11		**Chemical Products properly so called and Analogous** ...	**4,192**	**1,679**	**44**	**2,469**	...	...
			50	Manufacture of matches and explosive materials ...	254	27	8	219	...	...
			51	Manufacture of aerated and mineral waters ...	1	...	...	1	...	...
			52	Manufacture of dyes, paint and ink ...	1	1	...	...	...	...
			53	Manufacture and refining of vegetable and mineral oils ...	3,936	1,651	36	2,249	...	...
		12		**Food Industries** ..	**40,211**	**33,891**	**1,018**	**5,302**	...	..
			56	Rice pounders and huskers and flour grinders ...	15,230	9,816	402	5,012	...	...
			57	Bakers and biscuit makers ...	176	24	...	152	...	...
			58	Grain parchers, etc. ...	224	203	...	21	...	...
			59	Butchers ...	467	65	320	82	...	...
			60	Fish curers ...	8	...	...	8	...	...
			61	Butter, cheese and ghee makers ...	20	20	...	...	...	...
			62	Makers of sugar, molasses and gur ...	479	479	...	...	...	...
			63	Sweetmeat makers, preparers of jam and condiments, etc. ...	15	...	15	...	...	...

TABLE XV.—*Continued.*

Occupation or means of Livelihood.

COCHIN STATE. IMPERIAL SERIES.

PART D. DISTRIBUTION BY RELIGION.

CLASS.	SUB-CLASS.	ORDER.	GROUP.	OCCUPATION OR MEANS OF LIVELIHOOD.	TOTAL NUMBER OF WORKERS AND DEPENDENTS.	DISTRIBUTION BY RELIGION.				
						Hindu.	Musalman.	Christian.	Animist.	Others.
1	2	3	4	5	6	7	8	9	10	11
B. PREPARATION AND SUPPLY OF MATERIAL SUBSTANCES.	III. Industry.	12		**Food Industries.—contd.**						
			64	Brewers and distillers ...	5	...	...	5	...	...
			65	Toddy drawers ...	23,303	23,282	...	21	...	...
			66	Manufacturers of tobacco, opium and ganja ...	284	2	281	1	...	...
		13		**Industries of Dress and the Toilet** ..	**18,438**	**15,014**	**924**	**2,428**	...	**72**
			67	Hat, cap and turban makers ...	1	1	...	...	...	...
			68	Tailors, milliners, dress makers and darners, embroiderers on linen ...	3,954	1,673	620	1,589	...	72
			69	Shoe, boot and sandal makers ...	99	83	8	8	...	...
			70	Other industries pertaining to dress, gloves, socks, gaiters, belts, buttons, umbrellas, canes, etc. ...	36	33	...	3	...	...
			71	Washing, cleaning and dyeing ...	8,701	8,123	9	569	...	...
			72	Barbers, hair dressers and wig-makers ...	5,405	4,872	287	246	...	...
			73	Other industries connected with the toilet (tattooers, shampooers, bath houses, etc). ...	242	229	...	13	...	...
		14		**Furniture Industries** ..	**132**	**13**	**2**	**117**	...	...
			74	Cabinet makers, carriage painters, etc....	132	13	2	117	...	...
		15		**Building Industries** ..	**13,532**	**9,246**	**323**	**3,963**	...	...
			76	Lime burners, cement workers ...	541	389	...	152	...	...
			77	Excavators, plinth builders & well sinkers	20	15	5	...	...	...
			78	Stone and marble workers, masons and bricklayers ...	11,812	8,439	318	3,085	...	...
			79	Others (thatchers, building contractors, house painters, tilers, plumbers, locksmiths, etc.) ...	1,129	403	...	726	...	...
		16		**Construction of means of Transport** ..	**66**	**8**	**2**	**1**	**55**	...
			80	Cart, carriage, palki, etc., makers and wheelwrights ...	5	5	...	...	...	...
			82	Ship and boat builders ...	61	3	2	1	55	...
		17		**Production and Transmission of Physical Forces (Heat, Light, Electricity, Motive Power, etc.)** ..	**1**	**1**	...	...	...	...
			83	Gas works, electric light and ice factories..	1	1	...	...	...	...
		18		**Industries of Luxury and those pertaining to Literature and the Arts and Sciences** ...	**7,785**	**6,851**	**10**	**892**	...	**32**
			84	Printers, lithographers, engravers, etc ...	287	86	6	195	...	...
			85	Newspaper and magazine managers and editors, journalists, etc. ...	14	10	...	4	...	...
			86	Book binders and stitchers, envelope makers, etc. ...	157	38	...	93	...	26
			87	Makers of musical instruments ...	9	9	...	...	...	...

TABLE XV.—*Continued.*

Occupation or means of Livelihood.

COCHIN STATE IMPERIAL SERIES.

PART D. DISTRIBUTION BY RELIGION.

Class.	Sub-Class.	Order.	Group.	Occupation or means of Livelihood.	Total Number of Workers and Dependents.	Distribution by Religion. Hindu.	Musalman.	Christian.	Animist.	Others.
1	2	3	4	5	6	7	8	9	10	11
B. Preparation and Supply of Material Substances.	III. Industry.	18		**Industries of Luxury and those pertaining to Literature and the Arts and Sciences.—contd.**						
			88	Makers of watches and clocks and optical, photographic and surgical instruments ...	50	31	3	10	...	6
			89	Workers in precious stones and metals, enamellers, imitation jewellery makers, gilders, etc. ...	7,145	6,656	1	488	...	...
			90	Makers of bangles, rosaries, bead and other necklaces, spangles, lingams and sacred threads ...	32	17	...	15	...	...
			91	Toy, kite, cage, fishing tackle, etc., makers, taxidermists, etc. ...	89	4	...	85	...	...
			92	Others, including managers, persons other than performers employed in theatres and other places of public entertainment, employees of public societies, race course service, huntsmen, etc. ...	2	...	...	2	...	...
		19		**Industries concerned with Refuse matter** ..	**2,985**	**2,463**	**32**	**490**	...	...
			93	Sweepers, scavengers, dust and sweeping contractors ...	2,985	2,463	32	490	...	...
				Total Sub-Class III ...	**192,051**	**137,186**	**6,224**	**48,340**	**194**	**107**
	IV. Transport.	20		**Transport by Water** ..	**6,773**	**2,318**	**1,443**	**3,012**	...	**5**
			95	Ship owners and their employees, ship brokers, ships' officers, engineers, mariners and firemen ...	408	157	134	117	...	...
			96	Persons employed on the maintenance of streams, rivers and canals, (including construction) ...	18	...	18	...	...	...
			97	Boatowners, boatmen and towmen ...	6,347	2,156	1,291	2,895	...	5
		21		**Transport by Road** ..	**10,050**	**4,997**	**1,408**	**3,642**	**3**	...
			98	Persons employed on the construction and maintenance of roads and bridges .	1,458	1,436	13	6	3	...
			99	Cart owners and drivers, coachmen, stable boys, tramway, mailcarriage, etc., managers and employees (excluding private servants) ...	7,568	2.650	1,350	3.568	...	...
			100	Palki, etc., bearers and owners ...	31	15	...	16	...	...
			102	Porters and messengers ...	993	896	45	52	...	...
		22		**Transport by Rail** ...	**1,301**	**564**	**116**	**619**	...	**2**
			103	Railway employees of all kinds other than construction coolies ...	1,287	550	116	619	...	2
			104	Labourers employed on railway construction ...	14	14	...	...	...	...

TABLE XV.—*Continued.*

Occupation or means of Livelihood.

COCHIN STATE. IMPERIAL SERIES.

PART D. DISTRIBUTION BY RELIGION.

CLASS.	SUB-CLASS.	ORDER.	GROUP.	OCCUPATION OR MEANS OF LIVELIHOOD.	TOTAL NUMBER OF WORKERS AND DEPENDENTS	DISTRIBUTION BY RELIGION				
						Hindu.	Musalman.	Christian.	Animist.	Others.
1	2	3	4	5	6	7	8	9	10	11
B. PREPARATION AND SUPPLY OF MATERIAL SUBSTANCES.	IV. Transport	23		**Post Office, Telegraph and Telephone Services** ..	**732**	**545**	**18**	**169**	...	...
			105	Post Office, Telegraph and Telephone services ...	415	318	18	79	...	...
			105(a)	Anchal service * ...	317	227	...	90	...	...
				Total Sub-Class IV ..	**18,856**	**8,419**	**2,985**	**7,442**	**3**	**7**
	V. Trade	24		**Banks, Establishments of Credit, Exchange and Insurance** ..	**4,424**	**4,009**	**73**	**336**	...	**6**
			106	Bank managers, money lenders, exchange and insurance agents, money changers and brokers and their employees ...	4,424	4,009	73	336	...	6
		25		**Brokerage, Commission and Export** ..	**255**	**201**	**17**	**16**	...	**21**
			107	Brokers, commission agents, commercial travellers, warehouse owners and employees ...	255	201	17	16	...	21
		26		**Trade in Textiles** ..	**5,646**	**2,268**	**760**	**2,562**	...	**76**
			108	Trade in piece goods, wool, cotton, silk, hair and other textiles ...	5,646	2,258	750	2,562	...	76
		27		**Trade in Skins, Leather, and Furs** ..	**544**	**4**	**50**	**410**	...	**80**
			109	Trade in skins, leather, furs, feathers, horn, etc. ...	544	4	50	410	...	80
		28		**Trade in Wood** ..	**1,305**	**424**	**328**	**546**	...	**7**
			110	Trade in wood (not firewood), cork, bark, etc. ...	1,305	424	328	546	...	7
		29		**Trade in Metals** ..	**321**	**114**	**13**	**194**	...	...
			111	Trade in metals, machinery, knife, tool, etc., sellers ...	321	114	13	194	...	...
		30		**Trade in Pottery** ..	**217**	**113**	**55**	**44**	...	**5**
			112	Trade in pottery ...	217	113	55	44	...	5
		31		**Trade in Chemical Products** ..	**842**	**285**	**232**	**322**	...	**3**
			113	Trade in chemical products (drugs, dyes, paints, petroleum, explosives, etc.) ...	842	285	232	322	...	3

* Cochin State Postal Service.

TABLE XV.—*Continued.*

Occupation or means of Livelihood.

COCHIN STATE. IMPERIAL SERIES.

PART D. DISTRIBUTION BY RELIGION.

CLASS.	SUB-CLASS.	ORDER.	GROUP.	OCCUPATION OR MEANS OF LIVELIHOOD.	TOTAL NUMBER OF WORKERS AND DEPENDENTS.	DISTRIBUTION BY RELIGION				
						Hindu.	Musalman.	Christian.	Animist.	Others.
1	2	3	4	5	6	7	8	9	10	11
B. PREPARATION AND SUPPLY OF MATERIAL SUBSTANCES.	V. Trade	32		**Hotels, Cafes, Restaurants, etc.** ..	**9,690**	**8,022**	**638**	**995**	...	**35**
			114	Vendors of wine, liquors, aerated waters, etc. ...	6,203	5,856	...	312	...	35
			115	Owners and managers of hotels, cook-shops, sarais, etc., and their employees	3,487	2,166	638	683	...	...
		33		**Other trade in food stuffs** ..	**59,578**	**24,481**	**15,468**	**19,075**	...	**549**
			116	Fish dealers ...	11,842	3,725	4,716	3,247	...	154
			117	Grocers and sellers of vegetable oil, salt and other condiments ...	14,742	5,536	5,755	3,340	...	111
			118	Sellers of milk, butter, ghee, poultry, eggs, etc. ...	1,625	1,450	28	118	...	29
			119	Sellers of sweetmeats, sugar, gur and molasses ...	3,842	2,211	814	792	...	25
			120	Cardamom, betel-leaf, vegetables, fruit and areca nut sellers ...	11,347	2,940	1,726	6,477	...	204
			121	Grain and pulse dealers ...	13,813	8,071	1,466	4,250	...	26
			122	Tobacco, opium, ganja, etc., sellers ...	1,340	342	414	584	...	...
			123	Dealers in sheep, goats and pigs ...	459	32	427	...	...	...
			124	Dealers in hay, grass and fodder ...	563	174	122	267	...	...
		34		**Trade in Clothing and Toilet articles** ..	**336**	**76**	**19**	**241**	...	...
			125	Trade in ready made clothing and other articles of dress and the toilet (hats, umbrellas, socks, ready made shoes, perfumes, etc.) ...	336	76	19	241	...	...
		35		**Trade in furniture** ..	**1,537**	**432**	**374**	**731**	...	...
			126	Trade in furniture, carpets, curtains and bedding ...	945	122	263	560	...	...
			127	Hardware, cooking utensils, porcelain, crockery, glassware, bottles, articles for gardening, the cellar, etc. ...	592	310	111	171	...	...
		36		**Trade in Building Materials** ..	**1,585**	**765**	**144**	**676**	...	...
			128	Trade in building materials (stones, bricks, plaster, cement, sand, tiles, thatch, etc.) ...	1,585	765	144	676	...	...
		37		**Trade in means of Transport** ..	**797**	**435**	**246**	**116**	...	...
			129	Dealers and hirers of elephants, camels, horses, cattle, asses, mules, etc., sellers (not makers) of carriages, saddlery, etc. ...	797	435	246	116	...	...
		38		**Trade in Fuel** ..	**2,043**	**754**	**150**	**1,137**	...	**2**
			130	Dealers in firewood, charcoal, coal, cow dung, etc. ...	2,043	754	150	1,137	...	2

TABLE XV.—*Continued.*

COCHIN STATE. Occupation or means of Livelihood. IMPERIAL SERIES.

PART D. DISTRIBUTION BY RELIGION.

CLASS	SUB-CLASS	ORDER	GROUP	OCCUPATION OR MEANS OF LIVELIHOOD	TOTAL NUMBER OF WORKERS AND DEPENDENTS.	DISTRIBUTION BY RELIGION				
						Hindu.	Musalman.	Christian.	Animist.	Others.
1	2	3	4	5	6	7	8	9	10	11
B. PREPARATION AND SUPPLY OF MATERIAL SUBSTANCES	V. Trade	39		**Trade in Articles of Luxury and those Pertaining to Letters and the Arts and Sciences** ..	**1.118**	**777**	**29**	**287**	...	**25**
			131	Dealers in precious stones, jewellery (real and imitation) clocks, optical instruments, etc. ...	642	465	18	159	...	...
			132	Dealers in common bangles, bead necklaces, fans, small articles, toys, hunting and fishing tackle, flowers, etc. ...	346	285	9	27	...	25
			133	Publishers, booksellers, stationers, dealers in music, pictures, musical instruments and curiosities. ...	130	27	2	101	...	...
		40		**Trade in Refuse matter** ..	**54**	**54**	...	...	...	...
			134	Dealers in rags, stable refuse, etc. ...	54	54	...	...	...	...
		41		**Trade of other Sorts** ..	**15,214**	**5,428**	**1,078**	**8,612**	...	**96**
			135	Shop-keepers otherwise unspecified ...	14,450	4,788	971	8,595	...	96
			137	Conjurors, acrobats, fortune tellers, reciters, exhibitors of curiosities and wild animals ...	598	505	93	...	...	...
			138	Other trades (including farmers of pounds, tolls and markets) ...	166	135	14	17	...	...
				Total Sub-Class V. ..	**105,501**	**48,632**	**19,664**	**36,300**	...	**905**
				Total Class B. ..	**316,408**	**194,237**	**28,873**	**92,082**	**197**	**1,019**
C. PUBLIC ADMINISTRATION AND LIBERAL ARTS.	VI. Public force.	42		**Army** ..	**576**	**576**	...	...	...	...
			140	Army (Native States) ...	576	576	...	...	...	...
		44		**Police** ..	**1,164**	**845**	**146**	**173**	...	...
			142	Police ...	1,164	845	146	173	..	...
				Total Sub-Class VI ..	**1,740**	**1,421**	**146**	**173**	...	...
	VII. Public Administration.	45		**Public Administration** ..	**10,045**	**8,789**	**290**	**964**	...	**2**
			144	Service of the State (British) ...	71	50	...	19	...	2
			145	Service of Native and Foreign States ..						
			(a)	*Chiefs and their families* ...	304	303	...	1	...	...
			(b)	*Officers and servants of chiefs and their families* ...	1,473	1,445	2	26	...	..
			(c)	*Sirkar officers* ...	690	541	13	136	...	...
			(d)	*Clerical establishment* ...	2,477	2,341	12	124	...	...
			(e)	*Menials unspecified* ...	3,377	2,641	254	482	...	...
			(f)	*Service of States other than Cochin* ...	34	27	...	7	...	...
			146	Municipal and other local (not village) service ..						
			(a)	*Municipal service (clerical establishment)* ...	82	82	...	...	...	...
			(b)	*Do. ... other menials* ...	318	172	1	145	...	...

TABLE XV.—*Continued.*

Occupation or means of Livelihood.

COCHIN STATE. IMPERIAL SERIES.

PART D. DISTRIBUTION BY RELIGION.

CLASS	SUB-CLASS	ORDER	GROUP	OCCUPATION OR MEANS OF LIVELIHOOD	TOTAL NUMBER OF WORKERS AND DEPENDENTS	DISTRIBUTION BY RELIGION				
						Hindu.	Musalman.	Christian.	Animist.	Others.
1	2	3	4	5	6	7	8	9	10	11
C. PUBLIC ADMINISTRATION AND LIBERAL ARTS	VII. Public Administration	45		**Public Administration—contd.**						
			147	Village officials and servants other than watchmen ...	1,219	1,187	8	24	...	...
				Total Sub-Class VII ..	**10,045**	8,789	**230**	**964**	...	**2**
	VIII. Professions and liberal arts.	46		**Religion** ..	**10,648**	**8,463**	**615**	**1,563**	...	**7**
			148	Priests, ministers, etc. ...	2,699	2,455	79	165	...	...
			149	Religious mendicants, inmates of monasteries, etc. ...	155	15	...	140	...	...
			150	Catechists, readers, church and mission service ...	1,332	121	...	1,211	...	...
			151	Temple, burial or burning ground service, pilgrim conductors, circumcisers ...	6,462	5,872	536	47	...	7
		47		**Law** ..	**2,163**	**1,863**	**2**	**298**	...	...
			152	Lawyers of all kinds including kazis, law agents and mukhtiars ...	1,157	1,080	...	77	...	...
			153	Lawyers' clerks, petition writers, etc...	1,006	783	2	221	...	...
		48		**Medicine** ..	**4,881**	**3 517**	**250**	**1,118**	...	**1**
			154	Medical practitioners of all kinds, including dentists, oculists and veterinary surgeons ...	4,451	3,324	222	905	...	...
			155	Midwives, vaccinators, compounders, nurses, masseurs, etc. ...	430	193	28	208	...	1
		49		**Instruction** ..	**7,417**	**5,042**	**581**	**1,763**	...	**31**
			156	Professors and teachers of all kinds, and clerks and servants connected with education ...	7,417	5,042	581	1,763	...	31
		50		**Letters and Arts and Sciences** ..	**5,455**	**4,651**	**13**	791	...	..
			157	Public scribes, stenographers, etc. ...	69	69	...	...	...	...
			158	Architects, surveyors, engineers and their employees ...	617	298	13	306	...	...
			159	Others (authors, photographers, artists, sculptors, astronomers, meteorologists, botanists, astrologers, etc). ...	1,708	1,545	...	163	...	...
			160	Music composers and masters, players on all kinds of musical instruments (not military), singers, actors and dancers ...	3,061	2,739	...	322	...	...
				Total Sub-Class VIII ..	**30,564**	**23,536**	**1,461**	**5,528**	...	**39**
	IX. Persons living on their income.	51		**Persons Living on their income** ..	**1,129**	**904**	**97**	**116**	...	12
			161	Proprietors (other than of agricultural land) fund and scholarship holders and pensioners ...	1,129	904	97	116	...	12
				Total Sub-Class IX ..	**1,129**	**904**	**97**	**116**	...	12
				Total Class C ...	**43,478**	**34,650**	**1,994**	**6,781**	...	**53**

TABLE XV.—*Continued.*

Occupation or means of Livelihood.

COCHIN STATE. IMPERIAL SERIES.

PART D. DISTRIBUTION BY RELIGION.

CLASS.	SUB-CLASS.	ORDER.	GROUP.	OCCUPATION OR MEANS OF LIVELIHOOD.	TOTAL NUMBER OF WORKERS AND DEPENDENTS.	DISTRIBUTION BY RELIGION				
						Hindu.	Musalman.	Christian.	Animist.	Others.
1	2	3	4	5	6	7	8	9	10	11
D. MISCELLANEOUS.	X. Domestic service	52		**Domestic Service** ..	**5,573**	**3,512**	**365**	**1,674**	**1**	**21**
			162	Cooks, water carriers, door keepers, watchmen and other indoor servants	5,061	3,101	349	1,590	...	21
			163	Private grooms, coachmen, dog boys, etc.	512	411	16	84	1	...
				Total Sub-Class X ..	**5,573**	**3,512**	**365**	**1,674**	**1**	**21**
	XI. Insufficiently described occupation.	53		**General Terms which do not indicate a Definite Occupation** ..	**66,194**	**38,851**	**5,878**	**20,897**	**465**	**103**
			164	Manufacturers, business men and contractors otherwise unspecified ...	956	267	47	642	...	...
			165	Cashiers, accountants, book keepers, clerks and other employees in unspecified offices, warehouses and shops...	5,149	3,108	214	1,753	...	73
			166	Mechanics otherwise unspecified ...	20	7	7	6	...	...
			167	Labourers and wor men otherwise unspecified ...	60,070	35,469	5,610	18,496	465	30
				Total Sub-Class XI ..	**66,194**	**38,851**	**5.878**	**20.897**	**465**	**103**
	XII. Unproductive.	54		**Inmates of Jails, Asylums and Hospitals** ..	**157**	**76**	...	**81**	...	...
			168	Inmates of jails, asylums and hospitals	157	76	...	81	...	...
		55		**Beggars, Vagrants, Prostitutes** ..	**2,390**	**1,437**	**184**	**731**	**29**	**9**
			169	Beggars, vagrants, procurers, prostitutes, receivers of stolen goods, cattle poisoners ...	2, 390	1,437	184	731	29	9
				Total Sub-Class XII ..	**2,547**	**1,513**	**184**	**812**	**29**	**9**
				Total Class D ...	**74,314**	**43,876**	**6,427**	**23,383**	**495**	**133**
				Grand Total ...	**918,110**	**615,708**	**63,822**	**233092**	**4,177**	**1,311**

TABLE XV.

OCCUPATION OR MEANS OF LIVELIHOOD.

Part E.—Statistics of Industries.

COCHIN STATE. IMPERIAL SERIES.

TABLE XV.—Part E.

Statistics of employment in factories, mines, etc., in which at least 20 persons are employed.

Description of factory, mine, etc.	Whether using mechanical power or not.	Number of factories.	Factories employing	Total number of employees. Males.	Total number of employees. Females.	Details of persons employed. Direction, supervision and clerical work. Europeans and Anglo-Indians. Males.	Direction, supervision and clerical work. Europeans and Anglo-Indians. Females.	Direction, supervision and clerical work. Indians. Males.	Direction, supervision and clerical work. Indians. Females.	Skilled workmen. Europeans and Anglo-Indians. Males.	Skilled workmen. Europeans and Anglo-Indians. Females.	Skilled workmen. Indians. Males.	Skilled workmen. Indians. Females.	Unskilled labourers. Over 14. Males.	Unskilled labourers. Over 14. Females.	Unskilled labourers. Under 14. Males.	Unskilled labourers. Under 14. Females.	State of business at date of Census as compared with normal.
1	2	3	4	5	6	7	8	9	10	11	12	13	14	15	16	17	18	19
Printing Presses ...	Yes	1	From 50 to 100 persons	59	...	...	...	10	...	...	...	43	...	...	...	6	...	Somewhat brisker than usual
	No	3	20 to 50 „ ...	88	1	...	...	10	...	...	...	66	...	8	1	4	...	
	No	1	50 to 100 „ ...	60	...	...	...	1	...	...	...	29	...	28	...	2	...	
			Total „ ...	148	1	...	...	11	...	...	...	95	...	36	1	6	...	
Cocoanut Oil Mills ...	Yes	4	20 to 50 „ ...	143	5	...	...	18	...	...	...	40	...	83	5	2	...	Somewhat slacker than usual
	Yes	3	50 to 100 „ ...	155	1	...	...	17	...	2	...	43	...	90	1	3	...	
	Yes	2	100 to 200 „ ...	280	30	...	...	11	...	2	...	16	...	238	30	13	...	
			Total „ ...	578	36	...	...	46	...	4	...	99	...	411	36	18	...	
Flour Mill ..	Yes	1	20 to 50 „ ...	20	8	1	...	4	...	...	...	3	...	12	8	...	...	Normal
Rice Mill ...	Yes	2	20 to 50 „ ...	42	8	1	...	9	...	...	...	6	...	26	8	...	...	Much slacker than usual
Saw Mills ...	Yes	1	100 to 200 „ ...	175	...	3	...	7	...	3	...	77	...	85	...	...	...	Normal
	Yes	1	200 to 400 „ ...	249	...	2	...	2	...	2	...	40	...	203	...	...	...	
			Total „ ...	424	...	5	...	9	...	5	...	117	...	288	...	...	...	
Spinning & Weaving Mills..	No	1	100 to 200 „ ...	128	3	1	...	8	...	...	...	69	...	40	3	10	...	Brisker than usual
Iron works ...	Yes	2	20 to 50 „ ...	65	...	3	...	4	...	...	...	19	...	39	...	...	...	Normal
S. I. R. Loco shed ...	No	1	20 to 50 „ ...	22	1	..	...	...	...	...	...	2	...	20	1	...	...	Do
Tramway Workshop ...	Yes	1	20 to 50 „ ...	34	...	...	...	3	...	2	...	15	...	14	...	...	...	Brisker than usual

TABLE XV.—Part E.—*Continued.*

Statistics of employment in factories, mines, etc., in which at least 20 persons are employed.

Description of factory, mine, etc.	Whether using mechanical power or not	Number of factories	Factories employing	Total number of employees		Details of persons employed														State of business at date of Census as compared with normal.
						Direction, supervision and clerical work.				Skilled workmen.				Unskilled labourers.				
						Europeans and Anglo-Indians.		Indians.		Europeans and Anglo-Indians.		Indians.		Over 14.		Under 14.		
				Males.	Fe-males.	Males.	Females.	Males.	Females.	Males.	Females.	Males.	Females.	Males.	Females.	Males.	Females.	
1	2	3	4	5	6	7	8	9	10	11	12	13	14	15	16	17	18	19
Arrack Distillery ...	Yes	1	20 to 50 persons	41	1	...	...	7	...	...	...	22	1	12	...	...	...	Normal
Coir Rugs and matting Factory ...	Yes	1	50 to 100 „ ...	52	11	2	...	2	...	...	...	4	...	44	11	...	...	Slacker than usual
Ginger Bleaching Factory..	No	1	20 to 50 „ ...	26	...	...	...	2	...	...	...	20	...	4	...	...	...	Normal
Cask making Factory ...	No	1	20 to 50 „ ...	23	...	...	...	3	...	...	...	16	...	2	...	2	...	Do
Indian Fisheries Factory..	Yes	1	20 to 50 „ ...	24	3	4	...	...	...	3	...	...	...	17	2	...	1	Do
Tile and Brick Factories...	Yes	1	20 to 50 „ ...	28	8	...	...	2	...	1	...	6	...	17	6	2	2	Brisker than usual
	Yes	1	50 to 100 „ ...	68	5	...	...	6	...	...	...	4	...	39	5	19	...	
			Total „ ...	96	13	...	...	8	...	1	...	10	..	56	11	21	2	
	No	4	20 to 50 „ ...	99	26	...	...	8	...	...	...	2	...	76	24	18	2	
	No	9	50 to 100 „ ...	512	61	...	...	22	...	...	...	35	...	378	53	77	8	
			Total „ ...	611	87	...	...	30	...	...	...	37	...	451	77	90	10	
Rubber Plantations ...	No	3	100 to 200 „ ...	350	87	3	...	6	...	...	...	20	...	287	82	31	5	Do
	No	3	100 and over.. ...	2,266	491	7	...	15	...	...	...	695	...	1,256	311	293	180	
			Total „ ...	2,616	578	10	...	21	...	...	...	715	...	1,543	393	327	185	
Coffee Estates ...	No	10	20 to 50 „ ...	234	99	6	...	1	...	2	...	...	...	204	82	21	17	Somewhat slacker than usual
	No	5	50 to 100 „ ...	191	119	3	...	...	...	1	...	...	...	167	107	20	12	
			Total „ ...	425	218	9	...	1	...	3	...	...	...	371	189	41	29	
Grand total ...		[illegible]		5,434	968	36	...	178	...	18	...	1,292	1	3,389	740	521	227	

TABLE XVI.

OCCUPATION BY SELECTED CASTES, TRIBES OR RACES.

NOTE.— This Table differs from the standard form in that columns 9 to 12 of the latter have been omitted. The particulars required for those columns have not, through an oversight, been abstracted. The omission was noticed only when it was too late to supply it.

TABLE

OCCUPATION BY SELECTED

COCHIN STATE

CASTE, TRIBE OR RACE.	Traditional Occupation.	POPULATION DEALT WITH. Actual workers. Males.	Females.	Dependents. Males.	Females.	RECORDED 1 (a) Ordinary cultivation Males.	Females.	1 (b) Growers of special products and market gardening. Males.	Females.	1 (c) Forestry. Males.	Females.
1	2	3	4	5	6	7	8	9	10	11	12
HINDU.											
Ambalavasi ...	Temple servants ...	2,023	931	1.887	2,963	445	95	65	14	8	...
Arayan ...	Fishermen and boatmen ...	1,617	1,024	888	1,237	45	1	35	6	...	...
Brahman Malayali ...	Priests ...	1,757	82	1,661	3,117	1,076	61	...	...	1	...
do. Tamil ...	Do. ...	4,681	530	5,143	8,599	953	92	60	4	36	...
do. Konkini ...	Do. ...	2,706	258	1,874	3,684	224	24	35	3	2	...
do. Others ...	Do. ...	778	20	224	448	26	5	4	1	...	...
Chakkan ...	Oil-pressers ...	708	270	405	723	34	22	...	...	5	...
Devangan ...	Weavers ...	669	338	507	835	70	37	...	...	...	...
Iluvan ...	Toddy-drawers ...	55,536	33,704	47,281	71,982	27,380	16,846	1,436	374	661	6
Kadupattan ...	Salt-workers ...	3,919	2,199	3,156	5,050	2,617	1,354	100	18	20	2
Kaikolan ...	Weavers ...	1,222	699	789	1.411	250	51	...	...	1	...
Kammalan ...	Carpenters, masons, black-smiths, gold-smiths, bell-metal workers and leather workers	9,779	2 834	7,310	15,135	124	438	39	5	33	...
Kanakkan ...	Boatmen and agricultural labourers ...	2.186	1,788	1,604	1,949	521	638	...	...	6	...
Kaniyan ...	Astrologers ...	848	215	776	1,405	184	54	5	8	...	...
Kshatriya Malayali ...	Military and dominant ...	282	26	229	478	54	7	10	...	...	...
do. Others ...	Do. ...	186	26	119	248	6	...	...	...	1	...
Kudumi Chetti ...	General labourers.	3,938	1,699	2.562	4,172	1.889	435	95	8	24	1
Kusavan ...	Potters ...	1,217	846	612	882	74	23	...	...	2	...
Nayar ...	Military and agricultural ...	28,107	12.857	30613	50,129	18,364	6,953	788	320	179	...
Otta Naikkan ...	Earth-workers ...	913	752	455	686	206	252	19	...	1	...
Pandaran ...	Mendicants ...	1,139	713	747	1.116	194	61	6	...	...	...
Panan ...	Sorcerers and exorcists ...	856	558	633	853	75	126	...	...	...	2
Pandi Tattan ...	Goldsmiths ...	799	88	544	1.026	16	9	...	...	...	...
Parayan ...	Agricultural labourers and basket makers ...	3,086	2 099	1.046	2,110	891	797	34	...	10	...
Pulayan ...	Agricultural labourers ...	22 895	21.780	12,889	15,723	21,251	19,840	37	6	8	...
Valan ...	Boatmen and fishermen ...	2.497	1,723	1,549	2.068	49	7	...	4	...	...
Velan ...	Barbers and priests.	2,723	2 894	1.872	2 388	237	67	19	...	6	...
Velakkattalavan.	Barbers ...	972	566	652	1,061	108	41	...	2	2	3
Vellalan ...	Agriculturists ...	1,467	802	1,619	2,166	802	436	9	8	26	...
Veluttedan ...	Washermen ...	995	1,061	694	711	137	25	4	...	...	...
Vettuvan ...	Hunters ...	1.398	1,459	1,039	1,355	1.192	1.188	...	...	2	...
MUSALMAN.											
Jonakan ...		12.372	4,607	18,902	20,586	3,393	1,964	581	108	106	11
Ravuttan ...		2,414	1.069	1.697	3,050	648	514	3	...	28	...
CHRISTIAN.											
Anglo-Indian ...		644	217	597	988	54	23	13	1	1	...
European ...		48	4	8	16	...	...	10	...	...	...
Native Christian.		59,169	21,416	57,330	92,603	22,951	6,813	1,965	253	129	...
ANIMIST.											
Malayan ...		953	684	327	497	504	439	110	...	200	119
Jew ...		226	96	345	508	16	...	6	...	...	...

XVI.

CASTES, TRIBES OR RACES.

IMPERIAL SERIES.

PRINCIPAL OCCUPATION OF ACTUAL WORKERS (BY ORDERS.)

1 (d) Raising of farmstock.		1 (e) Raising of small animals.		2. Fishing and hunting		3. Mines.		4. Quarries of hard rocks.		5. Salt, etc.		6. Textiles.		7. Hides, skins and hard materials from the animal kingdom.		8. Wood.	
Males.	Females.	Males.	Females.	Males.	Females.	Males.	Females.	Males.	Females.	Males.	Females.	Males.	Females.	Males.	Females.	Males.	Females.
13	14	15	16	17	18	19	20	21	22	23	24	25	26	27	28	29	30
...	...	...	...	...	...	...	...	...	..	...	...	...	...	...	...	...	...
...	..	...	...	1142	576	...	...	...	...	...	...	32	377	...	...	4	...
...	...	...	...	...	...	...	...	...	...	...	...	...	...	...	...	...	...
...	...	...	...	...	...	...	...	...	...	...	...	1	...	...	...	...	...
...	...	...	...	...	...	...	...	...	...	...	...	31	5	1	...	...	...
...	...	...	...	...	...	...	...	...	...	...	...	...	...	...	...	...	...
...	...	...	...	...	...	...	...	...	...	...	...	6	9	...	...	...	...
...	...	...	...	...	...	...	...	...	...	...	...	525	223	...	...	...	...
709	29	...	...	85	5	...	...	...	...	...	...	2,838	7,700	...	...	816	1,103
82	1	...	...	...	...	...	...	...	...	...	...	3	1	...	...	2	3
3	...	...	...	...	...	...	...	...	...	...	...	870	570	...	...	...	...
4	...	...	...	...	...	...	...	...	...	...	...	1	118	231	23	5,156	1,257
9	1	...	...	440	18	...	...	...	...	...	...	32	568	...	...	9	429
2	...	...	...	...	...	...	...	...	...	...	...	8	39	...	...	36	16
...	...	...	...	...	...	...	...	...	...	...	...	...	...	...	...	...	...
1	2	...	...	...	...	...	...	...	...	...	...	...	...	...	...	...	...
4	...	...	...	146	5	...	...	...	...	...	...	69	254	...	...	...	...
...	...	...	...	...	...	...	...	...	...	...	...	...	..	...	...	...	...
50	...	1	..	4	...	...	...	...	...	...	...	18	126	...	...	2	1
13	...	...	...	...	...	...	...	...	...	...	...	...	...	...	...	...	...
8	...	...	...	..	...	...	...	...	...	...	...	...	...	...	...	13	70
6	1	...	...	1	...	...	...	...	...	...	...	...	...	...	...	411	333
...	...	...	...	...	...	...	...	...	...	...	...	...	...	...	...	...	...
20	2	...	...	...	...	...	...	...	...	...	...	85	41	8	6	1,944	1.239
248	19	1	...	25	229	...	...	...	...	...	...	3	1,009	1	...	88	305
...	...	...	...	1,649	...	...	...	...	...	...	...	255	492	...	...	...	4
7	...	...	...	10	3	...	...	...	...	...	...	9	6	...	...	120	6
3	...	...	...	...	...	...	...	...	..	...	...	...	...	...	...	...	...
20	...	...	...	...	...	...	...	...	..	...	...	4	6	...	...	...	...
...	...	...	...	...	...	...	..	...	...	...	...	...	...	...	...	...	...
21	...	...	...	..	...	...	...	...	...	...	...	...	...	...	...	1	63
42	...	...	...	89	...	...	...	...	...	...	...	197	1,042	...	...	360	313
87	...	...	...	...	...	...	...	...	...	...	...	91	44	...	...	25	15
...	...	...	...	3	...	...	...	...	...	...	...	17	76	5	...	191	6
...	...	...	...	...	...	...	...	...	...	...	..	...	...	...	...	...	...
66	3	9	...	1,707	111	...	...	...	...	...	...	3,758	5,469	40	...	2,918	147
24	...	...	...	..	...	...	...	...	...	...	...	...	22	...	..	8	...
...	...	...	...	...	...	...	...	...	...	...	..	1	...	...	...	...	...

TABLE
OCCUPATION BY SELECTED

COCHIN STATE.

CASTE, TRIBE OR RACE.	Traditional Occupation.	RECORDED: 9. Metals. Males.	9. Metals. Females.	10. Ceramics. Males.	10. Ceramics. Females.	11. Chemical products, properly so called and analogus. Males.	11. Females.	12. Food industries. Males.	12. Females.	13 industries of dress and the toilet. Males.	13. Females.	14. Furniture industries. Males.	14. Females.
		31	32	33	34	35	36	37	38	39	40	41	42
HINDU.													
Ambalavasi ...	Temple servants ...	...	...	...	...	...	...	...	33	1	...	...	...
Arayan ...	Fishermen and boatmen ...	...	...	...	...	...	...	...	6	20	9	...	...
Brahman Malayali ...	Priests ...	...	..	...	...	1	...	...	...	...	...	...	...
do. Tamil ...	Do.	...	...	...	...	2	...	...	...	2	...	...	...
do. Konkini ...	Do.	1	...	...	...	1	...	...	2	4	1	...	...
do. Others ...	Do.	...	...	...	...	...	...	1	...	...	...	1	...
Chakkan ...	Oil-pressers ...	...	...	...	...	203	175	7	20	...	...	...	...
Devangan ...	Weavers ...	...	...	...	...	...	...	...	12	...	...	...	...
Iluvan ...	Toddy drawers ...	4	...	34	17	200	6	7,183	2,585	299	180	...	...
Kadupattan ...	Salt-workers ...	...	...	...	...	...	...	52	321	7	4	...	...
Kaikolan ...	Weavers ...	...	...	...	...	1	15	4	35	1	...	...	...
Kammalan ...	Carpenters, masons, black-smiths, gold smiths bell-metal workers and leather workers ...	2,145	93	...	...	...	...	3	130	...	3	...	...
Kanakkan ...	Boatmen and agricultural labourers ...	1	...	...	...	...	...	...	25	3	5	...	...
Kaniyan ...	Astrologers ...	...	...	...	...	...	...	...	22	27	6	...	...
Kshatriya Malayali ...	Military and dominant	...	...	...	...	...	...	...	...	...	...	...	...
do. Others ...	Do.	...	...	...	...	...	...	1	...	1	2	1	...
Kudumi Chetti ...	General labourers.	1	...	...	1	4	...	44	634		...	...	...
Kusavan ...	Potters ...	...	...	1,105	754	...	...	..	6	...	...	...	...
Nayar ...	Military and agricultural ...	1	...	4	...	44	...	59	1,989	50	2	...	...
Otta Naikkan ...	Earth workers ...	...	...	28	...	...	...	...	1	...	...	...	...
Pandaran ...	Mendicants ...	...	...	...	8	..	...	...	...	1	...	...	...
Panan ...	Sorcerers and exorcists ...	...	...	...	...	...	...	2	5	18	18	...	...
Pan'di Tattan ...	Goldsmiths ...	11	...	...	...	...	...	...	6	...	...	...	...
Parayan ...	Agricultural labourers and basket makers ...	...	...	...	...	...	...	1	...	16	1	...	...
Pulayan ...	Agricultural labourers ...	...	...	...	...	...	...	2	37	5	2	...	...
Valan ...	Boatmen and fishermen ...	...	...	...	...	9	...	...	22	...	...	...	...
Velan ...	Barbers and priests.	...	...	...	1	...	...	1	1	1,323	2,275	...	...
Velakkattalavan.	Barbers ...	...	...	...	...	...	...	...	6	844	439	...	...
Vellalan ...	Agriculturists ...	...	...	...	4	...	1	44	46	15	...	...	...
Valuttedan ...	Washermen ...	...	...	...	...	...	...	...	1	840	1,051	...	...
Vettuvan ...	Hunter- ...	...	...	1	...	1	...	1	6	5	4	...	...
MUSALMAN.													
Jonakan ...		58	...	...	...	57	...	175	197	294	112	...	...
Ravuttan ...		...	...	3	...	...	...	84	48	12	7	...	...
CHRISTIAN.													
Anglo-Indian		71	...	...	...	...	...	3	4	37	64	3	...
European ...		...		...	...	...	...	...	...	...	...	..	...
Native Christian.		417	...	96	89	664	160	408	3,086	235	415	32	...
ANIMIST.													
Malayan ...		...	...	...	...	...	...	...	...	...	...	...	...
Jew ...		...	...	...	...	...	...	...	...	2	56	...	...

XVI.—*Continued.*

CASTES, TRIBES OR RACES

IMPERIAL SERIES.

PRINCIPAL OCCUPATION OF ACTUAL WORKERS (BY ORDERS).

15. Building industries.		16. Construction of means of transport		17. Production and transmission of physical forces.		18. Industries of luxury and those pertaining to literature and the arts and sciences.		19. Industries concerned with refuse matter.		20. Transport by water.		21. Transport by road.		22. Transport by rail		23. Post Office, Telegraph and Telephone services.	
Males.	Females.	Males.	Females.	Males.	Females.	Males.	Females.	Males.	Females.	Males.	Females.	Males.	Females.	Males.	Females.	Males	Females.
43	44	45	46	47	48	49	50	51	52	53	54	55	56	57	58	59	60
...	...	...	...	...	...	4	...	...	13	...	...	...	...	1	...	3	...
...	28	...	...	...	...	...	...	...	...	5	...	...	...	...	...	...	...
...	...	...	...	...	...	...	...	...	...	...	...	...	...	...	...	1	...
13	...	...	...	...	...	6	...	...	...	...	...	4	...	16	...	25	...
8	...	...	...	...	...	12	...	5	11	3	...	4	4	...	...	2	...
...	...	...	...	..	...	1	...	...	...	3	...	...	...	...	...	2	...
...	...	...	...	...	...	4	...	...	...	...	...	35	...	...	...	...	...
3	..	...	...	...	...	...	...	...	...	...	...	1	...	...	...	...	...
931	...	1	...	...	...	17	...	1	21	148	...	771	2	68	1	18	...
16	...	...	...	...	...	...	...	...	61	4	...	103	7	13	...	6	...
6	...	...	...	...	...	...	...	...	...	...	...	2	...	...	...	...	...
814	61	...	...	...	...	1,189	45	...	6	...	...	3	...	...	...	...	...
97	...	...	...	...	...	...	...	...	2	345	...	2	8	...	...	...	...
15	...	...	...	...	...	...	...	...	3	...	...	1	...	...	...	...	...
...	...	...	...	...	...	1	...	...	...	...	...	...	...	...	...	...	...
...	...	...	...	...	...	8	...	...	...	13	...	1	...	...	...	...	...
45	1	...	..	...	...	1	...	...	41	59	...	20	17	5	...	...	...
...	...	...	...	...	...	...	...	...	...	...	...	3	...	1	...	...	...
25	...	2	...	...	...	5	...	36	1,048	9	...	290	1	75	..	100	...
36	99	...	...	...	...	...	...	...	1	...	...	431	296	..	...	...	...
20	2	...	...	...	...	44	...	...	1	...	...	18	...	1	...	...	...
180	5	..	...	...	...	...	...	...	...	...	...	2	...	...	...	...	...
21	...	...	...	...	...	734	...	...	10	...	...	2	...	...	...	...	...
4	...	...	...	...	...	...	...	...	1	...	.	3	...	...	...	...	...
13	...	...	...	...	...	...	...	1	12	8	...	...	6	...	...	...	...
2	..	...	...	...	...	...	...	...	2	264	1	28	1	...	...	...	...
18	3	1	...	...	...	...	...	...	...	2	...	35	2	2	...	...	...
2	...	...	...	...	...	...	...	...	...	...	...	6	...	...	...	...	..
33	..	...	...	...	...	8	...	...	8	...	...	4	...	12	...	4	...
...	...	...	...	...	...	...	...	...	3	...	...	4	...	...	...	...	...
2	125	...	...	...	...	...	...	...	...	1	...	...	...	...	...	...	...
96	...	...	...	...	..	2	...	1	23	464	...	301	...	27	...	2	1
2	...	1	...	...	...	1	...	...	...	8	...	270	...	...	...	1	3
...	...	1	...	...	...	1	...	...	...	1	...	6	...	30	...	...	...
...	...	...	...	...	...	1	...	...	...	...	...	...	...	3	...	...	...
1,234	8	...	..	...	...	816	3	71	126	1,369	9	939	2	294	...	54	...
...	...	...	...	...	...	...	...	...	...	...	...	...	...	...	...	...	...
...	...	...	...	...	...	6	...	...	...	3	...	...	...	...	...	...	...

TABLE

OCCUPATION BY SELECTED

COCHIN STATE

CASTE, TRIBE OR RACE.	Traditional Occupation.	RECORDED PRINCIPAL OCCUPATION OF: 24. Banks, establishment of credit, exchange and insurance. Males.	24. Females.	25. Brokerage commission and export. Males.	25. Females.	26. Trade in textiles. Males.	26. Females.	27. Trade in skin leather and furs. Males.	27. Females.	28. Trade in wood. Males.	28. Females.	29. Trade in metals. Males.	29. Females.
		61	62	63	64	65	66	67	68	69	70	71	72
HINDU.													
Ambalavasi ...	Temple servants ...	11	13	...	...	...	...	...	...	...	...	...	...
Arayan ...	Fishermen and boatmen ...	...	...	...	...	...	...	...	...	...	...	...	...
Brahman Malayali ...	Priests ...	31	7	...	...	3	...	...	...	...	...	...	...
Do. Tamil ...	Do.	435	215	1	...	269	...	...	...	13	...	...	...
Do. Konkini ...	Do.	19	6	10	...	18	...	...	...	8	...	4	...
Do. Others ...	Do.	11	6	8	...	...	...	...	...	...	...	...	...
Chakkan ...	Oil-pressers ...	...	...	...	...	6	...	...	...	20	...	...	...
Devangan ...	Weavers ...	2	5	...	...	41	1	...	...	...	...	...	...
Iluvan ...	Toddy-drawers ...	3	4	...	2	201	32	...	1	48	...	7	...
Kadupattan ...	Salt-workers ...	3	5	...	...	1	1	...	...	9	...	...	...
Kaikolan ...	Weavers ...	1	6	...	...	48	...	...	...	2	...	...	...
Kammalan ..	Carpenters, masons, black-smiths, gold-smiths, bell-metal workers and leather workers ...	...	2	...	...	...	...	...	...	...	...	...	...
Kanakkan .	Boatmen and agricultural labourers ...	...	...	...	...	...	...	...	...	...	...	...	...
Kaniyan ...	Astrologers ...	...	...	...	...	...	...	...	...	...	...	...	...
Kshatriya, Malayali ...	Military and dominant ...	4	9	1	...	1	...	...	...	...	...	...	...
Do Others ...	Do.	8	3	18	...	9	...	...	...	...	...	1	...
Kudumi Chetti ...	General labourers .	...	...	8	...	...	4	...	...	1	...	...	...
Kusavan ...	Potters ...	...	...	...	...	...	...	...	...	...	...	...	...
Nayar ...	Military and agricultural ...	161	285	...	...	14	...	...	...	32	...	...	...
Otta Naikkan ...	Earth-workers ...	...	...	...	...	5	...	...	...	...	...	...	...
Pandaran ...	Mendicants ...	1	...	...	...	1	...	...	...	5	4	1	...
Panan ...	Sorcerers and exorcists ...	...	...	...	...	...	...	...	...	...	...	...	...
Pandi Tattan ...	Goldsmiths ...	...	2	...	...	...	...	...	...	...	...	...	...
Parayan ...	Agricultural labourers and basket makers ...	...	...	...	...	...	...	...	...	...	...	...	...
Pulayan ...	Agricultural labourers ...	...	...	...	...	...	...	...	...	...	...	...	...
Valan ..	Boatmen and fishermen ...	...	...	...	...	...	...	...	...	...	...	...	...
Velan ...	Barbers and priests	...	...	...	...	...	...	...	...	...	...	...	...
Velakkattalavan .	Barbers ...	1	4	...	...	...	...	...	...	...	...	...	...
Vellalan ...	Agriculturists ...	18	15	...	...	10	...	...	...	...	1	10	...
Veluttedan ...	Washermen ...	...	1	...	...	...	...	...	...	...	...	...	...
Vettuvan ...	Hunters ...	...	...	...	...	...	...	...	...	...	...	...	...
MUSALMAN.													
Jonakan ...		5	...	...	...	213	1	3	...	41	1	...	...
Ravuttan ...		22	...	...	...	71	...	23	...	13	...	5	...
CHRISTIAN.													
Anglo-Indian ...		...	...	...	...	11	...	...	...	3	...	...	...
European ...		...	...	...	...	...	...	...	...	...	...	...	...
Native Christian.		57	39	5	2	709	26	82	8	161	2	48	...
ANIMIST.													
Malayan ...		...	...	...	...	21	...	24	...	2	...	...	...
Jew ..		...	...	...	...	...	...	...	2	...	...	...	...

XVI.—*Continued.*
CASTES, TRIBES OR RACES.

IMPERIAL SERIES.

ACTUAL WORKERS (BY ORDERS.)

30. Trade in pottery.		31. Trade in chemical products.		32. Hotels cafes; restaurants, etc.		33. Other trade in food-stuffs.		34. Trade in clothing and toilet articles.		35. Trade in furniture.		36. Trade in building materials.		37. Trade in means of transport.		38. Trade in fuel.	
Males.	Females.	Males.	Females.	Males.	Females.	Males.	Females.	Males.	Females.	Males.	Females.	Males.	Females.	Males.	Females.	Males.	Females.
73	74	75	76	77	78	79	80	81	82	83	84	85	86	87	88	89	90
...	...	...	...	12	...	28	21	...	...	...	...	...	...	...	...	...	...
...	...	...	...	...	...	259	6	...	...	...	...	...	...	...	...	...	...
...	...	...	...	...	..	25	1	...	...	...	...	...	...	...	...	...	...
...	...	...	...	422	68	260	121	8	...	4	...	1	...	...	...	1	...
...	...	37	...	8	...	697	163	...	...	3	...	3	...	1	...	25	...
...	...	...	...	41	...	27	...	2	...	1	...	...	...	...	...	...	...
...	...	...	...	...	3	296	25	..	...	...	...	...	...	17	...	...	...
...	...	...	...	1	...	6	37	...	...	...	...	...	...	...	...	...	...
3	...	...	...	1,083	1,067	1,801	599	...	...	22	45	42	19	85	...	293	30
...	...	6	...	4	...	101	58	...	...	...	...	...	...	...	...	3	2
...	...	...	...	1	...	20	20	...	...	...	...	...	...	...	...	...	...
...	...	...	...	...	...	...	...	...	...	...	...	...	73	...	...	...	24
...	...	...	...	...	...	...	3	...	...	...	...	...	46	...	...	...	...
...	...	3	...	1	...	1	...	...	...	...	...	...	...	...	...	...	...
...	...	...	...	5	...	6	...	...	...	...	...	...	...	...	...	...	...
...	...	...	...	3	3	16	2	...	...	...	...	...	...	...	...	...	...
...	...	1	...	1	2	245	120	...	...	...	...	1	5	...	...	11	...
...	15	...	...	...	...	...	...	...	...	...	...	...	4	...	...	..	...
...	...	3	...	250	6	627	295	...	...	30	1	...	...	8	...	4	...
...	1	...	...	...	...	4	...	...	...	...	...	60	10	...	...	...	...
...	...	...	1	2	1	629	432	...	...	...	...	...	...	...	...	...	...
...	...	...	...	...	...	...	..	...	...	...	...	...	...	...	...	...	...
...	...	...	...	1	...	6	10	...	...	...	...	...	46	...	...	...	...
...	...	...	...	...	...	...	...	...	...	...	..	...	...	...	...	...	...
...	...	...	...	1	...	16	6	...	...	121	2	6	...	...	...	...	...
...	...	...	...	1	...	171	1,180	...	...	...	...	5	...	...	...	...	...
...	...	12	1	...	...	...	...	...	...	...	...	1	...	...	...	2	...
...	...	...	...	1	...	2	...	...	...	...	...	...	...	...	...	...	...
...	...	1	...	34	4	77	231	...	...	...	...	...		54	...	...	1
...	...	...	...	...	...	...	...	...	...	...	...	...	...	...	...	...	...
...	...	...	...	...	...	5	4	...	...	...	...	...	...	...	...	...	...
13	7	...	...	13	153	3,563	445	3	...	100	28	25	29	53	11	13	20
...	...	11	...	24	48	760	136	6	...	5	...	...	...	32	...	5	...
...	...	1	...	1	...	14	9	...	...	...	...	1	...	...	...	2	...
...	...	3	...	...	...	...	...	...	...	1	...	...	...	...	...	...	...
30	...	64	3	320	81	5,276	1,611	136	...	258	35	208	20	46	...	445	11
1	..	...	...	...	...	...	..	...	...	...	...	...	...	...	...	...	...
...	...	...	...	13	...	108	29	...	...	...	...	...	...	...	...	...	1

TABLE
OCCUPATION BY SELECTED

COCHIN STATE

CASTE, TRIBE OR RACE.	Traditional occupation.	RECORDED PRINCIPAL OCCUPATION OF — 39. Trade in articles of luxury and those pertaining to letters.		40. Trade in refuse matter.		41. Trade of other sorts.		42. Army.		44. Police		45. Public administration.	
		Males.	Females.	Males.	Females.	Males.	Females.	Males.	Females.	Males.	Females.	Males.	Females.
		91	92	93	94	95	96	97	98	99	100	101	102
HINDU.													
Ambalavasi ...	Temple servants ...	...	...	...	...	...	...	...	...	5	...	81	...
Arayan ...	Fishermen and boatmen ...	...	...	...	...	1	1	..	...	...	...	...	...
Brahman Malayali ...	Priests ...	...	...	...	...	2	1	...	...	...	...	17	...
Do. Tamil ...	Do.	26	...	...	...	176	...	7	...	31	...	605	...
Do. Konkini ...	Do.	67	...	...	...	770	...	...	...	...	...	15	...
Do. Others ...	Do.	2	...	...	...	1	...	...	...	...	...	15	...
Chakkan ...	Oil-Pressers ...	3	...	...	...	35	4	...	...	...	...	...	...
Devangan ...	Weavers ...	...	...	...	...	...	...	...	...	...	...	...	...
Iluvan ...	Toddy-drawers ...	1	1	7	16	22	1	...	...	...	...	30	...
Kadupattan ...	Salt-workers ...	...	...	...	...	10	...	...	...	2	...	19	...
Knikolan ...	Weavers ...	...	...	...	...	...	...	...	...	...	...	...	...
Kammalan ...	Carpenters, masons, black-smiths, gold-smiths, bell-metal workers and leather workers ...	...	...	...	...	...	...	...	...	...	...	...	...
Kanakkan ...	Boatmen and agricultural labourers...	...	...	...	...	...	...	...	...	...	...	...	...
Kaniyan ...	Astrologers ...	...	...	...	...	24	...	..	...	...	...	...	...
Kshatriya, Malayali .	Military and dominant ...	...	...	...	...	3	...	1	..	...	...	141	8
Do. Others ...	Do	...	...	...	...	23	2	11	..	...	...	4	...
Kudumi Chetty...	General labourers.	24	5	...	...	167	1	...	...	...	...	...	...
Kusavan ...	Potters ...	...	...	...	...	19	14	...	...	..	...	...	...
Nayar ...	Military and agricultural ..	10	7	...	...	99	1	228	...	285	...	2,064	206
Otta Naikkan ...	Earth-workers ...	...	...	...	...	1	1	...		...	...	...	...
Pandaran ...	Mendicants ...	22	26	...	...	6	3	...	...	...	...	1	...
Panan ...	Sorcerers and exorcists ...	...	...	...	...	61	11	...	...	...	...	...	...
Pandi Tattan ...	Gold smiths ...	...	...	...	...	...	...	..	...	...	...	...	...
Parayan ...	Agricultural labourers and basket makers ...	...	...	...	...	3	...	...	...	...	...	2	...
Pulayan ...	Agricultural labourers ...	...	...	...	...	..	...	...	...	...	...	...	...
Valan ...	Boatmen and fishermen ...	...	...	...	...	...	...	...	...	7	...	3	...
Velan ...	Barbers and priests.	...	...	...	...	81	3	...	...	...	...	...	...
Velakkattalavan .	Barbers ...	...	...	...	...	...	...	...	...	3	...	...	...
Vellalan ...	Agriculturists ...	...	...	...	...	...	...	...	...	9	...	45	...
Veluttedan ...	Washermen ...	...	...	...	...	...	...	...		...	...	3	...
Vettuvan ...	Hunters ...	...	...	...	...	...	...	...	...	...	...	...	...
MUSALMAN .													
Jonakan ...		3	4	...	...	152	26	...	..	8	..	14	...
Ravuttan ...		...	...	...	...	39	35	...	...	5	...	10	...
CHRISTIAN.													
Anglo-Indian ...		...	...	...	...	10	...	...	...	4	...	19	...
European ...		...	...	...	...	...	...	...	...	...	...	4	...
Native christian.		37	3	...	...	2,149	318	...	...	40	...	234	...
ANIMIST.													
Malayan ...		...	...	...	...	...	...	...	...	...	...	...	...
Jew.		9	...	...	...	19	1	...	...	...	...	...	...

XVI.—(*Continued.*)

CASTES, TRIBES OR RACES.

IMPERIAL SERIES.

ACTUAL WORKERS (BY ORDERS.)

46. Religion.		47. Law.		48. Medicine		49. Instruction.		50. Letters and arts and sciences.		51. Persons living principally on their income.		52. Domestic service.		53. General		54. Inmates of jails, asylums and hospitals.		55. Beggars prostitutes and vagrants.	
Males.	Females.	Males.	Females.	Males.	Females.	Males.	Females.	Males.	Females.	Males.	Females.	Males.	Females.	Males.	Females.	Males.	Females.	Males.	Females.
103	104	105	106	107	108	109	110	111	112	113	114	115	116	117	118	119	120	121	122
962	697	8	...	28	...	45	18	246	...	15	5	1	3	43	18	1	...	...	1
3	...	...	...	...	1	6	...	...	...	...	...	...	6	63	7	2	...	...	...
475	10	...	...	10	...	80	...	4	...	...	...	16	2	15	...	...	...	...	...
578	...	80	...	81	...	417	...	97	...	51	...	20	8	177	1	1	...	18	21
270	8	6	...	22	...	45	1	49	8	4	...	171	15	166	4	...	...	5	8
517	...	1	...	3	...	7	...	7	...	1	...	80	2	4	...	...	...	12	6
...	...	...	...	5	...	5	...	3	...	...	...	...	7	19	3	...	...	...	2
...	...	...	...	2	1	1	...	4	...	...	...	...	...	11	20	...	...	2	2
24	6	71	...	208	1	122	2	35	...	1	...	81	189	7,291	2,799	22	...	283	15
3	...	...	...	5	2	72	2	7	...	1	...	32	59	658	312	1	...	7	6
...	...	...	...	...	...	...	...	...	...	...	...	...	...	8	...	...	...	4	2
...	...	...	...	2	1	1	...	...	...	...	...	1	22	32	32	1	1	...	...
...	...	...	...	...	...	...	...	...	...	...	...	...	...	721	44	...	...	...	1
11	...	...	...	24	...	184	18	808	11	...	...	...	5	52	31	...	...	12	2
...	...	4	...	5	...	18	1	4	...	15	1	8	...	1	...	...	...	...	...
2	...	...	..	...	...	2	...	...	...	7	...	25	2	22	...	...	...	7	10
...	...	...	...	2	...	...	...	11	...	...	...	9	14	1,048	151	6	...	1	...
...	...	...	...	...	...	...	...	...	...	...	...	...	3	12	26	...	...	1	1
175	58	294	...	130	2	584	161	442	20	153	6	1,204	426	1,163	482	16	...	30	11
...	...	...	...	...	...	..	...	...	..	...	...	...	...	91	92	...	...	9	9
14	2	...	...	14	...	2	...	4	...	2	...	1	3	9	3	...	...	120	96
...	...	...	...	20	32	...	...	65	...	...	...	1	3	11	17	...	...	5	5
...	...	1	...	2	...	2	...	1	...	...	...	...	1	...	2	...	...	2	2
...	...	...	...	...	...	...	...	23	...	...	...	10	1	76	8	2	...	3	3
...	...	...	...	1	3	1	...	...	...	...	...	1	11	548	287	9	1	...	5
1	...	2	...	10	6	7	...	1	...	...	...	5	2	27	2	1	...	...	...
8	4	...	...	345	...	1	...	127	6	...	...	3	2	402	12	1	...	...	2
...	...	...	...	1	66	1	..	1	...	...	...	...	5	1	...	...	...	1	..
8	...	12	...	82	3	11	...	44	...	10	...	4	1	90	37	...	...	7	...
...	...	...	...	2	...	1	...	...	...	...	...	3	...	1	...	...	...	..	...
...	...	...	...	...	...	...	...	...	...	...	...	4	7	162	61	...	...	...	1
154	...	...	...	20	11	110	...	...	...	...	...	40	59	1,537	...	...	...	35	46
18	...	...	...	18	...	10	...	...	...	2	...	18	...	146	218	...	...	7	11
6	...	1	...	6	8	4	26	58	1	12	...	4	...	50	2	...	...	...	2
25	4	...	...	...	...	1	...	...	...	...	...	...	...	...	...	...	...	...	...
385	141	84	...	245	44	454	77	183	...	21	8	560	...	7,075	1,891	39	...	161	457
...	...	...	...	...	...	...	...	...	...	...	...	1	...	41	126	...	...	...	...
3	...	...	...	...	1	8	...	...	...	1	1	5	5	22	...	...	...	2	...

TABLE XVII.

CHRISTIANS BY SECT AND RACE.

NOTE.—The Government of India having decided that the term "Anglo-Indian" shall be used instead of "Eurasian", in the statistics of the present Census, all those who returned themselves as Eurasian have been entered under the head "Anglo-Indian", though the majority of the Eurasians of Cochin are not of British origin.

2. Those who returned themselves as "Feringis" have been classed under "Native Christians", as there is hardly any difference between them.

TABLE XVII.

Territorial Distribution of the Christian Population by Sect and Race.

Denominations.	Total.			Distribution by Race.							
				European and allied races.		Armenian.		Anglo-Indian.		Native.	
	Persons.	Males.	Females.	Males.	Females.	Males.	Females.	Males.	Females.	Males.	Females.
1	2	3	4	5	6	7	8	9	10	11	12
1. Anglican Communion	1,623	796	828	21	15	...	...	31	35	743	778
2. Baptist	44	24	20	...	...	...	...	6	3	18	17
3. Congregationalist	167	77	90	...	...	...	...	...	...	77	90
4. Lutheran	135	75	60	1	...	...	...	10	3	64	57
5. Methodist	6	2	4	...	...	...	...	2	4	...	...
6. Minor Protestant Denomination	36	19	17	...	...	...	...	...	...	19	17
7. Presbyterian	1	1	...	1	...	...	...	...	...	...	...
8. Protestants (unsecterian and unspecified) ...	349	142	207	...	...	...	...	...	...	142	207
9. Roman Catholic	97,787	50,228	47,559	33	5	...	...	1,192	1,160	49,003	46,394
10. Syrian (Roman)	100,166	50,271	49,895	...	...	...	...	...	...	50,271	49,895
11. Do (Jacobite)	20,025	9,904	10,121	...	...	...	...	...	...	9,904	10,121
12. Do (Reformed)	596	291	305	...	...	...	...	...	...	291	305
13. Do (Chaldean)	12,157	6,019	6,138	...	...	2	...	...	...	6,017	6,138
Total ...	233,093	117,849	115,244	56	20	2	...	1,241	1,205	115,549	114,019

TABLE XVII.

Territorial Distribution of the Christian Population by Sect and Race.

TABLE XVIII.

EUROPEANS, ARMENIANS AND ANGLO-INDIANS BY RACE AND AGE.

TABLE XVIII.

Europeans, Armenians and Anglo-Indians by Race and Age.

State.	Total.			Europeans and Allied Races.																									
				British subjects.													Others.												
				All ages.			0—12		12—15		15—30		30—50		50 and over		All ages			0—12		12—15		15—30		30—50		50 and over	
	Total.	Males.	Females.	Total.	Males.	Females.	Males.	Females.	Males.	Females.	Males.	Females.	Males.	Females.	Males.	Females.	Total.	Males.	Females.	Males.	Females.	Males.	Females.	Males.	Females.	Males.	Females.	Males.	Females.
1	2	3	4	5	6	7	8	9	10	11	12	13	14	15	16	17	18	19	20	21	22	23	24	25	26	27	28	29	30
Cochin ...	2,524	1,299	1,225	47	30	17	8	2	...	...	13	5	12	6	2	4	29	26	3	...	1	...	...	10	1	12	1	4	...

TABLE XVIII.—(*Continued.*)

Europeans and Allied Races.—(*Continued.*)																									
Armenians.													Anglo-Indians.												
All ages			0—12		12—15		15—30		30—50		50 and over		All ages			0—12		12—15		15—30		30—50		50 and over.	
Total.	Males.	Females.	Males.	Females.	Males.	Females.	Males.	Females.	Males.	Females.	Males.	Females.	Total.	Males.	Females.	Males.	Females.	Males.	Females.	Males.	Females.	Males.	Females.	Males.	Females.
31	32	33	34	35	36	37	38	39	40	41	42	43	44	45	46	47	48	49	50	51	52	53	54	55	56
2	2	...	...	...	...	...	...	...	1	...	1	...	2,446	1,241	1,205	454	375	95	95	330	385	248	229	119	121